the book of
Gay
&
Lesbian
quotations

ALSO BY PATRICIA JULIANA SMITH

En Travesti:
Women, Gender Subversion, and Opera
(with Corinne E. Blackmer)

Lesbian Panic:
Homoeroticism in Modern
British Women's Fictions

The Queer Sixties

the book of

Gay & Lesbian

quotations

compiled and edited by
patricia juliana smith

a new england publishing associates book

three rivers press

new york

Published by Three Rivers Press, 201 East 50th Street,
New York, New York 10022. Member of the Crown Publishing Group.

Random House, Inc. New York, Toronto, London, Sydney, Auckland
www.randomhouse.com

THREE RIVERS PRESS is a registered trademark of Random House, Inc.

Printed in the United States of America

Design by Meryl Sussman Levavi/Digitext, Inc.

Library of Congress Cataloging-in-Publication Data

The book of gay and lesbian quotations/compiled & edited by Patricia
   Juliana Smith.—1st ed.
      "A New England Publishing Associates book."
      Includes index.
      1. Gays—Quotations.   2. Lesbians—Quotations.   3. Quotations,
   English.   I. Smith, Patricia Juliana.
   PN6084.G35B66 1999
   808.88'2—dc21   98-41956

ISBN: 0-609-80262-3

10 9 8 7 6 5 4 3 2 1

First Edition

TO THE ROSE QUEEN

O, help me, heaven, to be decorative and do right.
—*RONALD FIRBANK,*
The Flower Beneath the Foot

Contents

contents

Acknowledgments

▼

I owe a great debt of thanks to my agent, Elizabeth Knappman, who persuaded me, in the course of a six-mile hike that I misunderstood to be only three miles, to undertake this task. Her unflagging support and nudging have been invaluable. My thanks, too, to PJ Dempsey, my editor at Crown Publishers, and her assistants Oona Schmid and Elizabeth Bird, who have kept me grounded in reality during the shaping of this text.

A special note of gratitude is due to Anita George, who provided me with her extraordinarily fine translations of a number of Sappho's poems and has graciously given me permission to reproduce them here. A number of colleagues, most particularly Lee Arnold, David William Forster, Beth Kattelman, François Lachance, Will Roscoe, and Gregory Woods, have been most helpful in providing me with quotations that might otherwise have slipped my notice.

As usual, I get by with a little help from my friends. Joe Bristow deserves special acknowledgment for being both an incredible source of information on gay and lesbian authors and a shoulder to cry on whenever I needed one. Various colleagues, including Blake Allmendinger, Helen Deutsch, Lowell Gallagher, Deborah Garfield, Jayne Lewis, Arthur Little, Anne Mellor, Tim Murphy, and Judith Rosen, have contributed significant kindness during the year in which this book came together, as have my graduate assistant Kate Taylor and several of my undergraduate students, including Rebecca Butterfield, Dat Tat "Dave" Pham, and Sharif Youssef. I thank Thomas Wortham, chair of the UCLA English Department, for his ongoing support and express my undying gratitude to department secretaries Jeanette Gilkison, *acknowledgments*

Rick Fagin, and Nora Elias for making sure that necessary documents and information got where they needed to go. My sister, Kate Lanehart, in her usual loving devotion, made sure that a crucial telephone call got to me when no one else knew where I was—otherwise this book might never have happened. Finally, I thank the "Rose Queen," to whom this is dedicated, for all the years of fashion, gossip, good food, and friendship.

Introduction

▼

I love them because it is a joy to find thoughts one
might have, beautifully expressed with much authority by someone recognized wiser than oneself.

—*MARLENE DIETRICH, on quotations,*
Marlene Dietrich's ABC (1962)

*S*ome years ago, one of my students presented me with
a novel idea that I had never really entertained
before. This young man, heterosexual and seemingly
quite naive, surely not the most brilliant I had ever encountered, told me that
he liked to take classes from gay and lesbian professors because "I think
they're a lot smarter than everyone else." The last thing I wanted to engage in
was a discussion of the putative intellectual superiority of homosexuals with
this somewhat enigmatic young man who had seemed a rather defensive and
confused fellow in class. I diplomatically responded that I really didn't think
there was any sort of verifiable evidence to suggest a correspondence between
intelligence and sexual preference. His reply nonetheless struck me as a truly
considerate and quite possibly true one: "I don't think it has anything to do

with genetics and all that, Dr. Smith. I just think that because society forces you to live in a different way from everyone else that you think about things a lot more than straight people do. You have to figure out why you're different and why other people are the way they are and what it all means. When you're straight, you don't have to think about things. You just take them for granted. But because you think about things more than straight people, you know more."

While I acknowledged that there were surely many exceptions to that paradigm—on both sides of the equation—there is, I think, some element of truth in it. Gays, lesbians, and other sexual outsiders do have a lot to think about, not merely about sex and sexuality but virtually all the aspects of that "normal" life into which we don't quite fit. And because many of the great minds of literary and cultural history have, in some sense, been "queer," they have left an enduring legacy of all the many matters they have thought about. And if there is a cultural stereotype about *opinionated* gays and lesbians, this book will do little to belie it, as it provides ample evidence of what many of the more outstanding representatives of gay and lesbian history have had to say on a wide variety of topics. We do have a lot to say; and contrary to yet another stereotype, we don't always agree with one another. A brief perusal of the entries under any given topic heading will reveal both congenial similarities and ferocious disagreements over time—which is as true of gays and lesbians in life as it is in literature. I have no doubt that a few will be affronted by my inclusion of the words of certain "politically incorrect" gay or lesbian figures. But they, too, have something to say; to exclude them is to give a less-than-true picture of the broad range of queer life and experience—or, even worse, it is to engage in a form of censorship, which has historically been the bane of virtually all gays and lesbians.

I look on this book, which I have "assembled" rather than "authored," as a collage of voices—*queer* voices, in a variety of senses—across many centuries, a celebration of the wit and wisdom of the sages of gay and lesbian culture. In this manner, I hope to present a quotations book of a sort that has not previously existed. Many quotations books of many sorts are available in libraries and bookstores; indeed, when one begins to sort through the vast array of such volumes, one might feel rather overwhelmed. There are quotations books to address a wide range of specific concerns, including books that focus on gay men, lesbians, and women in general, as well as that somewhat more ambiguous group that, for the purposes of this introduction, I shall deem "queer": an all-encompassing term that covers gay men, lesbians, bisexuals, transsexuals, transgendered individuals, and anyone else who falls outside the socially comfortable—and acceptable—boundaries of the "straight" world. But while a number of gay/lesbian/queer quotations books are in circulation, none of them provides what I would personally seek in such a book; and because I do not suppose that I am really so unique, I believe that others may have sensed this shortcoming as well.

It seems to me that most quotations books are a result of a choice between two seemingly opposed possibilities: one can be scholarly and as dry as dust, useful as a reference book but not much fun to read; otherwise, one can be outrageously amusing but, lacking documentation of its source, not very useful to the writer or speaker who might want to use a given quotation in another context. It occurs to me, though, that this either/or model need not be the only one. I think a quotations book can actually be amusing and informative simultaneously. It can provide the "wisdom of the ages," from Sappho and Socrates to the sages and celebrities of the present day, without compromising the perspectives and principles of *any* of the voices present here. And it can serve as an authoritative reference without boring to tears the reader who is, at the moment, seeking something other than erudition. For this reason, my arrangement of sources is almost diametrically opposed to that of what has become the norm for books of this sort. Virtually every gay and/or lesbian quotations book I have seen relies primarily on lines from queer celebrities du jour—often with apparently little recognition that many of these statements are merely paraphrases of older sources, most often Oscar Wilde—with a few tidbits from the "ancients" (Plato, Shakespeare, Wilde, Woolf, Forster, and others) thrown in for a touch of class. I have instead culled historical and literary sources, with the purpose of demonstrating a continuum of queer thought and culture over time, with some contemporary sources to add a touch of piquancy. It would be absurd to compare the relative literary merits of, say, Francis Bacon and Martina Navratilova—just as it would be to compare their relative athletic abilities. (And, I might add, the quotation from Bacon on tennis under "Sports" in this volume does, I think, quite amusingly point out the absurdity of the idea.) At the same time, I would like to think that both are vital parts of our rich and strange cultural heritage and that their very different insights are amply deserving of our regard.

This, then, is the task I have undertaken in bringing this book into being, one that seemed simple enough at the outset but, as I have since discovered, requires a number of difficult choices, some that will not please everyone. And while, as a lifelong queer myself, I no longer think it possible—or, for that matter, necessarily desirable—even to attempt to please all parties, I nonetheless think it tremendously important to explain the rationale behind some of the choices that are bound to displease some parties.

Some will object, no doubt, that I have included statements from individuals who should not be considered "gay," "lesbian," or otherwise "queer." Accordingly, I will offer this disclaimer: *The appearance of any individual's name in this text should not be taken as an indication that he or she is or was homosexual.* In some instances, enlightened minds who were or are, for all intents and purposes, heterosexual have had something insightful, sympathetic, and compelling to say about homosexuality and homosexuals. Their comments serve as vital pieces of the larger mosaic of queer history and culture and, I feel, should be incorporated here. Unlike editors of other gay- or lesbian-themed quotations books, I have not included the statements of famous homophobes of the media, the "religious" right wing, and contemporary politics. While it is important for all of us to remember that such attitudes exist, I see no reason to honor them with inclusion here; most of us have enough reminders of this in our everyday life as it is, and this book is meant to *celebrate* the greatness and variety of queer life, thought, and culture.

Such disclaimers having been made, I would like to add that there is significant documentation that *most* of the individuals quoted here, even those who were married or who had significant romantic relationships with members of the opposite sex, *were not exactly straight all—or most—of the time.* That some of these are among the most revered figures in the history of Western civilization may come as a shock to some. As an English professor and a literary critic, I have seen, with a combination of horror and amazement, the lengths to which otherwise learned and intelligent individuals will go to deny the queerness of William Shakespeare, Lord Byron, or even Virginia Woolf. I have also heard on many occasions some rather dubious arguments to the effect that even if, for example, E. M. Forster was homosexual in his private life, he always wrote about heterosexual relationships (except, of course, in his posthumously published novel, *Maurice*), so one can't apply anything he said to the concerns of homosexuality. I would counter such statements by suggesting that the very fact of one's queerness forces one into seeing *all* of life from a different perspective, outside the range of what society considers "normal." For that reason, even if the author is not discussing homosexuality directly—and let us not forget that for many decades, indeed many centuries, censorship laws forbade virtually all open discussion of this topic—his or her position outside the mainstream forces a "deviant" perspective on most aspects of life.

Along those lines, I would like to counter several other objections that might be made to my choices and arrangements of material. The first is that I have taken a number of these quotations out of context. Indeed, that is *precisely* what quotations books do. They provide a few sentences of the text, separated from the whole and without commentary to explain them. The only alternative to this is to present them within a completely different context, that of literary criticism; but, while not completely unrelated, a work of literary criticism serves a function very different from that of a reference book such as this. Some might argue that certain lines, particularly some concerning love and desire, originally appeared in narratives about heterosexual relationships; yet to say this is to disregard the simple fact that, as numerous literary scholars have demonstrated, for centuries gay and lesbian authors have had to disguise stories of same-sex love by means of a heterosexual mask in order to be able to present them in a public mode at all. Sadly, such an objection to their use in this text would indicate, too, the still all-too-common belief that love and desire between two persons of the same sex does not carry the same value, depth, reality, or "importance" as its heterosexual counterpart. Finally, as to the quotations from Shakespeare's works, let us not forget that his plays in their original mode of performance presented, at most, a curious simulacrum of heterosexuality: all the lines presented were spoken by male actors, often boys dressed as girls, sometimes boys dressed as girls dressed as boys. How, then, can one *really* claim that there is nothing "queer" in any of this? If the inherent "queerness" of many of the most cherished works of Western civilization makes any number of people truly uncomfortable, I have concluded—after years of patience and diplomacy in explaining these things—that the only reasonable response is to quote, with respect to all, the wisdom of that organization known as Queer Nation: *We're here, we're queer, get used to it.*

Related to these objections is one most often articulated by some academics, that homosexuality as we know it did not exist prior to the nineteenth century. As bizarre as this notion might seem to nonacademics, those whom Virginia Woolf lovingly and respectfully termed "the common reader," I have encountered it frequently enough in scholarly debate to be more than aware of its persistence. I am troubled by what strikes me as the self-defeating rhetoric of this argument, which implies that we are that impossibility, something new under the sun. Perhaps gay and lesbian *identity politics* as we now know them did not exist then—*what,* for that matter, *did* exist in its current form or under its present definitions even one hundred years ago?—but we *cannot* and *must not* deny that many people loved, desired, and made love to members of their own sex *long before* the most recent century, often at great personal risk. To do so is to forget, if not obliterate, our own cultural and social past; and I would refer the reader to the section entitled "Past, Present, Future" for George Santayana's oft-repeated dictum on what happens as a result of doing precisely that.

Finally, some might object that many of these quotations do not deal with homosexuality at all, but rather with matters that are common to most—if not all—human beings. This is in many ways true; that this should be an objection at all illustrates one of the ongoing problems of queer identity: because we are identified and made "other" as a result of our sexuality, many assume that all we ever think or talk about—or are entitled to talk about—is sex, as if other matters of life did not concern us as well. But we do not, for better or worse, spend all our time in bed; if truth be known, only a very small portion of our time is so occupied—alas. As I have already suggested, gays and lesbians, particularly those whose ideas are represented here, are notorious for their opinions on virtually everything, because, when you come right down to it, we are affected by the very same things that concern most other people. (Once, when asked to speak on the topic of lesbian pulp fictions, I suggested that those who run supermarkets do not quite realize that lesbians buy groceries. If they did, the publications of certain lesbian presses would be there right next to the Harlequin Romances—in massive quantities in some neighborhoods I've inhabited.)

For this reason, while some of the topics by which I have organized these quotations address concerns peculiar to queer life and sensibility, most do not. Truth, courage, childhood, age, lies, fidelity, religion, decorum, and life itself, to name but a few categories chosen at random, are part of everyone's life. Their function in this book is not to exclude anyone from the applicability of most of these very broad statements on the human condition. Rather, they serve, on the one hand, to illustrate how very much gays, lesbians, and other queers are part—a *vital* part—of the "big picture" of human existence. On the other hand, many of the entries show a peculiarly *queer* slant on social and cultural conditions that many take for granted, an alternative view on matters far too often accepted uncritically. Yet, paradoxically, as many of these quotations have been acknowledged by our larger culture as truths, it only goes to show, I would argue, the extent to which what we might term the homosexual sensibility has shaped Western civilization.

I admit to a certain whimsicality in the categorization of certain quotations. This is in keeping with a particular aspect of the homosexual sensibility of which I speak. Over the centuries, gays and lesbians have created a subversive form of rhetorical irony, commonly known as camp, by which a given statement can *seem* to support traditional values and the status quo, at least to the uninitiated, nonqueer public. Yet the excessiveness or convolutedness of the diction or syntax through which the statement is made gives a sly clue, in the manner of an inside joke, to one's kindred spirits that its *real* meaning parodies what it seems to assert. Usually camp works by treating serious matters as if they were trivial and trivial matters as if they were serious; in this manner, established values become inverted. Consequently, any number of the entries under a given heading can have two meanings simultaneously: whether they are "for" or "against" a given issue is not always clear to those unused to the rhetoric of camp. Accordingly, some of the entries may strike the casual reader as somewhat misplaced; at the same time, the same entries should provoke mirth in the cognoscenti of camp. To those who miss the jokes, I advise time and patience: breaking the codes is a sort of queer initiation rite. The textual pleasures of camp make the attempt worthwhile.

And so, gentle reader, I welcome you into the superb, diverse, contrary, raucous, poignant, contentious, rebellious, bitchy, and delightful realm of gay and lesbian thought and views. Enjoy—and be enlightened.

Achievement

▼

1. I believe in some one / Who will think of us / Many years from now. / And remember
   —SAPPHO (7th century BCE), Fragment 147; trans. Anita George

2. I've finished that chapel I was painting. The Pope is quite satisfied.
   —MICHELANGELO, on the Sistine Chapel, letter to his father, 1512

3. Bless thee, Bottom, bless thee! Thou art translated.
   —WILLIAM SHAKESPEARE, A Midsummer Night's Dream (1595)

4. How my achievements mock me!
   —WILLIAM SHAKESPEARE, Troilus and Cressida (1602)

5. She was a woman who, between courses, could be graceful with her elbows on the table.
   —HENRY JAMES, The Ambassadors (1903)

6. It is one of the consolations of middle-aged reformers that the good they inculcate must live after them if it is to live at all.
   —SAKI [H. H. Munro], "The Byzantine Omelette," Beasts and Super-Beasts (1914)

7. You can do anything in this world if you are prepared to take the consequences.
   —W. SOMERSET MAUGHAM, "The Circle" (1921)

8. I am an American and I have lived half my life in Paris, not the half which made me, but the half in which I made what I made.
   —GERTRUDE STEIN, An American and France (1930)

9. Nothing really matters but living—accomplishments are the ornaments of life, they come second.
   —WILLA CATHER, Lucy Gayheart (1935)

10. We have not crawled so very far / up our individual grass-blade / toward our individual star.
>   —H.D. [Hilda Doolittle], *The Walls Do Not Fall (1944)*

11. What is the victory of a cat on a hot tin roof?—I wish I knew. . . . Just staying on it, I guess, as long as she can.
>   —TENNESSEE WILLIAMS, *Cat on a Hot Tin Roof (1955)*

12. There is nothing like a rain of bombs to start one trying to assess one's own achievement.
>   —PATRICK WHITE, "The Prodigal Son" *(1958)*

13. I became one of the stately homos of England.
>   —QUENTIN CRISP, *The Naked Civil Servant (1968)*

14. I live no longer in the usual world. I have forsaken the familiar. And soon, by an extreme gesture, I shall cease altogether to be human and become legend like Jesus, Buddha, Cybele.
>   —GORE VIDAL, *Myra Breckinridge (1968)*

15. [*The Well of Loneliness*] became the "Lesbian bible."
>   —DEL MARTIN AND PHYLLIS LYON, *Lesbian / Woman (1972)*

16. I've always wanted to *be* somebody. But now I see I should have been more specific.
>   —JANE WAGNER *[words spoken by Lily Tomlin], The Search for Signs of Intelligent Life in the Universe (1985)*

17. [I] slept with four *Time* magazine covers.
>   —NED ROREM, *Nantucket Diary, 1973–1985 (1987)*

18. Fact is, for all I tell my sisters / I turned out terrific at it myself.
>   —DOROTHY ALLISON, "The Women Who Hate Me" *(1991)*

A c t i o n

▼

1. A man must make his opportunity, as oft as find it.
> —FRANCIS BACON, Advancement of Learning (1605)

2. The rarer action is / In virtue than in vengeance.
> —WILLIAM SHAKESPEARE, The Tempest (1611)

3. 'Tis not your saying that you love, / Can ease me of my smart; / Your actions must your words approve, / Or else you break my heart.
> —APHRA BEHN, "Song" (1684)

4. Actions are our epochs.
> —GEORGE GORDON, LORD BYRON, Manfred (1817)

5. Indeed, for my part, I shall be happy to leave / A world where action is not sister to the dream.
> —CHARLES BAUDELAIRE, "Le Reniement de Saint-Pierre," Les Fleurs du Mal (1857)

6. Action is not life, but a way of wasting some force, an enervation.
> —ARTHUR RIMBAUD, Une Saison en Enfer (1874)

7. I have never had to feel things. I have had to *do* them, to make myself felt.
> —HENRY JAMES, The American (1877)

8. Don't talk about action. It is the last resource of those who know not how to dream.
> —OSCAR WILDE, "The Critic as Artist" (1891)

9. Action is indeed the sole medium of expression for ethics.
> —JANE ADDAMS, Democracy and Social Ethics (1902)

10. Risk! Risk anything! Care no more for the opinions of others, for those voices. Do the hardest thing on earth for you. Act for yourself. Face the truth.
> —KATHERINE MANSFIELD (1922), The Journal of Katherine Mansfield (1927)

11. Trust the man who hesitates in his speech and is quick and steady in action, but beware of long arguments and long beards.
> —GEORGE SANTAYANA, Soliloquies in England (1922)

12. Efficiency should possess a sweeping gesture—even if that gesture may at moments sweep the ornaments off the mantelpiece.
> —*HAROLD NICOLSON, Small Talk (1937)*

13. I do want to get rich but I never want to do what there is to do to get rich.
> —*GERTRUDE STEIN, Everybody's Autobiography (1937)*

14. Is every human action, as you now think, / The fruit of imitation and thoughtlessness?
> —*LUIS CERNUDA, "La familia," Como quien espera el alba (1941–44)*

15. At any time you might act for my good. When people do that, it kills something precious between them.
> —*IVY COMPTON-BURNETT, Manservant and Maidservant (1947)*

16. No action is in itself good or bad, but only such according to convention.
> —*W. SOMERSET MAUGHAM, A Writer's Notebook (1949)*

17. One is always nearer by not keeping still.
> —*THOM GUNN, "On the Move" (1957)*

18. What you don't do can be a destructive force.
> —*ELEANOR ROOSEVELT (d. 1962), Tomorrow Is Now (1963)*

19. I had the correct instinct to fuck things up but no political philosophy to clarify a course of action.
> —*JILL JOHNSTON, Lesbian Nation (1973)*

20. Action is the antidote to despair.
> —*JOAN BAEZ, in Rolling Stone (1983)*

21. What you will do matters. All you need is to do it.
> —*JUDY GRAHN, Another Mother Tongue (1984)*

22. All this group ever does is trash what there is and dream about perfect little doll houses in the big separatist sky. I think it's time we started with the here and now and started talking about alliances and working to really change things instead of trying to define perfection.
> —*NORETTA KOERTGE, Valley of the Amazons (1984)*

23. We do not need, and indeed never will have, all the answers before we act. It is often only through taking action that we can discover some of them.
> —*CHARLOTTE BUNCH, Passionate Politics (1987)*

Adolescence

1. When you are seventeen you aren't really serious.
　　—ARTHUR RIMBAUD, "Roman" (1870)

2. The only unsatisfactory thing about Tommy's return was that she brought with her a girl she had grown fond of at school, a dainty, white, languid bit of a thing, who used violet perfumes and carried a sunshade. The Old Boys said it was a bad sign when a rebellious girl like Tommy took to being sweet and gentle to one of her own sex, the worst sign in the world.
　　—WILLA CATHER, "Tommy the Unsentimental" (1896)

3. The whole thing is metaphysics, music and adolescent eroticism; I shall never get over my adolescence.
　　—THOMAS MANN, letter to his brother Heinrich, 1901

4. In later life we look at things in a more practical way, in full conformity with the rest of society, but adolescence is the only period in which we learn anything.
　　—MARCEL PROUST, Remembrance of Things Past: Within a Budding Grove (1918)

5. She's shy—of the Violet persuasion, but that's not a bad thing in a young girl.
　　—RONALD FIRBANK, The Flower Beneath the Foot (1923)

6. Too chaste an adolescence makes for a dissolute old age.
　　—ANDRÉ GIDE, Journals, 21 January 1929

7. I was becoming more and more worried because I was not like other girls, so I felt that I had better get married as soon as my school days were over, and become normal, as it was supposed that a girl who had sweethearts and wanted to be married was wholly normal. My interest in girls persisted, however, and I could not get up much enthusiasm over the marriage idea.
　　—MARY CASAL, The Stone Wall (1930)

8. And so Ida went on growing older and then she was almost sixteen and a great many funny things happened to her.
　　—GERTRUDE STEIN, Ida (1941)

9. I am fourteen years old and that's the reason / I giggle and dote in season.

—STEVIE SMITH,
"The Conventionalist,"
Mother, What Is Man? (1942)

10. Held in the custody of childhood is a locked chest; the adolescent, by one means or another, tries to open it, the chest is opened: inside, there is nothing.
—YUKIO MISHIMA, "Cigarette"
(1946)

11. I was eleven, then I was sixteen. Though no honors came my way, those were lovely years.
—TRUMAN CAPOTE, *The Grass Harp*
(1951)

12. I tell you. As things are, I won't regret it when the teenage label's torn off the arse pockets of my drip-dry sky-blue jeans.
—COLIN MACINNES, *Absolute Beginners* (1959)

13. I'd the upbringing a nun would envy and that's the truth. Until I was fifteen I was more familiar with Africa than with my own body.
—JOE ORTON, *Entertaining Mr Sloane* (1963)

14. It's hard to be growing up in this climate where sex at its most crude and cold is O.K. but feeling is somehow indecent.

—MAY SARTON, *Mrs. Stevens Hears the Mermaids Singing* (1965)

15. Among the dire results of my "unnaturalness" I had been told that I should go blind and go mad. I believed this. In a kind of cold reasonableness, I tried to teach myself to type and play the piano with my eyes shut, against the time I should be blind.
—VALENTINE ACKLAND (d. 1969),
For Sylvia: An Honest Account
(1985)

16. A load of sticky jam with two adolescent girls embalmed in it.
—VIOLETTE LEDUC, *about her novel Thérèse et Isabelle; Mad in Pursuit* (1971)

17. I suppose I reached puberty officially at age fourteen, when I had my first wide-awake orgasm while staring at a magazine photograph of the Yale swimming team.
—RICHARD AMORY, in *Gay News*,
June 1976

18. Remember that as a teenager you are at the last stage in your life when you will be happy to hear that the phone is for you.
—FRAN LEBOWITZ, *Social Studies*
(1981)

Adventure

1. If we didn't live venturously, plucking the wild goat by the beard, and trembling over precipices, we should never be depressed, I've no doubt; but already should be faded, fatalistic and aged.
> —*VIRGINIA WOOLF, diary,*
> *26 May 1924*

2. How narrow is the line which separates an adventure from an ordeal.
> —*HAROLD NICOLSON, Small Talk*
> *(1937)*

3. Adventure is making the distant approach nearer.
> —*GERTRUDE STEIN, What Are*
> *Masterpieces (1940)*

4. The test of an adventure is that when you're in the middle of it, you say to yourself, "Oh, now I've got myself into an awful mess; I wish I were sitting quietly at home." And the sign that something's wrong with you is when you sit quietly at home wishing you were out having lots of adventure.
> —*THORNTON WILDER, The*
> *Matchmaker (1954)*

Adversity

1. I don't want the honey if it comes with the bee.
> —*SAPPHO (7th century BCE),*
> *Fragment 146; trans. Anita*
> *George*

2. A man is insensible to the relish of prosperity until he has tasted adversity.
> —*SA'DI, Gulistan (1258)*

3. Misery acquaints a man with strange bedfellows.
> —*WILLIAM SHAKESPEARE, The*
> *Tempest (1611)*

4. Adversity is the first path to Truth.
> —*GEORGE GORDON, LORD BYRON,*
> *Don Juan (1819–24)*

5. He knows himself, and all that's in him, who knows adversity.
—*HERMAN MELVILLE, Mardi (1849)*

6. Ill luck of any kind, or even ill treatment at the hands of others, is considered an offense against society, inasmuch as it makes people uncomfortable to hear of it. Loss of fortune, therefore, or loss of some dear friend on whom another was much dependent, is punished hardly less severely than physical delinquency.
—*SAMUEL BUTLER, Erewhon (1872)*

7. His misfortune made him more interesting, and even helped him to be the fashion.
—*HENRY JAMES, Washington Square (1890)*

8. Adversity, if a man is set down to it by degrees, is more supportable with equanimity by most people than any great prosperity arrived at in a single lifetime.
—*SAMUEL BUTLER (d. 1902), The Way of All Flesh (1903)*

9. It's a long old road, but I know I'm gonna find the end.
—*BESSIE SMITH, "Long Old Road" (1931)*

10. Hardship is vanishing, but so is style, and the two are more closely connected than the present generation supposes.
—*E. M. FORSTER, Two Cheers for Democracy (1951)*

A d v i c e

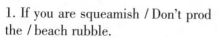

1. If you are squeamish / Don't prod the / beach rubble.
—*SAPPHO (7th century BCE), Fragment 84; trans. Mary Barnard (1958)*

2. Stop searching for the place where a late rose may linger.
—*HORACE (1st century BCE), Odes I, 38*

3. Make haste slowly.
—*DESIDERIUS ERASMUS, Adagia (1500)*

4. You should not seem to remember that there is such a thing as a man in the world, and you ought to imagine everybody to be of the same sex as yourself.
—*MATTHEW G. LEWIS, The Monk (1795)*

5. I have lived some thirty years on this planet, and I have yet to hear the first syllable of valuable or even earnest advice from my seniors.
— *HENRY DAVID THOREAU,*
"Economy," Walden (1854)

6. It is always a silly thing to give advice, but to give good advice is absolutely fatal.
— *OSCAR WILDE (d. 1900), in*
Richard Ellmann, ed., The Artist
as Critic: The Critical Writings of
Oscar Wilde (1969)

7. Astonish me!
— *SERGEI DIAGHILEV (1912), advice*
to Jean Cocteau; in Journals of
Jean Cocteau (1956)

8. Please send me some good advice in your next letter. I promise not to follow it.
— *EDNA ST. VINCENT MILLAY, letter,*
1913

9. In baiting a mouse-trap with cheese, always leave room for the mouse.
— *SAKI [H. H. Munro] (d. 1916),*
"The Infernal Parliament," The
Square Egg (1924)

10. I hope, for his own sake, that he has younger people than me at his disposal if he wishes to ask for bad advice, especially if he means to follow it.
— *MARCEL PROUST, Remembrance of*
Things Past: Cities of the Plain
(1922)

11. My advice to you is not to inquire why or whither, but just enjoy your ice-cream while it's on your plate— that's my philosophy.
— *THORNTON WILDER, The Skin of*
Our Teeth (1942)

12. Don't eat too many almonds; they add weight to the breasts.
— *COLETTE, Gigi (1944)*

13. She quoted a friend who used to say any advice is good as long as it is strong enough.
— *ALICE B. TOKLAS, about Gertrude*
Stein, letter to Carl Van Vechten,
3 September 1946

14. When love goes, bid him Godspeed. / And find another lover.
— *COUNTEE CULLEN (d. 1946),*
"Song in Spite of Myself," On
These I Stand (1947)

15. Save your money, dress better and catch a better husband.
— *EVELYN WAUGH, to Nancy*
Mitford; quoted in Harold Acton,
Nancy Mitford (1975)

16. If you have to be in a soap opera try not to get the worst role.
— *BOY GEORGE, in Face,*
December 1984

17. Never look backwards or you'll fall down the stairs.
— *RUDOLF NUREYEV (d. 1993),*
attributed

Affairs

1. Oh, what a dear ravishing thing is the beginning of an Amour!
    —*APHRA BEHN, The Emperor of the Moon (1687)*

2. The only difference between a caprice and a lifelong passion is that the caprice lasts a little longer.
    —*OSCAR WILDE, The Picture of Dorian Gray (1891)*

3. Romance at short notice was her specialty.
    —*SAKI [H. H. Munro], "The Open Window," Beasts and Super-Beasts (1914)*

4. No, I am in no muddles. . . . Dorothy I have not seen. Louise, no muddles (either Genoux or Loraine), Vera, no muddles. Lady Hillingdon, no muddles; don't know her; don't want to. Violet, no muddles; don't even know where she is; don't want to get into touch, thank you. Virginia [Woolf]—not a muddle exactly; she is a busy and sensible woman. But she does love me, and I did sleep with her at Rodmell. That does not constitute a muddle though.
    —*VITA SACKVILLE-WEST, letter to her husband, Harold Nicolson, 1926*

5. It was great fun, / But it was just one of those things.
    —*COLE PORTER, "Just One of Those Things" (1935 song)*

6. I can understand companionship. I can understand bought sex in the afternoon. I cannot understand the love affair.
    —*GORE VIDAL, in The Sunday Times (1973)*

Age and Aging

1. He who is of a calm and happy nature will hardly feel the pressure of age, but to him who is of an opposite disposition youth and age are equally a burden.
    —PLATO (4th century BCE), The Republic

2. You and I are past our dancing days.
    —WILLIAM SHAKESPEARE, Romeo and Juliet (1595)

3. My age is as a lusty winter, / Frosty but kindly.
    —WILLIAM SHAKESPEARE, As You Like It (1599–1600)

4. We grow old more through indolence, than through age.
    —CHRISTINA, QUEEN OF SWEDEN, Maxims (1660–80)

5. Threatening, terrifying is oncoming old age, but nothing will reverse and return!
    —NICOLAI GOGOL, Dead Souls (1842)

6. Thirty-five is a very attractive age. London society is full of women of the very highest birth who have, of their own free choice, remained thirty-five for years.

    —OSCAR WILDE, The Importance of Being Earnest (1895)

7. Wrecked on the lee shore of age.
    —SARAH ORNE JEWETT, The Country of Pointed Firs (1896)

8. The young have aspirations that never come to pass, the old have reminiscences of what never happened. It's only the middle-aged who are really conscious of their limitations.
    —SAKI [H. H. MUNRO], "Reginald at the Carlton," Reginald (1904)

9. She stands, I fear, poor thing, now for something younger than she looks.
    —RONALD FIRBANK, Valmouth (1919)

10. The older one grows the more one likes indecency.
    —VIRGINIA WOOLF, "The String Quartet" (1921)

11. It's pretty hard to retain the characteristics of one's sex after a certain age.
    —COLETTE, My Mother's House (1922)

12. Old age, believe me, is a good and pleasant thing. It is true that you

are gently shouldered off the stage, but then you are given such a comfortable front stall as spectator.
　　—*JANE HARRISON, Reminiscences of a Student's Life (1925)*

13. Tranquillity comes with years, and that horrid thing which Freud calls sex is expunged.
　　—*E. F. BENSON, Mapp and Lucia (1935)*

14. When one begins to think of oneself as growing old, one is already old.
　　—*ELSIE DE WOLFE, After All (1935)*

15. How foolish to think that one can ever slam the door in the face of age. Much wiser to be polite and gracious and ask him to lunch in advance.
　　—*NOËL COWARD, diary, 3 June 1956*

16. Old age is a great trial. . . . One has to be so damned *good!*
　　—*MAY SARTON, Kinds of Love (1970)*

17. Growing old is like being increasingly penalized for a crime you haven't committed.

　　—*ANTHONY POWELL, A Dance to the Music of Time: Temporary Kings (1973)*

18. Just when you began to feel that you could make good use of time, there was no time left to you.
　　—*LISA ALTHER, Kinflicks (1975)*

19. A woman who will tell her age will tell anything.
　　—*RITA MAE BROWN, Southern Discomfort (1982)*

20. I'm aging as well as a beach party movie.
　　—*HARVEY FIERSTEIN, Torch Song Trilogy (1982)*

21. I told Princess Margaret it was too bad she didn't like fags because it would mean she would have a very lonely old age. Fags are the only people who are kind to worldly old women.
　　—*TRUMAN CAPOTE (d. 1984), Answered Prayers (1986)*

22. Old age is somewhat like dieting. Every day there is less of us to be observed.
　　—*DORIS GRUMBACH, Fifty Days of Solitude (1994)*

AIDS

1. We're all going crazy, living this epidemic every minute, while the rest of the world goes on out there, all around us, as if nothing is happening, going on with their own lives and not knowing what it's like, what we're going through. We're living through war, but where they're living it's peacetime, and we're all in the same country.
   —*LARRY KRAMER, The Normal Heart (1986)*

2. The AIDS epidemic has rolled back a big rotting log and revealed all the squirming life underneath it, since it involves, all at once, the main themes of our existence: sex, death, power, money, love, hate, disease and panic. No American phenomenon has been so compelling since the Vietnam War.
   —*EDMUND WHITE, afterword to States of Desire: Travels in Gay America (1986 edition)*

3. AIDS obliges people to think of sex as having, possibly, the direst consequences: suicide. Or murder.
   —*SUSAN SONTAG, AIDS and Its Metaphors (1989)*

4. To have been oppressed in the fifties, freed in the sixties, exalted in the seventies, and wiped out in the eighties is a quick itinerary for a whole culture to follow. For we are witnessing not just the death of individuals but a menace to an entire culture. All the more reason to bear witness to the cultural moment.
   —*EDMUND WHITE, "Esthetics and Loss" (1989)*

5. It was the beginning of the end of the world but not everyone noticed right away. Some people were dying.
   —*SARAH SCHULMAN, People in Trouble (1990)*

6. The slow-witted approach to the HIV epidemic was the result of a thousand years of Christian malpractice and the childlike approach of the church to sexuality. If any single man was responsible, it was Augustine of Hippo who murdered his way to sainthood spouting on about the sins located in his genitals.
   —*DEREK JARMAN, At Your Own Risk: A Saint's Testament (1992)*

7. I have said it again and again. "Everyone who preached free love in the Sixties is responsible for AIDS." And we must accept moral responsibility for it. The idea that it is an accident, a historical accident, a

microbe that sort of fell from the heavens—absurd. We must face what we did.
—CAMILLE PAGLIA, *Sex, Art, and American Culture (1992)*

8. This disease will be the end of many of us, but not nearly all, and the dead will be commemorated and will struggle on with the living, and we are not going away. We won't die secret deaths anymore. The world only spins forward. We will be citizens. The time has come.
—TONY KUSHNER, *Angels in America, Part Two: Perestroika (1992)*

Ambition

1. Life's brief span forbids us from entering on far-reaching hopes.
—HORACE *(1st century BCE)*, *Odes I, 4*

2. They can because they think they can.
—VIRGIL, *Aeneid (19 BCE)*

3. Nature that fram'd us of four elements, / Warring within our breasts for regiment, / Doth teach us all to have aspiring minds.
—CHRISTOPHER MARLOWE, *Tamburlaine the Great (1587)*

4. 'Tis but a base, ignoble mind / That mounts no higher than a bird can soar.
—WILLIAM SHAKESPEARE, *2 Henry VI, (1592)*

5. As he was valiant, I honour him. But as he was ambitious, I slew him.
—WILLIAM SHAKESPEARE, *Julius Caesar (1599)*

6. Let not Ambition mock their useful toil, / Their homely joys, and destiny obscure.
—THOMAS GRAY, *"Elegy Written in a Country Churchyard" (1751)*

7. Stretching out to catch the stars, he forgets the flowers at his feet.
—JEREMY BENTHAM *(d. 1832)*, *Deontology (1834)*

8. We are all in the gutter, but some of us are looking at the stars.
—OSCAR WILDE, *Lady Windermere's Fan (1891)*

9. If a thing can be done why do it.
> —GERTRUDE STEIN (d. 1946), in
> Elizabeth Sprigge, Gertrude Stein
> (1957)

10. Ambition, old as mankind, the immemorial weakness of the strong.
> —VITA SACKVILLE-WEST, No
> Signposts in the Sea (1961)

11. Ambition if it feeds at all, does so on the ambition of others.
> —SUSAN SONTAG, The Benefactor
> (1963)

12. All men seek esteem; the best by lifting themselves, which is hard to do, the rest by shoving others down, which is much easier.
> —MARY RENAULT, The Praise
> Singer (1978)

13. I wanted to attempt something of ambition and size even if that meant I might be accused of straying too close to ambition's ugly twin, pretentiousness.
> —TONY KUSHNER, on his play
> Angels in America, in New York
> Times, 21 November 1993

Anger

1. Anger is a brief lunacy.
> —HORACE (1st century BCE),
> Epistles I, 2

2. No man is angry that feels not himself hurt.
> —FRANCIS BACON, "On Anger,"
> Essays (1625)

3. No vows are less sincere than those made in anger.
> —SARAH SCOTT, The History of
> Cornelia (1750)

4. Anger as soon as fed is dead—
/ 'Tis starving makes it fat.
> —EMILY DICKINSON, no. 1509
> (c. 1881), Complete Poems
> (1955)

5. Their anger dug out for itself a deep channel, so that future angers might more easily follow.
> —RADCLYFFE HALL, The Well of
> Loneliness (1928)

6. Rage cannot be hidden, it can only be dissembled.
> —JAMES BALDWIN, Notes of a Native
> Son (1955)

7. Great fury, like great whisky, requires long fermentation.

—TRUMAN CAPOTE, *Music for Chameleons (1980)*

8. Anger is loaded with information and energy.
　—AUDRE LORDE, *"The Uses of Anger," Sister Outsider (1984)*

9. I have suckled the wolf's lip of anger and I have used it for illumination, laughter, protection, fire in places where there was no light, no food, no sisters, no quarter.
　—AUDRE LORDE, *"The Uses of Anger," Sister Outsider (1984)*

A n i m a l s

1. Cheerfulness is proper to the cock, which rejoices over every little thing, and crows with varied and lively movements.
　—LEONARDO DA VINCI, *Notebooks (c. 1500)*

2. You spotted snakes with double tongue, / Thorny hedgehogs, be not seen; / Newts and blind-worms, do no wrong, / Come not near our fairy Queen.
　—WILLIAM SHAKESPEARE, *A Midsummer Night's Dream (1595)*

3. I think I could turn and live with animals, they are so placid and self-contain'd, / I stand and look at them long and long, / They do not sweat and whine about their condition, / They do not lie awake in the dark and weep for their sins, / They do not make me sick discussing their duty to God, / Not one is dissatisfied, not one is demented with the mania of owning things, / Not one kneels to another, nor to his kind that lived thousands of years ago, / Not one is respectable or unhappy over the whole earth.
　—WALT WHITMAN, *"Song of Myself," Leaves of Grass (1855)*

4. All animals, except man, know that the principal business of life is to enjoy it—and they do enjoy it as much as man and other circumstances will allow.
　—SAMUEL BUTLER (d. 1902), *The Way of All Flesh (1903)*

5. I am because my little dog knows me.
　—GERTRUDE STEIN, *The Geographical History of America (1936)*

6. More and more I am certain that the only difference between man and

animals is that men can count and animals cannot and if they count they mostly do count money.
    —GERTRUDE STEIN, *Everybody's Autobiography (1937)*

7. The best thing about animals is that they don't talk much.
    —THORNTON WILDER, *The Skin of Our Teeth (1942)*

8. Everyone's pet is the most outstanding. This begets mutual blindness.
    —JEAN COCTEAU, *Diary of an Unknown (1952)*

9. It is a terrible thing for an old lady to outlive her dogs.
    —TENNESSEE WILLIAMS, *Camino Real (1953)*

10. Shall we never have done with that cliché, so stupid that it could only be human, about the sympathy of animals for man when he is unhappy? Animals love happiness almost as much as we do. A fit of crying disturbs them, they'll sometimes imitate sobbing, and for a moment they'll reflect our sadness. But they flee unhappiness as they flee fever, and I believe that in the long run they are capable of boycotting it.
    —COLETTE (d. 1954), *Earthly Paradise (1966)*

11. If one is of the masculine gender, a poodle is the insignia of one's deviation.

    —MART CROWLEY, *The Boys in the Band (1968)*

12. No animal should ever jump up on the dining-room furniture unless absolutely certain that he can hold his own in the conversation.
    —FRAN LEBOWITZ, *Social Studies (1981)*

13. And as for the alleged "laws of nature," what about those lesbian seagulls on Catalina Island, off the coast of California? Or the fact that homosexuality and lesbianism existed among cats, dogs, primates, and other creatures?
    —PAULA CHRISTIAN, *The Cruise (1982)*

14. I would never wound a cat's feelings, no matter how downright aggressive I might be to humans.
    —A. L. ROWSE, *A Quartet of Cornish Cats (1982)*

15. Cats are autocrats of naked self-interest. They are both amoral and immoral, consciously breaking rules. Their "evil" look at such times is no human projection: the cat may be the only animal who savors the perverse or reflects on it.
    —CAMILLE PAGLIA, *Sexual Personae (1990)*

16. Penguins mate for life. Which doesn't exactly surprise me that much 'cause they all look alike—it's

not like they're gonna meet a better-looking penguin someday.
> —*ELLEN DEGENERES, in Mirabella (1992)*

17. She loved to smell Hollywood more than any other place we have been.
> —*LARS EIGHNER, on his dog, Travels with Lizabeth (1993)*

18. Consider two stereotypes: gay men and poodles or other "effemi-nate" dogs . . . [and] young girls and horses *(National Velvet)*, an interest that precedes the love of boys. Are lesbians supposedly fond of dogs? What is the lesbian pet of choice? . . . The image of the dog persuades us that queer passions, the perversities of women who love women and men who love men, are bred into the blood, are mute, domestic, and sub-human.
> —*WAYNE KOESTENBAUM, The Queen's Throat (1993)*

Antiquity

1. Had the Greeks held novelty in such disdain as we, what work of ancient date would now exist?
> —*HORACE (1st century BCE), Epistles II, I*

2. It is an unscrupulous intellect that does not pay to antiquity its due reverence.
> —*DESIDERIUS ERASMUS, Preface to Works of Hilary (1523)*

3. The isles of Greece, the isles of Greece! / Where burning Sappho loved and sung.

> —*GEORGE GORDON, LORD BYRON, Don Juan (1819–24)*

4. Woe betide the man who goes to antiquity for the study of anything other than ideal art, logic, and general method!
> —*CHARLES BAUDELAIRE (d. 1867), The Painter of Modern Life (1869)*

5. Whatever, in fact, is modern in our life we owe to the Greeks. Whatever is an anachronism is due to mediaevalism.

—OSCAR WILDE, "The Critic as
Artist" (1891)

6. It's beige! My color!
—ELSIE DE WOLFE (d. 1950) upon
first seeing the Acropolis, in
Jane S. Smith, Elsie de Wolfe
(1982)

7. It is time for dead languages to be
quiet.
—NATALIE CLIFFORD BARNEY, "On
Writing and Writers" (1962)

Appearance

1. Your behaviour is above your
seeming.
—HORACE WALPOLE, The Castle of
Otranto (1764)

2. Let us be grateful to the mirror for
revealing to us our appearance only.
—SAMUEL BUTLER, Erewhon (1872)

3. It is only shallow people who do
not judge by appearances. The true
mystery of the world is the visible,
not the invisible.
—OSCAR WILDE, The Picture of
Dorian Gray (1891)

4. We live, I regret to say, in an age of
surfaces.
—OSCAR WILDE, The Importance of
Being Earnest (1895)

5. I look like a discouraged beetle
battered by the rains of a spring
night. I look like a molting bird. I
look like a governess in distress. I
look—Good Lord, I look like an
actress on tour, and that speaks for
itself.
—COLETTE, Music Hall Sidelights
(1913)

6. Appearances are not held to be a
clue to the truth. But we seem to have
no other.
—IVY COMPTON-BURNETT,
Manservant and Maidservant
(1947)

7. It seems to me that invisibility is
the required provision of elegance.
Elegance ceases to exist when it is
noticed.
—JEAN COCTEAU, Diary of an
Unknown (1952)

8. Why not be one's self? That is the
whole secret of a successful appear-

ance. If one is a greyhound, why try to look like a Pekingese?
> —*EDITH SITWELL (d. 1964) in Elizabeth Salter and Allanah Harder, eds., Edith Sitwell (1976)*

9. All God's children are not beautiful. Most of God's children are, in fact, barely presentable.
> —*FRAN LEBOWITZ, Metropolitan Life (1978)*

Arguments and Quarrels

1. Myself when young did eagerly frequent / Doctor and Saint, and heard great Argument / About it and about: but evermore / Came out by the same Door as in I went.
> —*OMAR KHAYYÁM, Rubáiyát (11th–12th century); trans. Edward FitzGerald*

2. In a false quarrel there is no true valour.
> —*WILLIAM SHAKESPEARE, Much Ado About Nothing (1598)*

3. Rightly to be great / Is not to stir without great argument, / But greatly to find quarrel in a straw / When honour's at the stake.
> —*WILLIAM SHAKESPEARE, Hamlet (1600)*

4. How beggarly appear arguments before a defiant deed!
> —*WALT WHITMAN, "Song of Myself," Leaves of Grass (1855)*

5. Of all things in the world contention was most sweet to her.
> —*HENRY JAMES, The Bostonians (1886)*

6. I dislike arguments of any kind. They are always vulgar, and often convincing.
> —*OSCAR WILDE, The Importance of Being Earnest (1895)*

7. My dear sir, they don't debate. Each of them merely issues an ultimatum, and in what a tone! It all goes to show what extraordinary people they are, each more unequivocal than the other.
> —*COLETTE, "The Old Lady and the Bear" (1920)*

8. In time they quarreled, of course, and about an abstraction—as young people often do, as mature people almost never do.

—*WILLA CATHER, "Coming, Aphrodite!" Youth and the Bright Medusa (1920)*

9. Most quarrels amplify a misunderstanding.
—*ANDRÉ GIDE, Journals, 1920*

10. It is very often astonishing to each one quarreling to find out what the other one was remembering for quarreling. Mostly in quarreling not any one is finding out what the other one is remembering for quarreling, what the other one is remembering from quarreling.
—*GERTRUDE STEIN, The Making of Americans (1925)*

11. But brawling leads to laryngitis.
—*JEAN COCTEAU, Les enfants terribles (1929); trans. Rosamond Lehmann*

12. When an arguer argues dispassionately he thinks only of the argument.
—*VIRGINIA WOOLF, A Room of One's Own (1929)*

13. Those who attack always do so with greater fervor than those who defend.
—*ELEANOR ROOSEVELT, My Days (1938)*

14. Shouting has never made me understand anything.
—*SUSAN SONTAG, The Benefactor (1963)*

15. It was completely fruitless to quarrel with the world, whereas the quarrel with oneself was occasionally fruitful, and always, she had to admit, interesting.
—*MAY SARTON, Mrs. Stevens Hears the Mermaids Singing (1965)*

Art

1. All art constantly aspires towards the condition of music.
—*WALTER PATER, Studies in the History of the Renaissance (1873)*

2. He had looked out all the pictures to which an asterisk was affixed in those formidable pages of fine print in his Bädecker; his attention had been strained and his eyes dazzled,

and he had sat down with an aesthetic headache.
—HENRY JAMES, *The American*
(1877)

3. All that I desire to point out is the general principle that Life imitates Art far more than Art imitates Life.
—OSCAR WILDE, *"The Decay of Lying" (1891)*

4. The effort of art is to keep what is interesting in existence, to recreate it in the eternal.
—GEORGE SANTAYANA, *The Life of Reason (1906)*

5. A work of art that contains theories is like an object on which the price tag has been left.
—MARCEL PROUST (d. 1922), *Remembrance of Things Past: Time Regained (1927)*

6. Art is science made clear.
—JEAN COCTEAU, *"Le Coq et l'Arlequin," Le Rappel à l'Ordre (1926)*

7. There was so much sculpture that I should certainly have missed the indecencies if Major Poonby hadn't been considerate enough to point them out.
—J. R. ACKERLEY, *Hindoo Holiday (1932)*

8. Art is significant deformity.
—ROGER FRY (d. 1934), *in Virginia Woolf, Roger Fry (1940)*

9. The contemporary thing in art and literature is the thing which doesn't make enough difference to the people of that generation so that they can accept it or reject it.
—GERTRUDE STEIN, *"How Writing Is Written" (1935)*

10. Religion and art spring from the same root and are close kin. Economics and art are strangers.
—WILLA CATHER, *Commonweal, 17 April 1936*

11. I took Art at College as my second subject one semester. I'd have taken it as my first subject only Dad lost his money in religion so I had to learn a trade.
—EVELYN WAUGH, *The Loved One (1948)*

12. I suppose art is the only thing that can go on mattering once it has stopped hurting.
—ELIZABETH BOWEN, *Heat of the Day (1949)*

13. Fortunately art is a community effort—a small but select community living in a spiritualized world endeavoring to interpret the wars and solitudes of the flesh.
—ALLEN GINSBERG, *journal, 11 July 1954*

14. Much of modern art is devoted to lowering the threshold of what is terrible. By getting us used to what, formerly we could not bear to see or hear, because it was too shocking, painful, or embarrassing, art changes morals.
　　—SUSAN SONTAG, *On Photography*
　　　(1977)

15. Very few people possess true artistic ability. It is therefore both unseemly and unproductive to irritate the situation by making an effort. If you have a burning, restless urge to write or paint, simply eat something sweet and the feeling will pass.
　　—FRAN LEBOWITZ, *Metropolitan*
　　　Life (1978)

16. If Michelangelo were a heterosexual, the Sistine Chapel would have been painted basic white and with a roller.

—RITA MAE BROWN, *in New York Times, 15 May 1988*

17. Sometimes a person has to stop talking about art for a moment and take a look around.
　　—SARAH SCHULMAN, *People in*
　　　Trouble (1990)

18. Sometimes we forget that if we do not encourage new work now, we will lose all touch with the work of the past we claim to love. If art is not living in a continuous present, it is living in a museum, only those working now can complete the circuit between the past, present and future energies we call art.
　　—JEANETTE WINTERSON, *"Testimony*
　　　Against Gertrude Stein," Art
　　　[Objects]: Essays on Ecstasy and
　　　Effrontery (1995)

Artists

1. Let our artists rather be those who are gifted to discern the true nature of the beautiful and the graceful; then will youth dwell in a land of health, amid fair sights and sounds, and receive the good in everything; and beauty, the effulgence of works, shall flow into the eye and ear, like a health-giving breeze from a pure region, and insensibly draw the soul from earliest years into likeness and sympathy with the beauty of reason.
　　—PLATO *(4th century BCE)*,
　　　The Republic

2. In his very rejection of art Walt Whitman is an artist. He tried to produce a certain effect by certain means and he succeeded. . . . He stands apart, and the chief value of his work is in its prophecy, not in its performance. He has begun a prelude to larger themes. He is the herald to a new era. As a man he is the precursor of a fresh type. He is a factor in the heroic and spiritual evolution of the human being. If Poetry has passed him by, Philosophy will take note of him.
　　—OSCAR WILDE, *Pall Mall Gazette* (London), 25 January 1889

3. We work in the dark—we do what we can—we give what we have. Our doubt is our passion and our passion is our task. The rest is the madness of art.
　　—HENRY JAMES, *"The Middle Years" (1893)*

4. An artist has no need to express his mind directly in his work for it to express the quality of that mind; it has indeed been said that the highest praise of God consists in the denial of Him by the atheist, who finds creation so perfect that it can dispense with a creator.
　　—MARCEL PROUST, *Remembrance of Things Past: The Guermantes Way (1921)*

5. One must be a living man and a posthumous artist.

　　—JEAN COCTEAU, *"Le Coq et l'Arlequin," Le Rappel à l'Ordre (1926)*

6. It is very necessary to have makers of beauty left in a world seemingly bent on making the most evil ugliness.
　　—VITA SACKVILLE-WEST, *Country Notes (1940)*

7. The artist, like the idiot or clown, sits on the edge of the world, and a push may send him over it.
　　—OSBERT SITWELL, *The Scarlet Tree (1946)*

8. All men are creative but few are artists.
　　—PAUL GOODMAN, *Growing Up Absurd (1961)*

9. He had all an artist needs, except the spark from the gods.
　　—MARY RENAULT, *The Mask of Apollo (1966)*

10. An artist is someone who produces things that people don't need to have but that he—for some reason—thinks it would be a good idea to give them.
　　—ANDY WARHOL, *The Philosophy of Andy Warhol: From A to B and Back Again (1975)*

11. I have suffered far less from being a homosexual than I have from being a composer.

—*NED ROREM, in People,*
21 August 1978

12. So if you are a lesbian, be prepared. They'll take you seriously as an artist when you're dead. Then you can join the ranks of the angels like Stein, Cather, and Colette.
—*RITA MAE BROWN, Starting from*
Scratch (1988)

13. If we are to change our world view, images have to change. The artist now has a very important job to do. He's not a little peripheral figure entertaining rich people, he's really needed.
—*DAVID HOCKNEY, Hockney on*
Photography (1988)

B e a u t y

1. Mnasdika—Fair symmetry! / Better formed than soft Gyrinno.
—*SAPPHO (7th century BCE),*
Fragment 82(a); trans. Anita
George

2. O handsome lad, don't trust too much in your complexion.
—*VIRGIL, Eclogues (43–37 BCE)*

3. To me, fair friend, you never can be old / For as you were when first your eye I eyed, / Such seems your beauty still.
—*WILLIAM SHAKESPEARE,*
Sonnet 104 (1609)

4. There is no excellent beauty that hath not some strangeness in the proportion.

—*FRANCIS BACON, "Of Beauty,"*
The Essays (1625)

5. Just because the beautiful is always shocking, it would be absurd to suppose that that which is shocking is always beautiful.
—*CHARLES BAUDELAIRE (d. 1867),*
Le Spleen de Paris (1869)

6. It is better to be beautiful than to do good. But it is better to be good than ugly.
—*OSCAR WILDE, The Picture of*
Dorian Gray (1891)

7. It is a marvel that those red rose-leaf lips of yours should have been made no less for the music of song than for the madness of kissing.

—OSCAR WILDE, *letter to Lord Alfred Douglas (1893); used as evidence during his trial for "gross indecency"*

8. It is conventional to call "monster" any blending of dissonant element. I call "monster" every original inexhaustible beauty.

—ALFRED JARRY, *L'Ymagier (1894)*

9. I always say beauty is only sin deep.

—SAKI [H. H. Munro], *"Reginald's Choir Treat," Reginald (1904)*

10. The observer saw him in half-profiles, with one foot in its black patent leather advanced, one elbow resting on the arm of his basket-chair, the cheek nestled into the closed hand in a pose of easy grace, quite unlike the stiff subservient mien which was evidently habitual to his sisters. Was he delicate? His facial tint was ivory-white against the golden darkness of his clustering locks. Or was he simply a pampered darling, the object of a self-willed and partial love? Aschenbach inclined to think the latter. For in almost every artistic nature is inborn a wanton and treacherous proneness to side with the beauty that breaks hearts, to single out aristocratic pretensions and pay them homage.

—THOMAS MANN, *Death in Venice (1912)*

11. You are beautiful and faded, / Like an old opera tune / Played upon a harpsichord.

—AMY LOWELL, *"A Lady" (1914)*

12. These bewildering frightful beautifulnesses in this life—withal the same inherence which makes me someway Lesbian makes me the floor of the setting sun—strewn with overflowing gold and green vases of Fire and Turquoise—a sly and piercing annihilation-of-beauty, wonderful devastating to feel—oh, blighting breaking to feel—oh, deathly lovely to feel!

—MARY MACLANE, *I, Mary MacLane (1917)*

13. I went hunting wild / After the wildest beauty in the world.

—WILFRED OWEN, *"Strange Meeting" (1918)*

14. Perhaps it was because . . . the natural nearly always wore the guise of ugliness, that a certain element of artificiality seemed . . . necessary in beauty.

—WILLA CATHER, *"Paul's Case" (1920)*

15. I am waylaid by beauty.

—EDNA ST. VINCENT MILLAY, *"Assault" (1921)*

16. It has been said that beauty is a guarantee of happiness. Conversely, the possibility of pleasure can be the beginning of beauty.

—MARCEL PROUST (d. 1922),
Remembrance of Things Past:
The Captive (1923)

17. A thing of beauty is a boy forever.
—CARL VAN VECHTEN, *The Blind*
Bow-Boy (1923)

18. Beauty ought to look a little surprised: it is the emotion that best
suits her face. The beauty who does
not look surprised, who accepts her
position as her due—she reminds us
too much of a prima donna.
—E. M. FORSTER, *Aspects of the*
Novel (1927)

19. Seeing Mary in the glass she did
not turn round, but just smiled for a
moment at their two reflections. Mary
sat down in an arm-chair and
watched her, noticing the strong, thin
line of her thighs; noticing too the
curve of her breasts—slight and
compact, of a certain beauty.
—RADCLYFFE HALL, *The Well of*
Loneliness (1928)

20. O, beauty, are you not enough? /
Why am I crying after love?
—SARA TEASDALE, "Spring Night"
(1929)

21. The beauty of the world . . . has
two edges, one of laughter, one of
anguish, cutting the heart asunder.
—VIRGINIA WOOLF, *A Room of One's*
Own (1929)

22. Beauty is an ecstasy; it is as
simple as hunger. There is really
nothing to be said about it. It is like
the perfume of a rose: you can smell
it and that is all.
—W. SOMERSET MAUGHAM, *Cakes*
and Ale (1930)

23. All ugliness passes, and beauty
endures, excepting of the skin.
—EDITH SITWELL (1941), *in John*
Lehmann and Derek Parker, eds.,
Selected Letters (1970)

24. It is easy to be beautiful; it is difficult to appear so.
—FRANK O'HARA (d. 1966),
"Meditations in an Emergency"
(1967)

25. It's the daylight you gotta watch
out for. Face it, a thing of beauty is a
joy until sunrise.
—HARVEY FIERSTEIN, *Torch Song*
Trilogy (1981)

26. But tell me why it is that everybody is so good-looking now. In the
fifties, there were really good-looking
people and then all the rest who
weren't. Today, everybody is at least
attractive. How did it happen? Is it
because there's no wars to kill the
beauties?
—ANDY WARHOL, *diary,*
16 August 1982

27. There were people who were different like me inside. We could all

see our reflections in the faces of those who sat in this circle. I looked around. It was hard to say who was a woman, who was a man. Their faces radiated a different kind of beauty than I'd grown up seeing celebrated on television or in magazines. It's a beauty one isn't born with, but must fight to construct at great sacrifice.
— *LESLIE FEINBERG, Stone Butch Blues (1993)*

B e d

1. I was in love with my bed.
   — *WILLIAM SHAKESPEARE, The Two Gentlemen of Verona (1590–91)*

2. And I will make thee beds of roses / And a thousand fragrant posies.
   — *CHRISTOPHER MARLOWE (d. 1593), "The Passionate Shepherd to His Love" (1599)*

3. What angel wakes me from my flow'ry bed?
   — *WILLIAM SHAKESPEARE, A Midsummer Night's Dream (1595)*

4. There is no place like a bed for confidential disclosures between friends.
   — *HERMAN MELVILLE, Moby-Dick (1851)*

5. A bed, a nice fresh bed, with smoothly drawn sheets and a hot-water bottle at the end of it, soft to the feet like a live animal's tummy.
   — *COLETTE, Music Hall Sidelights (1913)*

6. For a long time I used to go to bed early.
   — *MARCEL PROUST, Remembrance of Things Past: Swann's Way (1913)*

7. The cool kindliness of sheets, that soon / Smooth away trouble; and the rough male kiss / Of blankets.
   — *RUPERT BROOKE, "The Great Lover" (1914)*

8. When my bed is empty, / Makes me feel awful mean and blue.
   — *BESSIE SMITH, "Empty Bed Blues" (1928)*

9. When we are in bed, or floating in water, is the only time when we are really out of pain.
　　—ROSE O'NEILL, *Garda (1929)*

10. Out on the lawn I lie in bed, / Vega conspicuous overhead.
　　—W. H. AUDEN, *Look, Stranger (1936)*

11. Musical beds is the faculty sport around here.

—EDWARD ALBEE, *Who's Afraid of Virginia Woolf (1962)*

12. Sleeping alone, except under doctor's orders, does much harm. Children will tell you how lonely it is sleeping alone. If possible you should always sleep with someone you love. You both recharge your mutual batteries free of charge.
　　—MARLENE DIETRICH, *Marlene Dietrich's ABC (1962)*

Belief and Disbelief

1. For what a man would like to be true, that he more readily believes.
　　—FRANCIS BACON, *Novum Organum (1620)*

2. The abdication of Belief / Makes the Behavior small— / Better an ignus fatuus / Than no illume at all.
　　—EMILY DICKINSON, *no. 1551 (c. 1882), Complete Poems (1955)*

3. To believe is very dull. To doubt is intensely engrossing.
　　—OSCAR WILDE (d. 1900), in *Oscariana (1911)*

4. What is faith but a kind of betting or a speculation after all? It should be, "I bet that my Redeemer liveth."

—SAMUEL BUTLER (d. 1902), *Note Books (1912)*

5. Through fear of resembling one another, through horror at having to submit, through uncertainty as well, through skepticism and complexity, there is a multitude of individual little beliefs for the triumph of strange little individuals.
　　—ANDRÉ GIDE, *Pretexts (1903)*

6. One must either accept some theory or else believe one's instinct or follow the world's opinion.
　　—GERTRUDE STEIN, *Q.E.D. (1903)*

7. When Cardinal Newman was a child he "wished he could believe

the Arabian Nights were true." When he came to be a man his wish seems to have been granted.
> —LYTTON STRACHEY, *Eminent Victorians (1918)*

8. It is desire that engenders belief and if we fail as a rule to take this into account, it is because most of the desires that create beliefs end only with our own life.
> —MARCEL PROUST (d. 1922) *Remembrance of Things Past: The Sweet Cheat Gone (1925)*

9. One can only believe, perhaps, in what one cannot see.
> —VIRGINIA WOOLF, *Orlando (1928)*

10. Not seeing is half-believing.
> —VITA SACKVILLE-WEST, *The Edwardians (1930)*

11. Life without faith is an arid business.
> —NOËL COWARD, *Blithe Spirit (1941)*

12. Faith, to my mind, is a stiffening process, a sort of mental starch, which ought to be applied as sparingly as possible.
> —E. M. FORSTER, *Two Cheers for Democracy (1951)*

13. If there were a verb meaning 'to believe falsely,' it would not have any significant first person, present indicator.

> —LUDWIG WITTGENSTEIN, *Philosophical Investigations (1953)*

14. Confronted with the impossibility of remaining faithful to one's beliefs, and the equal impossibility of becoming free of them, one can be driven to the most inhuman excesses.
> —JAMES BALDWIN, *Notes of a Native Son (1955)*

15. Questioning what seem to be the absurd beliefs of another group is a good way of recognizing the potential absurdity of many of one's own cherished beliefs.
> —GORE VIDAL, in *Nation*, 26 *April 1958*

16. The relation of faith between subject and object is unique in every case. Hundreds may believe, but each has to believe by himself.
> —W. H. AUDEN, *The Dyer's Hand (1962)*

17. You can make an audience see nearly anything, if you yourself believe in it.
> —MARY RENAULT, *The Mask of Apollo (1966)*

18. Every believer is an anarchist at heart. True believers would rather see governments topple and history rewritten than scuff the cover of their faith.

—JEANETTE WINTERSON, *Boating for Beginners (1985)*

19. Where there is no faith, devils are a necessity.
—RITA MAE BROWN, *Bingo (1988)*

20. Demons were simple. They believed in prayer and the potency of holy water. Thus they fled from both. But men—what did men believe?
—CLIVE BARKER, *Everville (1994)*

Bereavement

1. Now cracks a noble heart. Good night, sweet prince, / And flights of angels sing thee to thy rest!
—WILLIAM SHAKESPEARE, *Hamlet (1600–1601)*

2. No longer mourn for me when I am dead / Than you shall hear the surly sullen bell / Give warning to the world that I am fled / From this vile world with vilest worms to dwell. / Nay, if you read this line, remember not / the hand that writ it; for I love you so / That I in your sweet thoughts would be forgot / If thinking on me then should make you woe.
—WILLIAM SHAKESPEARE, *Sonnet 71 (1609)*

3. Green be the turf above thee, / Friend of my better days! / None knew thee but to love thee, / Nor named thee but to praise.

—FITZ-GREENE HALLECK, *"On the Death of J. R. Drake" (1820)*

4. When lilacs last in the dooryard bloom'd, / And the great stars early droop'd in the western sky in the night, / I mourn'd, and yet shall mourn with ever-returning spring.
—WALT WHITMAN, *"When lilacs last in the dooryard bloom'd" (1865–66)*

5. She had borne her about with her for years like an arrow sticking in her heart the grief, the anguish.
—VIRGINIA WOOLF, *Mrs. Dalloway (1925)*

6. Into the darkness they go, the wise and lovely. Crowned / With lilies and with laurel they go; but I am not resigned.
—EDNA ST. VINCENT MILLAY, *"Dirge Without Music" (1928)*

7. I am staying on here alone now.
— ALICE B. TOKLAS, *after the death of Gertrude Stein, letter to Julian Beck, 8 September 1946*

8. It takes time for the absent to assume their true shape in our thoughts. After death they take on a firmer outline and then cease to change.
— COLETTE *(d. 1954), Earthly Paradise (1966)*

9. A lady asked me why, on most occasions, I wore black. "Are you in mourning?" "Yes." "For whom are you in mourning?" "For the world."
— EDITH SITWELL *(d. 1964), Taken Care Of (1965)*

10. The ashes of grief have choked the song of mountains in me.
— PAUL MONETTE, *"New Year's at Lawrence's Grave," Love Alone: 18 Elegies for Rog (1988)*

11. You don't get over it because "it" is the person you loved.
— JEANETTE WINTERSON, *Written on the Body (1992)*

Biography and Autobiography

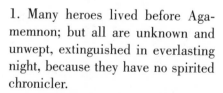

1. Many heroes lived before Agamemnon; but all are unknown and unwept, extinguished in everlasting night, because they have no spirited chronicler.
— HORACE *(1st century BCE) Odes 4, 9*

2. The life of any man written under the direction of his family, did nobody honour.
— HORACE WALPOLE, *letter, 1778*

3. I dislike modern memoirs. They are generally written by people who have either entirely lost their memories, or have never done anything worth remembering.
— OSCAR WILDE, *"The Critic as Artist" (1891)*

4. It simplifies even while seeking to enrich.
— HENRY JAMES *(d. 1916), on biography, in Leon Edel, Henry James, the Master 1901–1916 (1972)*

5. A biography is considered complete if it merely accounts for six or

seven selves, whereas a person may well have as many as a thousand.
—VIRGINIA WOOLF, *Orlando (1928)*

6. Discretion is not the better part of biography.
—LYTTON STRACHEY *(d. 1932), in Michael Holroyd, Lytton Strachey, Vol. 1 (1967)*

7. On reviewing my life, in tracing its course, I fill my cell with the pleasure of being what for want of a trifle I failed to be, recapturing, so that I may hurl myself into them as into dark pits, those moments when I strayed through the trap-ridden compartments of a subterranean sky.
—JEAN GENET, *Our Lady of the Roses (1949)*

8. Biography, if it is to enhance understanding, add to history or interpret character, must be constructive and not destructive.
—HAROLD NICOLSON, *in The Times, 20 March 1949*

9. Every autobiography is concerned with two characters, a Don Quixote, the Ego, and a Sancho Panza, the Self.
—W. H. AUDEN, *The Dyer's Hand (1962)*

10. Only when one has lost all curiosity has one reached the age to write an autobiography.
—EVELYN WAUGH, *A Little Learning (1964)*

11. To start writing about your life is, from one standpoint, to stop living it. You must avoid adventures today so as to make time for registering those of yesterday.
—NED ROREM, *Music from Inside Out (1967)*

12. An autobiography is an obituary in serial form with the last installment missing.
—QUENTIN CRISP, *The Naked Civil Servant (1968)*

13. All autobiography is self-indulgent.
—DAPHNE DU MAURIER, *Myself When Young (1977)*

14. Your life story would not make a good book. Do not even try.
—FRAN LEBOWITZ, *Metropolitan Life (1978)*

15. After a person dies, his biographers feel free to give him a glittering list of intimate friends. Anecdotes are so much tastier spiced with expensive names.
—LOUISE BROOKS, *Lulu in Hollywood (1982)*

Bisexuality

1. Two loves have I, of comfort and despair, / Which like two spirits do suggest me still. / The better angel is a man right fair, / The worser spirit a woman colored ill.
— *WILLIAM SHAKESPEARE, Sonnet 144 (1609)*

2. Without shame the man I like knows and avows the deliciousness of his sex, / Without shame the woman I like knows and avows hers.
— *WALT WHITMAN, "A Woman Waits for Me," Leaves of Grass (1855)*

3. Although my leaning toward the male sex was dominant, I also felt frequently drawn toward my own sex—an inclination which I could not correctly interpret until much later on. As a matter of fact I believe that bisexuality is almost a necessary factor in artistic production; at any rate, the tinge of masculinity within me helped me in my work.
— *KÄTHE KOLLWITZ, Diaries and Letters (1942)*

4. Well, I'm not going through life with one hand tied behind my back.
— *JAMES DEAN (d. 1955), when asked if he was gay, in Graham McCann, Rebel Males: Clift, Dean, and Brando (1978)*

5. Wicked bisexuals who break the hearts of innocent queens and then go waltzing back to Wifey.
— *CHRISTOPHER ISHERWOOD, The World in the Evening (1954)*

6. I imagine her as gloriously bisexual. I see her with three concubines and four lovers.
— *BRIGID BROPHY, The King of a Rainy Country (1956)*

7. I don't know what I am, darling, I've tried several varieties of sex. The conventional position makes me claustrophobic. And the others give me either stiff neck or lockjaw.
— *TALLULAH BANKHEAD (d. 1968), in Lee Israel, Miss Tallulah Bankhead (1972)*

8. A short note about bisexuality. You can't have your cake and eat it too. You can't be tied to male privilege with the right hand while clutching to your sister with the left.
— *RITA MAE BROWN, in Sisters, October 1972*

9. Bisexuality is not so much a copout as a fearful compromise.
— *JILL JOHNSTON, Lesbian Nation (1973)*

10. If you swing both ways, you really swing. I just figure you double your pleasure.
— *JOAN BAEZ, quoted in Sappho, May 1973*

11. What is new is not bisexuality, but rather the widening of our awareness and acceptance of human capacities for sexual love.
— *MARGARET MEAD, in Redbook (1975)*

12. There is no such thing as a homosexual or heterosexual person. There are only homo- or heterosexual acts. Most people are a mixture of impulses if not practices.
— *GORE VIDAL, "Tennessee Williams: Someone to Laugh at the Squares With" (1987)*

13. Homosexuality was invented by a straight world dealing with its own bisexuality.
— *KATE MILLETT, Flying (1990)*

Bodies

1. The function of muscle is to pull and not to push, except in the case of the genitals and the tongue.
— *LEONARDO DA VINCI, Notebooks (c. 1500)*

2. Thou seest I have more flesh than another man, and therefore more frailty.
— *WILLIAM SHAKESPEARE, 1 Henry IV (1596–97)*

3. Your body is the church where Nature asks to be reverenced.
— *MARQUIS DE SADE, L'Histoire de Juliette, ou les Prospérités du Vice (1797)*

4. Our bodies are our betters.
— *HERMAN MELVILLE, Mardi (1849)*

5. Every man is the builder of a temple, called his body, to the god he worships, after a style purely his own, nor can he get off by hammering marble instead. We are all sculptors and painters, and our material is our own flesh and blood and bones.
— *HENRY DAVID THOREAU, "Higher Laws," Walden (1854)*

6. If anything is sacred the human body is sacred.
— *WALT WHITMAN, "I Sing the Body Electric" (1855)*

7. We shift and bedeck and bedrape us, / Thou art noble and nude and antique.

    —ALGERNON CHARLES SWINBURNE,
      "Dolores" (1866)

8. Is nakedness indecent? No, not inherently. It is your thought, your sophistication, your fear, your respectability, that is indecent. There comes moods when these clothes of ours are not only irksome to wear, but are themselves indecent.

    —WALT WHITMAN, Specimen Days
      (1882)

9. How idiotic civilization is! Why be given a body if you have to keep it shut up in a case like a rare, rare fiddle?

    —KATHERINE MANSFIELD, "Bliss"
      (1920)

10. A curious and eager soul was imprisoned in all this lard, but by dint of never refusing himself a pheasant or a goose or his daily procession of Roman wines, he was his own bitter jailer.

    —THORNTON WILDER, The Bridge of
      San Luis Rey (1927)

11. That night she stared at herself in the glass; and even as she did so, she hated her body with its muscular shoulders, its small compact breasts, and its slender flanks of an athlete. All her life she must drag this body of hers like a monstrous fetter imposed on her spirit. This strangely ardent yet sterile body.

    —RADCLYFFE HALL, The Well of
      Loneliness (1928)

12. But when told that to appear naked in a drawing-room might be considered somewhat odd, since it was no longer the custom, she had argued that our bodies were very unimportant, only there so that people might perceive us. "We couldn't see each other without them, you know," she had said, smiling up at her mother.

    —RADCLYFFE HALL, A Saturday Life
      (1930)

13. I take no pleasure in women. I have never thought twice or even once of the shape of a woman; but men's bodies, in repose or in movement—especially the former, appeal to me directly and very generally.

    —T. E. LAWRENCE (d. 1935), in
      John Mack, A Prince of Our
      Disorder: The Life of T. E.
      Lawrence (1976)

14. To see you naked is to recall the Earth.

    —FEDERICO GARCÍA LORCA, "Casida
      de la mujer tendida," Diván del
      Tamarit (1936)

15. He's so fat he hasn't seen his privates in twenty years.

    —CARSON MCCULLERS, Ballad of
      the Sad Café (1951)

16. The human body is the best picture of the human soul.
—*LUDWIG WITTGENSTEIN (d. 1951),
Philosophical Investigations
(1953)*

17. This morning it occurred to me for the first time that my body, my faithful companion and friend, truer and better known to me than my own soul, may be after all only a sly beast who will end by devouring his master.
—*MARGUERITE YOURCENAR, Memoirs
of Hadrian (1951)*

18. I like a lad with a smooth body.
—*JOE ORTON, Entertaining Mr
Sloane (1964)*

19. The pearl wanted what I wanted. I was discovering the little male organ we all of us have. A eunuch taking heart again.
—*VIOLETTE LEDUC, Therese and
Isabelle (1968)*

20. Is not the most erotic part of the body wherever the clothing affords a glimpse?
—*ROLAND BARTHES, A Lover's
Discourse: Fragments (1977)*

21. Your traveled, generous thighs / between which my whole face has come and come—
—*ADRIENNE RICH, "Twenty-One
Love Poems," The Dream of a
Common Language (1978)*

22. Of course many bodybuilders are gay. . . . In effect, though different, it's similar in reversed process to drag. It's the opposite side but from almost the same source. The queen protects herself by dressing in women's clothes and the bodybuilder protects himself in muscles—so-called "men's clothes."
—*JOHN RECHY, in Gay Sunshine,
1978*

23. Your breasts, thighs, shoulders, mouth, voice, are the places / I live, whether or not I live with you.
—*MARILYN HACKER, Love, Death,
and the Changing of the Seasons
(1986)*

24. For me, what is working most in lesbian sensibility is the skin. The skin is tactile memory. It protects your interiority, your integrity. Your skin works like a synthesiser, transmuting words, emotions, and ideas. We have the imagination of our bodies, of our sex, and most of all of our skin, which synthesizes time and space. Imagination is travelling through our skin, all of its surfaces.
—*NICOLE BROSSARD, The Aerial
Letter (1988)*

25. Most people keep their brains / between their legs.
—*MORRISSEY, "Such a Little Thing
Makes Such a Big Difference"
(1989)*

26. The Puritans . . . forgot that we are born into flesh and in flesh must remain. Their women bind their breasts and cook plain food without salt, and the men are so afraid of their member uprising that they keep it strapped between their legs with bandages.

—*JEANETTE WINTERSON, Sexing the Cherry (1989)*

27. A waist is a terrible thing to mind.

—*JANE CAMINOS, That's Ms. Bulldyke to You, Charlie! (1992)*

Boredom and Ennui

1. Life is as tedious as a twice-told tale, / Vexing the dull ear of a drowsy man.

—*WILLIAM SHAKESPEARE, King John (1596)*

2. Society is now one polished horde, / Formed of two mighty tribes, the *Bores* and the *Bored.*

—*GEORGE GORDON, LORD BYRON, Don Juan (1819–24)*

3. Don't tell me that you have exhausted Life. When a man says that, one knows that life has exhausted him.

—*OSCAR WILDE, The Picture of Dorian Gray (1891)*

4. Boredom is the legitimate kingdom of the philanthropic.

—*VIRGINIA WOOLF, letter, 10 September 1918*

5. Sorrow, fear, physical pain, and excessive cold, I can still guarantee to stand up to all these with decent courage. But I abdicate in the face of boredom, which turns me into a wretched and, if necessary, ferocious creature.

—*COLETTE, "The Photographer's Missus" (1944)*

6. There is no greater bore than the travel bore. We do not in the least want to hear what he has seen in Hong Kong.

—*VITA SACKVILLE-WEST, Passenger to Teheran (1926)*

7. Miss Searle had always considered boredom an intellectual defeat.

—MARY RENAULT, *North Face* (1948)

8. Life in this society being, at best, an utter bore and no aspect of society being at all relevant to women, there remains to civic-minded, responsible, thrill-seeking females only to overthrow the government, eliminate the money system, institute complete automation and destroy the male sex.

—VALERIE SOLANIS, *SCUM Manifesto (1967–68)*

9. Boredom is just the reverse side of fascination: both depend on being outside rather than inside a situation, and one leads to the other.

—SUSAN SONTAG, *On Photography* (1977)

B u s i n e s s

▼

1. So long as money can answer, it were wrong in any business to put the life in danger.

—SA'DI, *Gulistan (1258)*

2. To business that we love we rise betime, / And go to't with delight.

—WILLIAM SHAKESPEARE, *Antony and Cleopatra (1606)*

3. Time is the measure of business.

—FRANCIS BACON, *"Of Dispatch," Essays (1625)*

4. Business! I think that there is nothing, not even crime, more opposed to poetry, to philosophy, ay, to life itself, than this incessant business.

—HENRY DAVID THOREAU, *Life Without Principle (1863)*

5. Things in this world are very roughly averaged; and although averaging is a useful, rapid way of dispatching business, it does undoubtedly waste a great deal which is too good for wasting.

—VERNON LEE, *Renaissance Fancies and Studies (1895)*

6. It is very vulgar to talk about one's business. Only people like stockbrokers do that, and then merely at dinner parties.

—OSCAR WILDE, *The Importance of Being Earnest (1895)*

7. Counting is the religion of this generation it is its hope and its salvation.

> —*GERTRUDE STEIN, Everybody's Autobiography (1937)*

8. A living is made, Mr. Kemper, by selling something that everybody needs at least once a year. Yes, sir! And a million is made by producing something that everybody needs every day. You artists produce something that nobody needs at any time.

> —*THORNTON WILDER, The Matchmaker (1954)*

9. [Commercialism is] doing well that which should not be done at all.

> —*GORE VIDAL, in Listener, 7 August 1975*

10. Being good in business is the most fascinating kind of art.

> —*ANDY WARHOL, The Philosophy of Andy Warhol: From A to B and Back Again (1975)*

11. Contrary to popular opinion, the hustle is not a new dance step—it is an old business procedure.

> —*FRAN LEBOWITZ, in Observer (1979)*

Butch and Butch/Femme

1. Miss Butler is tall and masculine, she wears always a riding habit, hangs her hat with the air of a sportsman in the hall, and appears in all respects as a young man if we except the petticoats which she still retains. Miss Ponsonby, on the contrary, is polite, so effeminate, fair and beautiful.

> —*Description of Eleanor Butler and Sarah Ponsonby (the Ladies of Llangollen), in the General Evening Post, 24 July 1790*

2. Not all masculine, but rather softly gentleman-like. I know how to please girls.

> —*ANNE LISTER, self-description; journal (1820), I Know My Own Heart, ed. Helena Whitbread (1988)*

3. When they still retain female garments, these women usually show traits of masculine simplicity . . . disdain for the pretty feminine artifices of the toilet . . . brusque, energetic

movements, the attitude of the arms, the direct speech, the inflexions of the voice, the masculine straightforwardness and sense of honor, and especially the attitude toward men, free from any suggestion either of shyness or audacity.

—*HAVELOCK ELLIS, Studies in the Psychology of Sex (1936)*

4. A great many women can feel and behave like men. Very few of them can behave like gentlemen.

—*RADCLYFFE HALL (d. 1943), quoted by Naomi (Micky) Jacob in Arena Three, September 1967*

5. Someday I expect the "discreet" lesbian will not turn her head on the streets at the sight of the "butch" strolling hand in hand with her friend in their trousers and definitive haircuts. But for the moment it still disturbs.

—*LORRAINE HANSBERRY, in The Ladder, May 1957*

6. What if you'd been raised as a boy and learned to be a man, and had to do it all inside a female body? What if you had all your feelings incarcerated under a pair of breasts? What would you do with yourself? How could you live? Who would be your lover?

—*ANN BANNON, Beebo Brinker (1962)*

7. Time enough later to teach her that it's better to be a real woman than an imitation man, and that when someone chooses a woman to go away with it's because a woman is what's preferred.

—*ISABEL MILLER [Alma Routsong], Patience and Sarah (1967)*

8. Miss Radclyffe Hall was a strange but impressive-looking woman, short of stature, with disproportionately large but handsomely shaped head and always with a perfect haircut. Her hands and feet were also large, as were the beautiful sapphires which she wore, one as a finger ring and one each as a cuff link. She wore beautifully tailored English suits, tight-fitting across the bosom and shoulders.

—*JANET FLANNER, Paris Was Yesterday 1925–1939 (1972)*

9. The butch is, ceremoniously speaking, Puck. Cross-dressing is a magical function, and the butch is the equivalent of the traditional cross-dresser who may also become a magician/shaman of the tribe. She is the one who cross-dresses, becomes a hunter or a sooth-sayer or a prophet or the first woman in a formerly all-male occupation. She keeps the idea of biological destiny untenable.

—*JUDY GRAHN, Another Mother Tongue (1984)*

10. I see all of a sudden that every butch is a femme; every femme is a butch. . . . I remember how it looks like femmes and butches went out of

style in this bar. I think . . . maybe I'm going out of style too.

—LEE LYNCH, *The Swashbuckler (1985)*

11. Only as a lesbian, I think: one minute covered in lace and nearly coming in a dressing room, the next minute charging down the street towards the punching bag.

—JESS WELLS, *The Dress and the Sharda Stories (1986)*

12. None of the butch women I was with . . . ever presented themselves to me as men; they did announce themselves as tabooed women who were willing to identify their passion for other women by wearing clothes that symbolized the taking of responsibility. Part of this responsibility was sexual expertise.

—JOAN NESTLE, *A Restricted Country (1987)*

13. Butch-femme relationships, as I experienced them, were complex erotic statements, not phony heterosexual replicas. They were filled with a deeply Lesbian language of stance, dress, gesture, loving, courage, and autonomy.

—JOAN NESTLE, *A Restricted Country (1987)*

14. There were . . . few butches in the '80s who would entertain the notion that they were men trapped in women's bodies, as butches in the 1950s sometimes did. For many of the neo-butches or -femmes the roles actually had little connection with the idealized butch and femme behaviors of their predecessors. . . . While distinctions in dress in 1980s butch/femme couples were not unusual, it was also common for both women in the couple to dress in a unisex style or to combine styles.

—LILLIAN FADERMAN, *Odd Girls and Twilight Lovers (1991)*

15. Apparently, in many minds the leap from the butch to the butcher knife is but a tiny one.

—LINDSY VAN GELDER, *on popular images of the homicidal lesbian, in Ms. magazine, January/February 1992*

16. I was real proud that in all those years I never hit another butch woman. See, I loved them too, and I understood their pain and their shame because I was so much like them. I loved the lines etched in their faces and hands and the curves of their work-weary shoulders. Sometimes I looked in the mirror and wondered what I would look like when I was their age. Now I know!

—LESLIE FEINBERG, *Stone Butch Blues (1993)*

17. I was the stonest of stone butches and loving every minute of it. My address book was thicker than most people's skins are.

—FRANKIE HUCKLENBROICH, *A Crystal Diary (1997)*

California

1. It is an odd thing, but everyone who disappears is said to be seen at San Francisco. It must be a delightful city, and possess all the attractions of the next world.
   —OSCAR WILDE, A Picture of
      Dorian Gray (1891)

2. California is a queer place—in a way, it has turned its back on the world, and looks into the void Pacific. It is absolutely selfish, very empty, but not false, and at least, not full of false effort.
   —D. H. LAWRENCE, letter,
      24 September 1923

3. What was the use of my having come from Oakland it was not natural to have come from there yes write about it if I like or anything if I like but not there, there is no there there.
   —GERTRUDE STEIN, Everybody's
      Autobiography (1937)

4. California is a tragic country—like Palestine, like every Promised Land.
   —CHRISTOPHER ISHERWOOD, in
      Horizon, 1947

5. They are a very decent generous lot of people out here and they don't expect you to listen. It's the secret of social ease in this country. They talk entirely for their own pleasure. Nothing they say is designed to be heard.
   —EVELYN WAUGH, The Loved One
      (1948)

6. Wherever I looked, there was nothing to see but more long streets and thousands of cars going along them, and dried-up country on each side of the streets. It was like the Sahara, only dirty.
   —MOHAMMED MRABET, of
      California, Look and Move On
      (1976)

7. The almost Oriental politeness of the West Coast is one of its distinctive regional features, in marked contrast to the contentiousness of the East Coast. So few human contacts in Los Angeles go unmediated by glass (either a TV screen or an automobile windshield) that the direct confrontation renders the participants docile, sweet, stunned.
   —EDMUND WHITE, States of Desire:
      Travels in Gay America (1980)

8. There are two modes of transport in Los Angeles: car and ambulance.

Visitors who wish to remain inconspicuous are advised to choose the latter.

—*Fran Lebowitz, Social Studies (1981)*

Camp

1. For a long time I found the celebrities of modern painting and poetry ridiculous. I loved absurd pictures, fanlights, stage scenery, mountebanks' backcloths, inn-signs, cheap colored prints; unfashionable literature, church Latin, pornographic books badly spelt, grandmothers' novels, fairy stories, little books for children, old operas, empty refrains, simple rhythms.

> —*Arthur Rimbaud, "Délires II: Alchimie du Verbe," Une Saison en Enfer (1878)*

2. The most I've had is just / A talent to amuse.

> —*Noël Coward, "If Love Were All" (1929 song)*

3. Irony is bitter truth / wrapped up in a little joke.

> —*H.D., The Walls Do Not Fall (1944)*

4. You can't camp about something you don't take seriously, you're not making fun of it, you're making fun *out* of it. You're expressing what's basically serious in terms of fun and artifice and elegance.

> —*Christopher Isherwood, the World in the Evening (1954)*

5. The relation between boredom and Camp taste cannot be overestimated. Camp taste is by its nature possible only in affluent societies, in societies or circles capable of experiencing the psychopathology of affluence.

> —*Susan Sontag, "Notes on 'Camp'" (1964)*

6. Camp is NOT a person, situation or activity; it is, rather, a relationship between the things and homosexuality . . . those elements in a person, situation or activity which express a gay sensibility or viewpoint. Camp, in fact, is the product of oppression, a *creative* means of dealing with an identity that is loaded down with stigma.

> —*Jack Babuscio, in Gay News, March 1976*

7. Bad taste makes the day go faster.
   —ANDY WARHOL, *in Houston*
   Home/Garden, November 1978

8. The strange thing about "camp" is that it has become fossilized. The mannerisms have never changed. If I were now to see a woman sitting with her knees clamped together, one hand on her hip and the other lightly touching her back hair, I should think, "Either she scored her last social triumph in 1926 or it is a man in drag."
   —QUENTIN CRISP, *in Guy*
   Kettelhack, ed., The Wit and
   Wisdom of Quentin Crisp (1984)

9. Camp is a homosexual sensibility with a soupçon of weariness.
   —NED ROREM, *Nantucket Diary,*
   1973–1985 (1987)

10. Camp is a lie that tells the truth.
    —PHILIP CORE, *Camp (1984)*

Caution

1. Wisely and slow; they stumble that run fast.
   —WILLIAM SHAKESPEARE, *Romeo*
   and Juliet (1595)

2. Those who prepare for all the emergencies of life beforehand may equip themselves at the expense of joy.
   —E. M. FORSTER, *Howards End*
   (1910)

3. She would take any amount of trouble to avoid trouble.
   —WILLA CATHER, *The Song of the*
   Lark (1915)

4. People wish to learn to swim and at the same time to keep one foot on the ground.
   —MARCEL PROUST (d. 1922),
   Remembrance of Things Past:
   The Sweet Cheat Gone (1925)

5. Everybody knows if you are too careful you are so occupied in being careful that you are sure to stumble over something.
   —GERTRUDE STEIN, *Everybody's*
   Autobiography (1937)

6. Set the foot down with distrust on the crust of the world—it is thin.

—EDNA ST. VINCENT MILLAY,
   "Huntsman, What Quarry?" The
   Underground System (1939)

7. A pervert like me, with the fattest file, for my age, in the vice depart-

ment's system, simply wants to avoid mud being stirred up needlessly.
   —COLIN MACINNES, *Absolute*
   Beginners (1959)

Censorship

1. Art made tongue-tied by authority.
   —WILLIAM SHAKESPEARE, *Sonnet 66*
   (1609)

2. If some books are deemed most baneful and their sale forbid, how, then, with deadlier facts, not dreams of doting men? Those whom books will hurt will not be proof against events. Events, not books, should be forbid.
   —HERMAN MELVILLE, *"The*
   Encantadas, Or Enchanted
   Islands," The Piazza Tales
   (1856)

3. The sign of a Philistine age is the cry of immorality against art.
   —OSCAR WILDE, *lecture to the art*
   students of the Royal Academy,
   30 June 1883

4. Particularly against books the Home Secretary is. If we can't stamp out literature in the country, we can

at least stop its being brought in from outside.
   —EVELYN WAUGH, *Vile Bodies*
   (1930)

5. To admit authorities, however heavily furred and gowned, into our libraries and let them tell us how to read, what to read, what value to place upon what we read, is to destroy the spirit of freedom which is the breath of those sanctuaries. Everywhere else we may be bound by laws and conventions—there we have none.
   —VIRGINIA WOOLF, *"How Should*
   One Read a Book," The Second
   Common Reader (1932)

6. The condition every art requires is, not so much freedom from restriction, as freedom from adulteration and from the intrusion of foreign matter.

—WILLA CATHER (d. 1947), On
Writing (1949)

7. In the present, amidst dangers
whose outcome we cannot foresee,
we get nervous about [freedom], and
admit censorship.
—E. M. FORSTER, Two Cheers for
Democracy (1951)

8. The film is apparently meaning-
less, but if it has any meaning it is
doubtless objectionable.
—BRITISH BOARD OF FILM CENSORS,
on banning Jean Cocteau's The
Seashell and the Clergyman
(1956)

Change

1. Nothing of him that doth
fade / But doth suffer a sea-
change / Into something rich and
strange.
—WILLIAM SHAKESPEARE, The
Tempest (1611)

2. He that will not apply new remedies must expect new evils; for time
is the greatest innovator.
—FRANCIS BACON, "Of
Innovations," Essays (1625)

3. Since 'tis Nature's law to change, /
Constancy alone is strange.
—JOHN WILMOT, EARL OF
ROCHESTER (d. 1680), "A
Dialogue Between Strephon
and Daphne" (1691)

4. What old people say you cannot
do, you try and find that you can. Old
deeds for old people, and new deeds
for new.
—HENRY DAVID THOREAU,
"Economy," Walden (1854)

5. Let that which stood in front go
behind, / Let that which was behind
advance to the front, / Let bigots,
fools, unclean persons, offer new
propositions, / Let the old propositions be postponed.
—WALT WHITMAN, "Reversals,"
Leaves of Grass (1856)

6. I seemed to feel a new man inside
my old skin, and I longed for a new
world.
—HENRY JAMES, The American
(1877)

7. All our lives long, every day
and every hour, we are engaged in

the process of accommodating our changed and unchanged selves to changed and unchanged surroundings; living, in fact, in nothing else than this process of accommodation; when we fail in it a little we are stupid, when we fail flagrantly we are mad, when we suspend it temporarily we sleep, when we give up the attempt altogether we die.
—*SAMUEL BUTLER (d. 1902), The Way of All Flesh (1903)*

8. Our heart changes, and this is the greatest cause of suffering in life.
—*MARCEL PROUST, Remembrance of Things Past: Swann's Way (1913)*

9. Like all weak men he laid an exaggerated stress on not changing one's mind.
—*W. SOMERSET MAUGHAM, The Moon and Sixpence (1919)*

10. If your laws forbid you, you must change your laws. If your church forbids you, you must change your church. And if your God forbids you, why then, you must change your God.
—*CLEMENCE DANE, A Bill of Divorcement (1921)*

11. Everything in life that we really accept undergoes a change.
—*KATHERINE MANSFIELD (1920), Journal of Katherine Mansfield (1927)*

12. We do not succeed in changing things according to our desire, but gradually our desire changes.
—*MARCEL PROUST (d. 1922), Remembrance of Things Past: The Sweet Cheat Gone (1925)*

13. Growth is exciting; growth is dynamic and alarming.
—*VITA SACKVILLE-WEST, Twelve Days (1928)*

14. New things are always ugly.
—*WILLA CATHER (d. 1947), in Phyllis C. Robinson, Willa (1982)*

15. We would rather be ruined than changed.
—*W. H. AUDEN, The Age of Anxiety (1948)*

16. The country's moral values, far from changing, seem to remain unnaturally constant.
—*JOE ORTON, The Good and Faithful Servant (1967)*

17. Try a boy for a change. You're a rich man. You can afford the luxuries of life.
—*JOE ORTON (d. 1967), What the Butler Saw (1969)*

18. I am in the world / to change the world.
—*MURIEL RUKEYSER, "Käthe Kollwitz" (1968)*

19. The moment of change is the only poem.

—ADRIENNE RICH, *"Images for
Godard" (1970)*

20. Most of us are about as eager to
be changed as we are to be born, and
go through our changes in a similar
state of shock.
 —JAMES BALDWIN, *The Price of the
 Ticket (1985)*

21. Has the world changed or have I
changed?
 —MORRISSEY, *"The Queen Is Dead"
 (1985)*

22. I change myself, I change the
world.
 —GLORIA ANZALDÚA,
 Borderlands/La Frontera (1987)

23. I'm doing well, especially since /
I moved away from here.

—JUDY GRAHN, *The Queen of
Swords (1987)*

24. Anything in history or nature
that can be described as changing
steadily can be seen as heading
toward disaster.
 —SUSAN SONTAG, *AIDS and Its
 Metaphors (1989)*

25. The queers of the sixties, like
those since, have connived with their
repression under a veneer of respectability. Good mannered city
queens in suits and pinstripes, so
busy establishing themselves, were
useless at changing anything.
 —DEREK JARMAN, *At Your Own
 Risk: A Saint's Testament (1992)*

Chaos   and   Confusion

▼

1. Actual life was chaos, but there
was always something terribly logical
in the imagination.
 —OSCAR WILDE, *The Picture of
 Dorian Gray (1891)*

2. What did art and virtue matter to
him compared with the advantages of
chaos?

—THOMAS MANN, *Death in Venice
(1912)*

3. The world is rather tiresome, I
must say—everything at sixes and
sevens—ladies in love with buggers,
buggers in love with womanisers, and
the price of coal going up too. Where
will it all end?

—LYTTON STRACHEY, *letter to Dora Carrington, 11 July 1919*

4. The fair sex? Which one is that?
—J. R. ACKERLEY, *The Prisoners of War (1935)*

5. She was always holding God's bag of tricks upside down.
—DJUNA BARNES, *Nightwood (1936)*

6. Chaos is a name for any order that produces confusion in our minds.
—GEORGE SANTAYANA, *Dominations and Powers (1951)*

7. I had nothing to offer anybody except my own confusion.
—JACK KEROUAC, *On the Road (1957)*

8. Is not the whole world a vast house of assignation of which the filing system has been lost?
—QUENTIN CRISP, *The Naked Civil Servant (1968)*

9. After one look at this planet any visitor from outer space would say, 'I WANT TO SEE THE MANAGER.'
—WILLIAM S. BURROUGHS, *The Adding Machine (1985)*

10. There were many, many questions that remained and which I had no energy or ability to continue to try and solve. I could only ignore them. I was not a satisfied woman. I was only quiet.
—SARAH SCHULMAN, *After Delores (1988)*

Character

1. They say best men are moulded out of faults, / And, for the most, become much more the better / For being a little bad.
—WILLIAM SHAKESPEARE, *Measure for Measure (1603)*

2. Most men are cowards, all men should be knaves.
—JOHN WILMOT, EARL OF ROCHESTER, *"A Satire Against Reason and Mankind" (1679)*

3. The care of our virtue we owe to ourselves; the preservation of our characters is due to the world.
—SARAH SCOTT, *A Description of Millenium Hall (1762)*

4. Pity the man who has a character to support—it is worse than a large family—he is silent poor indeed.
   —HENRY DAVID THOREAU, *Journal*,
   28 April 1841

5. What is character but the determination of incident? What is incident but the illustration of character?
   —HENRY JAMES, *"The Art of*
   Fiction" (1888)

6. I am afraid that he has one of those terribly weak natures that are not susceptible to influence.
   —OSCAR WILDE, *An Ideal Husband*
   (1895)

7. All the goodness, beauty and perfection of a human being belong to the one who knows how to recognize these qualities.
   —GEORGETTE LEBLANC, *Souvenirs*
   (1898); trans. Janet Flanner
   (1932)

8. It is not true that suffering ennobles the character; happiness does that sometimes, but suffering, for the most part, makes men petty and vindictive.

—W. SOMERSET MAUGHAM, *The*
   Moon and Sixpence (1919)

9. Some people are moulded by their admirations, others by their hostilities.
   —ELIZABETH BOWEN, *Death of the*
   Heart (1938)

10. One of the worst things about life is not how nasty the nasty people are. You know that already. It is how nasty the nice people are.
   —ANTHONY POWELL, *A Dance to the*
   Music of Time: The Kindly Ones
   (1962)

11. Intelligence is powerless to modify character.
   —QUENTIN CRISP, *The Naked Civil*
   Servant (1968)

12. Life makes great demands on people's characters, and gives them great opportunities to serve their own ends by the sacrifices of other people. Such ill doing may meet with little retribution, may indeed be hardly recognized, and I cannot feel so surprised if people yield to it.
   —IVY COMPTON-BURNETT, *in*
   Elizabeth Sprigge, The Life of Ivy
   Compton-Burnett (1973)

Children and Childhood

1. Alas! regardless of their doom, / The little victims play! / No sense have they of ills to come / Nor care beyond today.
—THOMAS GRAY, Ode on a Distant Prospect of Eton College (1742)

2. The female homosexual may chiefly be found in the haunts of boys. She is the rival in their play, preferring the rocking-horse, playing at soldiers, etc., to dolls and other girlish occupations. The toilet is neglected, and rough boyish manners are affected. Love of art finds a substitute in the pursuits of the sciences.
—RICHARD VON KRAFFT-EBING, Psychopathia Sexualis (1886)

3. Children begin by loving their parents; after a time they judge them; rarely, if ever, do they forgive them.
—OSCAR WILDE, A Woman of No Importance (1893)

4. Children are unaccountable little creatures.
—KATHERINE MANSFIELD, "Sixpence" (1921)

5. That most sensitive, most delicate of instruments—the mind of a little child!
—HENRY HANDEL RICHARDSON, The Fortunes of Richard Mahoney: Ultima Thule (1929)

6. She saw herself as a queer little girl, aggressive and awkward because of her shyness; a queer little girl who loathed sisters and dolls, preferring the stable-boys as companions, preferring to play with footballs and tops, and occasional catapults. She saw herself climbing the tallest beech trees, arrayed in old breeches illicitly come by. She remembered insisting with tears and some temper that her real name was William and not Wilhelmina.
—RADCLYFFE HALL, "Miss Ogilvy Finds Herself" (1934)

7. Childhood is the kingdom where no one dies.
—EDNA ST. VINCENT MILLAY, "Wine from These Grapes" (1934)

8. He is not like other children, not cruel, or savage. For this very reason he is called "strange."
—DJUNA BARNES, Nightwood (1936)

9. What is the use of being a little boy if you are going to grow up to be a man.
—GERTRUDE STEIN, *Everybody's Autobiography (1937)*

10. By the time I was six I was sure that I was born a man.
—CARSON MCCULLERS, *to Louis Untermeyer (1940); quoted by Virginia Spencer Carr, Introduction to Collected Stories of Carson McCullers (1987)*

11. All encounters with children are touched with social embarrassment.
—SYLVIA TOWNSEND WARNER, *"View Halloo" (1947)*

12. Certain gestures made in childhood seem to have eternal repercussions.
—ANAÏS NIN, *Under a Glass Bell (1948)*

13. Two things are terrible in childhood: helplessness (being in other people's power) and apprehension—the apprehension that something is being concealed from us because it was too bad to be told.
—ELIZABETH BOWEN, *Collected Impressions (1950)*

14. The hearts of small children are delicate organs. A cruel beginning in this world can twist them into curious shapes.
—CARSON MCCULLERS, *The Ballad of the Sad Café (1953)*

15. I am convinced that, except in a few extraordinary cases, one form or another of an unhappy childhood is essential to the formation of exceptional gifts.
—THORNTON WILDER, *interview, in Malcolm Cowley, ed., Writers at Work (1958)*

16. Every luxury was lavished on you—atheism, breastfeeding, circumcision.
—JOE ORTON, *Loot (1967)*

17. The trouble with children is that they are not returnable.
—QUENTIN CRISP, *The Naked Civil Servant (1968)*

18. I wasn't used to children and they were getting on my nerves. Worse, it appeared that I was a child, too. I hadn't known that before; I thought I was just short.
—FLORENCE KING, *on her first day in school, Confessions of a Failed Southern Lady (1985)*

19. The hardest part about being a kid is knowing you have got your whole life ahead of you.
—JANE WAGNER, *My Life, So Far (1994)*

Choice and Decision

1. Be content with what thou hast received, and smooth thy frowning forehead, for the door of choice is not open either to thee or me.
　　—HAFIZ (14th century), Ghazal 12 from the Divan

2. There's small choice in rotten apples.
　　—WILLIAM SHAKESPEARE, The Taming of the Shrew (1593)

3. I would prefer not to.
　　—HERMAN MELVILLE, "Bartleby the Scrivener" (1853)

4. Who is to decide between "Let it be" and "Force it"?
　　—KATHERINE MANSFIELD (1914), The Journal of Katherine Mansfield (1927)

5. The most decisive actions of our life—I mean those that are most likely to decide the whole course of our future—are, more often than not, unconsidered.
　　—ANDRÉ GIDE, The Counterfeiters (1925); trans. Dorothy Bussy

6. I didn't know what to do about life—so I did a nervous breakdown that lasted many months.
　　—MARGARET ANDERSON, My Thirty Years' War (1930)

7. Boredom helps one to make decisions.
　　—COLETTE, Gigi (1944)

8. If thou must choose / Between the chances, choose the odd.
　　—W. H. AUDEN, "Under Which Lyre" (1946)

9. But there comes a moment in everybody's life when he must decide whether he'll live among human beings or not—a fool among fools or a fool alone.
　　—THORNTON WILDER, The Matchmaker (1954)

10. There are no signposts in the sea.
　　—VITA SACKVILLE-WEST, No Signposts in the Sea (1961)

11. Once again she decided not to decide. She preferred being compelled into her decisions.
　　—LISA ALTHER, Kinflicks (1975)

12. People genuinely happy in their choices seem less often tempted to force them on other people than those who feel martyred and broken by their lives.
　　—JANE RULE, Lesbian Images (1975)

13. Once one discovers one is gay one must choose everything, from how to walk, dress and talk to where to live, with whom and on what terms.
—*EDMUND WHITE, States of Desire: Travels in Gay America (1980)*

14. Who can choose between the worst possibility / and the last.
—*JUNE JORDAN, "Roman Poem Number Thirteen" (1981)*

15. A peacefulness follows any decision, even the wrong one.
—*RITA MAE BROWN, Sudden Death (1983)*

16. I have a theory that every time you make an important choice, the part of you left behind continues the other life you could have had.
—*JEANETTE WINTERSON, Oranges Are Not the Only Fruit (1985)*

Cities

1. What is the city but the people?
—*WILLIAM SHAKESPEARE, Coriolanus (1608)*

2. A great city is that which has the greatest men and women.
—*WALT WHITMAN, "Song of the Broad-Axe," Leaves of Grass (1856)*

3. The way to live in New York is to move every three or four years. Then you always get the last thing.
—*HENRY JAMES, Washington Square (1890)*

4. Florence she found perfectly sweet, Naples a dream, but very whiffy. In Rome one had simply to sit still and feel.
—*E. M. FORSTER, Where Angels Fear to Tread (1902)*

5. Cities, like cats, will reveal themselves at night.
—*RUPERT BROOKE (d. 1915), Letters from America (1916)*

6. New York is the meeting place of the peoples, the only city where you can hardly find a typical American.
—*DJUNA BARNES, "Greenwich Village as It Is" (1916)*

7. In Paris, everybody wants to be an actor; nobody is content to be a spectator.

—JEAN COCTEAU, *Le Rappel à l'Ordre (1926)*

8. Paris is, according to its legends, the city where everyone loses his head, and his morals, lives through at least one *histoire d'amour,* ceases, quite, to arrive anywhere on time, and thumbs his nose at the Puritans.
—JAMES BALDWIN, *Notes of a Native Son (1955)*

9. Venice is like eating an entire box of chocolate liqueurs at one go.
—TRUMAN CAPOTE, *in Observer, 26 November 1961*

10. This desert town was man's own miracle of pure purposelessness.
—JANE RULE, *on Reno, The Desert of the Heart (1965)*

11. It was Berlin itself he was hungry to meet; the Berlin Wystan [Auden] had promised him. To Christopher, Berlin meant Boys.
—CHRISTOPHER ISHERWOOD, *Christopher and His Kind (1977)*

12. All of this—the shared apartment in the Village, the illicit relationship, the Friday-night train to a country house—was what he imagined life in New York to be, and he was intensely happy.
—JOHN CHEEVER, *"Torch Song," The Stories of John Cheever (1980)*

13. Everyone in Paris talks about love, but only two hundred people actually do it.
—LISA ALTHER, *Five Minutes in Heaven (1995)*

Civilization

1. We may have civilized bodies and yet barbarous souls.
—HERMAN MELVILLE, *Redburn (1849)*

2. Civilisation is not by any means an easy thing to attain to. There are only two ways by which man can reach it.

One is by being cultured, the other by being corrupt.
—OSCAR WILDE, *The Picture of Dorian Gray (1891)*

3. Since "unnatural" means "removed from nature," only the most civilized, because the least natural,

class of society can be expected to tolerate such a product of civilization.

> —VITA SACKVILLE-WEST, "Autobiography" (1920), in Nigel Nicholson, *Portrait of a Marriage (1973)*

4. Because our civilization is woven of so many diverse strands, the ideas which any one group accepts will be found to contain numerous contradictions.

> —MARGARET MEAD, *Coming of Age in Samoa (1928)*

5. Civilization is a method of living, an attitude of equal respect for all men.

> —JANE ADDAMS, *speech, Honolulu, 1933*

6. No civilization has in it any element which in the last analysis is not the contribution of an individual.

> —RUTH BENEDICT, *Patterns of Culture (1934)*

7. Civilized life exacts its toll.

> —IVY COMPTON-BURNETT, *A Heritage and Its History (1959)*

8. Nearly all great civilizations that perished did so because they had crystallized, because they were incapable of adapting themselves to new conditions, new methods, new points of view. It is as though people would rather die than change.

> —ELEANOR ROOSEVELT (d. 1962), *Tomorrow Is Now (1963)*

9. If civilization was left in female hands, we would still be living in grass huts.

> —CAMILLE PAGLIA, *Sex, Art, and American Culture (1992)*

Closet

1. Out of the dark confinement! out from behind the screen!

> —WALT WHITMAN, *"Song of the Open Road," Leaves of Grass (1855)*

2. They shut me up in Prose— / As when a little girl / They put me in the Closet— / Because they liked me 'still.'

> —EMILY DICKINSON, *no. 613 (c. 1862), Complete Poems (1955)*

3. From all I did and all I said / let no one try to find out who I was.
> —CONSTANTINE P. CAVAFY, "Hidden Things" (1908)

4. My private inclinations are not the concern of my reading public. I have no urge to martyr my reputation for the sake of self-indulgent exhibitionism.
> —NOËL COWARD, Song at Twilight (1966)

5. Believe it or not, there was a time in my life when I didn't go around announcing that I was a faggot.
> —MART CROWLEY, The Boys in the Band (1968)

6. Closets stand for prisons, not privacy.
> —ROBIN TYLER, recording Always a Bridesmaid Never a Groom (1979)

7. The walls of the closet are guarded by the gods of terror, and the inside of the closet is a house of mirrors.
> —JUDY GRAHN, Another Mother Tongue (1984)

8. The Gay closet has many points of discomfort. One is the sheer shame that life must be so secret, than one's citizenship is always dependent on how camouflaged as a heterosexual one appears. The necessary double life means that the Gay person can never simply stand flat-footed on the earth; there are always two people operating in one body, and one of them is a liar.
> —JUDY GRAHN, Another Mother Tongue (1984)

9. Only one thing has changed for certain. We have changed. We will never go back into the closet.
> —SARAH SCHULMAN, My American History (1994)

Compassion

1. Give nobody's heart pain so long as thou canst avoid it, for one sigh may set a whole world into a flame.
> —SA'DI, Gulistan (1258)

2. The quality of mercy is not strained; / It droppeth as the gentle rain from heaven / Upon the place beneath. It is twice blessed— / It

blesseth him that gives, and him that takes.
> —WILLIAM SHAKESPEARE, *The Merchant of Venice (1596–97)*

3. To look with mercy on the conduct of others is a virtue no less than to look with severity on your own.
> —MATTHEW G. LEWIS, *The Monk (1795)*

4. The drying up a single tear has more / Of honest fame, than shedding seas of gore.
> —GEORGE GORDON, LORD BYRON, *Don Juan (1819–24)*

5. Compassion the heart decides for itself.
> —HERMAN MELVILLE, *The Confidence-Man (1857)*

6. True kindness presupposes the faculty of imagining as one's own the suffering and joys of others.
> —ANDRÉ GIDE, *Pretexts (1903)*

7. And remember Mother's practical ethics: *one can drown in compassion if one answers every call it's another way of suicide.*
> —PATRICK WHITE, *The Eye of the Storm (1973)*

Complaint

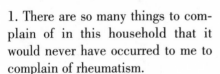

1. There are so many things to complain of in this household that it would never have occurred to me to complain of rheumatism.
> —SAKI [H. H. MUNRO], *"The Quest," The Chronicles of Clovis (1911)*

2. The world is disgracefully managed, one hardly knows to whom to complain.
> —RONALD FIRBANK, *Vainglory (1915)*

3. A woman of the world should always be the mistress of sorrow and not its servant. She may have a grief but never a grievance.
> —ELSIE DE WOLFE, *After All (1935)*

4. Grumbling is the death of love.
> —MARLENE DIETRICH, *Marlene Dietrich's ABC (1962)*

5. I personally think we developed language because of our deep inner need to complain.
> —JANE WAGNER [words spoken by Lily Tomlin], *The Search for Signs of Intelligent Life in the Universe (1985)*

Conformity

1. Wherever a man goes, men will pursue him and paw him with their dirty institutions, and, if they can, constrain him to belong to their desperate oddfellow society.
> —HENRY DAVID THOREAU, "The Village," Walden (1854)

2. We arrange our lives—even the best and boldest men and women that exist, just as much as the most limited—with reference to what society conventionally rules and makes right.
> —WALT WHITMAN, Notes Left Over (1881)

3. That habit of treading in ruts and trooping in companies which men share with sheep.
> —A. E. HOUSMAN, "The Editing of Juvenal" (1905)

4. It is not difficult to be unconventional in the eyes of the world when your unconventionality is but the convention of your set.
> —W. SOMERSET MAUGHAM, The Moon and Sixpence (1906)

5. Once conform, once do what other people do because they do it, and a lethargy steals over all the finer nerves and faculties of the soul.
> —VIRGINIA WOOLF, "Montaigne," The Common Reader (1925)

6. Miss Ogilvy had found as her life went on that in this world it is better to be one with the herd, that the world has no wish to understand those who cannot conform to its stereotyped pattern.
> —RADCLYFFE HALL, "Miss Ogilvy Finds Herself" (1934)

7. Nothing is more restful than conformity.
> —ELIZABETH BOWEN, Collected Impressions (1950)

8. Most of the men or women who have contributed to our civilization or our culture have been vilified in their day. . . . As we denounce the rebellious, the nonconformists, so we reward mediocrity so long as it mirrors herd standards.
> —TALLULAH BANKHEAD, Tallulah (1952)

9. Why conform to the standards of the cowshed? It's a thing you grow out of. With me behind you, boy, you'll grow out of it.
> —JOE ORTON, Entertaining Mr Sloane (1963)

10. Eccentricity is not, as dull people would have us believe, a form of madness. It is often a kind of innocent pride, and the man of genius and the aristocrat are frequently regarded as eccentrics because genius and aristocrat are entirely unafraid of and uninfluenced by the opinions and vagaries of the crowd.
—*EDITH SITWELL (d. 1964), Taken Care Of (1965)*

11. All reduction of people to objects, all imposition of labels and patterns to which they must conform, all segregation can lead only to destruction.
—*MAUREEN DUFFY, Rites (1969)*

12. I think the reward for conformity is that everyone likes you except yourself.
—*RITA MAE BROWN, Bingo (1988)*

Conscience

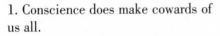

1. Conscience does make cowards of us all.
—*WILLIAM SHAKESPEARE, Hamlet (1600)*

2. Conscience: a chief pretence to cozen fools withal.
—*APHRA BEHN, The Rover (1677)*

3. If I were ambitious, I should not for so many years have been a prey to all the hell of conscientious scruples.
—*HORACE WALPOLE, The Castle of Otranto (1764)*

4. Conscience the awarder of its own doom.
—*HERMAN MELVILLE, Mardi (1849)*

5. Conscience makes egotists of us all.
—*OSCAR WILDE, The Picture of Dorian Gray (1891)*

6. People talk about conscience, but it seems to me one must bring it up to a certain point and leave it there. You can let your conscience alone if you're nice to the second housemaid.
—*HENRY JAMES, The Awkward Age (1899)*

7. The strongest feelings assigned to the conscience are not moral feelings at all; they express merely physical antipathies.
—*GEORGE SANTAYANA, The Life of Reason (1906)*

8. I believe I once considerably scandalized her by declaring that

clear soup was a more important factor in life than a clear conscience.
—SAKI, *"The Blind Spot," Beasts and Super-Beasts (1914)*

9. Conscience is the guardian in the individual of the rules which the community has evolved for its own preservation.
—W. SOMERSET MAUGHAM, *The Moon and Sixpence (1919)*

10. Asked by the chairman [of a military tribunal] the usual question: "I understand, Mr. Strachey, that you have a conscientious objection to war?" he replied (in his curious falsetto voice), "Oh no, not at all, only to *this* war." Better than this was his reply to the chairman's other stock question, which had previously never failed to embarrass the claimant. "Tell me, Mr. Strachey, what would you do if you saw a German soldier trying to violate your sister?" With an air of noble virtue: "I would try to get between them."

—ROBERT GRAVES, *on Lytton Strachey, Good-bye to All That (1929)*

11. Freedom of conscience entails more dangers than authority and despotism.
—MICHEL FOUCAULT, *Madness and Civilization (1965)*

12. There are some women . . . in whom conscience is so strongly developed that it leaves little room for anything else. Love is scarcely felt before duty rushes in to encase it, anger impossible because one must always be calm and see both sides, pity evaporates in expedients, even grief is felt as a sort of bruised sense of injury, a resentment that one should have grief forced upon one when one has always acted for the best.
—SYLVIA TOWNSEND WARNER, *"Total Loss" (1966)*

Contradiction

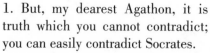

1. But, my dearest Agathon, it is truth which you cannot contradict; you can easily contradict Socrates.
—PLATO *(4th century BCE), Symposium*

2. Do I contradict myself? / Very well then I contradict myself, / (I am large, I contain multitudes).
—WALT WHITMAN, *"Song of Myself," Leaves of Grass (1855)*

3. The well-bred contradict other people. The wise contradict themselves.

> —OSCAR WILDE, "Phrases and Philosophies for the Use of the Young" (1894)

4. In me the tiger sniffs the rose.

> —SIEGFRIED SASSOON, The Heart's Journey (1928)

5. What I claim is to live to the full the contradiction of my time, which may well make sarcasm the condition of truth.

> —ROLAND BARTHES, Mythologies (1957)

6. I happen to feel that the degree of a person's intelligence is directly reflected by the number of conflicting attitudes she can bring to bear on the same topic.

> —LISA ALTHER, Kinflicks (1976)

C o n v e r s a t i o n

1. The more the pleasures of the body fade away, the greater to me is the pleasure and the charm of conversation.

> —PLATO (4th century BCE), The Republic

2. Whoever interrupts the conversation of others to make a display of his fund of knowledge, makes notorious his own stock of ignorance.

> —SA'DI, Gulistan (1258)

3. Ultimately, the bond of all companionship, whether in marriage or friendship, is conversation.

> —OSCAR WILDE, De Profundis (1897)

4. One is always wrong to open a conversation with the devil, for, however he goes about it, he always insists upon having the last word.

> —ANDRÉ GIDE, Journals, 1917

5. Do you know that conversation is one of the greatest pleasures in life? But it wants leisure.

> —W. SOMERSET MAUGHAM, "The Fall of Edward Barnard" (1921)

6. The primary use of conversation is to satisfy the impulse to talk.

> —GEORGE SANTAYANA, The Last Puritan (1935)

7. Conversation did not flow with the drink; it drowned in it.

—QUENTIN CRISP, *The Naked Civil Servant (1968)*

8. Their civil discussions weren't interesting, and their interesting discussions weren't civil.
—LISA ALTHER, *Kinflicks (1975)*

9. A conversation is a dialogue, not a monologue. That's why there are so few good conversations: due to scarcity, two intelligent talkers seldom meet.
—TRUMAN CAPOTE, *Music for Chameleons (1980)*

10. Polite conversation is rarely either.
—FRAN LEBOWITZ, *Social Studies (1981)*

Corruption

1. Lilies that fester smell far worse than weeds.
—WILLIAM SHAKESPEARE, *Sonnet 94 (1609)*

2. In an absolutely corrupt age, such as the one we are living in, the safest course is to do as the others do.
—MARQUIS DE SADE, *La Nouvelle Justine, ou les Malheurs de la Vertu (1795)*

3. Those who find ugly meanings in beautiful things are corrupt without being charming. This is a fault.
—OSCAR WILDE, *The Picture of Dorian Gray (1891)*

4. Corruption continues with us beyond the grave, and then plays merry hell with all ideals.
—DAPHNE DU MAURIER, *Mary Anne (1954)*

5. Big Business and Politics are twins, they are the monsters who kill everything, corrupt everything.
—ANAÏS NIN (1957), *The Diary of Anaïs Nin, Vol. 6 (1976)*

Courage

1. Courage is a kind of salvation.
   —*Plato (4th century BCE), The Republic*

2. Why, courage then! What cannot be avoided / 'Twere childish weakness to lament or fear.
   —*William Shakespeare, 3 Henry VI (1592)*

3. My courage was still more in my head than in my heart.
   —*John Cleland, Memoirs of a Woman of Pleasure (1749)*

4. Shame on the coward soul, which wants the courage neither to be a firm friend, or an open enemy.
   —*Matthew G. Lewis, The Monk (1795)*

5. An utterly fearless man is a far more dangerous comrade than a coward.
   —*Herman Melville, Moby-Dick (1851)*

6. I never wanted to be a hero, but on the other hand I am not anxious to cultivate cowardice.
   —*Gertrude Stein, Q.E.D. (1903)*

7. 'Tisn't life that matters! 'Tis the courage you bring to it.
   —*Hugh Walpole, Fortitude (1913)*

8. I suppose that none but those whose courage is unquestionable can venture to be effeminate.
   —*Ronald Firbank, Valmouth (1919)*

9. Life shrinks or expands in proportion to one's courage.
   —*Anaïs Nin (1941), The Diary of Anaïs Nin, Vol. 3 (1969)*

10. You become courageous by doing courageous acts. Courage is a habit.
   —*Mary Daly, in Minnesota Women's Press, 1993*

C r e a t i v i t y

▼

1. The noblest works and foundations have proceeded from childless men, who have sought to express the images of their minds, where those of their bodies have failed.
   —*FRANCIS BACON, "Of Parents and Children," Essays (1625)*

2. When woman's unmeasured bondage shall be broken, when she shall live for and through herself, man—hitherto detestable—having let her go, she, too, will be poet! Woman will find the unknown! Will her ideational worlds be different from ours? She will come upon strange, unfathomable, repellent, delightful things; we shall take them, we shall comprehend them.
   —*ARTHUR RIMBAUD, letter, 15 May 1871*

3. Creation for the joy of creation is the aim of the artist, and that is why the artist is a more divine type than the saint.
   —*OSCAR WILDE, in The Sketch, 9 January 1895*

4. One must die to life in order to be utterly a creator.
   —*THOMAS MANN, "Tonio Kröger" (1903)*

5. No one is ahead of his time, it is only that the particular variety of creating his time is the one that his contemporaries who also are creating their time refuse to accept.
   —*GERTRUDE STEIN, "Composition as Explanation" (1926)*

6. No one has ever written, painted, sculpted, modeled, built, or invented except literally to get out of hell.
   —*ANTONIN ARTAUD, Van Gogh, the Man Suicided by Society (1947)*

7. Creative writers are always greater than the causes that they represent.
   —*E. M. FORSTER, Two Cheers for Democracy (1951)*

8. The spirit of creation is simply the spirit of contradiction.
   —*JEAN COCTEAU, in Atlantic Monthly, June 1958*

9. All men are creative but few are artists.
   —*PAUL GOODMAN, Growing Up Absurd (1960)*

10. Jews and homosexuals are the outstanding creative minorities in contemporary urban culture. Creative, that is, in the truest sense; they

are creators of sensibilities. The two pioneering forces of modern sensibility are Jewish moral seriousness and homosexual aestheticism and irony.

—SUSAN SONTAG, "Notes on 'Camp' " (1964)

11. Under all the superficial praise of the "creative" is the desire to kill. It is the old war between the mystic and the nonmystic, a war to the death.

—MAY SARTON, Mrs. Stevens Hears the Mermaids Singing (1965)

12. Innovators are inevitably controversial.

—EVA LE GALLIENNE, The Mystic in the Theater (1965)

13. You will be wondering, putative reader, why I have reported all this. The answer is quite simple: it interests me, and you, forgive me, don't. I am not trying to tell you anything; I am at my childlike, priestlike task of creation.

—MAUREEN DUFFY, The Love Child (1971)

14. It is the creative potential itself in human beings that is the image of God.

—MARY DALY, Beyond God the Father (1973)

15. It is the lesbian in us who is creative, for the dutiful daughter of the fathers in us is only a hack.

—ADRIENNE RICH, "It Is the Lesbian in Us . . ." (1976)

16. Sexuality is part of our behavior. It's part of our world freedom. Sexuality is something that we ourselves create. It is our own creation, and much more than the discovery of a secret side of our desire. We have to understand that with our desires go new forms of relationships, new forms of love, new forms of creation. Sex is not a fatality; it's a possibility for creative life. It's not enough to affirm that we are gay but we must also create a gay life.

—MICHEL FOUCAULT (d. 1984), in Didier Eribon, Michel Foucault (1989)

17. Living in a state of psychic unrest, in a Borderland, is what makes poets write and artists create.

—GLORIA ANZALDÚA, Borderlands/La Frontera (1987)

18. Creativity comes from trust. Trust your instincts. And never hope more than you work.

—RITA MAE BROWN, Starting from Scratch (1988)

Crime

1. From a single crime know the nation.
   —*VIRGIL, Aeneid (19 BCE)*

2. As for myself, I walk abroad o'nights / And kill sick people groaning under walls: / Sometimes I go about and poison wells.
   —*CHRISTOPHER MARLOWE, The Jew of Malta (c. 1589)*

3. It is a crime, if a crime it is to be called, that produces no misery in society.
   —*JEREMY BENTHAM, on homosexuality, "Nonconformity" (c. 1774)*

4. 'Tis not the crime which holds your hand, but the punishment.
   —*MATTHEW G. LEWIS, The Monk (1795)*

5. Nobody ever commits a crime without doing something stupid.
   —*OSCAR WILDE, The Picture of Dorian Gray (1891)*

6. Starvation, and not sin, is the parent of modern crime.
   —*OSCAR WILDE (d. 1900), in The Epigrams of Oscar Wilde, ed. Alvin Redman (1954)*

7. I came to the conclusion many years ago that almost all crime is due to the repressed desire for aesthetic expression.
   —*EVELYN WAUGH, Decline and Fall (1928)*

8. There exists among the intolerably degraded the perverse and powerful desire to force into the arena of the actual those fantastic crimes of which they have been accused, achieving their vengeance and their own destruction through making the nightmare real.
   —*JAMES BALDWIN, Notes of a Native Son (1955)*

9. Crimes of which a people is ashamed constitute its real history. The same is true of man.
   —*JEAN GENET, The Screens (1961)*

10. I expect that rape and murder, either separately or mixed together, fill the fantasies of most men and all stylists. They are the supreme acts of ascendancy over others; they yield the only moments when a man is certain beyond all doubt that his message has been received. Of the few who live out these dreams, some

preface rape with murder so as to avoid embracing a partner who might criticize their technique.

—*QUENTIN CRISP, in Guy Kettelhack, ed., The Wit and Wisdom of Quentin Crisp (1984)*

Criminals

1. You may say that it is your misfortune to be criminal; I answer that it is your crime to be unfortunate.
    —*SAMUEL BUTLER, Erewhon (1872)*

2. Society often forgives the criminal, it never forgives the dreamer.
    —*OSCAR WILDE (d. 1900), in Oscariana (1911)*

3. "The man is a common murderer." "A common murderer, possibly, but a very uncommon cook."
    —*SAKI [H. H. Munro], "The Blind Spot," Beasts and Super-Beasts (1914)*

4. There are souls that are incurable and lost to the rest of society. Deprive them of one means of folly, they will invent ten thousand others. They will create subtler, wilder methods, methods that are absolutely DESPERATE. Nature herself is fundamentally antisocial, it is only by a usurpation of powers that the organized body of society opposes the *natural* inclination of humanity.

—*ANTONIN ARTAUD, General Security: The Liquidation of Opium (1925)*

5. Atrophy of feeling creates criminals.
    —*ANAÏS NIN (1940), The Diary of Anaïs Nin, Vol. 3 (1969)*

6. We know that their adventures are childish. They themselves are fools. They are ready to kill or be killed over a card-game in which an opponent—or they themselves—was cheating. Yet, thanks to such fellows, tragedies are possible.
    —*JEAN GENET, The Thief's Journal (1949)*

7. Strange and predatory and truly dangerous, car thieves and muggers—they seem to jeopardize all our cherished concepts, even our self-esteem, our property rights, our powers of love, our laws and pleasures. The only relationship we seem to have with them is scorn or bewilderment, but they belong somewhere on

the dark prairies of a country that is in the throes of self-discovery.
>—*JOHN CHEEVER (1955), John Cheever: The Journals (1991)*

8. All classes are criminal today. We live in an age of equality.
>—*JOE ORTON (d. 1967), Funeral Games (1968)*

9. The lyricism of marginality may find inspiration in the image of the "outlaw," the great social nomad, who prowls on the confines of a docile, frightened order.
>—*MICHEL FOUCAULT, Discipline and Punish: The Birth of the Prison (1975)*

Cruelty

1. Be not so severe as to cause shyness, nor so clement as to encourage boldness.
>—*SA'DI, Gulistan (1258)*

2. He hath a body able to endure / More than we can inflict: and therefore now / Let us assail his mind another while.
>—*CHRISTOPHER MARLOWE, Edward II (c. 1591)*

3. I must be cruel, only to be kind.
>—*WILLIAM SHAKESPEARE, Hamlet (1600–1601)*

4. But it is certain that when he makes water his urine is congeal'd ice.
>—*WILLIAM SHAKESPEARE, Measure for Measure (1603)*

5. Severity breedeth fear, but roughness breedeth hate. Even reproofs from authority ought to be grave, and not taunting.
>—*FRANCIS BACON, "Of Great Place," Essays (1625)*

6. Perhaps it was right to dissemble your love, / But—why did you kick me downstairs?
>—*ISAAC BICKERSTAFFE, "An Expostulation" (1789)*

7. Far from being a vice, cruelty is the primary feeling that nature imprints in us. The infant breaks its rattle, bites its nurse's nipple, and strangles a bird, well before reaching the age of reason.
>—*MARQUIS DE SADE, La Philosophie dans le Boudoir (1795)*

8. We like torturing people but without getting really into trouble by killing them.

> —*MARCEL PROUST, Remembrance of Things Past: Within a Budding Grove (1918); trans. C. K. Scott Moncrieff and Terence Kilmartin*

9. Are you then unable to recognize a sob unless it has the same sound as yours?

> —*ANDRÉ GIDE, Journals (1922)*

10. As to abuse—I thrive on it. Abuse, hearty abuse, is a tonic to all save men of indifferent health.

> —*NORMAN DOUGLAS, Some Limericks (1928)*

11. They threw mud / And I looked another way, pretending to smile.

> —*STEPHEN SPENDER, "My parents kept me from children who were rough" (1933)*

12. Unkindness almost always stands for the displeasure that one has in oneself.

> —*ADRIENNE MONNIER (1939), in The Very Rich Hours of Adrienne Monnier (1976); trans. Richard McDougall*

13. Cruelty is the luxury of those who have nothing to do, like drugs or racing stables.

> —*MARGUERITE YOURCENAR, Coup de Grâce (1939)*

14. All cruel people describe themselves as paragons of frankness.

> —*TENNESSEE WILLIAMS, The Milk Train Doesn't Stop Here Anymore (1963)*

15. When we think of cruelty, we must try to remember the stupidity, the envy, the frustration from which it has arisen.

> —*EDITH SITWELL (d. 1964), Taken Care Of (1965)*

Cruising

1. You only invite friends you pick up from the baths, Cotta. / Only men from the steam baths make up your guest list. / Cotta, I used to wonder why you never invite me— / Till I realized that in the nude I'm not up to scratch.

> —*MARTIAL (1st century), Satires, I.23; trans. James J. Wilhelm*

2. The phonographs of hades in the brain / Are tunnels that re-wind themselves, and love / A burnt match skating in a urinal.
— *HART CRANE, "The Tunnel," The Bridge (1930)*

3. The good love a park and the inept a railway station.
— *FRANK O'HARA, "Homosexuality" (1954)*

4. I saw you, Walt Whitman, childless, lonely old grubber, poking / among the meats in the refrigerator and eyeing the grocery boys.
— *ALLEN GINSBERG, "A Supermarket in California," Howl (1956)*

5. MIKE: . . . I'm to be at King's Cross station at eleven. I'm meeting a man in the toilet.
JOYCE: You always go to such interesting places.
— *JOE ORTON, The Ruffian on the Stair (1963)*

6. A Turkish bath, like the Quaker service, is a place of silent meeting. The silence is shared solely by men, men who come uniquely together not to speak but to act. More even than the army, the bath is by definition a male if not a masculine domain.
— *NED ROREM, The New York Diary of Ned Rorem (1967)*

7. Standing at the various bars with our token half-pints before us, we would eye each other surreptitiously, perhaps registering the fact that, with so many eagles about, if any Ganymede did arrive we would have to work fast.
— *J. R. ACKERLEY, My Father and Myself (1968)*

8. I wonder, sometimes, how much of the cruising was for the pleasure of my cruising partner's companionship and for the sport of pursuit and how much was actually for the pretty repetitive and superficial satisfactions of the act itself.
— *TENNESSEE WILLIAMS, Memoirs (1976)*

9. Cruising, he had long ago decided, was a lot like hitchhiking. It was best to dress like the person you wanted to pick up.
— *ARMISTEAD MAUPIN, Tales of the City (1978)*

10. The audience was liberally sprinkled with gay guys. . . . Soon a guy next to me touched me—no big deal, it was crowded. I wasn't even aware of him, at first. Then he started running his hand over my foot, and into my shoe. Well, I had never had my foot fondled by another guy before, besides which I was with a straight friend who thought I was straight as well, so what could I do?
— *JAMES SPADA, The Spada Report (1979)*

11. There's a club, if you'd like to go / you could meet somebody there who really loves you.

> —MORRISSEY, *"How Soon Is Now?"* (1984)

12. Sex was everywhere. The men who handled the vegetables in the outdoor markets, the bus conductors crossing back and forth over the wide grid of the city, baking in their seats. The midwesterners, the men from Oregon, the sailors—so many young men in white hanging around the corners of the frame. So many arms and legs pending, only waiting to be engaged.

—MICHAEL GRUMLEY (*d. 1988*), *Life Drawing (1991)*

13. The dive was the sex addict's quick fix, packed to the rafters with college boys and working-class youths under twenty-five. From street level you stepped into a writhing mass of tight boys in tighter pants. On those sultry August nights it was a sexual experience just getting a drink. Like a subway at rush hour you were crushed against one another.

> —HAROLD NORSE, *Memoirs of a Bastard Angel (1990)*

C u r i o s i t y

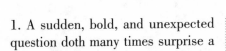

1. A sudden, bold, and unexpected question doth many times surprise a man and lay him open.

> —FRANCIS BACON, *"Of Cunning," Essays (1625)*

2. Too much curiosity lost Paradise.

> —APHRA BEHN, *The Lucky Chance (1686)*

3. Curiosity is one of those insatiable passions that grow by gratification.

> —SARAH SCOTT, *A Description of Millenium Hall (1762)*

4. It would be unnatural for a woman to quarrel with curiosity.

> —SARAH SCOTT, *A Description of Millenium Hall (1762)*

5. What we have to do is to be for ever curiously testing new opinions and courting new impressions, never acquiescing in a facile orthodoxy of Comte, or of Hegel, or of our own.

> —WALTER PATER, *Studies in the History of the Renaissance (1873)*

6. He had no curiosity. It was his chief defect.

—OSCAR WILDE, *The Picture of Dorian Gray (1891)*

7. Some men and women are inquisitive about everything, they are always asking, if they see any one with anything they ask what is that thing, what is it you are carrying, what are you going to be doing with that thing, why have you that thing, where did you get that thing, how long will you have that thing, there are many men and women who want to know about anything about everything.

—GERTRUDE STEIN, *The Making of the Americans (1925)*

8. We are all like Scheherazade's husband, in that we want to know what happens next.

—E. M. FORSTER, *Aspects of the Novel (1927)*

9. Perhaps the only misplaced curiosity is that which persists in trying to find out here, on this side of death, what lies beyond the grave.

—COLETTE, *The Pure and the Impure (1933)*

10. I think, at a child's birth, if a mother could ask a fairy godmother to endow it with the most useful gift, that gift should be curiosity.

—ELEANOR ROOSEVELT (d. 1962), in *Reader's Digest (1985)*

11. The curious are always in some danger. If you are curious you might never come home.

—JEANETTE WINTERSON, *Oranges Are Not the Only Fruit (1985)*

Custom

1. Since custom is the principal magistrate of man's life, let men by all means endeavor to obtain good customs.

—FRANCIS BACON, *"Of Custom and Education," Essays (1625)*

2. Most men's conscience, habits, and opinions are borrowed from convention and gather continually comforting assurances from the same social consensus that originally suggested them.

—George Santayana, *The Life of Reason (1906)*

3. Old-fashioned ways which no longer apply to changed conditions are a snare in which the feet of women have always become readily entangled.
　　—Jane Addams, *Newer Ideals of Peace (1907)*

4. There can be no relation more strange, more critical, than that between two beings who know each other only with their eyes, who meet daily, yes, even hourly, eye each other with a fixed regard, and yet by some whim or freak of convention feel constrained to act like strangers.
　　—Thomas Mann, *Death in Venice (1912)*

5. Centuries of custom, centuries of precedent! They pressed, they crushed, they suffocated. . . . They *must* swim against the current; it was ridiculous, preposterous that because she did not marry she should be forced to live a crippled existence. What real difference could it possibly make to her mother's loneliness if her daughter shared a flat with Elizabeth instead of with a husband? No difference at all, except in precedent.
　　—Radclyffe Hall, *The Unlit Lamp (1924)*

6. If you are way ahead with your head, you naturally are old fashioned and regular in your daily life.
　　—Gertrude Stein (d. 1946), quoted in John Malcolm Brinnin, *The Third Rose (1959)*

7. Convention was our safeguard: could one have stronger?
　　—Elizabeth Bowen, "A Day in the Dark" (1957)

8. Tradition, if not constantly recreated, can be as much a millstone as a mill-wheel.
　　—Colin MacInnes, *England, Half English (1961)*

9. Conventions, like clichés, have a way of surviving their own usefulness.
　　—Jane Rule, *The Desert of the Heart (1964)*

10. You can't break the mold and also be consoled for breaking it, old fool!
　　—May Sarton, *Mrs. Stevens Hears the Mermaids Singing (1965)*

Danger

1. In every sort of danger there are various ways of winning through, if one is ready to do and say anything whatever.
> —*SOCRATES, in Plato (4th century BCE), Apology*

2. A snake lurks in the grass.
> —*VIRGIL, Eclogues III (1st century BCE)*

3. The path is smooth that leadeth on to danger.
> —*WILLIAM SHAKESPEARE, Venus and Adonis (1593)*

4. God defend me from that Welsh fairy, / Lest he transform me to a piece of cheese!
> —*WILLIAM SHAKESPEARE, The Merry Wives of Windsor (1597–98)*

5. Perils commonly ask to be paid in pleasures.
> —*FRANCIS BACON, "Of Love," Essays (1625)*

6. A burnt child loves the fire.
> —*OSCAR WILDE, The Picture of Dorian Gray (1891)*

7. Without imagination, nothing is dangerous.
> —*GEORGETTE LEBLANC (1898), in Souvenirs (1932); trans. Janet Flanner*

8. People's sympathies seem generally to be with the fire so long as no one is in danger of being burned.
> —*SAMUEL BUTLER (d. 1902), Note Books (1912)*

9. It's not catastrophes, murders, or deaths, diseases, that age and kill us; it's the way people look and laugh, and run up the stairs of omnibuses.
> —*VIRGINIA WOOLF, Jacob's Room (1922)*

10. One does not discover new lands without consenting to lose sight of the shore for a very long time.
> —*ANDRÉ GIDE, The Counterfeiters (1926); trans. Dorothy Bussy*

11. To act is to be committed, and to be committed is to be in danger.
> —*JAMES BALDWIN, The Fire Next Time (1962)*

12. To access the damage is a dangerous act.
> —*CHERRÍE MORAGA, "La Guëra" (1983)*

13. Sometimes I think we can tell how important it is to risk by how dangerous it would be to do so.
—SONIA JOHNSON, *Going Out of Our Minds (1987)*

14. What you risk reveals what you value.
—JEANETTE WINTERSON, *Written on the Body (1992)*

Death

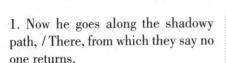

1. Now he goes along the shadowy path, / There, from which they say no one returns.
—CATULLUS *(1st century BCE), Carmina 3*

2. Pale Death strikes with impartial foot at the cottages of the poor and the turrets of kings.
—HORACE *(1st century BCE), Odes I, 4*

3. Dust into Dust, and under Dust to lie, / Sans Wine, sans Song, sans Singer, and—sans End!
—OMAR KHAYYÁM, RUBÁIYÁT *(11th–12th century); trans. Edward FitzGerald*

4. Yet let me kiss my Lord before I die, / And let me die with kissing of my Lord.
—CHRISTOPHER MARLOWE, *Tamburlaine the Great (1587)*

5. Men must endure / Their going hence, even as their coming hither.

—WILLIAM SHAKESPEARE, *King Lear (1605–6)*

6. To die is different from what any one supposed, and luckier.
—WALT WHITMAN, *"Song of Myself," Leaves of Grass (1855)*

7. All beauteous things for which we live / By laws of space and time decay. / But Oh, the very reason why / I clasp them, is because they die.
—WILLIAM CORY, *"Mimnermus in Church," Ionica (1858)*

8. Well! we are all *condamnés* as Victor Hugo says: we are all under sentence of death, but with a sort of indefinite reprieve.
—WALTER PATER, *Studies in the History of the Renaissance (1873)*

9. Death is only for the mediocre.
—ALFRED JARRY, *Gestes et Opinions du Docteur Faustroll Pataphysicien (1898)*

10. To die is to leave off dying and do the thing once and for all.
  —SAMUEL BUTLER (d. 1902), *Note Books (1912)*

11. Pray for the repose of His soul. He was so tired.
  —FREDERICK WILLIAM ROLFE ("Baron Corvo"), *Hadrian VII (1904)*

12. Death destroys a man: the idea of death saves him.
  —E. M. FORSTER, *Howards End (1910)*

13. There is no Death, / What seems so is transition.
  —MARIE CORELLI, *The Life Everlasting (1911)*

14. Naught broken save this body, lost but breath; / Nothing to shake the laughing heart's long peace there / But only agony, and that has ending; / And the worst friend and enemy is but Death.
  —RUPERT BROOKE, *"Peace" (1914)*

15. Waldo is one of those people who would be enormously improved by death.
  —SAKI [H. H. MUNRO], *"The Feast of Nemesis," Beasts and Super-Beasts (1914)*

16. In the happy no-time of his sleeping / Death took him by the heart.
  —WILFRED OWEN (d. 1918), *"Asleep," Poems (1920)*

17. The idea of dying is worse than dying itself, but less cruel than the idea that another has died.
  —MARCEL PROUST (d. 1922), *Remembrance of Things Past: The Captive (1923)*

18. A man's dying is more the survivors' affair than his own.
  —THOMAS MANN, *The Magic Mountain (1924)*

19. Like a light out of our heart, / You are gone.
  —H.D. [HILDA DOOLITTLE], *"Hymen," Collected Poems (1925)*

20. I shall not die of a cold. I shall die of having lived.
  —WILLA CATHER, *Death Comes for the Archbishop (1927)*

21. Our final experience, like our first, is conjectural. We move between two darknesses.
  —E. M. FORSTER, *Aspects of the Novel (1927)*

22. Against you I will fling myself, O Death!
  —VIRGINIA WOOLF, *The Waves (1931)*

23. There is only one way to be prepared for death: to be sated. In the soul, in the heart, in the spirit, in the flesh. To the brim.
  —HENRY DE MONTHERLANT, *Mors et Vita (1932)*

24. Death's not a separation or alteration or parting it's just a one-handled door.
—STEVIE SMITH, "Mrs. Simpkins," A
    Good Time Was Had by All
    (1937)

25. I face death alone willingly. I've tasted the best of life. It is pleasing to me to think that after I'm gone, thanks to me, mankind will be happier, better, and freer. For the benefit of future man, I created my work. I lived.
—ANDRÉ GIDE, Thésée (1946)

26. Funerals are pretty compared to death.
—TENNESSEE WILLIAMS, A Streetcar
    Named Desire (1947)

27. Let us try, if we can, to enter into death with open eyes.
—MARGUERITE YOURCENAR, Memoirs
    of Hadrian (1951)

28. I am neither impressed, nor frightened of death . . . The only thing that really saddens me over my demise is that I shall not be there to read the nonsense that will be written about me and my works and my motives.
—NOËL COWARD, diary,
    9 March 1955

29. Death is orgasm is rebirth is death is orgasm.

—WILLIAM S. BURROUGHS, The
    Ticket That Exploded (1962)

30. When I die, people will say it is the best thing for me. It is because they know it is the worst. They want to avoid the feeling of pity. As though they were the people most concerned!
—IVY COMPTON-BURNETT, The
    Mighty and Their Fall (1962)

31. Death is one moment, and life is so many of them.
—TENNESSEE WILLIAMS, The Milk
    Train Doesn't Stop Here Anymore
    (1963)

32. Audrey carried in *The Daily Telegraph*. Mother turned with avidity to the Deaths. When other helpers fail and comforts flee, when the senses decay and the mind moves in a narrower and narrower circle, when the grasshopper is a burden and the postman brings no letters, and even the Royal Family is no longer quite what it was, an obituary column stands fast.
—SYLVIA TOWNSEND WARNER, "Their
    Quiet Lives" (1966)

33. In all dying our ages are the same.
—MAUREEN DUFFY, "Der
    Rosenkavalier," The Venus Touch
    (1971)

34. Any woman's death diminishes me.

—*ADRIENNE RICH, "From an Old House in America," Poems: Selected and New (1974)*

35. Dying was apparently a weaning process; all the attachments to familiar people and objects had to be undone.
—*LISA ALTHER, Kinflicks (1975)*

36. Lesbians are everywhere, even in the morgue. We die like anyone else.
—*RITA MAE BROWN, foreword to Ginny Vida, Our Right to Love (1978)*

37. They've already got my ovaries, uterus, tubes—if I'm going, I'm going with my hair, guts, breasts, whatever I've got left. I'm going as a person, not as a patient. I'm going wanting to live, not wishing I were dead.
—*JANE CHAMBERS, Last Summer at Blue Fish Cove (1981)*

38. I don't want to die. I think death is a greatly overrated experience.
—*RITA MAE BROWN, Bingo (1988)*

39. But death—Their deaths have left me less defined: / It was their pulsing presence made me clear.
—*THOM GUNN, "The Missing," The Man with Night Sweats (1992)*

D e b t

1. He that dies pays all debts.
—*WILLIAM SHAKESPEARE, The Tempest (1611)*

2. There are some that account wife and children but as bills of charge.
—*FRANCIS BACON, "Of Marriage and Single Life," Essays (1625)*

3. Dreading that climax of all human ills / The inflammation of his weekly bills.
—*GEORGE GORDON, LORD BYRON, Don Juan (1819–24)*

4. It is only by not paying one's bills that one can hope to live in the memory of the commercial classes.
—*OSCAR WILDE, "Phrases and Philosophies for the Use of the Young" (1894)*

5. A man's indebtedness is not virtue; his repayment is.

—RUTH BENEDICT, *The Chrysanthemum and the Sword (1946)*

6. The first of the month falls every month, too, North or South. And

them white folks who sends bills never forgets to send them.
—LANGSTON HUGHES, *Simple Speaks His Mind (1950)*

Decadence

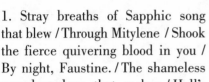

1. Stray breaths of Sapphic song that blew / Through Mitylene / Shook the fierce quivering blood in you / By night, Faustine. / The shameless nameless love that makes / Hell's iron gin / Shut on you like a trap that breaks / The soul, Faustine.
—ALGERNON CHARLES SWINBURNE, *"Faustine" (1866)*

2. Dandyism is an attempt to assert the absolute modernity of beauty.
—OSCAR WILDE, *The Picture of Dorian Gray (1891)*

3. His Hellenism once captivated me. But the *Attic* to him means nothing now but servants' bedrooms.
—RONALD FIRBANK, *The Princess Zoubaroff (1920)*

4. E. F. Benson never lived his life at all; only stayed with it and lunched with it.

—A. C. BENSON (d. 1925), *quoted in J. A. Gere and John Sparrow, eds., Geoffrey Madan's Notebooks (1981)*

5. Nonconformity and lust stalking hand and hand through the country, wasting and ravishing.
—EVELYN WAUGH, *Decline and Fall (1928)*

6. And as we are the reason for the 'Nineties' being gay, / We all wear a green carnation.
—NOËL COWARD, *"Green Carnation" (1929)*

7. Now, heaven knows, / Anything goes.
—COLE PORTER, *"Anything Goes" (1934)*

8. I was unwise enough to be photographed in bed wearing a Chinese

dressing-gown and an expression of advanced degeneracy.

> —NOËL COWARD, *Present Indicative* (1937)

9. Mauve is his favourite colour, and his gait / Suggests a peahen walking on hot bricks.

> —WILLIAM PLOMER, *"Playboy of the Demi-World: 1938" (1945)*

10. Eminence interested her far less than decadence; she understood that her readers felt an obscure, understandable pleasure reading about degradation but resented, in a perfectly human way, too long a tenure by the Famous in the pinnacles of success.

> —DORIS GRUMBACH, *The Missing Person (1981)*

Deception

1. I do indeed believe that to be an involuntary homicide is a less crime than to be a deceiver about beauty or goodness or justice as in the matter of law.

> —PLATO *(4th century BCE), The Republic*

2. Who can deceive a lover?

> —VIRGIL, *Aeneid (19 BCE)*

3. When we would deceive, we smile.

> —HERMAN MELVILLE, *Pierre (1852)*

4. When one is in love, one always begins by deceiving one's self, and one always ends by deceiving others. This is what the world calls a romance.

> —OSCAR WILDE, *The Picture of Dorian Gray (1891)*

5. Thea was still under the belief that if you clucked often enough, the hens would mistake you for one of themselves.

> —WILLA CATHER, *The Song of the Lark (1915)*

6. A deception that elevates us is dearer than a host of low truths.

> —MARINA TSVETAEVA, *"Pushkin and Pugachev" (1937)*

7. It's discouraging to think how many people are shocked by honesty and how few by deceit.

> —NOËL COWARD, *Blithe Spirit (1941)*

Decorum

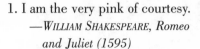

1. I am the very pink of courtesy.
   —*WILLIAM SHAKESPEARE, Romeo
   and Juliet (1595)*

2. Liberty plucks justice by the nose; / The baby beats the nurse, and quite athwart / Goes all decorum.
   —*WILLIAM SHAKESPEARE, Measure
   for Measure (1605)*

3. If a man be gracious and courteous to strangers, it shows he is a citizen of the world.
   —*FRANCIS BACON, "Goodness, and
   Goodness of Nature," Essays
   (1625)*

4. Society is smoothed to that excess, / That manners hardly differ more than dress.
   —*GEORGE GORDON, LORD BYRON,
   Don Juan (1819–24)*

5. Tact is after all a kind of mind-reading.
   —*SARAH ORNE JEWETT, The Country
   of Pointed Firs (1896)*

6. Being tactful in audacity is knowing how far one can go too far.
   —*JEAN COCTEAU, "Le Coq et
   l'Arlequin" (1918)*

7. But we can't possibly have a garden party with a man dead just outside the front gate.
   —*KATHERINE MANSFIELD, "The
   Garden Party" (1922)*

8. Please don't think me negligent or rude. I am both, in effect, of course, but please don't think me either.
   —*EDNA ST. VINCENT MILLAY (1920),
   in Allan Ross Macdougall, ed.,
   The Letters of Edna St. Vincent
   Millay*

9. One ought to go to a funeral instead of to church when one feels the need of being uplifted. People have on good black clothes, and they take off their hats and look at the coffin, and behave serious and reverent, and nobody dares to make a bad joke.
   —*THOMAS MANN, The Magic
   Mountain (1924)*

10. Whatsoever your Uncle Bob's failures were, he never tucked his serviette into his dickie.
   —*NOËL COWARD, The Café de la
   Paix (1939)*

11. Drawers are one thing, decorum is another.
   —*COLETTE, Gigi (1941)*

12. Shoddy table manners have broken up many a happy bond.
 —COLETTE, *Gigi (1941)*

13. Be pretty if you can, be witty if you must, but be gracious if it *kills* you.
 —ELSIE DE WOLFE *(d. 1950), in Mrs. Falk Feeley, A Swarm of Wasps (1983)*

14. Manners are especially the need of the plain. The pretty can get away with anything.
 —EVELYN WAUGH, *quoted in Observer, 15 April 1962*

15. He was very conscious of what a gentleman should or should not do; no gentleman looks out of a window; no gentleman wears a brown suit.
 —CECIL BEATON, *on Evelyn Waugh, The Strenuous Years (1973)*

16. At the moment I am debarred from the pleasure of putting her in her place by the fact that she has not got one.
 —EDITH SITWELL *(d. 1964), quoted in John Pearson, Façade (1978)*

17. I keep picturing poor dear Nancy Mitford as a house guest in some baronial estate in Wiltshire or Norfolk, having been shown all the blue-ribbon cattle and praising them later to her hostess, unable to use the taboo word "cows" for fear of causing offence and opting instead for "the bulls and their wives."
 —NOËL COWARD *(d. 1973), in William Marchant, The Privilege of His Company (1980)*

18. Nothing more rapidly inclines a person to go into a monastery than reading a book on etiquette. There are so many trivial ways in which it is possible to commit some social sin.
 —QUENTIN CRISP, *Manners from Heaven (1984)*

19. We must never confuse elegance with snobbery.
 —YVES SAINT LAURENT, *in Ritz (1984)*

20. No matter which sex I went to bed with, I never smoked on the street.
 —FLORENCE KING, *Confessions of a Failed Southern Lady (1985)*

21. You can't be truly rude until you understand good manners.
 —RITA MAE BROWN, *Starting from Scratch (1988)*

Democracy

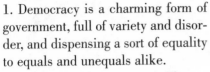

1. Democracy is a charming form of government, full of variety and disorder, and dispensing a sort of equality to equals and unequals alike.
　—*PLATO (4th century BCE), The Republic*

2. What is democracy?—an aristocracy of blackguards.
　—*GEORGE GORDON, LORD BYRON, diary, May 1821*

3. In no stable democracy do all men govern themselves. Though an army be all volunteers, martial law must prevail.
　—*HERMAN MELVILLE, Mardi (1847)*

4. Is a democracy, such as we know it, the last improvement possible in a government? Is it not possible to take a step further towards recognizing and organizing the rights of man?
　—*HENRY DAVID THOREAU, Civil Disobedience (1849)*

5. Democracy means simply the bludgeoning of the people by the people for the people.
　—*OSCAR WILDE, "The Soul of Man Under Socialism" (1895)*

6. What does democracy come down to? The persuasive power of slogans invented by wily self-seeking politicians.
　—*W. SOMERSET MAUGHAM, Christmas Holiday (1939)*

7. Democracy means / Everybody but me.
　—*LANGSTON HUGHES, "The Black Man Speaks," Jim Crow's Last Stand (1943)*

8. Knowledge—Zzzzzp! Money—Zzzzzp!—Power! That's the cycle democracy is built on!
　—*TENNESSEE WILLIAMS, The Glass Menagerie (1945)*

9. So two cheers for Democracy; one because it admits variety and two because it permits criticism. Two cheers are quite enough: there is no occasion to give three. Only Love the Beloved Republic deserves that.
　—*E. M. FORSTER, Two Cheers for Democracy (1951)*

10. Democracy in the contemporary world demands, among other things, an educated and informed people.
　—*ELIZABETH BISHOP, Brazil (1962)*

11. Democracy! Bah! When I hear that word I reach for my feather Boa!

—ALLEN GINSBERG (1960),
  Journals: Early Fifties Early
  Sixties (1977)

12. A democratic state is not proven by the welfare of the strong but by the welfare of the weak.
—JUNE JORDAN, "For the Sake of a
  People's Poetry," Passion (1980)

13. Democracy is an interesting, even laudable, notion and there is no question but that when compared to Communism, which is too dull, or Fascism, which is too exciting, it

emerges as the most palatable form of government.
—FRAN LEBOWITZ, Social Studies
  (1981)

14. Democracy is supposed to give you the feeling of choice, like Painkiller X and Painkiller Y. But they're both just aspirin.
—GORE VIDAL, in Observer,
  7 February 1982

15. Democracy is the fig leaf of elitism.
—FLORENCE KING, Reflections in a
  Jaundiced Eye (1989)

Depression

1. Man delights me not—no, nor woman neither.
—WILLIAM SHAKESPEARE, Hamlet
  (1600–1601)

2. I cannot remember the time when I have not longed for death. For years and years I used to watch for death as no sick man ever watched for the morning.
—FLORENCE NIGHTINGALE (1881),
  in Cecil Woodham-Smith,
  Florence Nightingale (1950)

3. I wake and feel the fell of dark, not day. / What hours, O what black hours we have spent / This night!
—GERARD MANLEY HOPKINS, "I
  wake and Feel the Fell of dark,
  not day" (c. 1885)

4. Sadness is almost never anything but a form of fatigue.
—ANDRÉ GIDE, Journals, 1922

5. Gaiety is forgetfulness of the self, melancholy is memory of the self: in

that state the soul feels all the power of its roots, nothing distracts it from its profound homeland and the look that it cast upon the outer world is gently dismayed.

> —ADRIENNE MONNIER (1942), in
> Richard McDougall, trans., The
> Very Rich Hours of Adrienne
> Monnier (1976)

6. And I thought, "My lord, one thing is certain, and that's that they'll make musicals one day about the glamour-studded 1950s." And I thought, my heaven, one thing is certain too, I'm miserable.

> —COLIN MACINNES, Absolute
> Beginners (1959)

7. Sometimes one has simply to endure a period of depression for what it may hold of illumination if one can live through it, attentive to what it exposes or demands.

> —MAY SARTON, Journal of a
> Solitude (1973)

8. Depression was a very active state really. Even if you appeared to an observer to be immobilized, your mind was in a frenzy of paralysis.

You were unable to function, but were actively despising yourself for it.

> —LISA ALTHER, Kinflicks (1975)

9. Depression is melancholy minus its charms—the animation, the fits.

> —SUSAN SONTAG, Illness as
> Metaphor (1978)

10. Depression is a very sensible reaction to just about everything we live in now.

> —CHRYSTOS, "Perhaps," in
> Christian McEwen and Sue
> O'Sullivan, eds., Out the Other
> Side (1988)

11. Depression—that is what we all hate. We the afflicted. Whereas the relatives and shrinks, the tribal ring, they rather welcome it: you are quiet and you suffer.

> —KATE MILLETT, The Loony-Bin
> Trip (1990)

12. Depression sits on my chest like a sumo wrestler.

> —SANDRA SCOPPETTONE, I'll Be
> Leaving You Always (1993)

Desire

1. Sweet Mother, I am no longer master of the loom. / Slave to desire, my heart yearns / And it's all the fault of a slender girl. / Blame Aphrodite.
> —SAPPHO (7th century BCE), *Fragment 102; trans. Anita George (1995)*

2. Thigh-spreader Eros shakes me again / Once more / Sweetbitter beast I cannot resist.
> —SAPPHO (7th century BCE), *Fragment 130; trans. Anita George*

3. The shepherd Corydon was yearning for handsome Alexis, / the plaything of his master, and he did not know what to hope for.
> —VIRGIL, *Eclogues (43–37 BCE)*

4. My heart is an anvil unto sorrow, / Which beats upon it like the Cyclops' hammers, / And with the noise turns up my giddy brain, / And makes me frantic for my Gaveston.
> —CHRISTOPHER MARLOWE, *Edward II (c. 1591)*

5. Is it not strange that desire should so many years outlive performance?
> —WILLIAM SHAKESPEARE, *2 Henry IV (1597–98)*

6. Being your slave, what should I do but tend / Upon the hours and times of your desire?
> —WILLIAM SHAKESPEARE, *Sonnet 57 (1609)*

7. All the desires of mutual love are virtuous.
> —APHRA BEHN, *"On Desire" (1684)*

8. Privation is the source of appetite.
> —SOR JUANA INÉS DE LA CRUZ *(1691), in Margaret Sayers Peden, trans., A Woman of Genius (1982)*

9. Will longing bring the thing desired?
> —HERMAN MELVILLE, *Mardi (1849)*

10. Rowing in Eden— / Ah, the Sea! / Might I but moor—Tonight / In thee!
> —EMILY DICKINSON, *no. 249 ("Wild Nights") (c. 1861), Complete Poems (1955)*

11. The delight that consumes the desire, / The desire that outruns the delight.
> —ALGERNON CHARLES SWINBURNE, *"Dolores" (1866)*

12. In the intimate dark there's never an ear, / Though the tulips stand on tiptoe to hear. / So give; ripe fruit must shrivel or fall. / As you are mine, Sweetheart, give all!
—AMY LOWELL, "Hora Stellatrix" (1912)

13. My God, but you keep me starved! You write "No Entrance Here," over all the doors. Hating bonds as you do, why should I be denied the rights of love if I leave you free?
—AMY LOWELL, "The Basket" (1914)

14. There is only one big thing— desire. And before it, when it is big, all is little.
—WILLA CATHER, The Song of the Lark (1915)

15. There is nothing like desire for preventing the thing one says from bearing any resemblance to what one has in mind.
—MARCEL PROUST, Remembrance of Things Past: The Guermantes Way (1921)

16. If fishes were wishes the ocean would be all of our desire. But they are not. We wish for land and sea and for a birthday and for cows and flowers. Our wishes have been expressed.
—GERTRUDE STEIN, "Did Nelly and Lilly Love You" (1922)

17. Dined with Virginia at Richmond. She is as delicious as ever.
—VITA SACKVILLE-WEST (on Virginia Woolf), diary entry, 22 February 1923

18. She looked at other women as though she would inhale them.
—RONALD FIRBANK, The Flower Beneath the Foot (1924)

19. From the satisfaction of desire there may arise, accompanying joy and as it were sheltering behind it, something not unlike despair.
—ANDRÉ GIDE, The Counterfeiters (1925)

20. I don't know how to say it . . . but . . . every time you say goodnight to me, and then go away, and shut the door of your room, I feel so terribly lost. . . . I stare at your door through the darkness . . . I keep on staring and staring . . . and I long to get up . . . open your door, creep up to your bed, and kneel beside it. I want to take your hand, and . . . and tell you . . . but I know I mustn't, so I have to clutch hard to my bed—I grip it so tight that it hurts. . . . Oh, I love you!
—CHRISTA WINSLOE, Girls in Uniform (1931)

21. She is bizarre, fantastic, nervous, like someone in a high fever. Her beauty drowned me.
—ANAÏS NIN, on June Miller (1931), The Diary of Anaïs Nin, Vol. 1 (1966)

22. There are mornings when all men experience with fatigue a flush of tenderness that makes them horny.
>   —*JEAN GENET, Our Lady of the Flowers (1949)*

23. I saw that lack of love contaminates. / You know I know you know I know you know.
>   —*THOM GUNN, "Carnal Knowledge" (1954)*

24. But lust too is a jewel / a sweet flower. . . .
>   —*ADRIENNE RICH, "Two Songs," Part I (1964)*

25. I think basically I think I want everyone and don't really want anybody.
>   —*MAUREEN DUFFY, The Love Child (1971)*

26. I desire, am only able to desire, myself.
>   —*VIOLETTE LEDUC, Mad in Pursuit (1971)*

27. In sex one wants or one does not want. And the grief, the sorrow of life is that one cannot make or coerce or persuade the wanting, cannot command it, cannot request it by mail order or finagle it through bureaucratic channels.
>   —*KATE MILLETT, Sita (1976)*

28. Our visions begin with our desires.
>   —*AUDRE LORDE, in Claudia Tate, ed., Black Women Writers at Work (1983)*

29. Whatsamatter honey? You sit in a puddle, or you just glad to see me?
>   —*HOLLY HUGHES, The Well of Horniness (1985)*

30. I feel as if I'm nothing but wetness, nothing but the thing between my legs.
>   —*PAT CALIFIA, "The Finishing School," Macho Sluts (1988)*

Difference

1. Different living is not living in different places / But creating in the mind a map.
>   —*STEPHEN SPENDER, "Different Living" (1933)*

2. The crucial differences which distinguish human societies and human beings are not biological. They are cultural.

—RUTH BENEDICT (1943), in
Margaret Mead, An
Anthropologist at Work (1959)

3. There is more difference within
the sexes than between them.
—IVY COMPTON-BURNETT, Mothers
and Sons (1955)

4. The founders and this people, who
set in diversity / The base of our
living.
—MURIEL RUKEYSER, "Young," One
Life (1957)

5. If you and I are no different, what
do we have to give each other? How
can we ever be friends?
—CHRISTOPHER ISHERWOOD, A
Single Man (1964)

6. This is a boy, sir. Not a girl. If
you're baffled by the difference it
might be as well to approach both
with caution.
—JOE ORTON (d. 1967), What the
Butler Saw (1969)

7. The only incontestable difference
is not that of sex or age or strength,
but that of the living and the dead.
—HÉLÈNE CIXOUS, Dedans (1969)

8. I was always right out there. I was
really quite popular. I was amusing
and I was pretty. I didn't look like
anybody else. People start out by
being put off by something that's different, but I very easily disarmed
them. Seduction—that's what I do. It

was: You think I'm different, well, I'll
show you how different I really am.
—TRUMAN CAPOTE, in New York
Times Magazine, 1978

9. There is no such thing as a value-
free concept of deviance; to say
homosexuals are deviant because
they are a statistical minority is to
stigmatize them. Nuns are rarely
classed as deviants for the same reason, although if they obey their vows
they clearly differ very significantly
from the great majority of people.
—DENNIS ALTMAN, The
Homosexualization of America
(1982)

10. Being women together was not
enough. We were different. Being
gay-girls together was not enough.
We were different. Being Black
together was not enough. We were
different. Being Black women together was not enough. We were different. Being Black dykes together
was not enough. We were different.
—AUDRE LORDE, Zami: A New
Spelling of My Name (1982)

11. It is not really difference the
oppressor fears so much as similarity.
—CHERRÍE MORAGA, "La Güera"
(1983)

12. Deviance is whatever is condemned by the community. Most
societies try to get rid of their deviants. Most cultures have burned
and beaten their homosexuals and

others who deviate from the sexual common. The queer are the mirror reflecting the heterosexual tribe's fear: being different, being other and therefore lesser, therefore sub-human, in-human, non-human.

—*GLORIA ANZALDÚA,*
Borderlands/La Frontera (1987)

Disappointment and Disillusionment

1. There is no misanthrope like a boy disappointed; and such was I, with the warm soul of me flogged out by adversity.

—*HERMAN MELVILLE, Redburn*
(1849)

2. She was usually in love with some-body, and, as her passion was never returned, she had kept all her illu-sions.

—*OSCAR WILDE, The Picture of*
Dorian Gray (1891)

3. I could not be more astonished if you told me there were fleas at the Ritz.

—*RONALD FIRBANK, The Flower*
Beneath the Foot (1923)

4. Disillusionment in living is find-ing out that nobody agrees with you not those that are fighting for you. Complete disillusionment is when you realize that no one can for they can't change. . . . This is then com-plete disillusionment in living, the complete realization that no one can believe as you do about anything.

—*GERTRUDE STEIN, The Making of*
Americans (1925)

5. Who ever is adequate? We all cre-ate situations each other can't live up to, then break our hearts at them because they don't.

—*ELIZABETH BOWEN, The Death of*
the Heart (1938)

6. Death from disillusion is not instantaneous, and there are no mercy killers for the disillusioned.

—*ANAÏS NIN (1946), The Diaries of*
Anaïs Nin, Vol. 4 (1971)

7. There's less in this than meets the eye.

—*TALLULAH BANKHEAD, Tallulah*
(1952)

8. There is no need to waste pity on young girls who are having their moments of disillusionment, for in another moment they will recover their illusion.
—COLETTE (d. 1954), *Earthly Paradise (1966)*

9. I am sick of the disparity between things as they are and as they should be. I'm tired. I'm tired of the truth and I'm tired of lying about the truth.

—EDWARD ALBEE, *The Death of Bessie Smith (1960)*

10. Nothing can be more deeply wounding than the disillusionments of a child or adolescent, but the disillusionments of an old man are old scars, slowly formed over the wounds of a long lifetime.
—WILLIAM PLOMER, *BBC broadcast, 14 December 1969*

Dissent

1. Say, Not so, and you will outcircle the philosophers.
—HENRY DAVID THOREAU, *Journal, 26 June 1840*

2. Were there none who were discontented with what they have, the world would never reach anything better.
—FLORENCE NIGHTINGALE, *Cassandra (1852)*

3. Discontent is the first step in the progress of a man or a nation.
—OSCAR WILDE, *A Woman of No Importance (1893)*

4. I have spent many years of my life in opposition and I rather like the role.
—ELEANOR ROOSEVELT, *letter to Bernard Baruch, 1952*

5. Some people always assume that if you mention a problem, you caused it.
—SONIA JOHNSON, *Going Out of Our Minds (1987)*

6. What do you mean, since when did I become such a radical fairy! Since I started knowing twits like you, you twit!
—LARRY KRAMER, *Just Say No (1989)*

Doctors

1. Is it not also true that no physician, in so far as he is a physician, considers or enjoins what is for the physician's interest, but that all seek the good of their patients? For we have agreed that a physician strictly so called, is a ruler of bodies, and not a maker of money, have we not?
   —SOCRATES (5th century BCE), in Plato (4th century BCE), The Republic

2. The more ignorant, reckless and thoughtless a doctor is, the higher his reputation soars even amongst powerful princes.
   —DESIDERIUS ERASMUS, Praise of Folly (1509)

3. By medicine life may be prolonged, yet death / Will seize the doctor too.
   —WILLIAM SHAKESPEARE, Cymbeline (1610)

4. Surgeons must be very careful / When they take the knife! / Underneath their fine incisions / Stirs the Culprit—Life!
   —EMILY DICKINSON, no. 108 (c. 1859), Complete Poems (1955)

5. I suppose one has a greater sense of intellectual degradation after an interview with a doctor than from any human experience.
   —ALICE JAMES, letter to William James, 27 September 1890

6. Even medical families cannot escape the more insidious forms of disease.
   —HENRY JAMES, Washington Square (1890)

7. Medicine being a compendium of the successive and contradictory mistakes of medical practitioners, when we summon the wisest of them to our aid, the chances are that we may be relying on as scientific truth the error of which will be recognized in a few years' time.
   —MARCEL PROUST, Remembrance of Things Past: The Guermantes Way (1921)

8. For what Harley Street specialist has time to understand the body, let alone the mind or both in combination, when he is a slave to thirteen thousand a year?
   —VIRGINIA WOOLF, Three Guineas (1938)

Doubt

1. Nothing more certain than incertainties; / Fortune is full of fresh variety: / Constant in nothing but inconstancy.
> —*RICHARD BARNFIELD, The Affectionate Shepherd (1594)*

2. Our doubts are traitors / And make us lose the good we oft might win / By fearing to attempt.
> —*WILLIAM SHAKESPEARE, Measure for Measure (1603)*

3. If a man will begin with certainties, he shall end in doubts; but if he will be content to begin with doubts, he shall end in certainties.
> —*FRANCIS BACON, The Advancement of Learning (1605)*

4. Doubt all things earthly, and intuitions of some things heavenly; this combination makes neither believer nor infidel, but makes a man who regards them both with equal eye.
> —*HERMAN MELVILLE, Moby-Dick (1851)*

5. People were always asking for good sound proofs; doubt springs eternal in the human breast, even in countries where the Inquisition can read your very thoughts in your eyes.
> —*THORNTON WILDER, The Bridge of San Luis Rey (1927)*

6. Like all self-possessed people, he was prey to doubt.
> —*BRUCE CHATWIN, What Am I Doing Here? (1989)*

Drag

1. Nay, faith, let not me play a woman; I have a beard coming.
> —*WILLIAM SHAKESPEARE, A Midsummer Night's Dream (1595)*

2. Dressing up meant the excitement and safety of disguise. You had to transform yourself as much as possible, so it was natural that you should

change your sex. [My mother] didn't
discourage this at all.
> —CHRISTOPHER ISHERWOOD,
> *Kathleen and Frank (1972)*

3. I've always thought I'd be particularly good in Romeo—as the nurse.
> —NOËL COWARD (d. 1973), in
> William Marchant, *The Pleasure
> of His Company (1975)*

4. There is more to be learned from wearing a dress for a day than there is from wearing a suit for life.
> —MARIO MIELI, *Homosexuality and
> Liberation: Elements of a Gay
> Critique (1980)*

5. The scorn directed against drags is especially virulent; they have become the outcasts of gay life, the "queers" of homosexuality. In fact, they are classic scapegoats. Our old fears about our sissiness, still with us though masked by the new macho fascism, are now located, isolated, quarantined through our persecution of the transvestite.
> —EDMUND WHITE, *States of Desire:
> Travels in Gay America (1980)*

6. There are easier things in this life than being a drag queen. But, I ain't got no choice. Try as I may, I just can't walk in flats.
> —HARVEY FIERSTEIN, *Torch Song
> Trilogy (1981)*

7. Did Mae West invent drag queens or did drag queens invent Mae West?

> —MICHAEL BRONSKI, *Culture Clash:
> The Making of Gay Sensibility
> (1984)*

8. Well any man who dresses up as a woman can't be all bad!
> —CHARLES LUDLAM, *The Mystery of
> Irma Vep (1984)*

9. If men really are turned on by all that awful underwear, leg and footwear, all that paint and headachy perfume, then maybe they should have been wearing it all along. . . . If what men want is our underwear, let them be welcome to it. It's a great swap for the shirts off their backs which we wear so comfortably.
> —JANE RULE, *A Hot-Eyed Moderate
> (1985)*

10. I'm terribly proud. You know, I've always been ripe material for the drag queens. In England, they love to do me. I went out of fashion for a while, because I wasn't very visible. But I know things must be going well, because they are starting to do me again!
> —DUSTY SPRINGFIELD, *on her 1980s
> comeback; quoted in US
> magazine, 2 May 1988*

11. If I had to wear high heels and a dress, I would be a mental case.
> —K. D. LANG, *quoted in The
> Advocate, 6 October 1992*

12. The Pope runs all over the world condemning homosexuality dressed in high drag. Now I ask you!

—*ROBIN TYLER, speech, March on Washington for Lesbian, Gay, and Bi Equal Rights, 25 April 1993*

D r e a m s

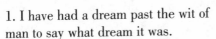

1. I have had a dream past the wit of man to say what dream it was.
   —*WILLIAM SHAKESPEARE, A Midsummer Night's Dream (1595)*

2. We are such stuff / As dreams are made on, and our little life / Is rounded with a sleep.
   —*WILLIAM SHAKESPEARE, The Tempest (1611)*

3. Our truest life is when we are in dreams awake.
   —*HENRY DAVID THOREAU, "The Inward Morning," A Week on the Concord and Merrimack Rivers (1849)*

4. We dream not ourselves, but the thing within us.
   —*HERMAN MELVILLE, Mardi (1849)*

5. Many will say it is a dream, and will not follow my inferences: but I confidently expect a time when there will be seen, running like a half-hid warp through all the myriad audible and visible worldly interests of America, threads of manly friendship, fond and loving, pure and sweet, strong and lifelong, carried to degrees hitherto unknown.
   —*WALT WHITMAN, Democratic Vistas (1871)*

6. A dream is always simmering below the conventional surface of speech and reflection.
   —*GEORGE SANTAYANA, The Life of Reason (1906)*

7. For to dream and then to return to reality only means that our qualms suffer a change of place and significance.
   —*COLETTE, Break of Day (1928)*

8. It is in our idleness, in our dreams, that the submerged truth sometimes comes to the top.
   —*VIRGINIA WOOLF, A Room of One's Own (1929)*

9. All men dream: but not equally. Those who dream by night in the dusty recesses of their minds wake in the day to find that it was vanity; but the dreamers of the day are dangerous men, for they may act their dream with open eyes to make it possible.

　—*T. E. LAWRENCE, Seven Pillars of Wisdom (1935)*

10. Dreams have only the pigmentation of fact.

　—*DJUNA BARNES, Nightwood (1936)*

11. But a man who doesn't dream is like a man who doesn't sweat. He stores up a lot of poison.

　—*TRUMAN CAPOTE, The Grass Harp (1951)*

12. What happens to a dream deferred?

　—*LANGSTON HUGHES, "Dream Deferred" (1951)*

13. I was not looking for my dreams to interpret my life, but rather for my life to interpret my dreams.

　—*SUSAN SONTAG, The Benefactor (1963)*

14. Oh, must we dream our dreams / and have them, too?

　—*ELIZABETH BISHOP, "Questions of Travel" (1965)*

D r i n k

1. Drink! for you know not whence you came, nor why: / Drink! for you know not why you go, nor where.

　—*OMAR KHAYYÁM, Rubáiyát (11th–12th century); trans. Edward FitzGerald*

2. Lechery, sir, it provokes, and unprovokes; it provokes the desire, but it takes away the performance.

　—*WILLIAM SHAKESPEARE, Othello (1605)*

3. Man, being reasonable, must get drunk; / The best of life is but intoxication.

　—*GEORGE GORDON, LORD BYRON, Don Juan (1819–24)*

4. Better sleep with a sober cannibal than a drunken Christian.

　—*HERMAN MELVILLE, Moby-Dick (1851)*

5. It is the hour for drunkenness! If you would not be the martyred slave of Time, drink without stopping! Drink wine, drink poetry, drink virtue, drink as you wish.
> —CHARLES BAUDELAIRE (d. 1867), Le Spleen de Paris (1869)

6. Malt does more than Milton can, / To justify God's ways to man.
> —A. E. HOUSMAN, A Shropshire Lad, no. 62 ["Terence, this is stupid stuff"] (1896)

7. I get no kick from champagne, / Mere alcohol doesn't thrill me at all
> —COLE PORTER, "I Get a Kick out of You" (1935)

8. Alcohol sobers me. After a few swallows of brandy I no longer think of you.
> —MARGUERITE YOURCENAR, Fires (1935)

9. Since the row with the actress who had shared her bed and her purse the need of drink had grown on her. And the horror and the terror of being alone. One of these days she would break—which of the village laws? Sobriety? Chastity? Or take something that did not properly belong to her?
> —VIRGINIA WOOLF, Between the Acts (1941)

10. I was rather drunk with what I had done. And I am always one to prefer being sober. I must be sober. It is so much more exciting to be sober, to be exact and concentrated and sober.
> —GERTRUDE STEIN (d. 1946), in John Malcolm Brinnin, The Third Rose (1959)

11. "Drink took to me," said Simple. "Whiskey just naturally likes me but beer likes me better."
> —LANGSTON HUGHES, Simple Speaks His Mind (1950)

12. Nothing is so musical as the sound of pouring bourbon for the first drink on a Sunday morning. Not Bach or Schubert or any of those masters.
> —CARSON MCCULLERS, Clock Without Hands (1953)

13. Pubs make you as drunk as they can, as soon as they can, and turn nasty when they succeed.
> —COLIN MACINNES, England, Half English (1961)

14. But you know, years ago everyone drank too much. Now it's drugs. Drinking was much more messy.
> —LARRY KRAMER, Faggots (1978)

15. Alcohol is an allergy of the body and an obsession of the mind.
> —RITA MAE BROWN, Starting from Scratch (1988)

Drugs

1. Everything one does in life, even love, occurs in an express train racing toward death. To smoke opium is to get out of the train while it is still moving. It is to concern oneself with something other than life or death.
  —*JEAN COCTEAU, Opium (1929)*

2. It is not opium which makes me work but its absence, and in order for me to feel its absence it must from time to time be present.
  —*ANTONIN ARTAUD, Appeal to Youth: Intoxication-Disintoxication (1934)*

3. The vaporish cocaine loosens the contours of their lives and sets their bodies adrift, and so they are untouchable.
  —*JEAN GENET, Our Lady of the Flowers (1949)*

4. Cocaine is not habit-forming. I should know—I've been using it for years.
  —*TALLULAH BANKHEAD, Tallulah (1952)*

5. Junk is the ideal product . . . the ultimate merchandise. No sales talk necessary. The client will crawl through a sewer and beg to buy.
  —*WILLIAM S. BURROUGHS, The Naked Lunch (1959)*

6. The fear of death is for all of us everywhere, but for the great intelligence of the opium eater it is beautifully narrowed into the crux of drugs.
  —*JOHN CHEEVER, Falconer (1977)*

7. I bought drugs like I bought designer clothes.
  —*BOY GEORGE, Take It Like a Man (1995)*

Duty and Dedication

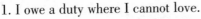

1. I owe a duty where I cannot love.
   —*APHRA BEHN, Abdelazar; or, the
   Moor's Revenge (1676)*

2. If you are chosen town clerk, for-
sooth, you cannot go to Tierra del
Fuego this summer; but you may go
to the land of infernal fire neverthe-
less.
   —*HENRY DAVID THOREAU,
   "Conclusion," Walden (1854)*

3. A man's foremost duty is not to get
collared.
   —*HENRY JAMES, Princess
   Casamassima (1886)*

4. Duty is what one expects from oth-
ers, it is not what one does oneself.
   —*OSCAR WILDE, A Woman of No
   Importance (1893)*

5. In practice it is seldom very hard
to do one's duty when one knows

what it is, but it is sometimes exceed-
ingly difficult to find this out.
   —*SAMUEL BUTLER (d. 1902), Note
   Books (1912)*

6. O, help me, heaven, to be decora-
tive and do right.
   —*RONALD FIRBANK, The Flower
   Beneath the Foot (1923)*

7. A devotion to humanity . . . is too
easily equated with a devotion to a
Cause, and Causes, as we know, are
notoriously bloodthirsty.
   —*JAMES BALDWIN, Notes of a Native
   Son (1955)*

8. Duties are what make life most
worth the living. Lacking them, you
are not necessary to anyone.
   —*MARLENE DIETRICH, in Steven
   Bach, Marlene Dietrich (1992)*

Education

1. Knowledge which is acquired under compulsion obtains no hold on the mind.
    —PLATO (4th century BCE), The Republic

2. Learning acquired in youth arrests the evil of old age; and if you understand that old age has wisdom for its food, you will conduct yourself in youth that your old age will not lack for nourishment.
    —LEONARDO DA VINCI, Notebooks (c. 1500)

3. Thou hast most traitorously corrupted the youth of the realm in erecting a grammar school.
    —WILLIAM SHAKESPEARE, 2 Henry VI (1597–98)

4. To spend too much time in studies is sloth.
    —FRANCIS BACON, "Of Studies," Essays (1625)

5. Alexander at the head of the world never tasted the true pleasure that boys of his own age have enjoyed at the head of a school.
    —HORACE WALPOLE, letter, 6 May 1736

6. My native purity had taken no root in education.
    —JOHN CLELAND, Memoirs of a Woman of Pleasure (1749)

7. What does education often do? It makes a straight-cut ditch of a free, meandering brook.
    —HENRY DAVID THOREAU, "Economy," Walden (1854)

8. Education is an admirable thing, but it is well to remember from time to time that nothing that is worth knowing can be taught.
    —OSCAR WILDE, "The Critic as Artist" (1891)

9. Laws and rules of conduct are for the state of childhood; education is an emancipation.
    —ANDRÉ GIDE, Journals, 1894

10. Ignorance is like a delicate exotic fruit; touch it and the bloom is gone. The whole theory of modern education is radically unsound. Fortunately, in England, at any rate, education produces no effect whatever.
    —OSCAR WILDE, The Importance of Being Earnest (1895)

11. Never learn anything until you find you have been made uncomfortable for a long while by not knowing it.
> —SAMUEL BUTLER (d. 1902), The Way of All Flesh (1903)

12. You can't expect a boy to be depraved till he's been to a good school.
> —SAKI [H. H. MUNRO], "A Baker's Dozen," Reginald in Russia (1910)

13. There are some things you learn better in calm, and some in storm.
> —WILLA CATHER, The Song of the Lark (1915)

14. I expect you'll be becoming a schoolmaster, sir. That's what most of the gentlemen does, sir, that gets sent down for indecent behaviour.
> —EVELYN WAUGH, Decline and Fall (1928)

15. I was asked to memorise what I did not understand; and, my memory being so good, it refused to be insulted in that manner.
> —ALEISTER CROWLEY, on geometry lessons, The Confessions of Aleister Crowley (1929)

16. Education is a state-controlled manufactory of echoes.
> —NORMAN DOUGLAS, How About Europe? (1929)

17. *Educated:* during the holidays from Eton.
> —OSBERT SITWELL, his entry in Who's Who (1929)

18. Teachers—a bunch of men all armed with the same information.
> —YUKIO MISHIMA, "Cigarette" (1946)

19. Let all the little poets be gathered together in classes / And let prizes be given to them by the Prize Asses.
> —STEVIE SMITH, "To School!" Harold's Leap (1950)

20. Spoon feeding in the long run teaches us nothing but the shape of the spoon.
> —E. M. FORSTER, in Observer, 7 October 1951

21. The college was not founded to give society what it wants. Quite the contrary.
> —MAY SARTON, The Small Room (1961)

22. The philosophical aim of education must be to get each one out of his isolated class and into the one humanity.
> —PAUL GOODMAN, Compulsory Miseducation (1964)

23. Assistant masters came and went. Some liked little boys too little and some too much.
> —EVELYN WAUGH, A Little Learning (1964)

24. Stand firm in your refusal to remain conscious during algebra. In real life, I assure you, there is no such thing as algebra.
　　—*FRAN LEBOWITZ, Social Studies (1981)*

25. It is very nearly impossible to become an educated person in a country so distrustful of the independent mind.
　　—*JAMES BALDWIN, The Price of the Ticket (1985)*

Egotism and Narcissism

1. Self-love, my liege, is not so vile a sin / As self-neglecting.
　　—*WILLIAM SHAKESPEARE, Henry V (1598–99)*

2. Why should I be angry with a man for loving himself better than me?
　　—*FRANCIS BACON, "Of Revenge," Essays (1625)*

3. I dote on myself, there is that lot of me and all so luscious.
　　—*WALT WHITMAN, "Song of Myself," Leaves of Grass (1855)*

4. To love oneself is the beginning of a life-long romance.
　　—*OSCAR WILDE, An Ideal Husband (1895)*

5. Sherard Blaw, the dramatist who had discovered himself, and who had given so ungrudgingly of his discovery to the world.
　　—*SAKI [H. H. Munro], The Unbearable Bassington (1912)*

6. Egoists always have the last word. Once and for all they establish the fact that their minds cannot be changed.
　　—*MARCEL PROUST, Remembrance of Things Past: Within a Budding Grove (1918)*

7. The sudden desire to look beautiful made her straighten her back. "Beautiful? For whom? Why, for myself, of course."
　　—*COLETTE, Cheri (1920)*

8. If you take passionate interest in a subject, it is hard not to believe yourself specially equipped for it.
　　—*ETHEL SMYTH, Streaks of Life (1922)*

9. Human altruism which is not egoism, is sterile.
　　—*MARCEL PROUST (d. 1922), Remembrance of Things Past: Time Regained (1926)*

10. Should I call myself an egoist? . . . Others have called me so. They merely meant I did not care for them.
—*L. P. HARTLEY, Simonetta Perkins (1925)*

11. He fell in love with himself at first sight and it is a passion to which he has always remained faithful. Self-love seems so often unrequited.
—*ANTHONY POWELL, A Dance to the Music of Time: The Acceptance World (1955)*

12. She invents dramas in which she always stars.
—*ANAÏS NIN (1931), The Diary of Anaïs Nin, Vol. 1 (1966)*

13. She was one of the most unimportantly wicked women of her time—because she could not let her time alone, and yet could never be a part of it. She wanted to be the reason for everything and so was the cause of nothing.
—*DJUNA BARNES, Nightwood (1936)*

14. I have often wished I had time to cultivate modesty. . . . But I am too busy thinking about myself.
—*EDITH SITWELL, in Observer, 30 April 1950*

15. She had learnt that it was impossible to discuss issues civilly with a person who insisted on referring to himself as "we."
—*LISA ALTHER, Kinflicks (1975)*

16. His sense of his deserts had grown. Now he was sure that what he desired, he deserved, and anyone who denied it merited punishment.
—*MARY RENAULT, The Praise Singer (1978)*

17. I never wanted to love you / I only wanted to see my face in yours.
—*WILLIAM FINN, March of the Falsettos (1981)*

E m o t i o n s   a n d   S e n t i m e n t a l i t y

▼

1. I hate and I love. Perhaps you ask why I do so. / I do not know, but I feel it happen and I am tormented.
—*CATULLUS (1st century BCE), Carmina 85*

2. Whatever makes an impression on the heart seems lovely to the eye.
—*SA'DI, Gulistan (1258)*

3. In their precise tracings-out and subtle causations, the strongest and

fieriest emotions of life defy all analytical insight.
—HERMAN MELVILLE, *Pierre (1851)*

4. I cannot repeat an emotion. No one can, except sentimentalists.
—OSCAR WILDE, *The Picture of Dorian Gray (1891)*

5. The important thing is being capable of emotions, but to experience only *one's own* would be a sorry limitation.
—ANDRÉ GIDE, *Journals, 12 May 1892*

6. Emotion is primarily about nothing, and much of it remains about nothing to the end.
—GEORGE SANTAYANA, *The Life of Reason (1906)*

7. Leisure requires the evidence of our own feelings, because it is not so much a quality of time as a peculiar state of mind. What being at leisure means is more easily felt than defined.
—VERNON LEE, *Limbo (1908)*

8. The emotions may be endless. The more we express them, the more we may have to express.
—E. M. FORSTER, *Abinger Harvest (1936)*

9. When she fell in love it was with a perfect fury of accumulated dishonesty; she became instantly a dealer in second-hand and therefore incalculable emotions.
—DJUNA BARNES, *Nightwood (1936)*

10. Sentimentality is only sentiment that rubs you up the wrong way.
—W. SOMERSET MAUGHAM *(1941), A Writer's Notebook (1949)*

11. Most affections are habits or duties we lack the courage to end.
—HENRY DE MONTHERLANT, *Queen After Death (1942)*

12. The unexpected sound of sobbing is demoralizing.
—COLETTE, *"The Photographer's Missus" (1944)*

13. Pity is the least of the emotions.
—TALLULAH BANKHEAD, *Tallulah (1952)*

14. If you have tears, prepare to cry elsewhere— / I know of no emotion we can share.
—THOM GUNN, *"Carnal Knowledge" (1954)*

15. Sentimentality, the ostentatious parading of excessive and spurious emotion, is the mark of dishonesty, the inability to feel.
—JAMES BALDWIN, *Notes of a Native Son (1955)*

16. True feeling justifies, whatever it may cost.

—MAY SARTON, *Mrs. Stevens Hears the Mermaids Singing (1965)*

17. Possibly this ledge I am constantly on the edge of slipping off is the verge of tears.
    —BRIGID BROPHY, *In Transit (1969)*

18. Do you know what *"le vice Anglais"*—the English vice—really is? Not flagellation, not pederasty—whatever the French believe it to be. It's our refusal to admit our emotions. We think they demean us, I suppose.
    —TERENCE RATTIGAN, *In Praise of Love (1973)*

19. If there is anybody I detest, it is weak-minded sentimentalists—all those melancholy people who, out of an excess of sympathy for others, miss the thrill of their own essence and drift through life without identity, like a human fog, feeling sorry for everyone.
    —JOHN CHEEVER, *"The Housebreaker of Shady Hill," The Stories of John Cheever (1980)*

20. Spilling your guts is just exactly as charming as it sounds.
    —FRAN LEBOWITZ, *Social Studies (1981)*

21. Our feelings are our most genuine paths to knowledge.
    —AUDRE LORDE, in Claudia Tate, ed., *Black Women Writers at Work (1983)*

22. In deep sadness there is no place for sentimentality.
    —WILLIAM S. BURROUGHS, *Queer (1985)*

23. No emotion is ever the final one.
    —JEANETTE WINTERSON, *Oranges Are Not the Only Fruit (1985)*

24. Pride is a tricky, glorious, double-edged feeling.
    —ADRIENNE RICH, *Blood, Bread, and Poetry (1986)*

25. Gay men may seek sex without emotion; lesbians often end up in emotion without sex.
    —CAMILLE PAGLIA, *Sex, Art, and American Culture (1992)*

Enemies

1. Whenever thy hand can reach it, tear out thy foe's brain, for such an opportunity washes anger from the mind.
   —SA'DI, *Gulistan (1258)*

2. 'Tis best to weigh / The enemy more might than he seems.
   —WILLIAM SHAKESPEARE, *Henry V (1598–99)*

3. You have many enemies, that know not / Why they are so, but, like to village curs, / Bark when their fellows do.
   —WILLIAM SHAKESPEARE, *King Henry VIII (1613)*

4. For my enemy is dead, a man divine as myself is dead.
   —WALT WHITMAN, *"Reconciliation" (1866)*

5. A man cannot be too careful in the choice of enemies.
   —OSCAR WILDE, *The Picture of Dorian Gray (1891)*

6. I am the enemy you killed, my friend.
   —WILFRED OWEN, *"Strange Meeting" (1918)*

7. Abatement in the hostility of one's enemies must never be thought to signify they have been won over. It only means that one has ceased to constitute a threat.
   —QUENTIN CRISP, *The Naked Civil Servant (1968)*

8. It is curious how often one prefers his enemies to his friends.
   —GORE VIDAL, *Reflections upon a Sinking Ship (1969)*

Equality

1. Is there no way for men to be, but women / Must be half-workers? We are bastards all.
  —*WILLIAM SHAKESPEARE, Cymbeline (1610)*

2. If love levels ranks, it raises them too.
  —*HORACE WALPOLE, The Castle of Otranto (1764)*

3. Gambling is the great leveler. All men are equal—at cards.
  —*NICOLAI GOGOL, Gamblers (1842)*

4. Where women walk in public processions in the streets the same as the men, / Where they enter the public assembly and take places the same as the men . . . / There the great city stands.
  —*WALT WHITMAN, "Song of the Broad Axe" (1856)*

5. Games in which all may win remain as yet in this world uninvented.
  —*HERMAN MELVILLE, The Confidence-Man (1857)*

6. Men their rights and nothing more; women their rights and nothing less.
  —*SUSAN B. ANTHONY, The Revolution (1868)*

7. If every one was equal, where would be the gratification I feel in getting a visit from a grandee?
  —*HENRY JAMES, Princess Casamassima (1886)*

8. The blending of Social Strata in masculine love seems to me one of its most pronounced, and socially hopeful, features. Where it appears, it abolishes class distinctions, and opens by a single operation the cataract-blinded eye to their futilities. . . . If it could be acknowledged and extended, it would do very much to further the advent of the right sort of Socialism.
  —*JOHN ADDINGTON SYMONDS, letter to Edward Carpenter, 21 January 1893*

9. All men are equal—all men, that is to say, who possess umbrellas.
  —*E. M. FORSTER, Howards End (1910)*

10. He educated Maurice, or rather his spirit educated Maurice's spirit, for they themselves became equal. Neither thought "Am I led; am I leading?" Love had caught him out of triviality and Maurice out of bewilderment in order that two imperfect souls might touch perfection.

—*E. M. FORSTER, Maurice (1914; published 1971)*

11. In America, everybody is, but some are more than others.
　　—*GERTRUDE STEIN, Everybody's Autobiography (1937)*

12. Never mind, dear, we're all made the same, though some more than others.
　　—*NOËL COWARD, The Café de la Paix (1939)*

Error

1. "I give the truths of tomorrow."
"I prefer the mistakes of today."
　　—*OSCAR WILDE, The Picture of Dorian Gray (1891)*

2. She had an unequaled gift of squeezing big mistakes into small opportunities.
　　—*HENRY JAMES, "Greville Fane," The Real Thing and Other Tales (1893)*

3. I do not mind lying, but I hate inaccuracy.
　　—*SAMUEL BUTLER (d. 1902), Note Books (1912)*

4. A little inaccuracy sometimes saves tons of explanation.
　　—*SAKI [H. H. Munro] (d. 1916), "Clovis on the Alleged Romance of Business," The Square Egg (1924)*

5. Sincerity is all that counts is a widespread modern heresy. Think again. Bolsheviks are sincere. Fascists are sincere. Lunatics are sincere. People who believe the earth is flat are sincere. They can't all be right. Better make certain first that you have something to be sincere about, and with.
　　—*TOM DRIBERG, in Daily Express, 1937*

6. Men have an extraordinarily erroneous opinion of their position in nature; and the error is ineradicable.
　　—*W. SOMERSET MAUGHAM, A Writer's Notebook (1949)*

7. Everybody winds up kissing the wrong person goodnight.
　　—*ANDY WARHOL, The Philosophy of Andy Warhol: From A to B and Back Again (1975)*

8. People are so busy dreaming the American Dream, fantasizing about what they *could* be or have a *right* to be, that they're all asleep at the switch. Consequently we are living in the Age of Human Error.

—*FLORENCE KING, Reflections in a Jaundiced Eye (1989)*

E t h i c s

1. Ethics, like natural selection, make existence possible. Aesthetics, like sexual selection, make life lovely and wonderful, fill it with new forms, and give it progress, variety and change.

—*OSCAR WILDE, "The Critic as Artist" (1891)*

2. Experience is of no ethical value. It is merely the name men give to their mistakes.

—*OSCAR WILDE, The Picture of Dorian Gray (1891)*

3. You can't learn too soon that the most useful thing about a principle is that it can always be sacrificed to expediency.

—*W. SOMERSET MAUGHAM, The Circle (1921)*

4. Today we live in a society suffering from ethical rickets.

—*RITA MAE BROWN, In Her Day (1976)*

5. Integrity pays, but not in cash.

—*JENNIFER STONE, "Lesbian Liberation," Mind over Media (1988)*

E v i l

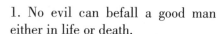

1. No evil can befall a good man either in life or death.
> —SOCRATES (d. 399 BCE), in Plato (4th century BCE), Apologia

2. The evil that men do lives after them; / The good is oft interred with their bones.
> —WILLIAM SHAKESPEARE, Julius Caesar (1600)

3. The philosophers may say what they like, I believe that poverty, illness and physical pain are really evil things which reason cannot conjure away from us.
> —CHRISTINA, QUEEN OF SWEDEN, Maxims (1660–80)

4. Violent evils require violent remedies.
> —WILLIAM BECKFORD, Vathek (1786)

5. Evil is a moral entity and not a created one, an eternal and not a perishable entity: it existed before the world; it constituted the monstrous, the execrable being who was also to fashion such a hideous world. It will hence exist after the creatures which people this world.
> —MARQUIS DE SADE, L'Histoire de Juliette, ou les Prospérités du Vice (1797)

6. Devils themselves are possessed by men, and not men by them.
> —HERMAN MELVILLE, Mardi (1849)

7. There are a thousand hacking at the branches of evil to one who is striking at the root.
> —HENRY DAVID THOREAU, "Economy," Walden (1854)

8. Evil is done without effort, naturally, it is the working of fate; good is always the product of an art.
> —CHARLES BAUDELAIRE (d. 1867), L'Art Romantique (1869)

9. We are never nearer to evil than when we believe a person is incapable of wrongdoing.
> —HENRY JAMES, The Europeans (1878)

10. I believe . . . that profit is not always what motivates man; that there are disinterested actions. By *disinterested* I mean: gratuitous. And that evil acts, what people call evil, can be as gratuitous as good acts.

—ANDRÉ GIDE, *Les Caves du
Vatican (1914)*

11. There was no treachery too base
for the world to commit; she knew
that.
—VIRGINIA WOOLF, *To the
Lighthouse (1927)*

12. There is no explanation for evil.
It must be looked upon as a neces-
sary part of the order of the universe.
To ignore it is childish, to bewail it is
senseless.
—W. SOMERSET MAUGHAM, *The
Summing Up (1938)*

13. Evil is unspectacular and always
human, / And shares our bed and
eats at our own table.
—W. H. AUDEN, *"Herman Melville"
(1939)*

14. It is not good enough to talk
about evil abstractly while lending

implicit support to traditional images
that legitimate specific social evils.
—MARY DALY, *Beyond God the
Father (1973)*

15. It isn't evil that's running the
earth, but mediocrity. The crime is
not that Nero played while Rome
burned, but that he played badly.
—NED ROREM, *The Final Diary:
1961–1972 (1974)*

16. For a long time, the lesbian has
been a personification of feminine
evil.
—ADRIENNE RICH, *"The Meaning of
Our Love for Women Is What We
Have Constantly to Expand"
(1977)*

17. In all men is evil sleeping; the
good man is he who will not awaken
it, in himself or in other men.
—MARY RENAULT, *The Praise
Singer (1978)*

Excess and Extremes

1. Excesses carry with them the prin-
ciples of their own destruction.
—JOHN CLELAND, *Memoirs of a
Coxcomb (1751)*

2. Moderation is a fatal thing: noth-
ing succeeds as excess.
—OSCAR WILDE, *A Woman of No
Importance (1893)*

3. Fanaticism consists in redoubling your effort when you have forgotten your aim.

> —GEORGE SANTAYANA, *Life of Reason (1906)*

4. All decent people live beyond their incomes nowadays, and those who aren't respectable live beyond other people's. A few gifted individuals manage to do both.

> —SAKI [H. H. Munro], *"The Match-Maker," The Chronicles of Clovis (1911)*

5. My candle burns at both ends, / It will not last the night / But oh my foes, and oh my friends / It gives a lovely light.

> —EDNA ST. VINCENT MILLAY, *"First Fig," A Few Figs from Thistles (1923)*

6. All extremes are dangerous.

> —VIRGINIA WOOLF, *"Montaigne," The Common Reader (1925)*

7. I like extravagance. Letters which give the postman a stiff back to carry, books which overflow from their covers, sexuality which bursts the thermometers.

> —ANAÏS NIN *(1933), The Diary of Anaïs Nin, Vol. 1 (1966)*

8. Excess on occasion is exhilarating. It prevents moderation from acquiring the deadening effect of habit.

> —W. SOMERSET MAUGHAM, *The Summing Up (1938)*

9. Let's not quibble! I'm the foe of moderation, the champion of excess. If I may lift a line from a die-hard whose identity is lost in the shuffle, "I'd rather be strongly wrong than weakly right."

> —TALLULAH BANKHEAD, *Tallulah (1952)*

10. Ours is a culture based on excess, on overproduction; the result is a steady loss of sharpness in our sensory experience. All the conditions of modern life—its material plenitude, its sheer crowdedness—conjoin to dull our sensory faculties.

> —SUSAN SONTAG, *Against Interpretation (1966)*

11. This woman did not fly to extremes; she lived there.

> —QUENTIN CRISP, *The Naked Civil Servant (1968)*

12. For myself, I would rather live with sins of excess than sins of denial.

> —JEANETTE WINTERSON, *Sexing the Cherry (1989)*

Experience

1. Experience never errs; what alone may err is our judgment.
   —*LEONARDO DA VINCI, Notebooks (c. 1500)*

2. I had rather have a fool to make me merry than experience to make me sad.
   —*WILLIAM SHAKESPEARE, As You Like It (1599–1600)*

3. The heart is forever inexperienced.
   —*HENRY DAVID THOREAU, "Rumors from an Aeolian Harp," A Week on the Concord and the Merrimack Rivers (1849)*

4. Experience, the only true knowledge.
   —*HERMAN MELVILLE, The Confidence-Man (1857)*

5. My experience of women is almost as large as Europe. And it is so intimate too. I have lived and slept in the same bed with English Countesses and Prussian Bauerinnen with a closeness of intimacy no one ever had before. . . . No woman has excited 'passions' among women more than I have.
   —*FLORENCE NIGHTINGALE, letter to Mary Clarke Mohl, 13 December 1861*

6. Not the fruit of experience, but experience itself, is the end. A counted number of pulses only is given to us of a variegated dramatic life.
   —*WALTER PATER, Studies in the History of the Renaissance (1873)*

7. Experience is never limited, and it is never complete; it is an immense sensibility, a kind of huge spider-web of the finest silken threads suspended in the chamber of consciousness, and catching every air-borne particle in its tissue.
   —*HENRY JAMES, "Art of Fiction" (1888)*

8. Experience is the name everyone gives to their mistakes.
   —*OSCAR WILDE, Lady Windermere's Fan (1892)*

9. Experience was to be taken as showing that one might get a five-pound note as one got a light for a cigarette; but one had to check the friendly impulse to ask for it in the same way.

—HENRY JAMES, *The Awkward Age*
   (1899)

10. I think the moon looked like a
piece of Majolica-Ware as it hung
above the trees, and I remember the
fire-flies darting in the garden below
were a new experience for me.
   —RONALD FIRBANK, *The Artificial*
      Princess (1915)

11. We do not receive wisdom. We
must discover it ourselves after experiences which no one else can have
for us and from which no one else
can spare us.
   —MARCEL PROUST, *Remembrance of*
      Things Past: Within a Budding
      Grove (1918)

12. Experience isn't interesting till it
begins to repeat itself—in fact, until
it does that, it hardly *is* experience.
   —ELIZABETH BOWEN, *Death of the*
      Heart (1938)

13. I have come to the conclusion,
after many years of sometimes sad
experience, that you cannot come to
any conclusion at all.
   —VITA SACKVILLE-WEST, *In Your*
      Garden Again (1953)

14. Experience is never at a bargain
price.
   —ALICE B. TOKLAS, *The Alice B.*
      Toklas Cook Book (1954)

15. Experience is a private, and a
very largely speechless affair.
   —JAMES BALDWIN, *Notes of a Native*
      Son (1955)

16. I've come through a land / You'll
never know.
   —RITA MAE BROWN, "The Bourgeois
      Question" (1967)

17. Experience is always larger than
language.
   —ADRIENNE RICH, *in American*
      Poetry Review,
      January–February 1991

18. This Western culture of ours
tends to sacrifice the full range of
experience to a lower common
denominator that's acceptable to
more people; we end up with
McDonald's instead of real food,
Holiday Inns instead of homes, and
USA Today instead of news and cultural analysis. And we do that with
the rest of our lives.
   —KATE BORNSTEIN, *Gender Outlaw*
      (1994)

Faces

1. A lovely face is the solace of wounded hearts and the key of locked-up gates.
   —SA'DI, *Gulistan (1258)*

2. Was this the face that launch'd a thousand ships, / And burnt the top-less towers of Ilium?
   —CHRISTOPHER MARLOWE, *The Tragical History of Dr. Faustus (c. 1592)*

3. I must to the barber's, monsieur, for methinks I am marvellous hairy about the face; and I am such a ten-der ass, if my hair do but tickle me I must scratch.
   —WILLIAM SHAKESPEARE, *A Midsummer Night's Dream (1595)*

4. God hath given you one face, and you make yourselves another.
   —WILLIAM SHAKESPEARE, *Hamlet (1600–1601)*

5. This face is a dog's snout sniffing for garbage, / Snakes nest in that mouth, I hear the sibilant threat.
   —WALT WHITMAN, *"Faces," Leaves of Grass (1855)*

6. She wore a fixed smile that wa'n't a smile; there wa'n't no light behind it, same's a lamp can't shine if it ain't lit.
   —WILLA CATHER, *"The Foreigner" (1900)*

7. A man's face is his autobiography. A woman's face is her work of fiction.
   —OSCAR WILDE (d. 1900), in *H. Montgomery Hyde, Oscar Wilde (1976)*

8. The features of our face are hardly more than gestures which force of habit made permanent. Nature, like the destruction of Pompeii, like the metamorphosis of a nymph into a tree, has arrested us in an accus-tomed movement.
   —MARCEL PROUST, *Remembrance of Things Past: Within a Budding Grove (1918)*

9. When she smiled the smile was only in the mouth and a little bitter: the face of an incurable yet to be stricken with its malady.
   —DJUNA BARNES, *Nightwood (1936)*

10. The face is the soul of the body.
    —LUDWIG WITTGENSTEIN (d. 1951), *Culture and Value (1980)*

11. Her face returned to childhood because it wore that expression of

inhuman innocence, of angelic hard-
ness which ennobles children's
faces.
> —COLETTE (d. 1954), The Other
> One (1960)

12. The face of Garbo is an Idea, that
of Hepburn an Event.
> —ROLAND BARTHES, Mythologies
> (1957)

13. To have a face, in the European
sense of the word, it would seem that
one must not only enjoy and suffer
but also desire to preserve the memory of even the most humiliating and
unpleasant experiences of the past.
> —W. H. AUDEN, The Dyer's Hand
> (1962)

14. The face of a lover is an unknown, precisely because it is invested with so much of oneself. It is
a mystery, containing, like all mysteries, the possibility of torment.
> —JAMES BALDWIN, Another Country
> (1962)

15. How does an inexpressive face
age? More slowly, one would suppose.
> —SUSAN SONTAG, Death Kit (1967)

16. Her face is closed as a nut, /
closed as a careful snail.
> —ELIZABETH BISHOP, "House Guest"
> (1969)

17. Time engraves our faces with all
the tears we have not shed.
> —NATALIE CLIFFORD BARNEY
> (d. 1972), in George Wickes, The
> Amazon of Letters (1976)

18. My face looks like a wedding-
cake left out in the rain.
> —W. H. AUDEN (d. 1973), in
> Humphrey Carpenter, W. H.
> Auden (1981)

19. Once you've had your face lifted,
you have to alter your entire past—
you have to be careful not to remember who Greta Garbo is. I couldn't
bear not to remember who Greta
Garbo is.
> —QUENTIN CRISP, How to Have a
> Lifestyle (1979)

Facts

1. My facts shall be falsehoods to the common sense. I would so state facts that they shall be significant, shall be myths or mythologic. Facts which the mind perceived, thoughts which the body thought—with these I deal.
   —HENRY DAVID THOREAU, Journal,
   9 November 1851

2. Facts fled before philosophy like frightened forest things.
   —OSCAR WILDE, The Picture of
   Dorian Gray (1891)

3. The fatal futility of Fact.
   —HENRY JAMES, The Spoils of
   Poynton (1897)

4. Albertine never related facts that were damaging to her, but always other facts which could be explained only by the former, the truth being rather a current which flows from what people say to us, and which we pick up, invisible though it is, than the actual thing they have said.
   —MARCEL PROUST, Remembrance of
   Things Past: Cities of the Plain
   (1922)

5. Everybody gets so much information all day long that they lose their common sense.
   —GERTRUDE STEIN (1946), in
   Elizabeth Sprigge, Gertrude Stein
   (1957)

6. Only / a fact could be so dreamlike
   —ADRIENNE RICH, "Like This
   Together," Necessities of Life
   (1966)

7. It is the spirit of the age to believe that any fact, no matter how suspect, is superior to any imaginative exercise, no matter how true.
   —GORE VIDAL, in Encounter,
   December 1967

8. Civilizations have been founded and maintained on theories which refused to obey facts.
   —JOE ORTON (d. 1967), What the
   Butler Saw (1969)

9. Anyone who knows a strange fact shares in its singularity.
   —JEAN GENET, Prisoner of Love
   (1986)

Falsehood

1. To tell a falsehood is like the cut of a sabre; for though the wound may heal, the scar of it will remain.
   —SA'DI, *Gulistan (1258)*

2. Man's mind is so formed that it is far more susceptible to falsehood than to truth.
   —DESIDERIUS ERASMUS, *Praise of Folly (1509)*

3. With devotion's visage / And pious action we do sugar o'er / The devil himself.
   —WILLIAM SHAKESPEARE, *Hamlet (1600–1601)*

4. The bad are frequently good enough to let you see how bad they are, but the good as frequently endeavor to get between you and themselves.
   —HENRY DAVID THOREAU, *Journal, 2 December 1851*

5. When one is pretending the entire body revolts.
   —ANAÏS NIN, *Under a Glass Bell (1948)*

6. The lie of compulsory female heterosexuality today afflicts not just feminist scholarship, but every profession, every reference work, every curriculum, every organizing attempt, every relationship or conversation over which it hovers. It creates, specifically, a profound falseness, hypocrisy, and hysteria in the heterosexual dialogue, for every heterosexual relationship is lived in the queasy strobe light of that lie.
   —ADRIENNE RICH, "Compulsory Heterosexuality and Lesbian Existence" (1980)

7. She calls a spade a delving instrument.
   —RITA MAE BROWN, *Southern Discomfort (1982)*

F a m e

1. Fame is like a river, that beareth up things light and swollen, and drowns things weighty and solid.
   —FRANCIS BACON, "Of Ceremonies and Respects," Essays (1625)

2. Fame is not always honest. Not seldom to be famous is to be widely known for what you are not.
   —HERMAN MELVILLE, Mardi (1849)

3. Fame is a bee. / It has a song— / It has a sting— / Ah, too, it has a wing.
   —EMILY DICKINSON (d. 1886), no. 1763, Complete Poems (1955)

4. We are nauseated by the sight of trivial personalities decomposing in the eternity of print.
   —VIRGINIA WOOLF, "THE MODERN ESSAY" (1925)

5. Celebrity: I picture myself as a marble bust with legs to run everywhere.
   —JEAN COCTEAU, "Des beaux-arts considérés comme un assassinat," Essai de critique Indirecte (1932)

6. Because I have conducted my own operas and love sheep-dogs; because I generally dress in tweeds, and sometimes, at winter afternoon concerts, have even conducted in them; because I was a militant suffragette and seized a chance of beating time to "The March of the Women" from the window of my cell in Holloway Prison with a tooth-brush; because I have written books, spoken speeches, broadcast, and don't always make sure my hat is on straight; for these and other equally pertinent reasons, in a certain sense I am well known.
   —ETHEL SMYTH, As Time Went On (1936)

7. Everybody worships me, it's nauseating.
   —NOËL COWARD, Present Laughter (1943)

8. In the future everyone will be world famous for fifteen minutes.
   —ANDY WARHOL, catalog for exhibition, Stockholm, 1968

9. If any reader of this book is in the grip of some habit of which he is deeply ashamed, I advise him not to give way to it in secret but to do it on television. No-one will pass him with averted gaze on the other side of the street. People will cross the road at the risk of losing their lives in order to say, "We saw you on the telly."
   —QUENTIN CRISP, in Guy Kettelhack, ed., The Wit and Wisdom of Quentin Crisp (1984)

10. My name has gotten to be a household word—at least in certain households. I think there are now people who know my name, but don't know what I do. I'm famous for being famous.

—*JOHN ASHBERRY, in PN Review,
1985*

11. But still I'd rather be Famous / than righteous or holy, any day.

—*MORRISSEY, "Frankly, Mr.
Shankly" (1985)*

Familiarity

1. Sweets grown common lose their dear delight.

—*WILLIAM SHAKESPEARE, Sonnet
102 (1609)*

2. The intimacy of shipboard, which is due to propinquity rather than any community of taste.

—*W. SOMERSET MAUGHAM, Rain
(1921)*

3. I like familiarity. In me it does not breed contempt. Only more familiarity.

—*GERTRUDE STEIN, in Reader's
Digest (1935)*

4. You do not notice changes in what is always before you.

—*COLETTE, My Apprenticeships
(1936)*

5. What's so phony nowadays is all this familiarity. Pretending there isn't any difference between people.

—*CHRISTOPHER ISHERWOOD, A
Single Man (1964)*

6. Familiarity breeds consent.

—*RITA MAE BROWN, In Her Day
(1976)*

7. Familiarity doesn't breed contempt, it *is* contempt.

—*FLORENCE KING, With Charity
Toward None (1992)*

Family

1. There are many kinds of conceit, but the chief one is to let people know what a very ancient and gifted family one descends from.
   —*Benvenuto Cellini,*
   Autobiography (1566)

2. A little more than kin and less than kind.
   —*William Shakespeare, Hamlet*
   (1600–1601)

3. After a good dinner one can forgive anybody, even one's own relations.
   —*Oscar Wilde, A Woman of No*
   Importance (1893)

4. Relations are simply a tedious pack of people, who haven't got the remotest knowledge of how to live, nor the smallest instinct about when to die.
   —*Oscar Wilde, The Importance of*
   Being Earnest (1895)

5. Blood may be thicker than water, but it is also a great deal nastier.
   —*Edith Somerville and Violet*
   Martin ["Martin Ross"], Some
   Experiences of an Irish R.M.
   (1898)

6. I believe that more unhappiness comes from this source than from any other—I mean from the attempt to prolong family connections unduly and to make people hang together artificially who would never naturally do so.
   —*Samuel Butler (d. 1902), Note*
   Books (1912)

7. We do not discuss the members of our family to their faces.
   —*Ivy Compton-Burnett, A House*
   and Its Head (1935)

8. Personal hatred and family affection are not incompatible; they often flourish and grow strong together.
   —*Willa Cather, Lucy Gayheart*
   (1935)

9. Families! I hate you! Shut-in homes, closed doors, jealous possessors of happiness.
   —*André Gide, Les Nouvelles*
   Nourritures (1936)

10. It will be a beautiful family talk, mean and worried and full of sorrow and spite and excitement.
    —*Ivy Compton-Burnett, A Family*
    and a Fortune (1939)

11. All men are brothers, but, thank God, they aren't all brothers-in-law.

—*ANTHONY POWELL, A Dance to the Music of Time: At Lady Molly's (1957)*

12. The family in the West is finished. . . . The odd group of strangers that make up every family no longer have any reason to live together, to suffer from one another's jagged edges.

—*GORE VIDAL, Rocking the Boat (1962)*

13. I think the ideal situation for a family is to be completely incestuous.

—*WILLIAM S. BURROUGHS, interview (1980), in Victor Bokris, With William Burroughs: A Report from the Bunker (1981)*

14. If Mr. Vincent Price were to be co-starred with Miss Bette Davis in a story by Mr. Edgar Allan Poe directed by Mr. Roger Corman, it could not fully express the pent-up violence and depravity of a single day in the life of the average family.

—*QUENTIN CRISP, Manners from Heaven (1984)*

15. Families composed of rugged individualists have to do things obliquely.

—*FLORENCE KING, Confessions of a Failed Southern Lady (1985)*

16. For men who want to flee Family Man America and never come back, there is a guaranteed solution: homosexuality is the new French Foreign Legion.

—*FLORENCE KING, Reflections in a Jaundiced Eye (1989)*

Fantasy   and   Imagination

1. Love came at night and placed beneath my covers / the sweet dream of a laughing boy, eighteen years old.

—*MELEAGER (1st century BCE), Musa Puerilis, no. 125; trans. Dennis Kratz*

2. My Oberon! What visions I have seen! / Methought I was enamour'd of an ass.

—*WILLIAM SHAKESPEARE, A Midsummer Night's Dream (1595)*

3. That night in a dream the Duke of Buckingham seemed to me to ascend into my bed, where he carried himself with much love towards me, after such rest wherein wearied men are wont exceedingly to rejoice; and likewise many seemed to me to enter the chamber who did see this.
> —WILLIAM LAUD, Archbishop of
> Canterbury, diary entry,
> August 1625

4. I dwell in Possibility— / A fairer house than Prose— / More numerous of Windows— / Superior—for Doors.
> —EMILY DICKINSON, no. 657
> (1862), Complete Poems (1955)

5. Because imagination created the world, it governs it.
> —CHARLES BAUDELAIRE (d. 1867),
> Le Spleen de Paris (1869)

6. It has been said that the great events of the world take place in the brain. It is in the brain, and the brain only, that the great sins of the world take place.
> —OSCAR WILDE, The Picture of
> Dorian Gray (1891)

7. Desire projected itself visually: his fancy, not quite yet lulled since morning, imaged the marvels and terrors of the manifold earth.
> —THOMAS MANN, Death in Venice
> (1911)

8. To strip our pleasures of imagination is to reduce them to their own dimensions, that is to say to nothing.
> —MARCEL PROUST, Remembrance of
> Things Past: Within a Budding
> Grove (1918)

9. An image is a stop the mind makes between uncertainties.
> —DJUNA BARNES, Nightwood
> (1936)

10. Imagination grows by exercise and contrary to common belief is more powerful in the mature than in the young.
> —W. SOMERSET MAUGHAM, The
> Summing Up (1938)

11. "We may as well imagine the scene." "No, my mind baulks at it." "Mine does worse. It constructs it."
> —IVY COMPTON-BURNETT, A Family
> and a Fortune (1939)

12. It is harder to kill a phantom than a reality.
> —VIRGINIA WOOLF (d. 1941),
> "Professions for Women" (1942)

13. I don't want realism. I want magic! Yes, yes, magic! I try to give that to people. I misrepresent things to them. I don't tell the truth, I tell what ought to be the truth. And if that is sinful, then let me be damned for it—Don't turn the light on!
> —TENNESSEE WILLIAMS, A Streetcar
> Named Desire (1947)

14. Is it lack of imagination that makes us come / to imagined places, not just stay at home?
> —ELIZABETH BISHOP, "Questions of Travel" (1965)

15. We live under continual threat of two equally fearful, but seemingly opposed, destinies: unremitting banality and inconceivable terror. It is fantasy, served out in large rations by the popular arts, which allows most people to cope with these twin specters.
> —SUSAN SONTAG, Against Interpretation (1966)

16. He should not be effeminate, indeed preferably normal . . . he should admit me but no one else; he should be physically attractive to me and younger than myself—the younger the better, as closer to innocence; finally he should be on the small side, lusty, circumsised, physically healthy and clean: no phimosis, halitosis, bromidosis. It may be thought that I had set myself a task so difficult of accomplishment as almost to put success purposely beyond my reach.
> —J. R. ACKERLEY, My Father and Myself (1968)

17. In spring a young man's fancy turns to a fancy young man.
> —MART CROWLEY, The Boys in the Band (1968)

18. Sex is more exciting on screen and between the pages than between the sheets anyway. Let the kids read about it and look forward to it, and then right before they're going to get the reality, break the news to them that they've already had the most exciting part, that it's behind them already. Fantasy love is much better than reality love.
> —ANDY WARHOL, The Philosophy of Andy Warhol: From A to B and Back Again (1975)

19. I imagine, starved to death, that I am making love to her in my first memory. I am in some summer house, in some country with a season of heat no other place on earth can match. It could be Alabama; it could be the Isle of Capri and I a wealthy, pre-war lesbian. . . . There is nothing inside the summer house but the two of us and that broken shard of teacup where a sleeping garter snake lies curled.
> —BERTHA HARRIS, Lover (1976)

20. Lots of sex is a fantasy.
> —DAVID HOCKNEY, David Hockney by David Hockney: My Early Years (1977)

21. Eroticism is a realm stalked by ghosts. It is the place beyond the pale, both cursed and enchanted.
> —CAMILLE PAGLIA, Sexual Personae (1990)

Fashion and Style

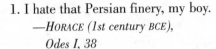

1. I hate that Persian finery, my boy.
—*Horace (1st century BCE),*
Odes I, 38

2. Costly thy habit as thy purse can buy, / But not expressed in fancy; rich, not gaudy.
—*William Shakespeare, Hamlet*
(1600–1601)

3. We worship not the Graces, nor the Parcae, but Fashion. She spins and weaves and cuts with full authority. The head monkey at Paris puts on a traveler's cap, and all the monkeys in America do the same.
—*Henry David Thoreau,*
"Economy," Walden (1854)

4. All fashions are charming, or rather relatively charming, each one being a new striving, more or less well conceived, after beauty, an approximate statement of an ideal, the desire for which constantly teases the unsatisfied human mind.
—*Charles Baudelaire (d. 1867),*
L'Art Romantique (1869)

5. Fashion, by which what is really fantastic becomes for a moment universal.
—*Oscar Wilde, The Picture of*
Dorian Gray (1891)

6. She would rather have perished than have looked dressed in her Sunday best.
—*Henry James, The Spoils of*
Poynton (1897)

7. Her frocks are built in Paris, but she wears them with a strong English accent.
—*Saki [H. H. Munro], "Reginald*
on Women," Reginald (1904)

8. His shoes exhaled the right *soupçon* of the harness-room; his socks compelled one's attention without losing one's respects.
—*Saki [H. H. Munro], "Ministers of*
Grace," The Chronicles of Clovis
(1911)

9. I know you! Your motto is "Silk socks and dubious feet."
—*Colette, The Other One (1929)*

10. Everybody looked overdressed or badly dressed—some, indeed, looked positively dirty beside him. His clothes seemed to melt into each other with the perfection of their cut and the quiet harmony of their color. Without a single point of emphasis everything was distinguished. . . . He was the personification of freshness and cleanliness and order.

—VIRGINIA WOOLF, "Beau
Brummell," The Second Common
Reader (1932)

11. It is not chic to be too chic.
—ELSIE DE WOLFE, After All (1935)

12. The trouble with most English-women is that they will dress as if they had been a mouse in some previous incarnation.
—EDITH SITWELL, "I Like to Wear
Dramatic Clothes" (1937)

13. Fashion seems to exist for an abstract person who is not you or me.
—ELIZABETH BOWEN, Collected
Impressions (1950)

14. Art produces ugly things which frequently become beautiful with time. Fashion, on the other hand, produces beautiful things which always become ugly with time.
—JEAN COCTEAU, New York World
Telegram & Sun,
21 August 1960

15. Marlene Dietrich and Roy Rogers are the only two living human beings who should be allowed to wear black leather pants.

—EDITH HEAD, in Saturday
Evening Post, 1963

16. While clothes with pictures and/or writing on them are not entirely an invention of the modern age, they are an unpleasant indication of the general state of things. I mean, be realistic. If people don't want to listen to you what makes you think they want to hear from your sweater?
—FRAN LEBOWITZ, Metropolitan
Life (1978)

17. Style is being yourself, but on purpose.
—QUENTIN CRISP, How to Have a
Lifestyle (1979)

18. I would go out tonight / but I haven't got a stitch to wear.
—MORRISSEY, "This Charming
Man" (1983)

19. The modern queer was invented by Tennessee Williams. Brando in blue jeans, sneakers, white T-shirt and leather jacket. When you saw that, you knew they were available.
—DEREK JARMAN, At Your Own
Risk: A Saint's Testament (1992)

Fathers

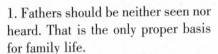

1. Fathers should be neither seen nor heard. That is the only proper basis for family life.
>   —OSCAR WILDE, An Ideal Husband (1895)

2. That is natural enough when nobody has had fathers they begin to long for them and then when everybody has had fathers they begin to long to do without them.
>   —GERTRUDE STEIN, Everybody's Autobiography (1937)

3. I stopped loving my father a long time ago. What remained was the slavery to a pattern.
>   —ANAÏS NIN, Under a Glass Bell (1948)

4. There is no change. That is your trouble. You want me to be altered by my father's death. And I have not been, and shall not be. I am what I am.
>   —IVY COMPTON-BURNETT, A Heritage and Its History (1959)

5. He admitted, I remember, his own early participation in the practice in which he thought it advisable to counsel moderation, then took occasion to add . . . that in the matter of sex there was nothing he had not done, no experience he had not tasted, no scrape he had not got into and out of, so that if we should ever be in want of help or advice we need never be ashamed to come to him and could always count on his understanding and sympathy.
>   —J. R. ACKERLEY (d. 1967), My Father and Myself (1968)

6. I lived in a normal family. I had no love for my father.
>   —JOE ORTON (d. 1967), What the Butler Saw (1969)

Fear

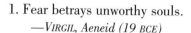

1. Fear betrays unworthy souls.
   —*VIRGIL, Aeneid (19 BCE)*

2. Were the diver to think on the jaws of the shark he would never lay hands on the precious pearl.
   —*SA'DI, Gulistan (1258)*

3. Just as courage imperils life, fear protects it.
   —*LEONARDO DA VINCI, Notebooks (c. 1500)*

4. Our fears do make us traitors.
   —*WILLIAM SHAKESPEARE, Macbeth (1606)*

5. I fear no bad angel and have offended no one.
   —*HORACE WALPOLE, The Castle of Otranto (1764)*

6. The bravest man amongst us is afraid of himself.
   —*OSCAR WILDE, The Picture of Dorian Gray (1891)*

7. That fear first created the gods is perhaps as true as anything so brief could be on so great a subject.
   —*GEORGE SANTAYANA, The Life of Reason (1906)*

8. And how am I to face the odds / Of man's bedevilment and God's? / I, a stranger and afraid / In a world I never made.
   —*A. E. HOUSMAN, no. 12, Last Poems (1922)*

9. Wisdom begins where the fear of God ends.
   —*ANDRÉ GIDE, diary, 15 January 1929*

10. Anything scares me, anything scares anyone but really after all considering how dangerous everything is nothing is really very frightening.
    —*GERTRUDE STEIN, The Autobiography of Alice B. Toklas (1933)*

11. I'm going to turn on the light and we'll be two people in a room looking at each other and wondering why on earth they were afraid of the dark.
    —*GALE WILHELM, We Too Are Drifting (1935)*

12. Proust has pointed out that the predisposition to love creates its own objects: is this not true of fear?
    —*ELIZABETH BOWEN, Collected Impressions (1950)*

13. Fear tastes like a rusty knife and do not let her into your house.
  —*JOHN CHEEVER, The Wapshot Chronicles (1957)*

14. As leaders we could not display fear. In the process we overcame our fears.
  —*DEL MARTIN AND PHYLLIS LYON, Lesbian / Woman (1972)*

15. I realize that if I wait until I am no longer afraid to act, write, speak, be, I'll be sending messages on a ouija board, cryptic complaints from the other side.
  —*AUDRE LORDE, The Cancer Journals (1980)*

16. Afraid is a country with no exit visas.
  —*AUDRE LORDE, "Diaspora" (1986)*

17. Fear of sexuality is the new, disease-sponsored register of the universe of fear in which everyone now lives.
  —*SUSAN SONTAG, AIDS and Its Metaphors (1989)*

18. Is it possible to be nostalgic about old fears?
  —*PETER ACKROYD, English Music (1992)*

Fidelity and Infidelity

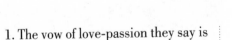

1. The vow of love-passion they say is no vow.
  —*PLATO (4th century BCE), The Symposium*

2. O heaven, were man / But constant, he were perfect!
  —*WILLIAM SHAKESPEARE, The Two Gentlemen of Verona (1590–91)*

3. Presume not on thy heart when mine is slain: / Thou gav'st me thine not to give back again.

  —*WILLIAM SHAKESPEARE, Sonnet 22 (1609)*

4. Constancy, that current coin for fools.
  —*APHRA BEHN, The Rover (1677)*

5. Then talk not of inconstancy / False hearts and broken vows; / If I, by miracle, can be / This live-long minute true to thee, / 'Tis all that heaven allows.

—JOHN WILMOT, EARL OF
ROCHESTER, *"Love and Love: A
Song" (c. 1677)*

6. What men call gallantry, and gods adultery, / Is much more common where the climate's sultry.
—GEORGE GORDON, LORD BYRON,
Don Juan (1819–24)

7. Those who are faithful know only the trivial side of love: it is the faithless who know love's tragedies.
—OSCAR WILDE, *The Picture of
Dorian Gray (1891)*

8. When one loves in a certain way, even betrayals become unimportant.
—COLETTE, *Claudine and Annie
(1903)*

9. Adultery introduces spirit into what might otherwise have been the dead letter of marriage.
—MARCEL PROUST (d. 1922),
*Remembrance of Things Past:
The Captive (1923)*

10. She was never attracted to anyone young and whole-hearted and free—she was, in fact, a congenital poacher.

—RADCLYFFE HALL, *The Well of
Loneliness (1928)*

11. You know, of course, that the Tasmanians, who never committed adultery, are now extinct.
—W. SOMERSET MAUGHAM, *The
Bread-Winner (1930)*

12. Lay your sleeping head, my love, / Human on my faithless arm.
—W. H. AUDEN, *"Lullaby" (1937)*

13. Adultery? Phooey!
—QUENTIN CRISP, *Manners from
Heaven (1984)*

14. Do they really think that because we're gay, young, and urban we don't have the same need for fidelity and intimacy that any other human beings do? When sex is as easy to get as a burger at McDonald's, it ain't too mysterious or marvelous, believe me.
—ANDREW HOLLERAN, in
M. Denneny, C. Ortleb, and
T. Steele, eds., *The View from
Christopher Street (1984)*

15. Monogamy is contrary to nature but necessary for the greater social good.
—RITA MAE BROWN, *Starting from
Scratch (1988)*

Flattery and Praise

1. He that loves to be flattered is worthy o' th' flatterer.
   —WILLIAM SHAKESPEARE, *Timon of Athens (1605)*

2. I will praise any man that will praise me.
   —WILLIAM SHAKESPEARE, *Antony and Cleopatra (1606)*

3. We begin to praise when we begin to see a thing needs our assistance.
   —HENRY DAVID THOREAU, *Journal, 20 June 1840*

4. The advantage of doing one's praising for oneself is that one can lay it on so thick and exactly in the right places.
   —SAMUEL BUTLER (d. 1902), *The Way of All Flesh (1903)*

5. The applause of silence is the only kind that counts.
   —ALFRED JARRY (d. 1907), *Dossiers Acénonètes du Collège de Pataphysique (1966)*

6. People ask you for criticism, but they only want praise.
   —W. SOMERSET MAUGHAM, *Of Human Bondage (1915)*

7. I can eat it with a spoon or with a soup ladle or anything and I like it.
   —GERTRUDE STEIN (d. 1946), on praise from critics, in Elizabeth Sprigge, *Gertrude Stein (1957)*

8. Disapproval from persons whose approval is as weightless as a man in space, is no worse than bouquets from them.
   —WILLIAM PLOMER, in *London magazine, October 1963*

9. The aim of flattery is to soothe and encourage us by assuring us of the truth of an opinion we have already formed about ourselves.
   —EDITH SITWELL (d. 1964), in Elizabeth Salter, *The Last Years of a Rebel (1967)*

10. It gives me no joy to be praised at the expense of a better artist, by someone who does not know the difference or who thinks me too vain to be aware of it myself.
    —MARY RENAULT, *The Mask of Apollo (1966)*

11. Praise requires constant renewal and expansion.
    —DORIS GRUMBACH, *Coming into the End Zone (1991)*

Food

1. Let them eat cake.
> —*MARIE ANTOINETTE, QUEEN OF*
> *FRANCE (d. 1793), attributed*

2. There is nothing to which men, while they have food and drink, cannot reconcile themselves.
> —*GEORGE SANTAYANA,*
> *Interpretations of Poetry and*
> *Religion (1900)*

3. Bouillabaisse is only good because cooked by the French, who, if they cared to try, could produce an excellent and nutritious substitute out of cigar stumps and empty matchboxes.
> —*NORMAN DOUGLAS, Siren Lands*
> *(1911)*

4. You needn't tell me that a man who doesn't love oysters and asparagus and good wines has got a soul, or a stomach either. He's simply got the instinct for being unhappy highly developed.
> —*SAKI [H. H. MUNRO], "The Match-*
> *Maker," The Chronicles of Clovis*
> *(1911)*

5. I cannot *live* / without a macaroon!
> —*EDNA ST. VINCENT MILLAY,*
> *Aria Da Capo (1920)*

6. Beneath the strain of expectation even the little iced sugar cakes upon the tea-table looked green with worry.
> —*RONALD FIRBANK, The Flower*
> *Beneath the Foot (1923)*

7. There are many ways of eating, for some eating is living for some eating is dying, for some thinking about ways of eating gives them the feeling that they have it in them to be alive and to be going on living, to some to think about eating makes them know that death is always waiting that dying is in them.
> —*GERTRUDE STEIN, The Making of*
> *Americans (1925)*

8. Ask for heron's eggs whipped with wine into an amber foam.
> —*RONALD FIRBANK (d. 1926) in*
> *Mervyn Hodder, Ronald Firbank:*
> *Memoirs and Critiques (1977)*

9. One cannot think well, love well, sleep well, if one has not dined well.
> —*VIRGINIA WOOLF, A Room of One's*
> *Own (1929)*

10. Cider and tinned salmon are the staple diet of the agricultural classes.
> —*EVELYN WAUGH, Scoop (1938)*

11. And now with some pleasure I find that it's seven; and must cook dinner. Haddock and sausage meat. I think it is true that one gains a certain hold on sausage and haddock by writing them down.
    —VIRGINIA WOOLF, diary,
    8 March 1941 [final entry]

12. This morning I paid seventy cents for two little old dried-up slivers of bacon and one cockeyed egg. It took me till noon to get my appetite back.
    —LANGSTON HUGHES, Simple Speaks His Mind (1950)

13. These are very nice ways to cook string beans but they interfere with the poor vegetable's leading a life of its own.
    —ALICE B. TOKLAS, The Alice B. Toklas Cook Book (1954)

14. What is sauce for the goose may be sauce for the gander, but is not necessarily sauce for the chicken, the duck, the turkey or the guinea hen.
    —ALICE B. TOKLAS, The Alice B. Toklas Cook Book (1954)

15. Dinner at the Huntercombes' possessed "only two dramatic features—the wine was a farce and the food a tragedy."
    —ANTHONY POWELL, A Dance to the Music of Time: The Acceptance World (1955)

16. "She should be thinking of higher things."
    "Nothing could be higher than food."
    —IVY COMPTON-BURNETT, The Mighty and Their Fall (1961)

17. Buddy, it's fruitcake weather!
    —TRUMAN CAPOTE, A Christmas Memory (1966)

18. There is such a thing as food and such a thing as poison. But the damage done by those who pass off poison as food is far less than that done by those who generation after generation convince people that food is poison.
    —PAUL GOODMAN, Five Years (1966)

19. At the table Su saw only division. The chicken on its platter seemed separated into two opposing armies, breasts against thighs—white meat for Bettina, dark for herself. The rolls pushed at their saucer's edges, one against one. The onions fell too neatly into two servings, the salad hunched equally on either side of the wooden servers; only the rice fluffed together as a unit and Su reached hungrily for it.
    —JUNE ARNOLD, Sister Gin (1972)

20. A lesbian's best friend is an upside down cake.
    —JILL JOHNSTON, Lesbian Nation (1973)

21. Food is an important part of a balanced diet.
> —*FRAN LEBOWITZ, Metropolitan Life (1978)*

22. The French would eat anything that couldn't outrun them.
> —*LISA ALTHER, Five Minutes in Heaven (1995)*

Fools and Folly

1. Wisdom at times is found in folly.
> —*HORACE (1st century BCE), Odes IV, 2*

2. The entire world is my temple, and a very fine one too, if I'm not mistaken, and I'll never lack priests to serve it as long as there are men.
> —*DESIDERIUS ERASMUS, the words of the Goddess of Folly, Praise of Folly (1509)*

3. Lord, what fools these mortals be!
> —*WILLIAM SHAKESPEARE, A Midsummer Night's Dream (1596)*

4. O that he were here to write me down an ass! But, masters, remember that I am an ass; though it be not written down, yet forget not that I am an ass.
> —*WILLIAM SHAKESPEARE, Much Ado About Nothing (1598)*

5. The folly of one man is the fortune of another.

> —*FRANCIS BACON, "Of Fortune," Essays (1625)*

6. Fools are more to be feared than the wicked.
> —*CHRISTINA, QUEEN OF SWEDEN, Maxims (1660–80)*

7. Folly does not amuse, or even employ one's notice long.
> —*JOHN CLELAND, Memoirs of a Coxcomb (1751)*

8. Give me the folly that dimples the cheek rather than the wisdom that curdles the blood.
> —*HERMAN MELVILLE, The Confidence-Man (1857)*

9. Any fool can make a rule / And every fool will mind it.
> —*HENRY DAVID THOREAU, Journal, 3 February 1860*

10. It is quite within a man's rights to be a fool once in a while.
> —*HENRY JAMES, Confidence (1880)*

11. This planet is largely inhabited by parrots, and it is easy to disguise folly by giving it a fine name.
—A. E. HOUSMAN, *"The Editing of Manilius" (1903)*

12. We must all indulge in a few follies if we are to make reality bearable.
—MARCEL PROUST, *Remembrance of Things Past: Within a Budding Grove (1918)*

13. You will do foolish things, but do them with enthusiasm.
—COLETTE (d. 1954), *in New York World-Telegram & Sun (1961)*

14. People do not wish to appear foolish; to avoid the appearance of foolishness, they were willing to remain actually fools.
—ALICE WALKER (1978), *in Gloria T. Hull, Patricia Bell Scott, and Barbara Smith, eds., All the Women Are White, All the Blacks Are Men, but Some of Us Are Brave (1982)*

Fortune   and   Fate

1. Avoid enquiring into what will be tomorrow, and count as gain each day that Fortune grants you.
—HORACE (1st century BCE), *Odes I, 11*

2. Fortune sides with him who dares.
—VIRGIL, *Aeneid (19 BCE)*

3. 'Tis all a Chequer-board of Nights and Days / Where Destiny with Men for Pieces plays: / Hither and thither moves, and mates, and slays, / And one by one back in the Closet lays.
—OMAR KHAYYÁM, *Rubáiyát (11th–12th century); trans. Edward FitzGerald*

4. The Moving Finger writes; and, having writ, / Moves on: nor all your Piety nor Wit / Shall lure it back to cancel half a Line, / Nor all your Tears wash out a Word of it.
—OMAR KHAYYÁM, *Rubáiyát (11th–12th century); trans. Edward FitzGerald*

5. When Fortune comes, seize her in front with a sure hand, because behind she is bald.

—*LEONARDO DA VINCI, Notebooks*
(c. 1500)

6. Let everyone witness how many different cards fortune has up her sleeve when she wants to ruin a man.
—*BENVENUTO CELLINI,*
Autobiography (1566)

7. Let us sit and mock the good housewife Fortune from her wheel, that her gifts may henceforth be bestowed equally.
—*WILLIAM SHAKESPEARE, As You*
Like It (1599–1600)

8. Fortune is like the market, where many times, if you can stay a little, the price will fall.
—*FRANCIS BACON, "Of Delay,"*
Essays (1625)

9. It is not enough to be in love, to be happy; since Fortune, who is capricious, and takes delight to trouble the repose of the most elevated and virtuous, has very little respect for passionate and tender hearts, when she designs to produce strange adventures.
—*APHRA BEHN, The History of*
Agnes De Castro (c. 1680)

10. Not entirely untempered to human nature are the most direful blasts of Fate.
—*HERMAN MELVILLE, Pierre (1852)*

11. Superiority to Fate / Is difficult to gain / 'Tis not conferred of Any / But possible to earn.
—*EMILY DICKINSON, no. 1081*
(c. 1866), Complete Poems (1955)

12. Fortune is a blind and fickle fostermother, who showers her gifts at random upon her nurslings. But we do her a grave injustice if we believe such an accusation. Trace a man's career from his cradle to his grave and mark how Fortune has treated him. You will find that when he is once dead she can for the most part be vindicated from the charge of any but very superficial fickleness. Her blindness is the merest fable; she can espy her favorites long before they are born.
—*SAMUEL BUTLER (d. 1902), The*
Way of All Flesh (1903)

13. Few evade full measure of their fate.
—*HART CRANE, "The River," The*
Bridge (1930)

14. Fate is not an eagle, it creeps like a rat.
—*ELIZABETH BOWEN, The House in*
Paris (1935)

15. Failure or success seem to have been allotted to men by their stars. But they retain the power of wriggling, of fighting with their star or against it, and in the whole universe

the only really interesting movement is this wriggle.
> —E. M. FORSTER, *Abinger Harvest* (1936)

16. A guardian angel comes when you are very young, and gives you special dispensation. From what? From the world. Yours might be luck. Mine is money.
> —JANE BOWLES, *Two Serious Ladies* (1943)

17. Destiny is over all of us, high or low.
> —IVY COMPTON-BURNETT, *The Mighty and Their Fall* (1961)

18. I asked for bread and was given a stone. It turned out to be precious.
> —QUENTIN CRISP, *How to Become a Virgin* (1981)

F r a u d

1. What he wanted in purity of heart, he supplied by exterior sanctity.
> —MATTHEW G. LEWIS, *The Monk* (1795)

2. "But the Emperor has nothing on at all!" cried a little child.
> —HANS CHRISTIAN ANDERSEN, *"The Emperor's New Clothes," Works* (1843)

3. The kind of fraud which consists in daring to proclaim the truth while mixing it with a large share of lies that falsify it, is more widespread than is generally thought.
> —MARCEL PROUST, *Remembrance of Things Past: Within a Budding Grove* (1918)

4. If there was a trick, there must be a trickster.
> —DOROTHY RICHARDSON, *Pilgrimage: The Tunnel* (1919)

5. "Oh dear," she said, "this is really all too bogus."
> —EVELYN WAUGH, *Vile Bodies* (1930)

6. Only God can tell the saintly from the suburban, / Counterfeit values always resemble the true.

—*W. H. Auden, "New Year Letter" (1941)*

7. Nothing ever made me more doubtful of T. E. Lawrence's genuineness than that he so heartily trusted two persons whom I knew to be bogus.

—*W. Somerset Maugham (1941), A Writer's Notebook (1949)*

8. You can't fake quality any more than you can fake a good meal.

—*William S. Burroughs, The Western Lands (1987)*

Freedom

1. As long as possible live free and uncommitted. It makes but little difference whether you are committed to a farm or the county jail.

—*Henry David Thoreau, "Where I Lived, and What I Lived For," Walden (1854)*

2. Blind and unwavering indiscipline at all times constitutes the real strength of all free men.

—*Alfred Jarry, Ubu Enchained (1899)*

3. To know how to free oneself is nothing; the arduous thing is to know what to do with one's freedom.

—*André Gide, The Immoralist (1902); trans. Dorothy Bussy*

4. The dangers of freedom are appalling.

—*Lytton Strachey, letter to Duncan Grant, 12 April 1907*

5. We have tasted space and freedom, frontiers falling as we went, / Now with narrow bonds and limits, never could we be content.

—*Vita Sackville-West, "Nomads" (1917)*

6. To enjoy freedom, if the platitude is pardonable, we have of course to control ourselves. We must not squander our powers, helplessly and ignorantly, squirting half the house in order to water a single rose-bush; we must train them, exactly and powerfully, here on the very spot.

—*Virginia Woolf, "How Should One Read a Book?" The Second Common Reader (1932)*

7. "Don't Fence Me In"
　　—COLE PORTER, *song title (1934)*

8. In the prison of his days / Teach the free man how to praise.
　　—W. H. AUDEN, *"In Memory of
　　W. B. Yeats" (1940)*

9. I cannot write too much upon how necessary it is to be completely conservative that is particularly traditional in order to be free.
　　—GERTRUDE STEIN, *Paris France
　　(1940)*

10. Liberty is the one thing no man can have unless he grants it to others.
　　—RUTH BENEDICT (1942), in
　　Margaret Mead, An
　　Anthropologist at Work (1959)

11. Freedom is not something that anybody can be given; freedom is something people take and people are as free as they want to be.
　　—JAMES BALDWIN, *Nobody Knows
　　My Name (1961)*

12. There's something contagious about demanding freedom.
　　—ROBIN MORGAN, *Sisterhood Is
　　Powerful (1970)*

13. She wanted to climb to the top of the tree and hang from its five-hundred-year-old branches and shout so that all the women could hear, even those who didn't listen any more: *All out come in free!*
　　—JUNE ARNOLD, *Sister Gin (1975)*

14. This is a celebration of individual freedom, not of homosexuality. No government has the right to tell its citizens when or whom to love. The only queer people are those who don't love anybody.
　　—RITA MAE BROWN, *speech,
　　opening of the Gay Olympics,
　　San Francisco, 28 August 1982*

15. In order to be able to live at all in America I must be unafraid to live anywhere in it, and I must be able to live in the fashion and with whom I choose.
　　—ALICE WALKER, *In Search of Our
　　Mothers' Gardens (1983)*

16. We don't yet have the political freedom to be able to be homosexuals only when we are making love with members of our own sex, but it is a freedom I know I'm working for.
　　—JANE RULE, *A Hot-Eyed Moderate
　　(1985)*

17. Of all the benefits of spinsterhood, the greatest is carte blanche. Once a woman is called "that crazy old maid" she can get away with everything.
　　—FLORENCE KING, *Reflections in a
　　Jaundiced Eye (1989)*

Friendship

1. Friendship is constant in all other things / Save in the office and affairs of love.
> —*WILLIAM SHAKESPEARE, Much Ado About Nothing (1598)*

2. It was a sparing speech of the ancients, to say that *a friend is another himself.*
> —*FRANCIS BACON, Essays (1625)*

3. Life becomes useless and insipid when we have no longer either friends or enemies.
> —*CHRISTINA, QUEEN OF SWEDEN, Maxims (1660–80)*

4. Friendship without love is only acquaintance, but with love, is heroic and exalted above all. Christian morality does not teach this, but the pagans praised it, and the greatest deeds of antiquity were accomplished by it.
> —*JOHANN JOACHIM WINCKELMANN (1762), in Hans Diepolder and Walter Rehm, eds., Johann Joachim Winckelmann: Briefe, Vol. 2 (1953–57); trans. Bradley Rose*

5. The same may be said of friendship at first sight as of love at first sight: it is the only true one, the only noble one.
> —*HERMAN MELVILLE, The Confidence-Man (1857)*

6. Laughter is not at all a bad beginning for a friendship, and it is far the best ending for one.
> —*OSCAR WILDE, The Picture of Dorian Gray (1891)*

7. The process of falling in love at first sight is as final as it is swift in such a case, but the growth of true friendship may be a lifelong affair.
> —*SARAH ORNE JEWETT, The Country of Pointed Firs (1896)*

8. Friendship is like money, easier made than kept.
> —*SAMUEL BUTLER (d. 1902), Note Books (1912)*

9. Friends are generally of the same sex, for when men and women agree, it is only in their conclusions; their reasons are different.
> —*GEORGE SANTAYANA, The Life of Reason (1906)*

10. The sacrifices of friendship were beautiful in her eyes as long as she was not asked to make them.
> —*SAKI [H. H. MUNRO], "Fur," Beasts and Super-Beasts (1914)*

11. I am treating you as my friend, asking you to share my present minuses in the hope that I can ask you to share my future pluses.
—KATHERINE MANSFIELD (d. 1923), in Leslie Moore, Katherine Mansfield: The Memories of L.M. (1971)

12. She's been my greatest friend for fifteen years. I know her through and through and I tell you that she hasn't got a single redeeming quality.
—W. SOMERSET MAUGHAM, Our Betters (1923)

13. Only solitary men know the full joys of friendship. Others have their family; but to a solitary and an exile his friends are everything.
—WILLA CATHER, Shadows on the Rock (1931)

14. I have lost friends, some by death—others by sheer inability to cross the street.
—VIRGINIA WOOLF, The Waves (1931)

15. But just as delicate fare does not stop you from craving for saveloys, so tried and exquisite friendship does not take away your taste for something new and dubious.
—COLETTE, "The Rainy Moon," Chambre d'Hôtel (1940)

16. To find a friend one must close one eye. To keep him—two.
—NORMAN DOUGLAS, An Almanac (1941)

17. I know of these romantic friendships of the English and the Germans. They are not Latin. I think they are very good if they do not go on too long. . . . It is a kind of love that comes to children before they know its meaning. In England it comes when you are almost men; I think I like that. It is better to have that kind of love for another boy than for a girl.
—EVELYN WAUGH, Brideshead Revisited (1945)

18. I hate the idea of causes, and if I had to choose between betraying my country and betraying my friend, I hope I should have the guts to betray my country.
—E. M. FORSTER, Two Cheers for Democracy (1951)

19. My only politics have been friendship.
—JEAN COCTEAU, Diary of an Unknown (1952)

20. It is wise to apply the oil of refined politeness to the mechanism of friendship.
—COLETTE (d. 1954), Earthly Paradise (1966)

21. We tiptoed around each other like heartbreaking new friends.
—JACK KEROUAC, On the Road (1957)

22. Love with its paraphernalia of sexuality, jealousy, nostalgia, and

exaltation was easier to recognize than friendship, which seemed to have (excepting athletic equipment) no paraphernalia at all.
—*JOHN CHEEVER, Bullet Park (1960)*

23. Sooner or later you've heard all your best friends have to say. Then comes the tolerance of real love.
—*NED ROREM, Music from Inside Out (1967)*

24. What I cannot love, I overlook. Is that real friendship?
—*ANAÏS NIN, The Diary of Anaïs Nin, Vol. 5 (1974)*

25. Friendship is a pretty full-time occupation if you really are friendly with somebody. You can't have too many friends because then you're just not really friends.
—*TRUMAN CAPOTE (d. 1984), in Lawrence Grobel, ed., Conversations with Truman Capote (1985)*

26. [Friendships] are easy to get out of compared to love affairs, but they are not easy to get out of compared to, say, jail.
—*FRAN LEBOWITZ, in Mirabella (1992)*

Gender and Androgyny

1. A woman's face with nature's own hand painted / Hast thou, the master-mistress of my passion.
—*WILLIAM SHAKESPEARE, Sonnet 20 (1609)*

2. It is well known that of every strong woman they say she has a masculine mind.
—*MARGARET FULLER, "The Great Lawsuit" (1843)*

3. Rearrange a 'Wife's' affection! / When they dislocate my Brain! /

Amputate my freckled bosom! / Make me bearded like a man!
—*EMILY DICKINSON, no. 1737 (1862), Complete Poems (1955)*

4. The home seems to me to be the proper sphere for the man. And certainly once a man begins to neglect his domestic duties he becomes painfully effeminate, does he not? And I don't like that. It makes men so very attractive.
—*OSCAR WILDE, The Importance of Being Earnest (1895)*

5. Oh, better I like to work out of doors than in the house. . . . I not care that your grandmother says it makes me like a man. I like to be like a man.

—WILLA CATHER, *My Antonia* (1918)

6. Different though the sexes are, they intermix. In every human being a vacillation from one sex to the other takes place, and often it is only the clothes that keep the male or female likeness, while underneath the sex is very opposite of what is above.

—VIRGINIA WOOLF, *Orlando* (1928)

7. Perhaps a mind that is purely masculine cannot create, any more than a mind that is purely feminine. It is fatal to be a man or woman pure and simple; one must be woman-manly or man-womanly.

—VIRGINIA WOOLF, *A Room of One's Own* (1929)

8. There was something different about the boy, a nervousness, a softness and tenderness which wasn't like a man's, although he wasn't the least bit effeminate looking—still—that thing was there.

—TENNESSEE WILLIAMS, *A Streetcar Named Desire* (1947)

9. What is most beautiful in virile men is something feminine; what is most beautiful in feminine women is something masculine.

—SUSAN SONTAG, "Notes on 'Camp' " (1964)

10. We are all monsters, if it comes to that, we women who chose to be something more and something less than women.

—MAY SARTON, *Mrs. Stevens Hears the Mermaids Singing* (1965)

11. The becoming of androgynous human persons implies a radical change in the fabric of human consciousness and in styles of human behavior.

—MARY DALY, *Beyond God the Father* (1973)

12. To me gender is not physical at all, but is altogether insubstantial. It is soul, perhaps, it is talent, it is taste, it is environment, it is how one feels, it is light and shade, it is inner music. . . . It is the essentialness of oneself.

—JAN MORRIS, *Conundrum* (1974)

13. I had reached the conclusion myself that sex was not a division but a continuum, that almost nobody was altogether of one sex or another, and that the infinite subtlety of the shading from one extreme to another was one of the most beautiful of nature's phenomena.

—JAN MORRIS, *Conundrum* (1974)

14. I didn't want to be a boy, ever, but I was outraged that his height and intelligence were graces for him and gaucheries for me.

—JANE RULE, Lesbian Images (1975)

15. We are all androgynous, not only because we are all born of a woman impregnated by the seed of a man but because each of us, helplessly and forever, contains the other—male in female, female in male, white in black and black in white.

—JAMES BALDWIN, The Price of the Ticket (1985)

16. There is something compelling about being both male and female, about having an entry into both worlds. I, like other queer people, am two in one body, both male and female. I am the embodiment of *hieros gamos:* the coming together of opposite qualities within.

—GLORIA ANZALDÚA, Borderlands/La Frontera (1989)

17. In the theory of gender I began from zero. There is no masculine power or privilege I did not covet. But slowly, step by step, decade by decade, I was forced to acknowledge that even a woman of abnormal will cannot escape her hormonal identity.

—CAMILLE PAGLIA, Sex, Art, and American Culture (1992)

Genius

1. Everybody hates a prodigy, detests an old head on young shoulders.

—DESIDERIUS ERASMUS, Praise of Folly (1509)

2. Genius is full of trash.

—HERMAN MELVILLE, Mardi (1849)

3. Genius is no more than childhood recaptured at will, childhood equipped now with man's physical means to express itself, and with the analytical mind that enables it to bring order into the sum of experience, involuntarily amassed.

—CHARLES BAUDELAIRE (d. 1867), L'Art Romantique (1869)

4. Genius lasts longer than beauty. That accounts for the fact that we all take such pains to overeducate ourselves.

—OSCAR WILDE, The Picture of Dorian Gray (1891)

5. Genius has been defined as a supreme capacity for making trouble. It might be more fitly described as a supreme capacity for getting its possessors into pains of all kinds, and

keeping them therein so long as the genius remains.
> —SAMUEL BUTLER (d. 1902), Note
> Books (1912)

6. There are two paths in life: one is the regular one, direct, honest. The other is bad, it leads through death— that is the way of genius!
> —THOMAS MANN, The Magic
> Mountain (1924)

7. It takes a lot of time to be a genius, you have to sit around so much doing nothing, really doing nothing.
> —GERTRUDE STEIN, Everybody's
> Autobiography (1937)

8. Genius is talent provided with ideals.
> —W. SOMERSET MAUGHAM, A
> Writer's Notebook (1949)

9. There are dancing motes or elements in genius which are impossible to pin down. One can only note

their action, marvel at what they leave behind.
> —ELIZABETH BOWEN, Collected
> Impressions (1950)

10. I would predicate that in all great works of genius masculine and feminine elements in the personality find expression, whether this androgynous nature is played out sexually or not.
> —MAY SARTON, Journal of a
> Solitude (1973)

11. Addicts of nonsense haven't the sense to see that men and women of genius educate themselves.
> —A. L. ROWSE, "Jane Austen as
> Social Realist," Portraits and
> Views (1979)

12. The difference between genius and stupidity is that even genius has limits.
> —RITA MAE BROWN, Bingo (1988)

Gifts and Giving

1. What with your friend you nobly share, / At least you rescue from your heir.
> —HORACE (1st century BCE),
> Odes IV, 7

2. Trust not the horse, O Trojans. Be it what it may, I fear the Grecians even when they offer gifts.
> —VIRGIL, Aeneid (19 BCE)

3. The hand of liberality is stronger than the arm of power.
> —SA'DI, *Gulistan (1258)*

4. I am not in the giving vein to-day.
> —WILLIAM SHAKESPEARE,
> *Richard III (1592–93)*

5. Rich gifts wax poor when givers prove unkind.
> —WILLIAM SHAKESPEARE, *Hamlet*
> *(1600–1601)*

6. Behold, I do not give lectures or a little charity. / When I give I give myself.
> —WALT WHITMAN, *"Song of*
> *Myself," Leaves of Grass (1855)*

7. Give crowns and pounds and guineas / But not your heart away; Give pearls away and rubies / But keep your fancy free.
> —A. E. HOUSMAN, *no. 13, A*
> *Shropshire Lad (1896)*

8. Unlike the alleged Good Woman of the Bible, I'm not above rubies.
> —SAKI [H. H. MUNRO], *"Reginald*
> *on Christmas Presents," Reginald*
> *(1904)*

9. When people grow gradually rich their requirements and standard of living expand in proportion, while their present-giving instincts often remain in the undeveloped condition of their earlier days. Something showy and not-too-expensive in a shop is their only conception of the ideal gift.
> —SAKI [H. H. MUNRO], *"Fur,"*
> *Beasts and Super-Beasts (1914)*

10. America I've given you all and now I'm nothing.
> —ALLEN GINSBERG, *"America,"*
> *Howl and Other Poems (1956)*

11. It is rare indeed that people give. Most people guard and keep; they suppose that it is they themselves and what they identify with themselves that they are guarding and keeping, whereas what they are actually guarding and keeping is their system of reality and what they assume to be.
> —JAMES BALDWIN, *The Fire Next*
> *Time (1963)*

12. There is only one real deprivation, I decided this morning, and that is not to be able to give one's gifts to those one loves most.
> —MAY SARTON, *Journal of a*
> *Solitude (1973)*

God

1. As flies to wanton boys are we to the gods. / They kill us for their sport.
> —*WILLIAM SHAKESPEARE, Hamlet (1600–1601)*

2. The reason the mass of men fear God, and *at bottom dislike Him,* is because they rather distrust His Heart, and fancy Him all brain like a watch.
> —*HERMAN MELVILLE, in Literary World, 17/24 August 1850*

3. Silent and amazed even when a little boy, / I remember I heard the preacher every Sunday put God in his statements, / As contending against some being or influence.
> —*WALT WHITMAN, "A Child's Amaze" (1867)*

4. No more gods! no more gods! Man is king, Man is God!—But the great Faith is Love!
> —*ARTHUR RIMBAUD, "Soleil et Chair" (1870)*

5. But God, if a God there be, is the substance of men which is man.
> —*ALGERNON CHARLES SWINBURNE, "Hymn of Man" (1871)*

6. An honest God's the noblest work of man.
> —*SAMUEL BUTLER (d. 1902), Further Extracts from the Notebooks (1934)*

7. God is the tangential point between zero and infinity.
> —*ALFRED JARRY (d. 1907), Gestes et Opinions du Docteur Faustroll Pataphysicien (1911)*

8. Her conception of God was certainly not orthodox. She felt towards him as she might have felt towards a glorified sanitary engineer; and in some of her speculations she seems hardly to distinguish between the Deity and the Drains.
> —*LYTTON STRACHEY, on Florence Nightingale, Eminent Victorians (1918)*

9. God, . . . we believe; we have told You we believe. . . . We have not denied You, then rise up to defend us. Acknowledge us, of God, before the whole world. Give us also the right to our existence!
> —*RADCLYFFE HALL, The Well of Loneliness (1928)*

10. It is much more difficult than one thinks not to believe in God.

—*ANDRÉ GIDE, Les Nouvelles Nourritures (1936)*

11. Evil can be condoned only if in the beyond it is compensated by good and God himself needs immortality to vindicate his ways to man.
    —*W. SOMERSET MAUGHAM, The Summing Up (1938)*

12. We know all their gods; they ignore ours. What they call our sins are our gods, and what they call their gods, we name otherwise.
    —*NATALIE CLIFFORD BARNEY, "Gods" (1962)*

13. If the concept of God has any validity or use, it can only be to make us larger, freer, and more loving. If God cannot do this, then it is time we got rid of Him.
    —*JAMES BALDWIN, The Fire Next Time (1963)*

14. The Lord is not my shepherd. I shall want.
    —*MAY SARTON, Mrs. Stevens Hears the Mermaids Singing (1965)*

15. I think there are innumerable gods. What we on earth call God is a little tribal God who has made an awful mess. Certainly forces operating through human consciousness control events.
    —*WILLIAM S. BURROUGHS, in Paris Review (1965)*

16. God is a gentleman. He prefers blondes.
    —*JOE ORTON, Loot (1966)*

17. It had become obvious that [God] was never going to do a thing I said.
    —*QUENTIN CRISP, The Naked Civil Servant (1968)*

18. May it not be that, just as we have to have faith in Him, God has to have faith in us and, considering the history of the human race so far, may it not be that "faith" is even more difficult for Him than it is for us?
    —*W. H. AUDEN, A Certain World (1970)*

19. Why indeed must "God" be a noun? Why not a verb—the most active and dynamic of all?
    —*MARY DALY, Beyond God the Father (1973)*

20. When God hands you a gift, he also hands you a whip; and the whip is intended for self-flagellation solely.
    —*TRUMAN CAPOTE, Music for Chameleons (1980)*

21. When I found out I thought God was white, and a man, I lost interest.
    —*ALICE WALKER, The Color Purple (1982)*

22. I think it pisses God off if you walk by the color purple in a field somewhere and don't notice it.
    —*ALICE WALKER, The Color Purple (1982)*

23. I never go to confession; God doesn't want us to confess, he wants us to challenge him.

 —*JEANETTE WINTERSON, The Passion (1987)*

24. I have met a great many people on their way towards God and I wonder why they have chosen to look for him rather than themselves.

 —*JEANETTE WINTERSON, Sexing the Cherry (1989)*

Goodness

1. How far that little candle throws his beams! / So shines a good deed in a naughty world.

 —*WILLIAM SHAKESPEARE, The Merchant of Venice (1596–97)*

2. If I knew for a certainty that a man was coming to my house with the conscious design of doing me good, I should run for my life.

 —*HENRY DAVID THOREAU, "Economy," Walden (1854)*

3. How sick one gets of being "good," how much I should respect myself if I could burst out and make everyone wretched for twenty-four hours; embody selfishness.

 —*ALICE JAMES, letter to William James, 11 December 1889*

4. To be good, according to the vulgar standard of goodness, is obviously quite easy. It merely requires a certain amount of sordid terror, a certain lack of imaginative thought, and a certain low passion for middle-class respectability.

 —*OSCAR WILDE, "The Critic as Artist" (1891)*

5. How lovely goodness is in those who, stepping lightly, go smiling through the world.

 —*VIRGINIA WOOLF, "The String Quartet" (1921)*

6. Loving-kindness is the better part of goodness. It lends grace to the sterner qualities of which this consists.

 —*W. SOMERSET MAUGHAM, The Summing Up (1938)*

7. O I am a cat that likes to / Gallop about doing good.

 —*STEVE SMITH (d. 1971), "The Galloping Cat," Scorpion (1972)*

Gossip and Slander

1. There are a great many of these accusers, and they have been accusing me now for a great many years, and what is more, they approached you at the most impressionable age, when some of you were children or adolescents; and literally won their case by default, because there was no one to defend me.
　　—SOCRATES, on trial for charges of corrupting the youth of Athens (399 BCE); in Plato (4th century BCE), Apology

2. Rumor goes forth at once, Rumor than whom / No other speedier evil thing exists; / She thrives by rapid movement, and acquires / Strength as she goes; small at the first from fear, / She presently uplifts herself aloft, / And stalks upon the ground and hides her head / Among the clouds.
　　—VIRGIL, Aeneid (19 BCE)

3. Be thou as chaste as ice, as pure as snow, thou shalt not escape calumny.
　　—WILLIAM SHAKESPEARE, Hamlet (1600–1601)

4. Hurl calumnies boldly; something is sure to stick.
　　—FRANCIS BACON (d. 1626), De Dignitate et Augmentis Scientiarum (1632)

5. As you know, no one over thirty years of age is afraid of tittle-tattle. I myself find it much less difficult to strangle a man than to fear him.
　　—CHRISTINA, QUEEN OF SWEDEN, Maxims (1660–80)

6. Rumor is seldom at a loss for answers.
　　—HERMAN MELVILLE, The Confidence-Man (1857)

7. There is only one thing in the world worse than being talked about, and that is not being talked about.
　　—OSCAR WILDE, The Picture of Dorian Gray (1891)

8. As a wicked man I am a complete failure. Why there are lots of people who say I have never really done anything wrong in the whole course of my life. Of course they only say it behind my back.
　　—OSCAR WILDE, Lady Windermere's Fan (1892)

9. It is perfectly monstrous the way people go about, nowadays, saying things against one behind one's back that are absolutely and entirely true.

—OSCAR WILDE, *A Woman of No
Importance (1893)*

10. The censorious said that she
slept in a hammock and understood
Yeats's poems, but her family denied
both stories.
  —SAKI [H. H. MUNRO], *"The Jesting
  of Arlington Stringham," The
  Chronicles of Clovis (1911)*

11. Coffee and rolls took on the
nature of an orgy. We positively scin-
tillated. Anecdotes of the High Born
were poured out, sweetened and
sipped: we gorged on scandals of
High Birth generously buttered.
  —KATHERINE MANSFIELD *(d. 1923),
  "The Sisters of the Baroness," In
  a German Pension (1926)*

12. The telephone shone as brightly
as a weapon kept polished by daily
use.
  —COLETTE, *The Last of Cheri
  (1926)*

13. Gossip is the art-form of the man
and woman in the street, and the
proper subject for gossip, as for all
art, is the behaviour of mankind.
  —W. H. AUDEN, in *Listener,
  22 December 1937*

14. All courtiers gossip madly, it's
part of their business.
  —DAPHNE DU MAURIER, *Mary Anne
  (1954)*

15. I don't care what anybody says
about me as long as it isn't true.
  —TRUMAN CAPOTE, *interview, in
  David Frost, The Americans
  (1970)*

16. I'm enormously less interested in
whom you sleep with than I am in
with whom you're prepared to die.
  —TI-GRACE ATKINSON, *Amazon
  Odyssey (1974)*

17. Can you suggest any suitable
aspersions to spread abroad about
Mrs Thatcher? It is idle to suggest
she has unnatural relations with Mrs
Barbara Castle; what is needed is
something socially lower; that she
eats asparagus with knife and fork, or
serves instant mash potatoes.
  —SYLVIA TOWNSEND WARNER, *letter,
  29 January 1976*

18. Gossip is irresponsible commu-
nication.
  —RITA MAE BROWN, *A Plain Brown
  Rapper (1976)*

Government

1. It is with government as with medicine, its only business is the choice of evils.

> —*JEREMY BENTHAM, An Introduction to the Principles of Morals and Legislation (1789)*

2. The mechanism that directs government cannot be virtuous, because it is impossible to thwart every crime, to protect oneself from every criminal without being criminal too; that which directs corrupt mankind must be corrupt itself; and it will never be by means of virtue, virtue being inert and passive, that you will maintain control over vice, which is ever active: the governor must be more energetic than the governed.

> —*MARQUIS DE SADE, L'Histoire de Juliette, ou les Prospérités du Vice (1797)*

3. A thousand years scarce serve to form a state; / An hour may lay it in the dust.

> —*GEORGE GORDON, LORD BYRON, Childe Harold's Pilgrimage (1812–18)*

4. I heartily accept the motto, "That government is best which governs least"; and I should like to see it acted up to more rapidly and systematically. Carried out, it finally amounts to this, which I also believe,—"That government is best which governs not at all."

> —*HENRY DAVID THOREAU, On the Duty of Civil Disobedience (1849)*

5. Man is about the same, in the main, whether with despotism, or whether with freedom.

> —*WALT WHITMAN, "Democracy in the New World," Notes Left Over (1881)*

6. The form of government that is most suitable to the artist is no government at all.

> —*OSCAR WILDE, "The Soul of Man Under Socialism" (1891)*

7. We all know that Prime Ministers are wedded to the truth, but like other married couples they sometimes live apart.

> —*SAKI [H. H. Munro], The Unbearable Bassington (1912)*

8. I work for a government I despise for ends I think criminal.

—JOHN MAYNARD KEYNES,
letter to Duncan Grant,
15 December 1917

9. The important thing for government is not to do things which individuals are doing already, and to do them a little better or a little worse; but to do those things which at present are not done at all.
—JOHN MAYNARD KEYNES, "The
End of Laissez-Faire" (1926)

10. Man is a social rather than political animal; he can exist without a government.
—GEORGE SANTAYANA, Obiter
Scripta (1936)

11. Distrust of authority should be the first civic duty.
—NORMAN DOUGLAS, An Almanac
(1942)

12. Since people will never cease trying to interfere with the liberties of others in pursuing their own, the State can never wither away.
—W. H. AUDEN, "Henry James: An
American Scene" (1946)

13. To govern is to choose how the revenue from taxes is to be spent.
—GORE VIDAL, "Homage to Daniel
Shays" (1972)

14. I think the Reagan and Bush administrations will be remembered one hundred years hence as the people who could have stopped the plague but chose not to because the right people were dying.
—RITA MAE BROWN, Venus Envy
(1993)

Greatness

1. To have a great man for a friend seems pleasant to those who have never tried it; those who have, fear it.
—HORACE (1st century BCE),
Epistles I, 18

2. Be not afraid of greatness. Some are born great, some achieve greatness, and some have greatness thrust upon 'em.
—WILLIAM SHAKESPEARE, Twelfth
Night (1601)

3. All great rising is by a winding stair.

—FRANCIS BACON, *"Of Great
Place," Essays (1625)*

4. He or she is greatest who con-
tributes the greatest original practi-
cal example.
　—WALT WHITMAN, *"By Blue
　Ontario's Shores," Leaves of
　Grass (1855)*

5. We all like people who do things,
even if we only see their faces on a
cigar-box lid.
　—WILLA CATHER, *The Song of the
　Lark (1915)*

6. Born of the sun they travelled a
short while towards the sun, / And
left the vivid air signed with their
honour.
　—STEPHEN SPENDER, *"I Think
　Continually of Those Who Were
　Truly Great" (1933)*

7. The great man is too often all of a
piece; it is the little man that is a
bundle of contradictory elements.
　—W. SOMERSET MAUGHAM, *The
　Summing Up (1938)*

8. I distrust Great Men. They produce a desert of uniformity around
them and often a pool of blood too,
and I always feel a little man's pleasure when they come a cropper.
　—E. M. FORSTER, *Two Cheers for
　Democracy (1951)*

9. Few great men could pass
Personnel.
　—PAUL GOODMAN, *Growing Up
　Absurd (1960)*

10. Greatness is not the effect of
which inspiration is the cause. We
are all inspired, but we are all not
great.
　—NED ROREM, *Music from Inside
　Out (1967)*

11. I didn't and don't want to be a
"feminine" version or a diluted version or a special version or a sub-
sidiary version or an ancillary
version, or an adapted version of the
heroes I admire. I want to be the
heroes themselves.
　—JOANNA RUSS, *The Female Man
　(1975)*

Guilt

1. Mountains and hills, come, come and fall on me, / And hide me from the heavy wrath of God.
> —CHRISTOPHER MARLOWE, *The Tragical History of Dr. Faustus (c. 1592)*

2. So full of artless jealousy is guilt / It spills itself in fearing to be spilt.
> —WILLIAM SHAKESPEARE, *Hamlet (1600–1601)*

3. Can guilt dwell with innocent beauty and virtuous modesty?
> —HORACE WALPOLE, *The Castle of Otranto (1764)*

4. Guilt and courage are incompatible.
> —MATTHEW G. LEWIS, *The Monk (1795)*

5. Guilt has a vital power, which gives it life, until it is held up to scorn.
> —WALT WHITMAN, *Franklin Evans; or, the Inebriate (1846)*

6. Part of the public horror of sexual irregularity so-called is due to the fact that everyone knows himself essentially guilty.
> —ALEISTER CROWLEY, *The Confessions of Aleister Crowley (1929)*

7. There is a sort of man who pays no attention to his good actions, but is tormented by his bad ones. This is the type that most often writes about himself.
> —W. SOMERSET MAUGHAM, *The Summing Up (1938)*

8. I used so much hair spray that I feel personally responsible for global warming.
> —DUSTY SPRINGFIELD, *in New York Times Magazine, 29 October 1995*

Happiness

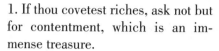

1. If thou covetest riches, ask not but for contentment, which is an immense treasure.

—SA'DI, Gulistan (1258)

2. How bitter a thing it is to look into happiness through another man's eyes!

—WILLIAM SHAKESPEARE, As You Like It (1599–1600)

3. The greatest happiness of the greatest number is the foundation of morals and legislation.

—JEREMY BENTHAM, The Commonplace Books (1781–85)

4. Happiness lies neither in vice nor in virtue; but in the manner we appreciate the one and the other, and the choice we make pursuant to our individual organization.

—MARQUIS DE SADE, L'Histoire de Juliette, ou les Prospérités du Vice (1797)

5. Do you see O my brothers and sisters? / It is not chaos or death—it is form, union, plan—it is eternal life—it is Happiness.

—WALT WHITMAN, "Song of Myself," Leaves of Grass (1855)

6. Happiness was my fate, my remorse, my worm: my life would always be too large to be dedicated to force and to beauty.

—ARTHUR RIMBAUD, "Alchimie du Verbe," Une Saison en Enfer (1873)

7. Ah! Those strange people who have the courage to be unhappy! Are they unhappy, by the way?

—ALICE JAMES (1889), in Anna Robeson Burr, Alice James (1934)

8. The good ended happily, and the bad unhappily. That is what fiction means.

—OSCAR WILDE, The Importance of Being Earnest (1895)

9. Nothing is more fatal to happiness than the remembrance of happiness.

—ANDRÉ GIDE, The Immoralist (1902); trans. Dorothy Bussy

10. Happiness is the only sanction of life: where happiness fails, existence remains a mad lamentable experiment.

—GEORGE SANTAYANA, The Life of Reason (1906)

11. It takes patience to appreciate domestic bliss; volatile spirits prefer unhappiness.
> —GEORGE SANTAYANA, *The Life of Reason (1906)*

12. He's simply got the instinct for being unhappy highly developed.
> —SAKI [H. H. MUNRO], *"The Match-Maker," The Chronicles of Clovis (1911)*

13. Happiness, to some, elation; / Is, to others, mere stagnation.
> —AMY LOWELL, *"Happiness" (1914)*

14. Shall I give you my recipe for happiness? I find everything useful and nothing indispensable. I find everything wonderful and nothing miraculous. I reverence the body. I avoid first causes like the plague.
> —NORMAN DOUGLAS, *South Wind (1917)*

15. That is happiness; to be dissolved into something complete and great.
> —WILLA CATHER, *My Antonia (1918)*

16. Happiness serves hardly any other purpose than to make unhappiness possible.
> —MARCEL PROUST (d. 1922), *Remembrance of Things Past: Time Regained (1927)*

17. The sharing of joy, whether physical, emotional, psychic or intellectual, forms a bridge between the sharers which can be the basis for understanding much of what is not shared between them, and lessens the threat of their difference.
> —AUDRE LORDE, *Uses of the Erotic (1978)*

18. In Hollywood if you don't have happiness you send out for it.
> —REX REED, in *J. R. Colombo, Hollywood the Bad (1979)*

Hatred

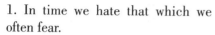

1. In time we hate that which we often fear.
> —WILLIAM SHAKESPEARE, Antony
> and Cleopatra (1606)

2. For thou art so possessed with murd'rous hate / That 'gainst thyself thou stick'st not to conspire.
> —WILLIAM SHAKESPEARE, Sonnet 10
> (1609)

3. Now Hatred is by far the longest pleasure; / Men love in haste, but they detest at leisure.
> —GEORGE GORDON, LORD BYRON,
> Don Juan (1819–24)

4. Haters are thumbscrews, Scotch boots, and Spanish inquisitions to themselves. He who hates is a fool.
> —HERMAN MELVILLE, Mardi (1849)

5. It were treason to our love / And a sin to God above / One iota to abate / Of a pure impartial hate.
> —HENRY DAVID THOREAU, "Indeed,
> Indeed, I Cannot Tell" (1852)

6. It does not matter much what a man hates, provided he hates something.
> —SAMUEL BUTLER (d. 1902), Note
> Books (1912)

7. I tell you there is such a thing as creative hate!
> —WILLA CATHER, The Song of the
> Lark (1915)

8. For it was not her one hated but the idea of her, which undoubtedly had gathered in to itself a great deal that was not Miss Killman; had become one of those spectres with which one battles in the night; one of those spectres who stand astride us and suck up half our life-blood, dominators and tyrants; for no doubt with another throw of the dice, had the black been uppermost and not the white, she would have loved Miss Killman! But not in this world. No.
> —VIRGINIA WOOLF, Mrs Dalloway
> (1926)

9. I had rather be hated for what I am than be beloved for what I am not.
> —ANDRÉ GIDE, letter to Edmund
> Gosse, 16 January 1927

10. Rejection is a form of self-assertion. You have only to look back upon yourself as a person who hates this or that to discover what it is that you secretly love.
> —GEORGE SANTAYANA, "My Father,"
> Persons and Places: The
> Background of My Life (1944)

11. One of the reasons people cling to their hates so stubbornly is because they seem to sense, once hate is gone, that they will be forced to deal with pain.
—JAMES BALDWIN, *Notes of a Native Son (1955)*

12. What we need is hatred. From it are our ideas born.
—JEAN GENET, *The Blacks (1958)*

13. They say that oppression engenders hate. They are heard on all sides crying hate hate.
—MONIQUE WITTIG, *Les Guérillères (1969)*

14. Hate generalizes, love specifies.

—ROBIN MORGAN, *The Anatomy of Freedom (1982)*

15. Anger, used, does not destroy. Hatred does.
—AUDRE LORDE, "Eye to Eye," *Sister Outsider (1984)*

16. Behind the hatred there lies / a murderous desire for love.
—MORRISSEY, "The Boy with the Thorn in His Side" (1985)

17. Insecurity breeds treachery: if you are kind to people who hate themselves, they will hate you as well.
—FLORENCE KING, *With Charity Toward None (1992)*

Heaven   and   Hell

1. And that inverted Bowl they call the Sky, / Whereunder crawling cooped we live and die, / Lift not your hands to it for help—for it / As impotently moves as you or I.
—OMAR KHAYYÁM, *Rubáiyát (11th–12th century); trans. Edward FitzGerald*

2. Hell hath no limits, nor is circumscrib'd / In one self place; for

where we are is Hell, / And where Hell is, there must we ever be.
—CHRISTOPHER MARLOWE, *The Tragical History of Dr. Faustus (c. 1592)*

3. Heaven will not be trifled with.
—HORACE WALPOLE, *The Castle of Otranto (1764)*

4. There is no other hell for man than the stupidity and wickedness of his own kind.

> —*MARQUIS DE SADE, L'Histoire de Juliette, ou les Prospérités du Vice (1797)*

5. Hell is a democracy of devils, where all are equals.

> —*HERMAN MELVILLE, Redburn (1849)*

6. You promise heavens free from strife, / Pure truth, and perfect change of will; / But sweet, sweet is this human life, / So sweet, I fain would breathe it still; / Your chilly stars I can forgo, / This warm kind world is all I know.

> —*WILLIAM CORY, "Mimnermus in Church," Ionica (1858)*

7. I believe that I am in hell, therefore I am there.

> —*ARTHUR RIMBAUD, "Nuit de l'Enfer," Une Saison en Enfer (1874)*

8. Men have feverishly conceived a heaven only to find it insipid, and a hell to find it ridiculous.

> —*GEORGE SANTAYANA, The Life of Reason (1906)*

9. Heaven is neither a place nor a time.

> —*FLORENCE NIGHTINGALE (d. 1910), in Edward Tyas, The Life of Florence Nightingale, Vol. 2 (1913)*

10. You know what the dead do in heaven? They sit on their golden chairs and sicken for home.

> —*CLEMENCE DANE, A Bill of Divorcement (1921)*

11. Hell is of this world and there are men who are unhappy escapees from hell, escapees destined ETER-NALLY to reenact their escape.

> —*ANTONIN ARTAUD, "General Security: The Liquidation of Opium" (1925)*

12. Heaven is a near / translatable thing.

> —*H.D. [HILDA DOOLITTLE], "Chance Meeting," Red Roses for Bronze (1931)*

13. We have no guarantee that the afterlife will be any less exasperating than this one, have we?

> —*NOËL COWARD, Blithe Spirit (1941)*

14. It is a curious thing that every creed promises a paradise which will be absolutely uninhabitable for any-one of civilised taste.

> —*EVELYN WAUGH, Put Out More Flags (1942)*

15. Eternity—waste of time.

> —*NATALIE CLIFFORD BARNEY, "Gods" (1962)*

16. It is an open question whether any behavior based on fear of eternal

punishment can be regarded as ethical or should be regarded as merely cowardly.
—*MARGARET MEAD, in Redbook, February 1971*

17. This life soon be over, I say. Heaven last all ways.
—*ALICE WALKER, The Color Purple (1982)*

History

1. History is busy with us.
—*MARIE ANTOINETTE, QUEEN OF FRANCE, to the revolutionary tribunal, 14 October 1793*

2. As soon as histories are properly told there is no more need of romances.
—*WALT WHITMAN, preface, Leaves of Grass (1855)*

3. Wherever men have lived there is a story to be told, and it depends chiefly on the story-teller or historian whether that is interesting or not.
—*HENRY DAVID THOREAU, Journal, 18 March 1860*

4. The beginning of my history is— love. It is the beginning of every man and every woman's history, if they are only frank enough to admit it.
—*MARIE CORELLI, Wormwood (1890)*

5. Anybody can make history. Only a great man can write it.
—*OSCAR WILDE, "The Critic as Artist" (1891)*

6. It has been said that though God cannot alter the past, historians can; it is perhaps because they can be useful to Him in this respect that He tolerates their existence.
—*SAMUEL BUTLER, Erewhon Revisited (1901)*

7. History is always written wrong, and so always needs to be rewritten.
—*GEORGE SANTAYANA, The Life of Reason (1906)*

8. The history of every country begins in the heart of a man or woman.
—*WILLA CATHER, O Pioneers! (1913)*

9. Human beings are too important to be treated as mere symptoms of the past.
—*LYTTON STRACHEY, Eminent Victorians (1918)*

10. Now in fighting history we find acknowledgments.
> —GERTRUDE STEIN, *"Didn't Nelly and Lilly Love You" (1922)*

11. History is attractive to the more timid of us [because] we can recover self-confidence by snubbing the dead.
> —E. M. FORSTER, *Abinger Harvest (1936)*

12. To walk into history is to be free at once, to be at large among people.
> —ELIZABETH BOWEN, *The House in Paris (1935)*

13. History to the defeated / May say Alas but cannot help nor pardon.
> —W. H. AUDEN, *"Spain 1937" (1937)*

14. But I belong to history, as she belongs to me; and I'm enlightened, yet what's the use of light?
> —PIER PAOLO PASOLINI, *Le Cenere di Gramsci (1957)*

15. World events are the work of individuals whose motives are often frivolous, even casual.
> —GORE VIDAL, *Rocking the Boat (1962)*

16. History creates confusion, even in its own time.
> —JEAN COCTEAU, *in Sunday Times, 20 October 1963*

17. History is in the shit sense. You have left it behind you.
> —BRIGID BROPHY, *In Transit (1969)*

18. History is not kind to us / we restitch it with living.
> —AUDRE LORDE, *"On my way out I passed over you and the Verrazano Bridge" (1986)*

19. I want to be a witness to my own time because I've had a sneaking suspicion lately that I'm going to live a lot longer than most of the people I meet. If I'm gonna be the only one still around to say what happened, I'd better pay close attention. Now.
> —SARAH SCHULMAN, *Rat Bohemia (1995)*

Homosexuality

1. Dionysus, please give to Cle-
oboulus / this wise advice: accept
our love.
>   —ANACREON (5th century BCE),
>   Fragment PMG 357; trans.
>   Dennis Kratz

2. The mightiest kings have had their
minions; / Great Alexander lov'd
Hephaestion, / The conquering Her-
cules for Hylas wept, / And for Pa-
troclus stern Achilles droop'd. / And
not kings only but the wisest men; /
The Roman Tully lov'd Octavius, /
Grave Socrates wild Alcibiades.
>   —CHRISTOPHER MARLOWE,
>   Edward II (c. 1591)

3. O my friends, can there be an
extravagance to equal that of imagining that a man must be a monster
deserving to lose his life because he
has preferred enjoyment of the ass-
hole to that of the cunt, because a
young man with whom he finds two
pleasures, those of being at once
lover and mistress, has appeared to
him preferable to a young girl, who
promises him half as much! He shall
be a villain, a monster, for having
wished to play the role of a sex not
his own! Indeed! Why then has
Nature created him susceptible of
this pleasure?
>   —MARQUIS DE SADE, La Philosophie
>   dans le Boudoir (1795)

4. It is so true that a woman may be
in love with a woman, and a man with
a man. It is pleasant to be sure of it,
because it is undoubtedly the same
love that we shall feel when we are
angels.
>   —MARGARET FULLER, Woman in the
>   Nineteenth Century (1845)

5. The institution of the dear love of
comrades.
>   —WALT WHITMAN, "I Hear It Was
>   Charged Against Me" (1860)

6. The love of men for each other—
so tender, heroic, constant; / That has
come all down the ages, in every
clime, in every nation, / Always so
true, so well assured of itself, over-
leaping barriers of age, of rank, of
distance, / Flag of the camp of
Freedom.
>   —EDWARD CARPENTER, "A Mightier
>   than Mammon," Towards
>   Democracy (1883)

7. The love that dare not speak its
name.
>   —LORD ALFRED DOUGLAS, "Two
>   Loves" (1894)

8. I hold the conviction that as centuries go on, and the sexes become more nearly merged on account of their increasing resemblances, I hold the conviction that such connections will to a very large extent cease to be regarded as merely unnatural, and will be understood far better, at least in their intellectual if not in their physical aspects.

> —VITA SACKVILLE-WEST, "Autobiography" (1920), in Nigel Nicholson, Portrait of a Marriage (1973)

9. She told many then the way of being gay, she taught very many then little ways they could use in being gay. She was living very well, she was gay then, she went on living then, she was regular in being gay, she always was living very well and was gay very well and was telling about little ways one could be learning to use in being gay, and later was telling them quite often, telling them again and again.

> —GERTRUDE STEIN, "Miss Furr and Miss Skeene" (1922)

10. There was nothing abnormal about it when homosexuality was the norm.

> —MARCEL PROUST, Remembrance of Things Past: Cities of the Plain (1922)

11. You understand that in homosexuality, just as in heterosexuality, there are all shades and degrees, from radiant health to sullen sickness, from simple expansiveness to all the refinements of vice.

> —ANDRÉ GIDE, Corydon (1924)

12. You're neither unnatural, nor abominable, nor mad; you're as much a part of what people call nature as anyone else; only you're unexplained as yet—you've not got your niche in creation.

> —RADCLYFFE HALL, The Well of Loneliness (1928)

13. But the intuition of those who stand midway between the two sexes is so ruthless, so poignant, so accurate, so deadly as to be in the nature of an added scourge.

> —RADCLYFFE HALL, The Well of Loneliness (1928)

14. Homosexuality is assuredly no advantage, but it is nothing to be ashamed of, no vice, no degradation; it cannot be classified as an illness.

> —SIGMUND FREUD, letter, 9 April 1935; The Letters of Sigmund Freud (1961)

15. What is this love we have for the invert, boy or girl? It was they who were spoken of in every romance that we ever read.

> —DJUNA BARNES, Nightwood (1936)

16. This place rumord to have been Sodom is blessed / In the Lord's eyes.

—ROBERT DUNCAN, *"This Place*
Rumord to Have Been Sodom"
(1960)

17. Show me a happy homosexual,
and I'll show you a gay corpse.
—MART CROWLEY, *The Boys in the*
Band (1968)

18. Buggery is spiritually valuable
because of its difficulties and tor-
ments.
—W. H. AUDEN *(d. 1973), in*
Humphrey Carpenter, W. H.
Auden, a Biography (1981)

19. More leant-upon than leanings,
I'd have thought.
—DAVID GARNETT, *in response to a*
question whether he, as a member
of the Bloomsbury group, had
had "homosexual leanings";
quoted in the Sunday Times
(London), 16 March 1980

20. Sexual orientation is only one
aspect of homosexuality, which is
really a personality, a sensitivity. A
spirit. It cannot be ignored like a
pimple or repressed like the urge to
eat a chocolate-covered cherry; it
cannot be isolated from one's personality.
—RICHARD FRIEDEL, *The Movie*
Lover (1981)

21. Practising? Certainly not. I'm
perfect.

—QUENTIN CRISP, *in response to a*
U.S. immigration officer's
question as to whether he was
a "practising homosexual";
quoted in the Sunday Times,
20 January 1982

22. I assume everyone is gay unless
I'm told otherwise.
—HARVEY FIERSTEIN, *in Life,*
January 1984

23. If you removed all of the homosexuals and homosexual influence
from what is generally regarded as
American culture, you would be
pretty much life with *Let's Make a*
Deal.
—FRAN LEBOWITZ, *in Leigh W.*
Rutledge, Unnatural Quotations
(1988)

24. Oddly, the homosexual is a far
more threatening figure than the
androgyne. Society after society has
passed laws against homosexuals,
but not against androgynes. Homosexuals are more menacing, in
part simply because they exist.
—CATHARINE R. STIMPSON, *Where*
the Meanings Are (1988)

25. Gay men have no automatic lin-
eage. Unlike straight men, who can
be initiated into the rituals of manhood by their fathers and brothers,
we must create our own models and
our own rites of passage. We self-
consciously assume the roles of

teacher and student, mentor and pro-
tégé . . . and in some instances, master and slave.
> —*JOHN PRESTON (d. 1993), Flesh*
> *and the Word 3 (1995)*

26. Since the most important element
of any concept is that its originating
question be appropriately framed,
any theory demanding an explanation for homosexuality is a problem-
atic one because it maintains our
existence as a category of deviance. I
mean, no one is running around trying to figure out why some people
like sports, for example.
> —*SARAH SCHULMAN, My American*
> *History (1994)*

H o p e

1. In the time of trouble avert not thy
face from hope, for the soft marrow
abideth in the hard bone.
> —*HAFIZ Divan (14th century),*
> *Ghazal 107, Divan*

2. The miserable have no other medicine / But only hope.
> —*WILLIAM SHAKESPEARE, Measure*
> *for Measure (1603)*

3. Hope is the most sensitive part of
a poor wretch's soul; whoever raises
it only to torment him is behaving
like the executioners in Hell who,
they say, incessantly renew old
wounds and concentrate their attention on that area of it that is already
lacerated.
> —*MARQUIS DE SADE, letter,*
> *20 February 1781*

4. Hope is a strange invention— / A
Patent of the Heart— / In unremitting action— / Yet never wearing
out—
> —*EMILY DICKINSON, no. 1392*
> *(c. 1877), Complete Poems*
> *(1955)*

5. Hope costs nothing.
> —*COLETTE, Claudine at School*
> *(1900)*

6. To hope for Paradise is to live in
Paradise, a very different thing from
actually getting there.
> —*VITA SACKVILLE-WEST, Passenger*
> *to Teheran (1926)*

7. For what human ill does not dawn
seem to be an alternative?
> —*THORNTON WILDER, The Bridge of*
> *San Luis Rey (1927)*

Hosts and Guests

1. A host is like a general: calamities often reveal his genius.
   —HORACE (1st century BCE), Satires II, 8

2. Unbidden guests / Are often welcomest when they are gone.
   —WILLIAM SHAKESPEARE, 1 Henry VI (1592)

3. Good company, good wine, good welcome / Can make good people.
   —WILLIAM SHAKESPEARE, The Tempest (1611)

4. It is nothing won to admit men with an open door, and to receive them with a shut and reserved countenance.
   —FRANCIS BACON, The Advancement of Learning (1605)

5. Nowadays the host does not admit *you* to his hearth, but has got the mason to build one for yourself somewhere in his alley, and hospitality is the art of *keeping* you at the greatest distance.
   —HENRY DAVID THOREAU, "House-Warming," Walden (1854)

6. I'm sure I don't know half the people who come to my house. Indeed, from all I hear, I shouldn't like to.
   —OSCAR WILDE, An Ideal Husband (1895)

7. Mother Ubu, you are very ugly today. Is it because we have company?
   —ALFRED JARRY, Ubu Roi (1896)

8. I hate guests who complain of the cooking and leave bits and pieces all over the place and cream-cheese sticking to the mirrors.
   —COLETTE, Cheri (1920)

9. When her guests were awash with champagne and with gin, / She was recklessly sober, as sharp as a pin.
   —WILLIAM PLOMER, "Slightly Foxed, or The Widower of Bayswater," Collected Poems (1960)

House and Home

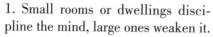

1. Small rooms or dwellings discipline the mind, large ones weaken it.
   —*LEONARDO DA VINCI, Notebooks (c. 1500)*

2. [Strawberry Hill] is a little plaything house that I got out of Mrs Chenevix's shop, and is the prettiest bauble you ever saw. It is set in enamelled meadows, with filigree hedges. . . . Thank God! the Thames is between me and the Duchess of Queensbury.
   —*HORACE WALPOLE, letter, 8 June 1747*

3. Plasticity loves new moulds because it can fill them, but for a man of sluggish mind and bad manners there is decidedly no place like home.
   —*GEORGE SANTAYANA, The Life of Reason (1906)*

4. I know of nothing more significant than the awakening of men and women throughout our country to the desire to improve their houses. Call it what you will—awakening, development, American Renaissance—it is a most startling and promising condition of affairs.
   —*ELSIE DE WOLFE, The House in Good Taste (1913)*

5. Many a man who thinks to found a home discovers that he has merely opened a tavern for his friends.
   —*NORMAN DOUGLAS, South Wind (1917)*

6. Safe upon the solid rock the ugly houses stand: / Come and see my shining palace on the sand!
   —*EDNA ST. VINCENT MILLAY, "Second Fig," A Few Figs from Thistles (1921)*

7. To one of my intense inter-uterine nature there is no measuring the shock that the loss of a house can cause.
   —*MARGARET ANDERSON, My Thirty Years' War (1930)*

8. In the matter of furnishing, I find a certain absence of ugliness far worse than ugliness.
   —*COLETTE, Gigi (1945)*

9. She was more than ever proud of the position of the bungalow, so almost in the country.

—ANGUS WILSON, *"A Flat Country Christmas" (1957)*

10. A flowerless room is a soulless room, to my way of thinking; but even one solitary little vase of a living flower may redeem it.

> —VITA SACKVILLE-WEST *(d. 1962), Vita Sackville-West's Garden Book (1983)*

11. There was no need to do any housework after all. After the first four years the dirt doesn't get any worse.

> —QUENTIN CRISP, *The Naked Civil Servant (1968)*

12. Being offended is the natural consequence of leaving one's home.

> —FRAN LEBOWITZ, *Social Studies (1981)*

13. It was a Victorian parlor maid's nightmare, marked by the kind of decor involving the word "throw." Throw pillows, throw covers, throw cloths. . . . Next to throw, the operative word was "occasional." Occasional tables, occasional chairs, occasional lamps; footstools, hassocks, stacked trays, wheeled tea-carts, and enough card tables to start a gambling den.

> —FLORENCE KING, *Confessions of a Failed Southern Lady (1985)*

Human   Nature

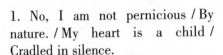

1. No, I am not pernicious / By nature. / My heart is a child / Cradled in silence.

> —SAPPHO *(7th century BCE), Fragment 120; trans. Anita George*

2. In all of us, even in good men, there is a lawless wild-beast nature, which peers out in sleep.

> —PLATO *(4th century BCE), The Republic*

3. Now I believe I can hear the philosophers protesting that it can only be misery to live in folly, illusion, deception and ignorance, but it isn't—it's human.

> —DESIDERIUS ERASMUS, *Praise of Folly (1509)*

4. To each his suff'rings, all are men, / Condemn'd alike to groan; / The tender for another's pain, / Th' unfeeling for his own.

—THOMAS GRAY, *Ode on a Distant
Prospect of Eton College (1742)*

5. This world is a comedy to those
that think, a tragedy to those that
feel.
> —HORACE WALPOLE, *letter to Anne,
> Countess of Upper Ossory,
> 16 August 1776*

6. Cats and monkeys—monkeys and
cats—all human life is there!
> —HENRY JAMES, *The Madonna of
> the Future (1879)*

7. No practice is entirely vicious
which has not been extinguished
among the comeliest, most vigorous,
and most cultivated races of mankind
in spite of centuries of endeavor to
extirpate it. If a vice in spite of such
efforts can still hold its own among
the most polished nations, it must be
founded on some immutable truth or
fact in human nature, and must have
some compensatory advantage which
we cannot afford altogether to dispense with.
> —SAMUEL BUTLER (d. 1902), *The
> Way of All Flesh (1903)*

8. Were they normal? What a question to ask! And it is always those
who know nothing about human nature, who are bored by psychology
and shocked by physiology, who
ask it.
> —E. M. FORSTER, *Howards End
> (1910)*

9. There are only two classes of people, the magnanimous, and the rest.
> —MARCEL PROUST, *Remembrance of
> Things Past: Swann's Way
> (1913)*

10. In or about December, 1910,
human character changed.
> —VIRGINIA WOOLF, "Mr Bennett
> and Mrs Brown" (1923)

11. There are, I have discovered, two
kinds of people in this world, those
who long to be understood and those
who long to be misunderstood. It is
the irony of life that neither is grati-
fied.
> —CARL VAN VECHTEN, *The Blind
> Bow-Boy (1923)*

12. There is no surer way of calling
the worst out of anyone than that of
taking their worst as being their true
selves, no surer way of bringing out
the best than by only accepting that
as being true of them.
> —E. F. BENSON, *Rex (1925)*

13. The young man who has not wept
is a savage, and the old man who will
not laugh is a fool.
> —GEORGE SANTAYANA, *Dialogues in
> Limbo (1925)*

14. I have never been able to accept
the two great laws of humanity—that
you're always being suppressed if
you're inspired and always being
pushed into a corner if you're exceptional. I won't be cornered and I
won't stay suppressed.

—MARGARET ANDERSON, *My Thirty Years' War (1930)*

15. No man needs curing of his individual sickness; his universal malady is what he should look to.
—DJUNA BARNES, *Nightwood (1936)*

16. The desires of the heart are as crooked as corkscrews / Not to be born is the best for man.
—W. H. AUDEN, *"Letter to William Coldstream, Esq." (1937)*

17. Well, of course, people are only human. . . . But it really does not seem much for them to be.
—IVY COMPTON-BURNETT, *A Family and a Fortune (1939)*

18. There's nothing that makes you so aware of the improvisation of human existence as a song unfinished. Or an old address book.
—CARSON MCCULLERS, *The Ballad of the Sad Café (1951)*

19. We're all of us guinea pigs in the laboratory of God. Humanity is just a work in progress.
—TENNESSEE WILLIAMS, *Camino Real (1953)*

20. I have learned that neither kindness or cruelty by themselves, or independent of each other, create any effect beyond themselves.
—EDWARD ALBEE, *The Zoo Story (1958)*

21. Once she had loved her fellow human beings; she did not love them now, she had seen them do too many unpleasant things.
—L. P. HARTLEY, *Facial Justice (1960)*

22. One can redeem skeletons and abandoned cities as human. But not a lost, dehumanized nature.
—SUSAN SONTAG, *Death Kit (1967)*

23. Misanthropy is a realistic attitude toward human nature that falls short of the incontinent emotional dependency expressed by Barbra Streisand's anthem to insecurity, "Peepul who need peepul are the luckiest peepul in the world."
—FLORENCE KING, *With Charity Toward None (1992)*

24. If you are a human being, you might as well face it. You are going to rub a lot of people the wrong way.
—JANE WAGNER, *My Life, So Far (1994)*

H u m o r

1. And if I laugh at any mortal thing, / 'Tis that I may not weep.
   —*GEORGE GORDON, LORD BYRON, Don Juan (1819–24)*

2. A laugh's the wisest, easiest answer to all that's queer.
   —*HERMAN MELVILLE, Moby-Dick (1851)*

3. Humor is so blessed a thing, that even in the least virtuous product of the human mind, if there can be found but nine good jokes, some philosophers are clement enough to affirm that those should redeem all the wicked thoughts, though plenty as the populace of Sodom.
   —*HERMAN MELVILLE, The Confidence-Man (1857)*

4. How fatally the entire want of humor cripples the mind.
   —*ALICE JAMES (1889), in Anna Robeson Burr, Alice James (1934)*

5. Laughter is not at all a bad beginning for a friendship, and it is far the best ending for one.
   —*OSCAR WILDE, The Picture of Dorian Gray (1891)*

6. It is difficult to like anybody else's idea of being funny.
   —*GERTRUDE STEIN, Everybody's Autobiography (1937)*

7. Humour teaches tolerance.
   —*W. SOMERSET MAUGHAM, The Summing Up (1938)*

8. A total absence of humor renders life impossible.
   —*COLETTE, Gigi (1952)*

9. I have a fine sense of the ridiculous, but no sense of humor.
   —*EDWARD ALBEE, Who's Afraid of Virginia Woolf? (1962)*

10. I used to think that everything was just being funny but now I don't know. I mean, how can you tell?
    —*ANDY WARHOL, in Vogue, March 1970*

11. Seriousness is the refuge of the shallow. There are events and personal experiences that call forth seriousness but they are fewer than most of us think.
    —*RITA MAE BROWN, Starting from Scratch (1988)*

Hypocrisy

1. Hypocrite reader, my likeness, my brother!
   —*Charles Baudelaire*, "Au Lecteur," *Les fleurs du mal* (1857)

2. I hope you have not been leading a double life, pretending to be wicked and being really good all the time. That would be hypocrisy.
   —*Oscar Wilde*, *The Importance of Being Earnest* (1895)

3. That vice pays homage to virtue is notorious; we call it hypocrisy.
   —*Samuel Butler* (d. 1902), *The Way of All Flesh* (1903)

4. A criminal is twice a criminal when he adds hypocrisy to his crime.
   —*Marie Corelli*, *Free Opinions* (1905)

5. The true hypocrite is the one who ceases to perceive his deception, the one who lies with sincerity.
   —*André Gide*, *Journal of "The Counterfeiters"* (1921)

6. Hypocrisy is the most difficult and nerve-racking vice that any man can pursue; it needs an unceasing vigilance and a rare detachment of spirit. It cannot, like adultery or gluttony, be practiced at spare moments; it is a whole-time job.
   —*W. Somerset Maugham*, *Cakes and Ale* (1930)

7. The only thing worse than a liar is a liar that's also a hypocrite!
   —*Tennessee Williams*, *The Rose Tattoo* (1951)

Ideals

1. If you have built castles in the air, your work need not be lost; that is where they should be. Now put the foundations under them.
   —*HENRY DAVID THOREAU,*
   "Conclusion," Walden (1854)

2. A map of the world that does not include Utopia is not worth even glancing at, for it leaves out the one country at which Humanity is always landing.
   —*OSCAR WILDE, "The Soul of Man*
   Under Socialism" (1895)

3. Ideal society is a drama enacted exclusively in the imagination.
   —*GEORGE SANTAYANA, The Life of*
   Reason (1906)

4. You can tell the ideals of a nation by its advertisements.
   —*NORMAN DOUGLAS, South Wind*
   (1917)

5. The ideal has many names, and beauty is but one of them.
   —*W. SOMERSET MAUGHAM, Cakes*
   and Ale (1930)

6. Noble values, in the end, are always overcome; history tells the story of their defeat over and over again.
   —*HENRY DE MONTHERLANT, La*
   Maître de Santiago (1947)

7. Positive ideals are becoming a curse, for they can seldom be achieved without someone being killed or maimed or interned.
   —*E. M. FORSTER, Two Cheers for*
   Democracy (1951)

Ideas

1. Do not despise my opinion, when I remind you that it should not be hard for you to stop sometimes and look into the stains of walls, or ashes of a fire, or clouds, or mud or like places, in which, if you consider them well, you may find really marvellous ideas.

—*LEONARDO DA VINCI, Notebooks*
(c. 1500)

2. The difficulty lies, not in the new ideas, but in escaping from the old ones, which ramify, for those brought up as most of us have been, into every corner of our minds.
—*JOHN MAYNARD KEYNES, The*
General Theory of Employment,
Interest and Money (1936)

3. One can live in the shadow of an idea without grasping it.
—*ELIZABETH BOWEN, The Heat of*
the Day (1949)

4. Like an enormous walnut in feeble, jittery squirrel hands, an idea, bigger and closer than any idea he had ever known, had been revolving in his mind for several days.
—*PATRICIA HIGHSMITH, Strangers on*
a Train (1950)

5. I had never been as resigned to ready-made ideas as I was to ready-made clothes, perhaps because, although I couldn't sew, I could think.
—*JANE RULE, Lesbian Images*
(1975)

6. The most interesting ideas are heresies.
—*SUSAN SONTAG, in Salmagundi,*
fall-winter 1975

7. There are no new ideas. There are only new ways of making them felt.
—*AUDRE LORDE, "Poetry Is Not a*
Luxury" (1977)

8. Talk uses up ideas. . . . Once I have spoken them aloud, they are lost to me, dissipated into the noisy air like smoke. Only if I bury them, like bulbs, in the rich soil of silence do they grow.
—*DORIS GRUMBACH, Fifty Days of*
Solitude (1994)

Identity   and   Individuality

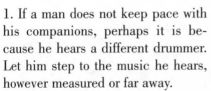

1. If a man does not keep pace with his companions, perhaps it is because he hears a different drummer. Let him step to the music he hears, however measured or far away.
—*HENRY DAVID THOREAU,*
"Conclusion," Walden (1854)

2. I / is another.
—*ARTHUR RIMBAUD, letter,*
13 May 1871

3. At every single moment of one's life one is what one is going to be no less than what one has been.

—OSCAR WILDE, *De Profundis*
(1897)

4. Do you know what individuality
is? . . . Consciousness of will. To be
conscious that you have a will and
can act.
—KATHERINE MANSFIELD, *journal
entry*, 30 September 1922

5. Rose is a rose is a rose is a rose.
—GERTRUDE STEIN, *"Sacred
Emily," Geography and Plays*
(1922)

6. A strong sense of identity gives
man an idea he can do no wrong; too
little accomplishes the same.
—DJUNA BARNES, *Nightwood*
(1936)

7. The minute you or anybody else
knows what you are you are not it,
you are what you or anybody else
knows you are and as everything in
living is made up of finding out what
you are it is extraordinarily difficult
really not to know what you are and
yet to be that thing.
—GERTRUDE STEIN, *Everybody's
Autobiography* (1937)

8. You were no locomotive, Sunflower, you were a sunflower! / And
you Locomotive, you are a locomotive, forget me not!

—ALLEN GINSBERG, *"Sunflower
Sutra," Howl and Other Poems*
(1956)

9. Every man carries with him
through life a mirror, as unique and
impossible to get rid of as his
shadow.
—W. H. AUDEN, *The Dyer's Hand*
(1962)

10. Promiscuous homosexuals (out-
laws with dual identities—tomorrow
they will go to offices and athletic
fields, classrooms and construction
sites) are the shock troops of the sexual revolution.
—JOHN RECHY, *The Sexual Outlaw*
(1977)

11. If we, as lesbians and gay men,
continue to speak of ourselves and
conceive of ourselves as women and
as men, we are instrumental in main-
taining heterosexuality.
—MONIQUE WITTIG, *"The Straight
Mind"* (1980)

12. Identity would seem to be the
garment with which one covers the
nakedness of the self: in which case,
it is best that the garment be loose, a
little like the robes of the desert,
through which one's nakedness can
always be felt, and, sometimes, dis-
cerned. This trust in one's nakedness
is all that gives one the power to
change one's robes.
—JAMES BALDWIN, *The Price of the
Ticket* (1985)

Ignorance

1. Nothing is so good for an ignorant man as silence, and if he knew this he would no longer be ignorant.
   —SA'DI, *Gulistan (1258)*

2. It is well known, that among the blind the one-eyed man is king.
   —DESIDERIUS ERASMUS, *Adagia (1500)*

3. O thou monster ignorance, how deformed dost thou look!
   —WILLIAM SHAKESPEARE, *Love's Labour's Lost (1594–95)*

4. Such horrid Ignorance benights the Times, / That Wit and Honour are become our Crimes.
   —KATHERINE PHILIPS, *"The Prince of Phancy" (1664)*

5. Ignorance is not innocence.
   —CHRISTINA, QUEEN OF SWEDEN, *Maxims (1660–80)*

6. Where ignorance is bliss, / 'Tis folly to be wise.
   —THOMAS GRAY, *Ode on a Distant Prospect of Eton College (1742)*

7. Ignorance and bungling with love are better than wisdom and skill without.
   —HENRY DAVID THOREAU, *A Week on the Concord and Merrimack Rivers (1849)*

8. Ignorance is the parent of fear.
   —HERMAN MELVILLE, *Moby-Dick (1851)*

9. There is that indescribable freshness and unconsciousness about an illiterate person that humbles and mocks the power of the noblest expressive genius.
   —WALT WHITMAN, preface, *Leaves of Grass (1855)*

10. As towards most other things of which we have but little personal experience (foreigners, or socialists, or aristocrats, as the case may be), there is a degree of vague ill-will towards what is called *Thinking*.
    —VERNON LEE, *Hortus Vitae (1904)*

11. A so-called Lesbian alliance can be of rarefied purity, and those who do not believe it are merely judging in ignorance of the facts.
    —ELISABETH CRAIGIN, *Either Is Love (1937)*

12. Too many of our countrymen rejoice in stupidity, look upon ignorance as a badge of honor. They con-

demn everything they don't understand.

    —*TALLULAH BANKHEAD, Tallulah (1952)*

13. At my back I hear the word—"homosexual"—and it seems to split my world in two. . . . It is ignorance, our ignorance of one another, that creates this terrifying erotic chaos. Information, a crumb of information, seems to light the world.

    —*JOHN CHEEVER, diary entry, 1966; John Cheever: The Journals (1991)*

14. I pounded on my car and screamed, "They misspelled it! They misspelled it!" For some reason, that offended me more than anything else.

    —*ELAINE NOBLE, after finding "Lesbean" scratched on her car; quoted in The Advocate, 6 October 1992*

Illness

1. She says her blood is nothing but rose-water.

    —*RONALD FIRBANK, Valmouth (1918)*

2. Disease makes men more physical, it leaves them nothing but body.

    —*THOMAS MANN, The Magic Mountain (1924)*

3. The diseases which destroy a man are no less natural than the instincts which preserve him.

    —*GEORGE SANTAYANA, Dialogues in Limbo (1925)*

4. Those who have never been ill are incapable of real sympathy for a great many misfortunes.

    —*ANDRÉ GIDE, Journals, 25 July 1930*

5. Her illness seemed to be one prolonged mistake. Her self looked, wildly smiling, out of her body: what was happening in here was too terrible to acknowledge; she had to travesty it and laugh it off. Unserene, she desperately kept her head.

    —*ELIZABETH BOWEN, The House in Paris (1935)*

6. Remembering that Alison was not well, Leonora tried to look sickly also, as that was her notion of the proper behavior in a sickroom.

    —*CARSON MCCULLERS, Reflections in a Golden Eye (1941)*

7. Every invalid is a prisoner.
—*MARGUERITE YOURCENAR, Memoirs of Hadrian (1951)*

8. Illness is the night-side of life, a more onerous citizenship. Everyone who is born holds dual citizenship, in the kingdom of the well and in the kingdom of the sick. Although we prefer to use only the good passport, sooner or later each of us is obliged, at least for a spell, to identify ourselves as citizens of that other place.
—*SUSAN SONTAG, Illness as Metaphor (1978)*

Imprisonment

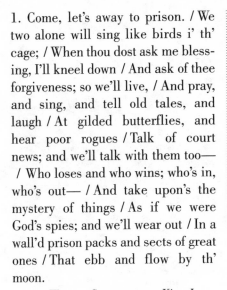

1. Come, let's away to prison. / We two alone will sing like birds i' th' cage; / When thou dost ask me blessing, I'll kneel down / And ask of thee forgiveness; so we'll live, / And pray, and sing, and tell old tales, and laugh / At gilded butterflies, and hear poor rogues / Talk of court news; and we'll talk with them too— / Who loses and who wins; who's in, who's out— / And take upon's the mystery of things / As if we were God's spies; and we'll wear out / In a wall'd prison packs and sects of great ones / That ebb and flow by th' moon.
—*WILLIAM SHAKESPEARE, King Lear (1605–6)*

2. My very chains and I grew friends, / So much a long communion tends / To make us what we are: even I / Regain'd my freedom with a sigh.
—*GEORGE GORDON, LORD BYRON, "The Prisoner of Chillon" (1816)*

3. Under a government which imprisons any unjustly, the true place for a just man is also prison.
—*HENRY DAVID THOREAU, Civil Disobedience (1849)*

4. I never saw a man who looked / With such a wistful eye / Upon that little tent of blue / Which prisoners call the sky.
—*OSCAR WILDE, The Ballad of Reading Gaol (1898)*

5. Anyone who has been to an English public school will always feel comparatively at home in prison. It is the people brought up in the gay intimacy of the slums who find prison so soul-destroying.

—EVELYN WAUGH, *Decline and Fall*
(1928)

6. Up to that time I had never conceived the possibility of anybody
being in prison, anybody whose business it was not naturally because of
natural or accidental crime to be in
prison, and in California in those
days even natural or accidental
crime did not mean prison. And now
in 1943 the large part of the men of a
whole nation are in prison. . . .
Anybody can be a prisoner now. . . .
Oscar Wilde and the Ballad of
Reading Gaol was the first thing that
made me realise that it could happen, being in prison.
  —GERTRUDE STEIN, *Wars I Have
    Seen (1946)*

7. It was better to be in a jail where
you could bang the walls than in a
jail you could not see.
  —CARSON MCCULLERS, *The Member
    of the Wedding (1946)*

8. Here is all straight and narrow as
a tomb / Oh shut me not within a little room.
  —STEVIE SMITH, *"The Commuted
    Sentence," Harold's Leap (1950)*

9. Caged birds accept each other but
flight is what they long for.
  —TENNESSEE WILLIAMS, *Camino
    Real (1953)*

10. I met a man . . . who was celebrated because he had spent half his
life in prison. He had then written a
book about it which displeased the
prison authorities and won a literary
prize. But this man's life was over.
He was fond of saying that, since to
be in prison was simply not to live,
the death penalty was the only mer-
ciful verdict any jury could deliver. I
remember thinking that, in effect, he
had never left prison. Prison was all
that was real to him; he could speak
of nothing else.
  —JAMES BALDWIN, *Giovanni's Room
    (1956)*

11. Before, I had been vaguely conscious of something rotten somewhere; prison crystallized this. The
old whore society lifted up her skirts,
and the stench was pretty foul. Not
that the actual prison treatment was
bad; but it was a revelation of what
really lies under the surface of our
industrialized society.
  —JOE ORTON (d. 1967), on his
    imprisonment for "malicious
    damage" to library books; quoted
    in John Lahr, introduction, Joe
    Orton: The Complete Plays
    (1976)

12. Outside of this cell we may have
our oppressors, yes, but not inside.
Here no one oppresses the other. The
only thing that seems to disturb me
. . . because I'm exhausted, or conditioned, or perverted . . . is that someone wants to be nice to me, without
asking anything back for it.
  —MANUEL PUIG, *Kiss of the Spider
    Woman (1978)*

Inanimate Objects

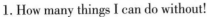

1. How many things I can do without!
   —SOCRATES (5th century BCE), upon
   goods in the marketplace; in
   Diogenes Laertius (3rd century
   BCE), Vitae Philosophorum

2. I have loved ships, as I have loved men.
   —HERMAN MELVILLE, Mardi (1849)

3. That irregular and intimate quality of things made entirely by the human hand.
   —WILLA CATHER, Death Comes for
   the Archbishop (1927)

4. Tools have their own integrity.
   —VITA SACKVILLE-WEST, "Summer,"
   The Land (1927)

5. I instinctively like to acquire and store up what promises to outlast me.
   —COLETTE, Break of Day (1928)

6. It matters less to venerate things than to live with them on terms of good friendship.

   —ADRIENNE MONNIER (1938), in
   Richard McDougall, trans., The
   Very Rich Hours of Adrienne
   Monnier (1976)

7. After inside upheavals, it is important to fix on imperturbable things. Their imperturbableness, their air that nothing has happened renews our guarantee.
   —ELIZABETH BOWEN, The Death of
   the Heart (1938)

8. I think that cars today are almost the exact equivalent of the great Gothic cathedrals: I mean the supreme creation of an era, conceived with passion by unknown artists, and consumed in image if not in usage by a whole population which appropriates them as a purely magical object.
   —ROLAND BARTHES, Mythologies
   (1957)

9. Why grab possessions like thieves, or divide them like socialists when you can ignore them like wise men?
   —NATALIE CLIFFORD BARNEY, "My
   Country 'tis of Thee" (1962)

Innocence

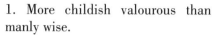

1. More childish valourous than manly wise.
   —*CHRISTOPHER MARLOWE,*
   Tamburlaine the Great (1587)

2. He is reported to be so strict an observer of chastity that he knows not in what consists the difference of man and woman.
   —*MATTHEW G. LEWIS, The Monk*
   (1795)

3. Innocence is my redress.
   —*HERMAN MELVILLE, The*
   Confidence-Man (1857)

4. Nothing looks so like innocence as an indiscretion.
   —*OSCAR WILDE, Lady Windermere's*
   Fan (1892)

5. All happiness is a form of innocence.
   —*MARGUERITE YOURCENAR, Alexis*
   (1929)

6. The innocent are so few that two of them seldom meet—when they do meet, their victims lie strewn all round.
   —*ELIZABETH BOWEN, The Death of*
   the Heart (1938)

7. There is so little basic difference between total innocence and complete degradation.
   —*MARGUERITE YOURCENAR, Coup de*
   Grâce (1939)

8. No, it is not only our fate but our business to lose innocence, and once we have lost that, it is futile to attempt a picnic in Eden.
   —*ELIZABETH BOWEN, "Out of a*
   Book" (1946)

9. Innocence is not pure so much as pleased, / Always expectant, bright-eyed, self-enclosed.
   —*MAY SARTON, "Giant in the*
   Garden" (1953)

10. Anyone who insists on remaining in a state of innocence long after that innocence is dead turns himself into a monster.
    —*JAMES BALDWIN, Notes of a Native*
    Son (1955)

11. I am not innocent. Innocence is a science of the sublime. And I am only at the very beginning of the apprenticeship.
    —*HÉLÈNE CIXOUS, Vivre*
    l'Orange/To Live the Orange
    (1979)

Intellectuals and Academics

1. Ask a wise man to dinner and he'll upset everyone by his gloomy silence or tiresome questions. Invite him to a dance and you'll have a camel prancing about. Haul him off to a public entertainment and his face will be enough to spoil the people's entertainment.
   —*DESIDERIUS ERASMUS, In Praise of Folly (1509)*

2. Annabel was accounted a beauty and intellectually gifted; she never played herring, and was reputed to have read Maeterlinck's *Life of the Bee*. If you abstain from tennis and read Maeterlinck in a small country village, you are of necessity intellectual.
   —*SAKI [H. H. MUNRO], "Reginald at the Theatre," Reginald (1904)*

3. A scholar's heart is a dark well in which are buried many aborted feelings that rise to the surface as arguments.
   —*NATALIE CLIFFORD BARNEY, Adventures of the Mind (1929)*

4. I've been called many things, but never an intellectual.
   —*TALLULAH BANKHEAD, Tallulah (1952)*

5. Everybody's always talking about people breaking into houses but there are more people in the world who want to break out of houses.
   —*THORNTON WILDER, The Matchmaker (1955)*

6. Intellectuals incline to be individualists, or even independents, are not team conscious and tend to regard obedience as a surrender of personality.
   —*HAROLD NICOLSON, in Observer, 12 October 1958*

7. The word "Intellectual" suggests straight away / A man who's untrue to his wife.
   —*W. H. AUDEN, "New Year Letter" (1961)*

8. Universities are filled with poets and novelists conducting demure and careful lives in imitation of Eliot and Forster and those others who (through what seems to have been discretion) made it.
   —*GORE VIDAL, Rocking the Boat (1962)*

Judgment

1. Forbear to judge, for we are sinners all.
    —*WILLIAM SHAKESPEARE, 2 Henry VI*
    (1592)

2. What judgment shall I dread, doing no wrong?
    —*WILLIAM SHAKESPEARE, The*
    Merchant of Venice (1596–97)

3. Take the whole populace for a judge, and you will long wait for a unanimous verdict.
    —*HERMAN MELVILLE, Mardi (1849)*

4. You must not judge by the work, but by the work in connection with the surroundings.
    —*SAMUEL BUTLER (d. 1902), The*
    Way of All Flesh (1903)

5. Other people's appetites easily appear excessive when one doesn't share them.
    —*ANDRÉ GIDE, The Counterfeiters*
    (1925); trans. Dorothy Bussy

6. If it has to choose who is to be crucified, the crowd will always save Barrabas.
    —*JEAN COCTEAU, Le Rappel à*
    l'Ordre (1926)

7. When we come to judge others it is not by ourselves as we really are that we judge them, but by an image that we have formed of ourselves from which we have left out everything that offends our vanity or would discredit us in the eyes of the world.
    —*W. SOMERSET MAUGHAM, The*
    Summing Up (1938)

8. What right have they to judge? To judge you they must have the capacity to feel as you feel. And who has? One in a thousand. You alone know how you have felt. And you alone know how unequal the battle has always been that your will has had to fight.
    —*TERENCE RATTIGAN, The Deep*
    Blue Sea (1952)

Justice and Injustice

1. It is said Socrates commits a crime by corrupting the young men and not recognizing the gods that the city recognizes, but some other new religion.
> —PLATO (4th century BCE),
> Apologia

2. Mankind censure injustice, fearing that they may be victims of it and not because they shrink from committing it.
> —PLATO (4th century BCE), The
> Republic

3. If you study the history and records of the world you must admit that the source of justice was the fear of injustice.
> —HORACE (1st century BCE),
> Satires I, 3

4. Use every man after his desert, and who should scape whipping?
> —WILLIAM SHAKESPEARE, Hamlet
> (1600–1601)

5. It is due to Justice that man is a God to man and not a wolf.
> —FRANCIS BACON (d. 1626), De
> Dignitate et Augmentis
> Scientiarum (1632)

6. Under a government which imprisons any unjustly, the true place for a just man is also a prison.
> —HENRY DAVID THOREAU, Civil
> Disobedience (1849)

7. Justice is my being allowed to do whatever I like. Injustice is whatever prevents my doing so.
> —SAMUEL BUTLER (d. 1902), Note
> Books (1912)

8. When the sense of justice seeks to express itself quite outside the regular channels of established government, it has set forth on a dangerous journey inevitably ending in disaster.
> —JANE ADDAMS, Twenty Years at
> Hull House (1910)

9. Justice and judgment lie often a world apart.
> —EMMELINE PANKHURST, My Own
> Story (1914)

10. Many die, many kill their bodies and souls, but they cannot kill the justice of God, even they cannot kill the eternal spirit. From their very degradation that eternal spirit will rise up to demand of the world compassion and justice.

—RADCLYFFE HALL, *The Well of*
Loneliness (1928)

11. Jesus would be framed and in jail
if he was living today.
—CARSON MCCULLERS, *The Heart Is*
a Lonely Hunter (1940)

12. Justice cannot be for one side
alone, but must be for both.

—ELEANOR ROOSEVELT,
"*My Day*," *newspaper column,*
15 October 1947

13. Social justice and compassion
are compatible with an intelligent
respect for private enterprise and law
and order.
—CAMILLE PAGLIA, *Sex, Art, and*
American Culture (1992)

Knowledge and Wisdom

1. We are in fact convinced that if we
are ever to have pure knowledge of
anything, we must get rid of the body
and contemplate things by themselves with the soul by itself. It
seems, to judge from the argument,
that the wisdom which we desire and
upon which we profess to have set
our hearts will be attainable only
when we are dead and not in our lifetime.
—SOCRATES (5th century BCE), *in*
Plato, Phaedo

2. I would rather excel in the knowledge of what is excellent, than in the
extent of my power.
—ALEXANDER THE GREAT
(4th century BCE), *in Plutarch*
(1st century), *Lives*

3. Knowledge is power.

—FRANCIS BACON, "*De Haeresibus*,"
Meditationes Sacrae (1597)

4. He that knew all that ever learning
writ, / Knew only this—that he knew
nothing yet.
—APHRA BEHN, *The Emperor of the*
Moon (1687)

5. Not by constraint or severity shall
you have access to true wisdom, but
by abandonment, and childlike
mirth. If you would know aught, be
gay before it.
—HENRY DAVID THOREAU, *Journal,*
23 June 1840

6. Suspect first and know next. True
knowledge comes but by suspicion
and revelation.
—HERMAN MELVILLE, *The*
Confidence-Man (1857)

7. There are only two kinds of people who are really fascinating—people who know absolutely everything, and people who know absolutely nothing.
>—OSCAR WILDE, *The Picture of Dorian Gray (1891)*

8. It is far safer to know too little than too much. People will condemn the one, though they will resent being called upon to exert themselves to follow the other.
>—SAMUEL BUTLER *(d. 1902), The Way of All Flesh (1903)*

9. Children with Hyacinth's temperament don't know better as they grow older; they merely know more.
>—SAKI *[H. H. Munro] (d. 1916), "Hyacinth," The Toys of Peace (1919)*

10. Can I ever know you / Or you know me?
>—SARA TEASDALE, *"The Mystery" (1920)*

11. It is a great nuisance that knowledge can be acquired only by hard work.
>—W. SOMERSET MAUGHAM, *Cakes and Ale (1930)*

12. To appear to be on the inside and know more than others about what is going on is a great temptation for most people. It is a rare person who is willing to seem to know less than he does.
>—ELEANOR ROOSEVELT, *This I Remember (1949)*

13. What we imagine knowledge to be: / dark, salt, clear, moving, utterly free.
>—ELIZABETH BISHOP, *"At the Fishhouses," A Cold Spring (1955)*

14. To know all is not to forgive all. It is to despise everybody.
>—QUENTIN CRISP, *The Naked Civil Servant (1968)*

15. I don't know nothing, I think. And glad of it.
>—ALICE WALKER, *The Color Purple (1982)*

Language

1. You taught me language, and my profit on't / Is I know how to curse.
>—*WILLIAM SHAKESPEARE, The Tempest (1611)*

2. No language is rude that can boast polite writers.
>—*AUBREY BEARDSLEY (d. 1898), The Story of Venus and Tannhäuser or Under the Hill (1907)*

3. "Basta!" his master replied with all the brilliant glibness of the Berlitz school.
>—*RONALD FIRBANK, The Flower Beneath the Foot (1923)*

4. Perhaps of all the creations of man language is the most astonishing.
>—*LYTTON STRACHEY, introduction to George Rylands, Words and Poetry (1928)*

5. All true language / is incomprehensible.
>—*ANTONIN ARTAUD, Ci-Gît (1947)*

6. Philosophy is a struggle against the bewitching of our minds by means of language.
>—*LUDWIG WITTGENSTEIN (d. 1951), Philosophical Investigations (1953)*

7. The root function of language is to control the universe by describing it.
>—*JAMES BALDWIN, Notes of a Native Son (1955)*

8. Any refusal of language is death.
>—*ROLAND BARTHES, Mythologies (1957)*

9. It is said that life and death are under the power of language.
>—*HÉLÈNE CIXOUS, Dedans (1969)*

10. Only where there is language is there world.
>—*ADRIENNE RICH, "The Demon Lover" (1969)*

11. Language is a skin: I rub my language against the other. It is as if I had words instead of fingers, or fingers at the tip of my words. My language trembles with desire.
>—*ROLAND BARTHES, A Lover's Discourse: Fragments (1977)*

12. Language is the road map of a culture. It tells you where its people come from and where they are going.
>—*RITA MAE BROWN, Starting from Scratch (1988)*

13. I didn't use language to make a war-zone of my heart.
> —*JEANETTE WINTERSON, Sexing the Cherry (1989)*

14. Language, as symbol, determines much of the nature and quality of our experience.
> —*SONIA JOHNSON, The Ship That Sailed into the Living Room (1991)*

15. The basic agreement between human beings, indeed what makes them human and makes them social, is language.
> —*MONIQUE WITTIG, "On the Social Contract," The Straight Mind (1992)*

16. Language casts sheaves of reality upon the social body, stamping it and violently shaping it.
> —*MONIQUE WITTIG, "The Mark of Gender," The Straight Mind (1992)*

Last   Words

▼

1. Crito, I owe a cock to Asclepius. Will you repay him?
> —*SOCRATES (399 BCE), in Plato (4th century BCE), Phaedo*

2. Courage! I have shown it for years; think you I shall lose it at the moment when my sufferings are to end?
> —*MARIE ANTOINETTE, QUEEN OF FRANCE, on the way to the guillotine (1793)*

3. Let us go in; the fog is rising.
> —*EMILY DICKINSON (1886), attributed*

4. One of us must go.
> —*OSCAR WILDE (1900), of himself and the wallpaper, attributed.*

5. Tell the boys to follow, to be faithful, to take me seriously.
> —*HENRY JAMES (1916), in H. Montgomery Hyde, Henry James at Home (1969)*

6. If this is dying, then I don't think much of it.
> —*LYTTON STRACHEY (1932), in Michael Holroyd, Lytton Strachey (1967)*

7. I've still so much music in my head. I have said nothing. I have so much to say.

> —*MAURICE RAVEL (1937), in Jourdan-Morhange, Ravel et Nous (1945)*

8. What is the answer? . . . In that case, what is the question?

> —*GERTRUDE STEIN (1946), in Alice B. Toklas, What Is Remembered (1963)*

9. Dying is a very dull, dreary affair. And my advice to you is to have nothing whatever to do with it.

> —*W. SOMERSET MAUGHAM (d. 1965), in Robin Maugham, Escape from the Shadows (1972)*

10. I don't want to be remembered as an old queen who died of AIDS.

> —*LIBERACE (d. 1987), in News of the World, 11 October 1987*

L a w

1. Amongst the learned the lawyers claim first place, the most self-satisfied class of people, as they roll their rock of Sisyphus and string together six hundred laws in the same breath, no matter whether relevant or not, piling up opinion on opinion and gloss upon gloss to make their profession seem the most difficult of all. Anything which causes trouble has special merit in their eyes.

> —*DESIDERIUS ERASMUS, In Praise of Folly (1509)*

2. The laws can't be enforced against the man who is the laws' master.

> —*BENVENUTO CELLINI, Autobiography (1566)*

3. Wrest once the law to your authority; / To do a great right do a little wrong.

> —*WILLIAM SHAKESPEARE, The Merchant of Venice (1596–97)*

4. Every law is an evil, for every law is an infraction of liberty.

> —*JEREMY BENTHAM, Principals of Morals and Legislation (1789)*

5. Are not laws dangerous which inhibit the passions? Compare the centuries of anarchy with those of the strongest legalism in any country you like and you will see that it is only when the laws are silent that the greatest actions appear.

—*MARQUIS DE SADE, L'Histoire de Juliette, ou les Prospérités du Vice (1797)*

6. It is not desirable to cultivate a respect for the law, so much as for the right. The only obligation which I have a right to assume is to do at any time what I think right.
—*HENRY DAVID THOREAU, Civil Disobedience (1849)*

7. No suicides permitted here, and no smoking in the parlour.
—*HERMAN MELVILLE, Moby-Dick (1851)*

8. It's a poor rule that won't work both ways.
—*HENRY JAMES, The American (1877)*

9. It is indeed a burning shame that there should be one law for men and another law for women. I think there should be no law for anybody.
—*OSCAR WILDE, in The Sketch, 9 January 1895*

10. "France or Italy. . . . There homosexuality is no longer criminal."

"You mean that a Frenchman could share with a friend and yet not go to prison?"

"Share? Do you mean unite? If both are of age and avoid public indecency, certainly."

"Will the law ever be that in England?"

"I doubt it. England has always been disinclined to accept human nature."
—*E. M. FORSTER, Maurice (1914; published 1971)*

11. Let God and man decree / Laws for themselves and not for me.
—*A. E. HOUSMAN, no. 12, Last Poems (1922)*

12. Do what thou wilt shall be the whole of the law.
—*ALEISTER CROWLEY, The Confessions of Aleister Crowley (1929)*

13. People starting with the idea that certain things are right and are the law, come to believe that others are right because they are the law.
—*W. SOMERSET MAUGHAM, A Writer's Notebook (1949)*

14. My law-givers are Erasmus and Montaigne, not Moses and Paul.
—*E. M. FORSTER, Two Cheers for Democracy (1951)*

15. Even an attorney of moderate talent can postpone doomsday year after year, for the system of appeals that pervades American jurisprudence amounts to a legalistic wheel of fortune, a game of chance, somewhat fixed in the favor of the criminal, that the participants play interminably.

—TRUMAN CAPOTE, *In Cold Blood*
(1965)

16. I remember how surprised I was when my first novel was about to be published and I was informed that I could be sued for anything any one of my characters said. "But I often don't agree with what they say," I protested. The lawyer was not interested in the clear distinction I make

between my voice and the voices of my characters. Neither, I have found, are many of my readers.
—JANE RULE, "Sexuality in
Literature," *Outlander (1981)*

17. The law is simply expediency wearing a long white dress.
—QUENTIN CRISP, *Manners from
Heaven (1984)*

Lesbians and Lesbianism

1. Without any men, you still manage to commit adultery.
—MARTIAL *(1st century), Satires,
I.90 ("To a Butch Lesbian");
trans. James J. Wilhelm*

2. In pity to our Sex sure thou wert sent, / That we might Love, and yet be Innocent: / For sure no Crime with thee we can commit; / Or if we shou'd—thy Form excuses it.
—APHRA BEHN, "To the Fair
Clarinda, Who Made Love to Me,
Imagin'd More Than Woman. By
Mrs. B." (1688)

3. I love, & only love, the fairer sex & thus beloved by them in turn, my heart revolts from any other love than theirs.

—ANNE LISTER, *journal (1821), I
Know My Own Heart, ed. Helena
Whitbread (1988)*

4. I cannot help thinking surely it was not platonic. Heaven forgive me, but I look within myself & doubt. I feel the infirmity of our nature and hesitate to pronounce such attachments uncemented by something more tender still than friendship.
—ANNE LISTER, *on the Ladies of
Llangolen; journal (1822), I
Know My Own Heart, ed. Helena
Whitbread (1988)*

5. The love of women for each other—so rapt, intense, so confiding close, so burning-passionate, / To

unheard deeds of sacrifice, of daring and devotion, prompting.

—*EDWARD CARPENTER, "A Mightier than Mammon," Towards Democracy (1883)*

6. The loves of women for each other grow more numerous each day, and I have pondered much why these things were. That so little should be said about them surprises me, for they are everywhere. . . . In these days, when any capable and careful woman can honorably earn her own support, there is no village that has not its examples of "two hearts in counsel," both of which are feminine.

—*FRANCES E. WILLARD, Glimpses of Fifty Years (1889)*

7. For the love between women is nothing like the love of men. I love you for yourself and not for myself. I desire from you only your smiling lips and the brightness of your gaze.

—*RENÉE VIVIEN (d. 1909), "Bona Dea" (1983)*

8. "More than once," Sir Oliver dryly replied, "I even married, *en seconde noces,* a Lesbian . . ."

"A native of Lesbos? Just fancy that!" the Baroness marvelled, appraising a passing débutante, a young girl in a mousseline robe of palest Langue de chat.

—*RONALD FIRBANK, The Artificial Princess (1915)*

9. These Sapphists love women; friendship is never untinged with amorosity.

—*VIRGINIA WOOLF, diary, 21 December 1925*

10. In my day I was a Pioneer and a Menace. [Lesbianism] was not then as it is now, chic . . . but as daring as a Crusade; for where now it leaves a woman talkative, so that we have not a Secret among us, then it left her in Tears and Trepidation. Then one had to lure them to the Breast, and now you have to smack them, back and front, to wean them at all.

—*DJUNA BARNES, Ladies Almanack (1928)*

11. [The] close resemblance [of two women] guarantees similarity in volupté. The love takes courage in her certainty of a body whose secrets she knows, whose preferences her own body has taught her.

—*COLETTE, Ces Plaisirs (1932)*

12. If Nature is to be invoked, one can say that all women are naturally homosexual. The lesbian, in fact, is distinguished by her refusal of the male and her liking for feminine flesh; but every adolescent female fears penetration and masculine domination, and she feels a certain repulsion for the male body; on the other hand the female body is for her as for the male, an object of desire.

—SIMONE DE BEAUVOIR, *The Second Sex (1949)*

13. The Lesbian is one of the least known members of our culture. Less is known about her—and less accurately—than about the Newfoundland dog.
    —SYDNEY ABBOTT AND BARBARA LOVE, *Sappho Was a Right-on Woman (1972)*

14. Once a woman is known as a Lesbian, both she and society often feel that no other fact about her can rival the sexual identification. . . . No matter what a Lesbian achieves, her sexuality will remain her *primary* identity.
    —SYDNEY ABBOTT AND BARBARA LOVE, *Sappho Was a Right-on Woman (1972)*

15. The Lesbian is every woman.
    —DEL MARTIN AND PHYLLIS LYON, *Lesbian/Woman (1972)*

16. All women are lesbians except those who don't know it naturally they are but don't know it yet I am a woman who is a lesbian because I am a woman.
    —JILL JOHNSTON, *Lesbian Nation (1973)*

17. The male party line concerning Lesbians is that women become Lesbians out of reaction to men. This is a pathetic illustration of the male

ego's inflated proportions. I became a Lesbian because of women, because women are beautiful, strong and compassionate.
    —RITA MAE BROWN, *A Plain Brown Rapper (1976)*

18. The lesbian gaze is a transgressive act.
    —MICHEL FOUCAULT, *in Donald F. Bouchard, ed., Language, Counter-Memory, Practice (1977)*

19. Two women in a ring of flesh, as if they were continually giving birth to each other, may go back as far as Sappho, but as a symbol they have more in common with war than with peace, fission rather than fusion, destructive of all holy clichés: motherhood, the family, maple syrup, our bacon wrapper flag!
    —JANE RULE, *Contract with the World (1980)*

20. Lesbian existence comprises both the breaking of a taboo and the rejection of a compulsory way of life. It is also a direct or indirect attack on the male right of access to women.
    —ADRIENNE RICH, *"Compulsory Heterosexuality and Lesbian Existence" (1980)*

21. It's those two new girls on the block, Harold, something about the way they walk, something about the way they talk . . . something about

the way they look . . . at each other.
. . . Harold, I could swear they're
Lebanese!

—HOLLY HUGHES, *The Well of
Horniness (1985)*

22. One of the first things a typical
lesbian learns is that there is no such
thing as a typical lesbian.

—YVONNE ZIPTER, *Diamonds Are a
Dyke's Best Friend (1988)*

23. A lesbian who does not reinvent
the world is a lesbian in the process
of disappearing.

—NICOLE BROSSARD, *The Aerial
Letter (1988); trans. Marlene
Wildeman*

Liberation

1. The shallow consider liberty a
release from all law, from every constraint. The wise see in it, on the contrary, the potent Law of Laws.

—WALT WHITMAN, *"Freedom,"
Notes Left Over (1881)*

2. Everywhere a new motive of life
dawns. / With the liberation of Love,
and with it of Sex, with the sense that
these are things—and the joy of
them—not to be dreaded or barred,
but to be made use of, wisely and
freely, as a man makes use of his
most honoured possession, / Comes a
new gladness.

—EDWARD CARPENTER, *"A Mightier
than Mammon," Towards
Democracy (1883)*

3. Ah! For a little directness to liberate the soul!

—E. M. FORSTER, *A Room with a
View (1908)*

4. We all have to rise in the end, not
just one or two who were smart
enough, had will enough for their
own salvation, but all the halt, the
maimed and the blind of us which is
most of us.

—MAUREEN DUFFY, *The Microcosm
(1966)*

5. The liberation of language is
rooted in the liberation of ourselves.

—MARY DALY, *Beyond God the
Father (1973)*

6. I love every "lib" movement there
is, because after the "lib" the things
that were always mystique become
understandable and boring, and then
nobody has to feel left out if they're
not part of what is happening.

—ANDY WARHOL, *The Philosophy of Andy Warhol: From A to B and Back Again (1975)*

7. Which me will survive all these liberations.
   —AUDRE LORDE, *"From a Land Where Other People Live" (1975)*

8. First you have to liberate the children (because they're the future) and then you have to liberate the men (because they've been so deformed by the system) and then if there's any liberation left you can take it into the kitchen and eat it.
   —JOANNA RUSS, *On Strike Against God (1980)*

9. It's so strange, you know, in the early seventies, one day half the women's movement came out as lesbians. It was like we were all sitting around and the ice cream came, and all of a sudden I looked around and everyone ran out for ice cream.
   —SARAH SCHULMAN, *The Sophie Horowitz Story (1984)*

L i e s

1. Marry, sir, they have committed false report, moreover they have spoken untruths, secondarily they are slanders, sixth and lastly they have belied a lady, thirdly they have verified unjust things, and to conclude, they are lying knaves!
   —WILLIAM SHAKESPEARE, *Much Ado About Nothing (1598)*

2. A mixture of a lie doth ever add pleasure.
   —FRANCIS BACON, *"Of Truth," Essays (1625)*

3. And, after all, what is a lie? 'Tis but / The truth in masquerade; and I defy / Historian—heroes—lawyers— priests, to put / A fact without some leaven of a lie.
   —GEORGE GORDON, LORD BYRON, *Don Juan (1819–24)*

4. Sometimes a lie is heavenly, and truth infernal.
   —HERMAN MELVILLE, *Pierre (1852)*

5. Young as he was, his instinct told him that the best liar is he who makes the smallest amount of lying go the longest way.
   —SAMUEL BUTLER (d. 1902), *The Way of All Flesh (1903)*

6. Lies are essential to humanity. They play perhaps as great a role as

the pursuit of pleasure, and are indeed controlled by this pursuit.
>—*MARCEL PROUST (d. 1922),*
>*Remembrance of Things Past:*
>*The Sweet Cheat Gone (1925)*

7. One of those telegrams of which the model had been wittily invented by M. de Guermantes: "Impossible to come, lie follows."
>—*MARCEL PROUST (d. 1922),*
>*Remembrance of Things Past:*
>*Time Regained (1926)*

8. Never to lie is to have no lock to your door.
>—*ELIZABETH BOWEN, The House in*
>*Paris (1935)*

9. In the theater lying is looked upon as an occupational disease.
>—*TALLULAH BANKHEAD, Tallulah*
>*(1952)*

10. Lying is the only art form that the public sanctions and instinctively prefers to reality.

>—*JEAN COCTEAU, Diary of an*
>*Unknown (1952)*

11. Mendacity is a system that we live in. Liquor is one way out an' death's the other.
>—*TENNESSEE WILLIAMS, Cat on a*
>*Hot Tin Roof (1955)*

12. Life is a system of half-truths and lies, / Opportunistic, convenient evasion.
>—*LANGSTON HUGHES, "Elderly*
>*Politicians" (1958)*

13. He will lie even when it is inconvenient, the sign of the true artist.
>—*GORE VIDAL, Two Sisters (1970)*

14. Lying is an elementary means of self-defense.
>—*SUSAN SONTAG, in Saturday*
>*Review, 23 September 1972*

15. Lying is done with words, and also with silence.
>—*ADRIENNE RICH, On Lies, Secrets,*
>*and Silences (1979)*

Life

1. The unexamined life is not worth living for a human being.
>—*SOCRATES, in Plato*
>*(4th century BCE), Apologia*

2. Too late is tomorrow's life; live for today.
>—*MARTIAL (1st century),*
>*Epigrams I, 15*

3. While I thought I was learning how to live, I have been learning how to die.
—*Leonardo da Vinci, Notebooks (c. 1500)*

4. It is a tale / Told by an idiot, full of sound and fury; / Signifying nothing.
—*William Shakespeare, Macbeth (1606)*

5. He did not think that it was necessary to make a hell of this world to enjoy paradise in the next.
—*William Beckford, Vathek (1786)*

6. Every man's life is a fairy-tale written by God's finger.
—*Hans Christian Andersen, preface, Works (1843)*

7. There are certain queer times and occasions in this strange mixed affair we call life when a man takes his whole universe for a vast practical joke.
—*Herman Melville, Moby-Dick (1851)*

8. You promise heavens free from strife, / Pure truth, and perfect change of will; / But sweet, sweet is this human life, / So sweet, I fain would breathe it still.
—*William Cory, "Mimnermus in Church," Ionica (1858)*

9. This life is a hospital in which every patient is possessed with a desire to change his bed.
—*Charles Baudelaire (d. 1867), Le Spleen de Paris (1869)*

10. Life is the farce which everyone has to perform.
—*Arthur Rimbaud, "Mauvais Sang," Une Saison en Enfer (1874)*

11. Life, Lady Stutfield, is simply a *mauvais quart d'heure* made up of exquisite moments.
—*Oscar Wilde, A Woman of No Importance (1893)*

12. Life is like playing a violin solo in public and learning the instrument as one goes on.
—*Samuel Butler, speech at the Somerville Club, 27 February 1895*

13. For he who lives more lives than one / More deaths than one must die.
—*Oscar Wilde, The Ballad of Reading Gaol (1898)*

14. To live is like to love—all reason is against it, and all healthy instinct for it.
—*Samuel Butler (d. 1902), Note Books (1912)*

15. Live all you can; it's a mistake not to. It doesn't so much matter what you do in particular, so long as you have had your life. If you haven't had that, what *have* you had?
—*Henry James, The Ambassadors (1903)*

16. To live solely for dress, or for what people so curiously misname "pleasure," to be spoken of invariably as "the aesthetic Lady Georgia" . . . is surely not to exhaust all the possible emotions of life?
>—RONALD FIRBANK, "A Tragedy in Green" (1907)

17. Life is easy to chronicle, but bewildering to practice, and we welcome "nerves" or any other shibboleth that will cloak our personal desires.
>—E. M. FORSTER, A Room with a View (1908)

18. There is no cure for birth and death save to enjoy the interval.
>—GEORGE SANTAYANA, Soliloquies in England (1922)

19. If you wish to live, you must first attend your own funeral.
>—KATHERINE MANSFIELD (d. 1923), in Antony Alpers, Katherine Mansfield (1954)

20. Life is not a series of gig lamps symmetrically arranged; life is a luminous halo, a semi-transparent envelope surrounding us from the beginning of consciousness to the end.
>—VIRGINIA WOOLF, "Modern Fiction," The Common Reader (1925)

21. Life is falling sideways.
>—JEAN COCTEAU, Opium (1930)

22. I have always had something to live besides a private life.
>—MARGARET ANDERSON, My Thirty Years' War (1930)

23. It's not true that life is one damn thing after another—it's one damn thing over and over.
>—EDNA ST. VINCENT MILLAY, letter to A. D. Fiske, 24 October 1930

24. What if—what if Life itself were the sweetheart?
>—WILLA CATHER, Lucy Gayheart (1935)

25. Love and life cannot help but marry and stay married with an exhausting violence of fidelity.
>—KATE O'BRIEN, Mary Lavelle (1936)

26. When we speak the word "life," it must be understood we are not referring to life as we know it from its surface of fact, but to that fragile, fluctuating center which forms never reach.
>—ANTONIN ARTAUD, The Theater and Its Double (1938)

27. *Weep for the lives your wishes never led.*
>—W. H. AUDEN, "Anthem for St. Cecilia's Day" (1941)

28. As regards plots I find real life no help at all. Real life seems to have no plots.

—Ivy Compton-Burnett, *quoted in Rosamund Lehmann et al., Orion I (1945)*

29. All of life is a foreign country.
—Jack Kerouac, *letter, 24 June 1949*

30. To face life without hope can mean to live without despair.
—Terence Rattigan, *The Deep Blue Sea (1952)*

31. Life was never life to me unless my heart stood still.
—Margaret Anderson, *The Fiery Fountains (1953)*

32. One of the real troubles with living is that living is so banal.
—James Baldwin, *Giovanni's Room (1956)*

33. Most people's lives—what are they but trails of debris, long long trails of debris with nothing to clean it all up but, finally, death?
—Tennessee Williams, *Suddenly, Last Summer (1958)*

34. We are involved in a life that passes understanding and our highest business is our daily life.
—John Cage, *"Where Are We Going? And What Are We Doing?" Silence (1961)*

35. Life was meant to be lived and curiosity must be kept alive. One must never, for whatever reason, turn one's back on life.
—Eleanor Roosevelt, *The Autobiography of Eleanor Roosevelt (1961)*

36. I have had such an uneventful life that there is little to say.
—Ivy Compton-Burnett, *A Family and a Fortune (1962)*

37. Human beings . . . they go on being born and dying, dying and being born. It's kind of boring, isn't it?
—Yukio Mishima, *"Sword" (1963)*

38. What is life? It is the flash of a firefly in the night. It is the breath of a buffalo in the wintertime. It is as the little shadow that runs across the grass and loses itself in the sunset.
—Truman Capote, *In Cold Blood (1965)*

39. Persons who merely have-a-life customarily move in a dense fluid. That's how they're able to conduct their lives at all. Their living depends on not seeing.
—Susan Sontag, *Death Kit (1967)*

40. You don't get to choose how you're going to die. Or when. You can only decide how you're going to live. Now.
—Joan Baez, *Daybreak (1968)*

41. Life was a funny thing that happened to me on the way to the grave.
—QUENTIN CRISP, *The Naked Civil Servant (1968)*

42. Life is a publicity stunt. A shill. You've been had.
—KATE MILLETT, *Flying (1974)*

43. Life is something to do when you can't get to sleep.
—FRAN LEBOWITZ, *in Observer, 1979*

44. Life is painful, nasty and short . . . in my case it has only been painful and nasty.
—DJUNA BARNES *(d. 1982), in Hank O'Neal, Life Is Painful, Nasty and Short (1991)*

45. You play, you win. You play, you lose. You play.
—JEANETTE WINTERSON, *The Passion (1987)*

46. Our lives are written in disappearing ink.
—MICHELLE CLIFF, *"Monster" (1991)*

47. Life ain't the movies.
—DOROTHY ALLISON, *Two or Three Things I Know for Sure (1995)*

Literature

1. There is no such thing as a moral or an immoral book. Books are well written, or badly written.
—OSCAR WILDE, *The Picture of Dorian Gray (1891)*

2. Literature is the record of our discontent.
—VIRGINIA WOOLF, *"The Evening Party" (1918)*

3. To turn events into ideas is the function of literature.
—GEORGE SANTAYANA, *Little Essays (1921)*

4. Remarks are not literature.
—GERTRUDE STEIN, *to Ernest Hemingway, The Autobiography of Alice B. Toklas (1933)*

5. It is noble sentiments that bad literature gets written.
—ANDRÉ GIDE, *Journal, 2 September 1940*

6. Surely it was time someone invented a new plot, or that the author came out of the bushes.
> —VIRGINIA WOOLF, *Between the Acts (1941)*

7. Literature is the orchestration of platitudes.
> —THORNTON WILDER, *in Time, 12 January 1953*

8. Novels, except as aids to masturbation, play no part in contemporary life.
> —GORE VIDAL, *Rocking the Boat (1962)*

9. Some books are undeservedly forgotten; none are undeservedly remembered.
> —W. H. AUDEN, *The Dyer's Hand (1962)*

10. The lesbian, without a literature, is without life. Sometimes pornographic, and sometimes a mark of fear, sometimes a sentimental flourish, she . . . floats in space . . . without that attachment to earth where growth is composed.
> —BERTHA HARRIS, *quoted in Adrienne Rich, "It is the Lesbian in Us . . ." (1976)*

11. To misappropriate Oscar Wilde's remark about the English and fox-hunting: *lesbian literature is the pursuit of the inedible by the unspeakable.* It is also the pursuit of the unspeakable by the inedible; and it is this particularly.
> —BERTHA HARRIS, *in Heresies, fall 1977*

12. Keats and Yeats are on your side / while Wilde is on mine.
> —MORRISSEY, *"Cemetry Gates" (1985)*

13. I suspect one of the reasons we create fiction is to make sex exciting.
> —GORE VIDAL, *in the Times Literary Supplement, 2 October 1987*

14. Don't ask to live in tranquil times. Literature doesn't grow there.
> —RITA MAE BROWN, *Starting from Scratch (1988)*

15. There is the view that poetry should improve your life. I think people confuse it with the Salvation Army.
> —JOHN ASHBERRY, *in International Herald Tribune, 2 October 1989*

16. Literature is a peculiarly public product of a particularly private endeavor.
> —VALERIE MINER, *Rumors from the Cauldron (1991)*

17. If I believe in anything, rather than God, it's that I am a part of something that goes back to *Antigone*

and that whatever speaks the truth of our hearts can only make us stronger.
> —PAUL MONETTE, *The Politics of Silence (1993)*

18. Literature is the lie that tells the truth.
> —DOROTHY ALLISON, *in The New York Times Book Review (1994)*

L o s s

1. Poor Catullus, stop this folly, / And what you see is lost consider to be lost.
> —CATULLUS *(1st century BCE), Carmina 8*

2. He who possesses most must be most afraid of loss.
> —LEONARDO DA VINCI, *Notebooks (c. 1500)*

3. It is a hard thing to have loved; it is a hard thing not to have loved. But harder than all else is to lose (or fail to gain) one's lover.
> —CHARLES MATURIN, *Melmoth the Wanderer (1820)*

4. 'Tis better to have loved and lost than never to have lost at all.
> —SAMUEL BUTLER *(d. 1902), The Way of All Flesh (1903)*

5. Give me a dozen such heartbreaks, if that would help me to lose a couple of pounds.
> —COLETTE, *Cheri (1920)*

6. The true paradises are paradises we have lost.
> —MARCEL PROUST *(d. 1922), Remembrance of Things Past: Time Regained (1926)*

7. He's lost him completely, as though he had never existed. / Through fantasy, through hallucination, / he tries to find his lips in the lips of other young men, / he longs to feel his kind of love once more.
> —CONSTANTINE P. CAVAFY, *"In Despair" (1923)*

8. They lose least who have least to lose.
> —ROSE O'NEILL, *Garda (1929)*

9. The loss of love is a terrible thing; / They lie who say death is worse.
> —COUNTEE CULLEN *(d. 1946), "Variations on a Theme (The Loss of Love)," On These I Stand (1947)*

10. We only keep what we lose.
    —MAY SARTON, "O Saisons!
    O Châteaux!" (1948)

11. It is better to be drunk with loss and to beat the ground, than to let the deeper things gradually escape.
    —IVY COMPTON-BURNETT (1969),
    quoted in Hilary Spurling, Ivy
    (1984)

12. So many things seem filled with the intent / to be lost that their loss is no disaster.

    —ELIZABETH BISHOP, "One Art"
    (1969)

13. All the agony of that severance fresh as a dismembered limb.
    —KATE MILLETT, Sita (1976)

14. I still miss those I loved who are no longer with me but I find I am grateful for having loved them. The gratitude has finally conquered the loss.
    —RITA MAE BROWN, Starting from
    Scratch (1988)

L o v e

1. You could mend my heart completely: / Let your lovely face gleam back at me / Touched by tears of Eros.
    —SAPPHO (7th century BCE),
    Fragment 4; trans. Anita George

2. When desire, having rejected reason and overpowered judgment which leads to right, is set in the direction of the pleasure which beauty can inspire, and when again under the influence of its kindred desires it is moved with violent motion towards the beauty of corporeal forms, it acquires a surname from this very violent motion, and is called love.
    —SOCRATES (5th century BCE), in
    Plato (4th century BCE),
    Phaedrus

3. Human nature was originally one and we were a whole, and the desire and the pursuit of the whole is called love.
    —PLATO (4th century BCE),
    Symposium

4. Love conquers all [Omnia vincit Amor].
    —VIRGIL, Eclogues (43–37 BCE)

5. Words have no language which can utter the secrets of love; and beyond the limits of expression is the expounding of desire.

> —HAFIZ *(14th century), Ghazal 46, The Divan*

6. Who ever loved, that loved not at first sight?

> —CHRISTOPHER MARLOWE, *Hero and Leander (1593)*

7. Come live with me, and be my love, / And we will all the pleasures prove, / That valleys, groves, hills and fields, / Woods or steepy mountain yields.

> —CHRISTOPHER MARLOWE *(d. 1593),* "The Passionate Shepherd to His Love" *(1599)*

8. The course of true love never did run true.

> —WILLIAM SHAKESPEARE, *A Midsummer Night's Dream (1596)*

9. I do love nothing in the world so well as you. Is not that strange?

> —WILLIAM SHAKESPEARE, *Much Ado About Nothing (1598)*

10. Let me not to the marriage of true minds / Admit impediments. Love is not love / Which alters when it alteration finds, / Or bends with the remover to remove. / O no, it is an ever fixèd mark / That looks on tempests and is never shaken; / It is the star to every wand'ring barque, /

Whose worth's unknown although his height be taken.

> —WILLIAM SHAKESPEARE, *Sonnet 116 (1609)*

11. If you remember the power you have over me, you will also remember that I have been in possession of your love for twelve years; I belong to you so utterly, that it will never be possible for you to lose me; and only when I die shall I cease loving you.

> —CHRISTINA, QUEEN OF SWEDEN *(17th century), letter to Ebba Sparre, her lady-in-waiting; in Margaret Goldsmith, Christina of Sweden (1935)*

12. No bridegroom's nor crown-conqueror's mirth / To mine compar'd can be: / They have but pieces of the earth, / I've all the world in thee.

> —KATHERINE PHILIPS, "To My Excellent Lucasia, on Our Friendship" *(1664)*

13. [Love,] That cordial drop heaven in our cup has thrown / To make the nauseous draught of life go down.

> —JOHN WILMOT, EARL OF ROCHESTER, "A letter from Artemisa in the Town to Chloe in the Country" *(1679)*

14. Love's a thin Diet, nor will it keep out Cold.

> —APHRA BEHN, *The Lucky Chance (1687)*

15. Love, that made me timid, taught me to be tender too.

—JOHN CLELAND, *Memoirs of a Woman of Pleasure (1749)*

16. In love, or unhappy—it is the same thing. Is anybody unhappy about another unless they are in love with them?
    —HORACE WALPOLE, *The Castle of Otranto (1764)*

17. Camerado, I give you my hand! / I give you my love more precious than money, / I give you myself before preaching or law; / Will you give me yourself?
    —WALT WHITMAN, *"Song of the Open Road," Leaves of Grass (1855)*

18. I love thee, I love but thee, / With a love that shall not die. / Till the sun grows old, / And the stars are cold, / And the leaves of the Judgment Book unfold.
    —BAYARD TAYLOR, *"Bedouin Song" (1855)*

19. 'Till I loved / I never lived—Enough.
    —EMILY DICKINSON, *no. 549 (c. 1862), Complete Poems (1955)*

20. Love must be reinvented.
    —ARTHUR RIMBAUD, *"Une Saison en Enfer" (1873)*

21. "The Love that dare not speak its name" in this century is such a great affection of an elder for a younger man as there was between David and Jonathan, such as Plato made the very basis of his philosophy, and such as you find in the sonnets of Michelangelo and Shakespeare. It is that deep, spiritual affection that is as pure as it is perfect. . . . It is in this century misunderstood . . . and on account of it I am placed where I am now.
    —OSCAR WILDE, *statement made at his trial for "indecent acts" (Regina v. Wilde and Taylor), 30 April 1895*

22. Love clamors far more incessantly and passionately at a closed gate than an open one!
    —MARIE CORELLI, *The Master Christian (1900)*

23. Not to believe in love is a great sign of dullness.
    —GEORGE SANTAYANA, *The Life of Reason (1906)*

24. Love felt and returned, love which our bodies exact and our hearts have transfigured, love which is the most real thing that we shall ever meet.
    —E. M. FORSTER, *A Room with a View (1908)*

25. Are there many things in this cool-hearted world so utterly exquisite as the pure love of one woman for another?
    —MARY MACLANE, *I, Mary MacLane (1917)*

26. There can be no peace of mind in love, since the advantage one has secured is never anything but a fresh starting-point for further desires.

—*MARCEL PROUST, Remembrance of Things Past: Within a Budding Grove (1918)*

27. In its early stage love is shaped by desire; later on it is kept alive by anxiety. In painful anxiety as in joyful desire, love insists upon everything. It is born and it thrives only if something remains to be won.

—*MARCEL PROUST (d. 1922), Remembrance of Things Past: The Captive (1923)*

28. We love only what we do not completely possess.

—*MARCEL PROUST (d. 1922), Remembrance of Things Past: The Captive (1923)*

29. I know I am but summer to your heart, / and not the full four seasons of the year.

—*EDNA ST. VINCENT MILLAY, "I Know I Am But Summer" (1923)*

30. It is love, not reason, that is stronger than death.

—*THOMAS MANN, The Magic Mountain (1924)*

31. Love is a game—yes? / I think it is a drowning.

—*AMY LOWELL, XIX, "Twenty-four Hokku on a Modern Theme" (1925)*

32. I'd always rather be with people who loved me too little rather than with people who loved me too much.

—*KATHERINE MANSFIELD (1919), The Journal of Katherine Mansfield (1927)*

33. Could loving, as people called it, make her and Mrs Ramsay one? for it was not knowledge but unity she desired, not inscriptions on tablets, nothing that could be written in any language known to men, but intimacy itself, which is knowledge, she had thought, leaning her head on Mrs Ramsay's knee.

—*VIRGINIA WOOLF, To the Lighthouse (1927)*

34. Love had a thousand shapes.

—*VIRGINIA WOOLF, To the Lighthouse (1927)*

35. I love my love with a y because she is my bride / I love her with a d because she is my love beside

—*GERTRUDE STEIN, "Before the Flowers of Friendship Faded Friendship Faded" (1931)*

36. What is the main thing in love? to know and to hide. To know about the one you love and to hide that you love. At times the hiding (shame) overpowers the knowing (passion). The passion for the hidden—the passion for the revealed.

—*MARINA TSVETAEVA, The House at Old Pimen (1934)*

37. It was a great holiness, a religion, as all great loves must be.
—*ELSIE DE WOLFE, After All (1935)*

38. I loved you, so I drew these tides of men into my hands and wrote my will across the sky and stars.
—*T. E. LAWRENCE, dedication,
Seven Pillars of Wisdom (1935)*

39. When you love someone all your saved-up wishes start coming out.
—*ELIZABETH BOWEN, The Death of
the Heart (1938)*

40. I'm glad it cannot happen twice, the fever of first love.
—*DAPHNE DU MAURIER, Rebecca
(1938)*

41. Like love we don't know where or why.
—*W. H. AUDEN, "Law Like Love"
(1939)*

42. If love is the best thing in life, then the best part of love is the kiss.
—*THOMAS MANN, Lotte in Weimar
(1939)*

43. I'll love you, dear, I'll love you /
Till China and Africa meet.
—*W. H. AUDEN, "As I Walked Out
One Evening" (1940)*

44. I go where I love and where I am loved.
—*H.D. [HILDA DOOLITTLE], The
Flowering of the Rod (1946)*

45. Between women love is contemplative; caresses are intended less to gain possession of the other than gradually to re-create the self through her; separateness is abolished, there is no struggle, no victory, no defeat; in exact reciprocity each is at once subject and object, sovereign and slave; duality becomes mutuality.
—*SIMONE DE BEAUVOIR, The Second
Sex (1949)*

46. Love makes use of the worst traps. The least noble. The rarest. It exploits coincidence.
—*JEAN GENET, Our Lady of the
Flowers (1949)*

47. In real love you want the other person's good. In romantic love you want the other person.
—*MARGARET ANDERSON, The Fiery
Fountains (1953)*

48. Most of us would rather love than be loved. Almost everyone wants to be the lover. And the curt truth is that, in a deep secret way, the state of being beloved is intolerable to many. The beloved fears and hates the lover, and with the best of reasons. For the lover is forever trying to strip bare his beloved. The lover craves any possible relation with the beloved, even if this experience can cause him only pain.
—*CARSON MCCULLERS, The Ballad
of the Sad Café (1953)*

49. A lot of strange things have been done in the name of love. In the search for love. And for the love of women. Crazy, silly, unreasonable things.
> —ANN BANNON, *Journey to a Woman (1960)*

50. How do you know that love is gone? If you said that you would be there at seven, you get there by nine and he or she has not called the police yet—it's gone.
> —MARLENE DIETRICH, *Marlene Dietrich's ABC (1962)*

51. Love, like a sense of humor, is now claimed by everyone even though Love, like a sense of humor, is rather more rare than not, and to most of us poor muddlers unbearable at full strength.
> —GORE VIDAL, *Rocking the Boat (1962)*

52. I am the least difficult of men. All I want is boundless love.
> —FRANK O'HARA (d. 1966), *"Meditations in an Emergency" (1967)*

53. Love is the only effective counter to death.
> —MAUREEN DUFFY, *Wounds (1969)*

54. The pain of love is the pain of being alive. It's a perpetual wound.
> —MAUREEN DUFFY, *Wounds (1969)*

55. Love is the wild card of existence.
> —RITA MAE BROWN, *In Her Day (1976)*

56. To try to write love is to confront the *muck* of language: that region of hysteria where language is both *too much* and *too little*, excessive and impoverished.
> —ROLAND BARTHES, *A Lover's Discourse (1977)*

57. If love is the answer, could you rephrase the question?
> —LILY TOMLIN, in *Cosmopolitan, February 1980*

58. The love expressed between women is particular and powerful because we have had to love in order to live; love has been our survival.
> —AUDRE LORDE, quoted in Mari Evans, *Black Women Writers (1983)*

59. Loving you is like living in the war years.
> —CHERRÍE MORAGA, *Loving in the War Years (1983)*

60. Everyone wants Love to follow them / down their road.
> —JUDY GRAHN, *The Queen of Swords (1987)*

61. This idea that love overtakes you is nonsense. This is but a polite man-

ifestation of sex. To love another you have to undertake some fragment of their destiny.

—QUENTIN CRISP, in
New Statesman & Society,
9 August 1991

62. Why is it that the most unoriginal thing we can say to one another is still the thing we long to hear? "I love you" is always a quotation.

—JEANETTE WINTERSON, Written on the Body (1992)

63. Love demands expression. It will not stay still, stay silent, be good, be modest, be seen and not heard, no. It will break out in tongues of praise, the high note that smashes the glass and spills the liquid.

—JEANETTE WINTERSON, Written on the Body (1992)

Lovers

1. We that are true lovers run into strange capers.

—WILLIAM SHAKESPEARE, As You Like It (1599–1600)

2. They say all lovers swear more performance than they are able and yet reserve an ability that they never perform, vowing more than the perfection of ten and discharging less than the tenth part of one.

—WILLIAM SHAKESPEARE, Troilus and Cressida (1602)

3. Do you suppose you will find in me your ideal? / Do you think it is so easy to have me become your lover?

—WALT WHITMAN, "Are You the New Person Drawn to Me?" Leaves of Grass (1855)

4. One doesn't want a lover one pities.

—HENRY JAMES, Roderick Hudson (1876)

5. Lovers lying two and two / Ask not whom they sleep beside, / And the bridegroom all night through / Never turns him to the bride.

—A. E. HOUSMAN, poem 12, A Shropshire Lad (1896)

6. You are my lover and I am your mistress and kingdoms and empires

and governments have tottered and succumbed before now to that mighty combination.

> —*VIOLET TREFUSIS, letter to Vita Sackville-West, March 1919*

7. Lovers should also have their days off.

> —*NATALIE CLIFFORD BARNEY (d. 1972), in George Wickes, The Amazon of Letters (1976)*

8. The lover who does not forget *sometimes* dies from excess, fatigue, and the strain of memory.

> —*ROLAND BARTHES, A Lover's Discourse: Fragments (1977)*

9. For lovers, touch is metamorphosis. All the parts of their bodies seem to change, and seem to become something different and better.

> —*JOHN CHEEVER, "The Bus to St. James's," The Stories of John Cheever (1978)*

10. Secretly, we wish anyone we love will think exactly the way we do.

> —*KIM CHERNIN, In My Mother's House (1983)*

11. Lovers are not at their best when it matters. Mouths dry up, palms sweat, conversation flags and all the time the heart is threatening to fly from the body once and for all. Lovers have been known to have heart attacks. Lovers drink too much from nervousness and cannot perform. They do not stroke the favoured cat and their face-paint comes loose. This is not all. Whatever you have set store by, your dress, your dinner, your poetry, will go wrong.

> —*JEANETTE WINTERSON, The Passion (1987)*

12. As your lover describes you, so you are.

> —*JEANETTE WINTERSON, Sexing the Cherry (1989)*

Macho

1. You see that guy with the long, uncut hair, Decianus? / The one you're afraid of because of is glowering scowl? / The one who gabs about the Curii and other great heroes of the past? / Well, don't be afraid of that butch front. Yesterday he was a bride.

> —*MARTIAL (1st century), Satires I, 24; trans. James J. Wilhelm*

2. We'll have a swashing and a martial outside, / As many other mannish cowards have / That do outface it with their semblances.
　　—WILLIAM SHAKESPEARE, *As You Like It (1599–1600)*

3. The whole generation is womanized; the masculine tone is passing out of the world.
　　—HENRY JAMES, *The Bostonians (1886)*

4. Virility has now become self-conscious.
　　—VIRGINIA WOOLF, *A Room of One's Own (1929)*

5. He may have hair upon his chest / But, sister, so has Lassie.
　　—COLE PORTER, "I Hate Men," *Kiss Me Kate (1948)*

6. This sounds like a He-fellow, don't you think? / It sounds like that. I belch, I bawl, I drink.
　　—EDITH SITWELL, "One-Way Song" *(1954)*

7. On motorcycles, up the road, they come: / Small, black, as flies hanging in heat, the Boys.
　　—THOM GUNN, "On the Move" *(1957)*

8. Then we went over to Studio 54. Stevie introduced me to Roy Cohn who was with four beautiful boys, but butch-looking. A boy is "butch" if he weighs over 170 and he's an all-American football-type, a spilling-out masculine man.
　　—ANDY WARHOL, *diary, 7 October 1977*

9. Those who believe machismo reeks of violence alone choose to forget it once stood for honor as well.
　　—EDMUND WHITE, *States of Desire: Travels in Gay America (1980)*

10. The American *ideal* . . . of sexuality appears to be rooted in the American ideal of masculinity. This idea has created cowboys and Indians, good guys and bad guys, punks and studs, tough guys and softies, butch and faggot, black and white. It is an ideal so paralytically infantile that it is virtually forbidden—as an unpatriotic act—that the American boy evolve into the complexity of manhood.
　　—JAMES BALDWIN, *The Price of the Ticket (1985)*

11. If there was anything I loved better than a big penis it was a bigger penis.
　　—LITTLE RICHARD, in *Spin, March 1987*

12. Gay men are guardians of the masculine impulse. To have anonymous sex in a dark alleyway is to pay homage to the dream of male freedom. The unknown stranger is a wan-

dering pagan god. The altar, as in pre-history, is anywhere you kneel.

—*CAMILLE PAGLIA, Sex, Art, and American Culture (1992)*

Marriage

1. A young man married is a man that's marr'd.
    —*WILLIAM SHAKESPEARE, All's Well That Ends Well (1604–5)*

2. He that hath wife and children hath given hostages to fortune; for they are impediments to great enterprises, either of virtue or mischief.
    —*FRANCIS BACON, "Of Marriage and Single Life," Essays (1625)*

3. Other things titillate me more keenly than the pale pleasures of marriage.
    —*CHRISTINA, QUEEN OF SWEDEN (1654), in Edgar H. Cohen, Mademoiselle Libertine (1970)*

4. Oh how fatal are forced marriages! / How many ruins one such match pulls on!
    —*APHRA BEHN, The Lucky Chance (1686)*

5. Man and wife are often nothing better than assistants in each other's ruin.

—*SARAH SCOTT, A Description of Millenium Hall (1762)*

6. It is as unjust to possess a woman exclusively as to possess slaves.
    —*MARQUIS DE SADE, La Philosophie dans le Boudoir (1795)*

7. Better be an old maid, a woman with herself for a husband, than the wife of a fool.
    —*HERMAN MELVILLE, Mardi (1849)*

8. Do you dream that men ever have the marrying of themselves? Juxtaposition marries men.
    —*HERMAN MELVILLE, Pierre (1852)*

9. Marriage is the only chance (and it is but a chance) offered to women for escape from this death . . . and how eagerly and ignorantly it is embraced.
    —*FLORENCE NIGHTINGALE, "Cassandra" (1852)*

10. Pussy said to Owl, "You elegant fowl! / How charmingly sweet you

sing! / O let us be married! too long we have tarried: / But what shall we do for a ring?"

> —EDWARD LEAR, "The Owl and the
> Pussy-Cat," Nonsense Songs
> (1871)

11. Marriage, to women as to men, must be a luxury, not a necessity; an incident in life, not all of it.

> —SUSAN B. ANTHONY, speech, 1875

12. Men marry because they are tired; women, because they are curious: both are disappointed.

> —OSCAR WILDE, The Picture of
> Dorian Gray (1891)

13. In married life three is company and two none.

> —OSCAR WILDE, The Importance of
> Being Earnest (1895)

14. There was no need. I have three pets at home which answer the same purpose as a husband. I have a dog which growls every morning, a parrot which swears all the afternoon, and a cat that comes home late at night.

> —MARIE CORELLI (d. 1924),
> explaining why she never
> married, in James Crichton-
> Browne, What the Doctor
> Thought (1930)

15. Death and marriage are raging through this College with such fury that I ought to be grateful for having escaped both.

> —A. E. HOUSMAN, letter,
> 29 May 1925

16. So that is marriage, Lily thought, a man and a woman looking at a girl throwing a ball.

> —VIRGINIA WOOLF, To the
> Lighthouse (1927)

17. The honeymoon wasn't such a ghastly experience really; it was afterwards that was really awful.

> —NOËL COWARD, Private Lives
> (1930)

18. That is partly why women marry—to keep up the fiction of being in the hub of things.

> —ELIZABETH BOWEN, The House in
> Paris (1935)

19. Most everybody in the world climbs into their graves married.

> —THORNTON WILDER, Our Town
> (1938)

20. Anyone who marries three girls from St. Louis hasn't learned much.

> —GERTRUDE STEIN (d. 1946), on
> Ernest Hemingway; quoted in
> James R. Mellow, Charmed
> Circle: Gertrude Stein and
> Company (1974)

21. A multitude of men who love only men marry and become fathers. Fed to satiety with the overflowing bounty of woman in a single wife, they don't so much as lay a hand on another woman. Among the world's devoted husbands men of this kind are not few. If they have children, they become more mother than father to

them. Some women prefer a peaceful life, and such men.
—*YUKIO MISHIMA, Thirst for Love [Forbidden Colors] (1953)*

22. The best part of married life is the fights. The rest is merely so-so.
—*THORNTON WILDER, The Matchmaker (1954)*

23. I cannot abide the Mr. and Mrs. Noah attitude towards marriage; the animals went in two by two, forever stuck together with glue.
—*VITA SACKVILLE-WEST, No Signposts in the Sea (1961)*

24. Marriage excuses no one the freak's roll-call.
—*JOE ORTON (d. 1967), What the Butler Saw (1969)*

25. Have you taken up transvestism? I'd no idea our marriage teetered on the brink of fashion.
—*JOE ORTON (d. 1967), What the Butler Saw (1969)*

26. Marriage is but for a little while. It is alimony that is forever.
—*QUENTIN CRISP, The Naked Civil Servant (1968)*

27. Admittedly *some* are best served when the struggle for power narrows to but one other person and the duel endures for a lifetime as mate attempts to destroy mate in that long wrangling for supremacy which is

called marriage. Most human beings, however, prefer the short duet, lasting anywhere from five minutes with a stranger to five months with a lover.
—*GORE VIDAL, Myra Breckinridge (1968)*

28. The great secret of a successful marriage is to treat all disasters as incidents and none of the incidents as disasters.
—*HAROLD NICOLSON (d. 1968), in Jonathon Green, ed., A Dictionary of Contemporary Quotations (1982)*

29. There is . . . that story, perhaps apocryphal, of Maurice [Bowra]'s decision to get married. When he announced that he had at last chosen a girl, a friend remonstrated: "But you can't marry anyone as plain as that." Maurice answered, "My dear fellow, buggers can't be choosers."
—*FRANCIS KING, in Hugh Lloyd-Jones, Maurice Bowra: A Celebration (1974)*

30. But it was always a fairly well-kept secret that if you were married to somebody you didn't have enough room in bed and might have to face bad breath in the morning.
—*ANDY WARHOL, The Philosophy of Andy Warhol: From A to B and Back Again (1975)*

31. Marriage is lonelier than solitude.

—*ADRIENNE RICH, "Paula Becker to Clare Westhoff" (1975–76)*

32. That was their marriage then— not the highest paving of the stair, the clatter of Italian fountains, the wind in the alien olive trees, but this: a jay-naked male and female discussing their bowels.

—*JOHN CHEEVER, Falconer (1977)*

33. The desire to make a good appearance, of course, is typical of singles everywhere, whether straight or gay. Vanity, alas, is less characteristic of couples of either variety. Domestic bliss usually creates an eyesore.

—*EDMUND WHITE, States of Desire: Travels in Gay America (1980)*

34. The long-term accommodation that protects marriage and other such relationships is forgetfulness.

—*ALICE WALKER, You Can't Keep a Good Woman Down (1981)*

35. There were those who claimed that love, if it be allowed at all, must be kept tame by marriage vows and family ties so that its fiery heat warms the hearth but does not burn down the house.

—*JEANETTE WINTERSON, Sexing the Cherry (1989)*

Memory and Remembrance

1. I have more memories than if I had lived for a thousand years.

—*CHARLES BAUDELAIRE, "Spleen," Les Fleurs du Mal (1857)*

2. I shall remember while the light lives yet / And in the night time I shall not forget.

—*ALGERNON CHARLES SWINBURNE, "Erotion" (1866)*

3. Memory is the diary that we all carry about with us.

—*OSCAR WILDE, The Importance of Being Earnest (1895)*

4. Some memories are realities, and better than anything that can ever happen to one again.

—*WILLA CATHER, My Antonia (1918)*

5. Even though our lives wander, our memories remain in one place.

—*MARCEL PROUST (d. 1922), Remembrance of Things Past: Time Regained (1926)*

6. These things were permanent, they could not be dissolved. They were memories that cannot hurt.
　—DAPHNE DU MAURIER, *Rebecca*
　(1938)

7. In memory everything seems to happen to music.
　—TENNESSEE WILLIAMS, *The Glass*
　Menagerie (1945)

8. The charm, one might say the genius, of memory is that it is choosy, chancy and temperamental.
　—ELIZABETH BOWEN, *in Vogue,*
　1955

9. People who remember court madness through pain, the pain of the perpetually recurring death of their innocence; people who forget court another kind of madness, the madness of the denial of pain and the hatred of innocence; and the world is mostly divided between madmen who remember and madmen who forget.
　—JAMES BALDWIN, *Giovanni's Room*
　(1956)

10. Life is all memory, except for the one present moment that goes by you so quickly you hardly catch it going.
　—TENNESSEE WILLIAMS, *The Milk*
　Train Doesn't Stop Here Any
　More (1962)

11. I have a memory like an elephant. In fact elephants often consult me.
　—NOËL COWARD *(d. 1973), in J. K.*
　Galbraith, A Life in Our Times
　(1981)

12. Old memories are so empty when they can not be shared.
　—JEWELLE GOMEZ, *"No Day Too*
　Long" (1981)

13. We shouldn't have talked so much, it occurred to me now; we should just have fucked our brains out. Because the memories left over from that were simple: no narrative, few details, just a blur of bliss across the brain.
　—EMMA DONOGHUE, *Hood (1995)*

M e n

1. A man perfect to the last detail.
   —HORACE (1st century BCE),
      Satires 1, 5

2. My men, like satyrs grazing on the lawns, / Shall with their goat feet dance an antic hay.
   —CHRISTOPHER MARLOWE,
      Edward II (c. 1591)

3. God made him, and therefore let him pass for a man.
   —WILLIAM SHAKESPEARE, The
      Merchant of Venice (1596–97)

4. Let me have men about me that are fat, / Sleek-headed men and such as sleep a-nights. / Yon Cassius has a lean and hungry look. / He thinks too much. Such men are dangerous.
   —WILLIAM SHAKESPEARE, Julius
      Caesar (1599)

5. The noblest works and foundations have proceeded from childless men.
   —FRANCIS BACON, "Of Parents and
      Children," Essays (1625)

6. As all boys are rascals, so are all men.
   —HERMAN MELVILLE, The
      Confidence-Man (1857)

7. There is something positively brutal about the good temper of most modern men.
   —OSCAR WILDE, A Woman of No
      Importance (1893)

8. There is something tragic about the enormous number of young men there are in England at the present moment who start life with perfect profiles, and end by adopting some useful profession.
   —OSCAR WILDE, "Phrases and
      Philosophies for the Use of the
      Young" (1894)

9. The three most important things a man has are, briefly, his private parts, his money, and his religious beliefs.
   —SAMUEL BUTLER (d. 1902),
      Further Extracts from the
      Notebooks (1934)

10. Many things I thought of then, / Battle, and the love of men, / Cities entered, oceans crossed, / Knowledge gained and virtue lost. . . .
   —A. E. HOUSMAN, no. 31 ["Hell
      Gate"], Last Poems (1922)

11. It's only if a man's a gentleman that he won't hesitate to do an ungentlemanly thing.

—W. SOMERSET MAUGHAM, *The Constant Wife (1927)*

12. I hate men. / I can't abide 'em even now and then.
—COLE PORTER, *"I Hate Men," Kiss Me Kate (1948)*

13. Don't accept rides from strange men, / and remember that all men are strange as hell.

—ROBIN MORGAN, *"Letter to a Sister Underground," Sisterhood is Powerful (1970)*

14. Men deem themselves weighty and women light. Therefore it is simple to tie a stone round their necks and drown them should they become too troublesome.
—JEANETTE WINTERSON, *Sexing the Cherry (1989)*

Middle   Class

1. You are the majority—in number and intelligence; therefore you are the force—which is justice. Some are scholars, others are owners; a glorious day will come when the scholars will be owners and the owners scholars. Then your power will be complete, and no man will protest against it.
—CHARLES BAUDELAIRE *(d. 1867), "Salon of 1846: To the Bourgeois," Curiosités Esthétiques (1868)*

2. I simply contend that the middle-class ideal which demands that people be affectionate, respectable, honest and content, that they avoid excitements and cultivate serenity is the ideal that appeals to me, it is in short the ideal of affectionate family life, of honorable business methods.
—GERTRUDE STEIN, *Q.E.D. (1903)*

3. Why! Why! Why is the middle-class so stodgy—so utterly without a sense of humour!
—KATHERINE MANSFIELD, *"Bliss" (1920)*

4. The British Bourgeoisie / Is not born, / And does not die, / But, if it is ill, / It has a frightened look in its eyes.
—OSBERT SITWELL, *"At the House of Mrs Kinfoot" (1921)*

5. For generations the British bourgeoisie have spoken of themselves as gentlemen, and by that they have meant, among other things, a self-respecting scorn of irregular perquisites. It is the quality that distinguishes the gentleman from both the artist and the aristocrat.

—*EVELYN WAUGH, Decline and Fall
(1928)*

6. He'd been mistaken in thinking that if he killed himself the sordid bourgeois world would perish with him.

—*YUKIO MISHIMA, "Raisin Bread"
(1948)*

7. The petit-bourgeois is a man unable to imagine the Other. If he comes face to face with him, he blinds himself, ignores and denies him, or else transforms him into himself.

—*ROLAND BARTHES, Mythologies
(1957)*

M i n d

▼

1. When people will not weed their own minds, they are apt to be overrun with nettles.

—*HORACE WALPOLE, letter to
Caroline, Countess of Ailesbury,
10 July 1779*

2. In the wild struggle for existence, we want to have something that endures, and so we fill our minds with rubbish and facts, in the silly hope of keeping our place. The thoroughly well-informed man—that is the modern ideal. And the mind of the thoroughly well-informed man is a dreadful thing. It is like a bric-à-brac shop, all monsters and dust, with everything priced above its proper value.

—*OSCAR WILDE, The Picture of
Dorian Gray (1891)*

3. Such a cultivated mind doesn't really attract me. . . . No, no, the mind I love must still have wild places, a tangled orchard where dark damsons drop in the heavy grass, an overgrown little wood, the chance of a snake or two (real snakes), a pool that nobody's fathomed the depth of—and paths threaded with those little flowers planted by the mind.

—KATHERINE MANSFIELD *(1920),*
Journal of Katherine Mansfield
(1927)

4. The intellect . . . often, alas, acts
the cannibal among the other faculties so that often, where the Mind is
biggest, the Heart, the Senses,
Magnanimity, Charity, Tolerance,
Kindliness, and the rest of them
scarcely have room to breathe.
—VIRGINIA WOOLF, *Orlando (1928)*

5. Nothing mattered except states of
mind, chiefly our own.

—JOHN MAYNARD KEYNES, *Essays in*
Biography (1933)

6. Mrs. Benson and I certainly did
not belong in the same cage, but so
fascinating was her mind that I could
have groped about in it for ever.
—ETHEL SMYTH, *As Time Went On*
(1936)

7. It is in our minds that we live
much of our life.
—IVY COMPTON-BURNETT, *A*
Heritage and Its History (1959)

M i n o r i t i e s

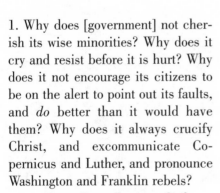

1. Why does [government] not cherish its wise minorities? Why does it
cry and resist before it is hurt? Why
does it not encourage its citizens to
be on the alert to point out its faults,
and *do* better than it would have
them? Why does it always crucify
Christ, and excommunicate Co-
pernicus and Luther, and pronounce
Washington and Franklin rebels?
—HENRY DAVID THOREAU, *Civil*
Disobedience (1849)

2. The warm heart of any human
being that saw the black man first not
as a black but as a man.

—WILLIAM PLOMER, *Turbott Wolfe*
(1926)

3. We need every human gift and
cannot afford to neglect any gift
because of artificial barriers of sex or
race or class or national origin.
—MARGARET MEAD, *Male and*
Female (1949)

4. A minority is only thought of as a
minority when it constitutes some
kind of threat to the majority, real or
imaginary. And no threat is ever *quite*
imaginary.

—CHRISTOPHER ISHERWOOD, A
  Single Man (1964)

5. I'm with you, little minority sister.
  —CHRISTOPHER ISHERWOOD, A
  Single Man (1964)

6. It frequently happens that when the dominant culture loses a vision or actively suppresses it, this lost knowledge arises again among those excluded from that culture.
  —KIM CHERNIN, *The Obsession*
  (1981)

7. Although Jews would doubtless be Jews if there was no anti-Semitism, same-sexers would think little or nothing at all about their preference if society ignored it. So there is a difference between the two estates. But there is no difference in the degree of hatred felt by the Christian majority for Christ-killers and Sodomites. In the German concentration camps, Jews wore yellow stars while homosexuals wore pink triangles.
  —GORE VIDAL, *Pink Triangle and*
  Yellow Star (1982)

8. We recognized ourselves as exotic sister-outsiders who might gain little from banding together. Perhaps our strength might lay in our fewness, our rarity.
  —AUDRE LORDE, *on black lesbians*
  in the 1950s; Zami: A New
  Spelling of My Name (1982)

9. Homophobia divides black people as political allies, it cuts off political growth, stifles revolution, and perpetuates patriarchal domination.
  —CHERYL CLARKE, *in Barbara*
  Smith, Home Girls (1983)

10. All of us would do well to stop fighting each other for our space at the bottom, because there ain't no more room.
  —CHERYL CLARKE, *"Lesbianism: An*
  Act of Resistance," in Cherríe
  Moraga and Gloria Anzaldúa,
  This Bridge Called My Back
  (1983)

11. In this country, lesbianism is a poverty—as is being brown, as is being a woman, as is being just plain poor. The danger lies in ranking the oppressions.
  —CHERRÍE MORAGA, *"La Guëra"*
  (1983)

12. The lesbian is to the American Indian what the Indian is to the Caucasian—invisible.
  —PAULA GUNN ALLEN, *in Trudy*
  Darty and Sandee Porter,
  Women-Identified Women (1984)

13. Idealization of a group is a natural consequence of separation from the group; in other words, it is a by-product of alienation.
  —PAULA GUNN ALLEN, *The Sacred*
  Hoop (1986)

Money

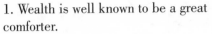

1. Wealth is well known to be a great comforter.
> —*PLATO (4th century BCE), The Republic*

2. All else—valor, a good name, glory, everything in heaven and earth—is secondary to the charm of riches.
> —*HORACE (1st century BCE), Satires II, 3*

3. Make money, money by right means if you can, but if not, by any means make money.
> —*VIRGIL (1st century BCE), Epistulae*

4. Nothing comes amiss, so money comes withal.
> —*WILLIAM SHAKESPEARE, The Taming of the Shrew (1593)*

5. What a world of vile ill-favoured faults / Looks handsome in three hundred pounds a year!
> —*WILLIAM SHAKESPEARE, The Merry Wives of Windsor (1597–98)*

6. Money is like muck, not good except it be spread.
> —*FRANCIS BACON, "Of Seditions and Troubles," Essays (1625)*

7. Money speaks sense in a language all nations understand.
> —*APHRA BEHN, The Rover (1681)*

8. It has been said that the love of money is the root of all evil. The want of money so quite as truly.
> —*SAMUEL BUTLER, Erewhon (1872)*

9. Money's a horrid thing to follow, but a charming thing to meet.
> —*HENRY JAMES, The Portrait of a Lady (1881)*

10. It is better to have a permanent income than to be fascinating.
> —*OSCAR WILDE, "The Model Millionaire" (1887)*

11. Money is like a sixth sense without which you cannot make a complete use of the other five.
> —*W. SOMERSET MAUGHAM, Of Human Bondage (1915)*

12. I must say I hate money, but it's the lack of it I hate most.
> —*KATHERINE MANSFIELD (d. 1923), in Antony Alpers, Katherine Mansfield (1954)*

13. Money dignifies what is frivolous if unpaid for.

—Virginia Woolf, *A Room of One's Own (1929)*

14. Money is only useful when you get rid of it. It is like the odd card in "Old Maid"; the player who is finally left with it has lost.

—Evelyn Waugh, in *Commonweal, 11 March 1949*

15. The differences between a little money and no money at all is enormous—and can shatter the world. And the difference between a little money and an enormous amount of money is very slight—and that, also, can shatter the world.

—Thornton Wilder, *The Matchmaker (1954)*

16. Money, it turned out, was exactly like sex, you thought of nothing else if you didn't have it and thought of other things if you did.

—James Baldwin, *Esquire, May 1961*

17. My mother taught me never to speak about money when there was a shirtful, and I've always been very reluctant to speak about it when there was any scarcity, so I cannot paint much of a picture of what ensued in the next six months.

—John Cheever, "The Housebreaker of Shady Hill," *The Stories of John Cheever (1980)*

Morality

1. A system of morality which is based on relative emotional values is a mere illusion, a thoroughly vulgar conception which has nothing sound in it and nothing true.

—Socrates *(5th century BCE)*, in Plato *(4th century BCE), Phaedo*

2. Who but the learned and dull moral fool / Could gravely have foreseen, man ought to live by rule?

—Aphra Behn, "The Golden Age" *(1684)*

3. All universal moral principles are idle fancies.

—Marquis de Sade, *The 120 Days of Sodom (1784)*

4. Do not be too moral. You may cheat yourself out of much life so.

Aim above morality. Be not simply good, be good for something.
> —HENRY DAVID THOREAU, *letter to Mr. B., 7 March 1848*

5. Morality is the weakness of the mind.
> —ARTHUR RIMBAUD, *"Une Saison en Enfer" (1873)*

6. Morality is simply the attitude we adopt towards people whom we personally dislike.
> —OSCAR WILDE, *An Ideal Husband (1895)*

7. I never came across anyone in whom the moral sense was dominant who was not heartless, cruel, vindictive, log-stupid, and entirely lacking in the smallest sense of humanity. Moral people, as they are termed, are simply beasts.
> —OSCAR WILDE (d. 1900), in Hesketh Pearson, *Oscar Wilde (1946)*

8. Morality turns on whether the pleasure precedes or follows the pain.
> —SAMUEL BUTLER (d. 1902), *Note Books (1912)*

9. You are so afraid of losing your moral sense that you are not willing to take it through anything more dangerous than a mud-puddle.
> —GERTRUDE STEIN, *Q.E.D. (1903)*

10. I think she must have been very strictly brought up, she's so desperately anxious to do the wrong thing correctly.
> —SAKI [H. H. MUNRO], *"Reginald on Worries," Reginald (1904)*

11. One becomes moral as soon as one is unhappy.
> —MARCEL PROUST, *Remembrance of Things Past: Within a Budding Grove (1918)*

12. Nothing is good for everyone, but only relatively to some people.
> —ANDRÉ GIDE, *The Counterfeiters (1925); trans. Dorothy Bussy*

13. Why, I wish to know, is it perfectly moral for me to copulate with a personage whose sexual organs are different from my own, and perfectly immoral for me to copulate with a personage whose sexual organs are not different?
> —LYTTON STRACHEY (d. 1932), *The Really Interesting Question (1972)*

14. We have an overall moral policy in this clinic from which even I am not exempt. Whilst you're with us I shall expect you to show an interest in no one's sexual organs but your own.
> —JOE ORTON (d. 1967), *What the Butler Saw (1969)*

15. Morality, like language, is an invented structure for conserving and

communicating order. And morality is learned, like language, by mimicking and remembering.

> —*JANE RULE, Lesbian Images (1975)*

16. Our chief taboos are no longer conscious. They do not appear as themselves in our laws, and for the most part are not spoken of directly. But when we break them or even think of breaking them, our unconscious knowledge that we are violating sacred rules causes us to feel as if our lives are threatened, as if we may not be allowed to live.

> —*SONIA JOHNSON, From Housewife to Heretic (1981)*

17. The more immoral we become in big ways, the more puritanical we become in little ways.

> —*FLORENCE KING, Lump It or Leave It (1990)*

Mothers

1. All women become like their mothers. That is their tragedy. No man does. That's his.

> —*OSCAR WILDE, The Importance of Being Earnest (1895)*

2. Few misfortunes can befall a boy which bring worse consequences than to have a really affectionate mother.

> —*W. SOMERSET MAUGHAM (1896), A Writer's Notebook (1949)*

3. The thirty-seventh dramatic situation: To become aware that one's mother is a virgin.

> —*ALFRED JARRY, L'Amour Absolu (1899)*

4. Mothers at present bring children into the world, but this performance is apt to mark the end of their capacities. They can't even attend to the elementary animal requirements of their offspring. It is quite surprising how many children survive in spite of their mothers.

> —*NORMAN DOUGLAS, South Wind (1917)*

5. We buried her . . . this mother with whom I fought so desperately, whom I loved so dearly, and of whose presence I grow daily more and more conscious.

> —*ETHEL SMYTH, Impressions That Remained (1919)*

6. I do love you so much, my mother. . . . If I didn't keep calling you mother, anybody reading this would think I was writing to my sweetheart. And he would be quite right.

> —*EDNA ST. VINCENT MILLAY, letter to her mother, 1921*

7. I made [Vita] give up having Taloola [*sic*] Bankhead to luncheon. She says that she is the most accomplished Lesbian in England and I certainly don't approve of V. knowing such an accomplished personality who talks in such a disgusting way.

> —*VICTORIA, LADY SACKVILLE (mother of Vita Sackville-West), diary entry, 15 March 1924; quoted in Susan Mary Alsop, Lady Sackville (1979)*

8. I don't know what I am; no one's ever told me that I'm different and yet I know that I'm different—that's why, I suppose, you've felt as you have done. And for that I forgive you, though whatever it is, it was you and my father who made this body—but what I will never forgive is your daring to try and make me ashamed of my love. I'm not ashamed of it, there's no shame in me.

> —*RADCLYFFE HALL, protagonist Stephen Gordon to her mother, The Well of Loneliness (1928)*

9. Oh! mothers aren't fair—I mean it's not fair of nature to weigh us down with them and yet expect us to be our own true selves. The handicap's too great.

> —*HENRY HANDEL RICHARDSON, "Two Hanged Women" (1934)*

10. Mother love, particularly in America, is a highly respected and much publicised emotion and when exacerbated by gin and bourbon it can become extremely formidable.

> —*NOËL COWARD, Future Indefinite (1954)*

11. She would imprison the child in her house by force of love.

> —*PATRICK WHITE, The Tree of Man (1955)*

12. Bury her naked? My own mum? It's a Freudian nightmare.

> —*JOE ORTON, Loot (1967)*

13. But Gide hasn't got a mother!

> —*E. M. FORSTER (d. 1970), to J. R. Ackerley, explaining his reluctance to be as open about his homosexuality as André Gide; in Peter Parker, Ackerley (1989)*

14. There is no intimacy between woman and woman which is not preceded by a long narrative of the mother.

> —*BERTHA HARRIS, Lover (1976)*

15. Looking back I wonder if I didn't do it a tiny bit to spite my mother.

> —*CHRISTOPHER ISHERWOOD, in Gay News, May 1976*

16. I grow old, old / without you, Mother, landscape / of my heart.

—*OLGA BROUMAS, "Little Red Riding Hood," Beginning with O (1977)*

17. I am a reflection of my mother's secret poetry as well as of her hidden angers.

—*AUDRE LORDE, Zami: A New Spelling of My Name (1982)*

18. I fear, as any daughter would, losing myself back into the mother.

—*KIM CHERNIN, In My Mother's House (1983)*

19. Yes, Mother. . . . I can see you are flawed. You have not hidden it. That is your greatest gift to me.

—*ALICE WALKER, Possessing the Secret of Joy (1992)*

Music

1. And now I'll sing / beautifully / songs of delight / to my girlfriends.

—*SAPPHO (7th century BCE), Fragment 160; trans. Anita George*

2. The man that hath no music in himself, / Nor is not moved with concord of sweet sounds, / Is fit for treasons, stratagems, and spoils; / The motions of his spirit are dull as night, / And his affections dark as Erebus. / Let no such man be trusted.

—*WILLIAM SHAKESPEARE, The Merchant of Venice (1596–97)*

3. There's no way to stop my singing in this world but to cut my throat.

—*HERMAN MELVILLE, Moby-Dick (1851)*

4. Men profess to be lovers of music, but for the most part they give no evidence in their opinions and lives that they have heard it. It would not leave them narrow-minded and bigoted.

—*HENRY DAVID THOREAU, Journal, 5 August 1851*

5. Music is essentially useless, as life is.

—*GEORGE SANTAYANA, The Life of Reason (1906)*

6. From you, Beethoven, Bach, Mozart, / The substance of my dreams took fire. / You built cathedrals in my heart, / And lit my pinnacled desire.

—SIEGFRIED SASSOON, "Dead
  Musicians" (1918)

7. Without music I should wish to
die.
  —EDNA ST. VINCENT MILLAY, letter,
    1920

8. Listening to music feels like a triumphant expedition into the Future;
but into a Future which is happening now.
  —CLEMENTINA (KIT) ANSTRUTHER-
    THOMSON (d. 1921), Art and Man
    (1923)

9. [Music] a pederast might hum
when raping a choirboy.
  —MARCEL PROUST (d. 1922), of
    Fauré's Romances sans Paroles;
    in Musical Quarterly, 1924

10. Tchaikovsky thought of committing suicide for fear of being discovered as a homosexual, but today, if
you are a composer and *not* homosexual, you might as well put a bullet
through your head.
  —SERGEI DIAGHILEV (d. 1929), in
    Vernon Duke, Listen Here!
    (1963)

11. Extraordinary how potent cheap
music is.
  —NOËL COWARD, Private Lives
    (1930)

12. Words are wearisome and worn,
while the arabesques of music are
forever new.

—COLETTE, My Apprenticeships
  (1936)

13. A piece for orchestra without
music.
  —MAURICE RAVEL (d. 1937), of his
    Boléro, in R. Nichols, Ravel
    (1977)

14. The whole problem can be stated
quite simply by asking, "Is there a
meaning to music?" My answer
would be, "Yes." And "Can you state
in so many words what the meaning
is?" My answer to that would be
"No."
  —AARON COPLAND, What to Listen
    for in Music (1939)

15. Music can be made anywhere, is
invisible and doesn't smell.
  —W. H. AUDEN, "In Praise of
    Limestone" (1951)

16. Music melts all the separate
parts of our bodies together.
  —ANAÏS NIN, Winter of Artifice
    (1945)

17. It is not possible to write real
music about an unreal emotion.
  —VIRGIL THOMSON, in New York
    Herald Tribune, 10 April 1949

18. In the evenings the art of building gave way to that of music, which
is architecture, too, though invisible.
  —MARGUERITE YOURCENAR, Memoirs
    of Hadrian (1951)

19. The power and magic of music lie in its intangibility and its limitlessness. It suggests images, but leaves us free to choose them and to accommodate them to our pleasure.
>—*WANDA LANDOWSKA (d. 1959), in Denise Resout, ed., Landowska on Music (1964)*

20. Music is edifying, for from time to time it sets the soul in operation.
>—*JOHN CAGE, Silence (1961)*

21. Music, that vast and inevitable structure.
>—*EDITH SITWELL (d. 1964), Taken Care Of (1965)*

22. False notes can be forgiven, false music cannot.
>—*NADIA BOULANGER (d. 1979), in Don G. Campbell, Reflections of Boulanger (1982)*

23. The worst part of being gay in the twentieth century is all that damn disco music to which one has to listen.
>—*QUENTIN CRISP, Manners from Heaven (1984)*

24. The music that they constantly play / IT SAYS NOTHING TO ME ABOUT MY LIFE.
>—*MORRISSEY, "Panic" (1986)*

25. Only dead people need loud music, you know.
>—*ALICE WALKER, The Temple of My Familiar (1989)*

M y t h

1. As anyone will say, / My tongue tells myths / Greater than any man's.
>—*SAPPHO (7th century BCE), Fragment 18; trans. Anita George*

2. Wickedness is a myth invented by good people to account for the curious attractiveness of others.
>—*OSCAR WILDE, "Phrases and Philosophies for the Use of the Young" (1894)*

3. Myth is neither a lie nor a confession: in is an inflexion.
>—*ROLAND BARTHES, Mythologies (1957)*

4. No more masks! No more mythologies!

> —MURIEL RUKEYSER, "The Poem as
> Mask," The Speed of Darkness
> (1968)

5. PRENTICE: Many men imagine that a preference for women is, *ipso facto,* a proof of virility.

RANCE *(nodding, sagely):* Someone should really write a book on these folk-myths.

> —JOE ORTON (d. 1967), What the
> Butler Saw (1969)

6. So little is known about the Lesbian that even Lesbians themselves are caught up in the myths and stereotypes so prevalent in our society.

> —DEL MARTIN AND PHYLLIS LYON,
> Lesbian /Woman (1972)

7. The thing I came for . . . the thing itself and not the myth.

> —ADRIENNE RICH, "Diving into the
> Wreck" (1973)

8. Myths hook and bind the mind because at the same time they set the mind free: they explain the universe while allowing the universe to go on being unexplained.

> —JEANETTE WINTERSON, Boating for
> Beginners (1985)

Nature

1. Oh, the powers of nature! She knows what we need, and the doctors know nothing.

> —BENVENUTO CELLINI,
> Autobiography (1566)

2. Nature is of itself a wonderful instructress: One has but to abandon oneself to its impulses and there is no fear of making any very wide mistakes.

> —JOHN CLELAND, Memoirs of a
> Coxcomb (1751)

3. Wolves which batten upon lambs, lambs consumed by wolves, the strong who immolate the weak, the weak victims of the strong: there you have Nature, there you have her intentions, there you have her scheme: a perpetual action and reaction, a host of vices, a host of virtues,

in one word, a perfect equilibrium resulting from the equality of good and evil on earth.

> —MARQUIS DE SADE, *Justine, ou les Malheurs de la Vertu (1791)*

4. The earth is not a mere fragment of dead history, stratum upon stratum like the leaves of a book, to be studied by geologists and antiquaries chiefly, but living poetry like the leaves of a tree, which precede flowers and fruit—not a fossil earth, but a living earth.

> —HENRY DAVID THOREAU, *"Spring," Walden (1854)*

5. Nature is a temple in which living columns / sometimes utter confused words. / Man walks through it among forests of symbols, / which watch him with knowing eyes.

> —CHARLES BAUDELAIRE, *"Correspondences," Les Fleurs du Mal (1857)*

6. After you have exhausted what there is in business, politics, conviviality, and so on—have found that none of these finally satisfy, or permanently wear—what remains? Nature remains.

> —WALT WHITMAN, *"New Themes Entered Upon," Specimen Days and Collect (1882)*

7. The more we study art, the less we care for nature. What art really reveals to us is nature's lack of design, her curious crudities, her

extraordinary monotony, her absolutely unfinished condition.

> —OSCAR WILDE, *"The Decay of Lying" (1891)*

8. It is strange that there are times when I feel the stars are not at all *solemn:* they are secretly gay.

> —KATHERINE MANSFIELD *(1920), Journal of Katherine Mansfield (1927)*

9. A vacuum is a hell of a lot better than some of the stuff that nature replaces it with.

> —TENNESSEE WILLIAMS, *Cat on a Hot Tin Roof (1955)*

10. By the time I was eleven years old, I had been taught that nature, far from abhorring a Vacuum, positively adores it.

> —EDITH SITWELL *(d. 1964), Taken Care Of (1965)*

11. We will look upon the earth and her sister planets as being with us, not for us. One does not rape a sister.

> —MARY DALY, *Beyond God the Father (1973)*

12. Now, nature, as I am only too well aware, has her enthusiasts, but on the whole, I am not to be counted among them. To put it rather bluntly, I am not the type who wants to go back to the land—I am the type who wants to go back to the hotel.

> —FRAN LEBOWITZ, *Social Studies (1981)*

Need

1. The true creator is necessity, who is the mother of our invention.
>—*PLATO (4th century BCE), The Republic*

2. Necessity is the mistress and guardian of nature. Necessity is the theme and artificer of nature, the bridle, and eternal law.
>—*LEONARDO DA VINCI, Notebooks (c. 1500)*

3. Necessity will make us all forsworn.
>—*WILLIAM SHAKESPEARE, Love's Labour's Lost (1594–95)*

4. The art of our necessities is strange, / And can make vile things precious.
>—*WILLIAM SHAKESPEARE, King Lear (1605–6)*

5. There is something wrong about the man who wants help. There is somewhere a deep defect, a want, in brief, a need, a crying need, somewhere about that man.
>—*HERMAN MELVILLE, The Confidence-Man (1857)*

6. Lord, forgive me if my need / Sometimes shapes a human creed.
>—*COUNTEE CULLEN, "Heritage," On These I Stand (1925)*

7. It is inevitable that when one has a great need of something one finds it. What you need you attract like a lover.
>—*GERTRUDE STEIN (d. 1946), in Elizabeth Sprigge, Gertrude Stein (1957)*

8. I have always depended on the kindness of strangers.
>—*TENNESSEE WILLIAMS, A Streetcar Named Desire (1947)*

9. You gotta have a swine to show you where the truffles are.
>—*EDWARD ALBEE, Who's Afraid of Virginia Woolf? (1963)*

Night and Evening

1. The iron tongue of midnight hath told twelve. / Lovers, to bed; 'tis almost fairy time.
> —*WILLIAM SHAKESPEARE, A Midsummer Night's Dream (1595)*

2. Press close bare-bosom'd night—press close magnetic nourishing night! / Night of south winds! night of the large few stars! / Still nodding night! mad naked summer night.
> —*WALT WHITMAN, "Song of Myself," Leaves of Grass (1855)*

3. Wild Nights—Wild Nights! / Were I with thee / Wild Nights should be / Our luxury!
> —*EMILY DICKINSON, no. 249 ("Wild Nights") (c. 1861), Complete Poems (1955)*

4. "Anyhow," Mme. de Cambremer went on, "I have a horror of sunsets, they're so romantic, so operatic."
> —*MARCEL PROUST, Remembrance of Things Past: Cities of the Plain (1922)*

5. The night is a skin pulled over the head of day that the day may be in torment.
> —*DJUNA BARNES, Nightwood (1936)*

6. Tropical nights are hammocks for lovers.
> —*ANAÏS NIN (1940), The Diary of Anaïs Nin, Vol. 3 (1969)*

7. The long sweetness of the simultaneity, yours and mine, ours and mine, / The mosquitoey summer night light.
> —*JOHN ASHBERRY, "Here Everything Is Still Floating," Shadow Train (1981)*

8. My nights are rich with mystery, my dreams breathless with expectation.
> —*JANE CHAMBERS, Last Summer at Blue Fish Cove (1981)*

Obedience and Disobedience

1. Every good servant does not all commands.
   —*WILLIAM SHAKESPEARE, Cymbeline (1610)*

2. If we obey God, we must disobey ourselves.
   —*HERMAN MELVILLE, Moby-Dick (1851)*

3. No man, not even a doctor, ever gives any other definition of what a nurse should be than this—"devoted and obedient." This definition would do just as well for a porter. It might even do for a horse. It would not do for a policeman.
   —*FLORENCE NIGHTINGALE, Notes on Nursing (1859)*

4. To the States or any one of them, or any city of the States. / *Resist much, obey little.*
   —*WALT WHITMAN, "To the States" (1860)*

5. Disobedience, in the eyes of any one who has read history, is man's original virtue. It is through disobedience that progress has been made, through disobedience and through rebellion.
   —*OSCAR WILDE, "The Soul of Man Under Socialism" (1895)*

6. We have taken this action, because as women we realize that the condition of our sex is so deplorable that it is our duty even to break the law in order to call attention to the reasons why we do so.
   —*EMMELINE PANKHURST, on trial for her actions in the cause of women's suffrage, 1908*

7. "She still seems to me in her own way a person born to command," said Luce. . . .
   "I wonder if anyone is born to obey," said Isabel.
   "That may be why people command rather badly, that they have no suitable material to work on."
   —*IVY COMPTON-BURNETT, Parents and Children (1941)*

Opera

1. I like Wagner's music better than anybody's. It is so loud that one can talk the whole time without other people hearing what one says.
—*Oscar Wilde, The Picture of Dorian Gray (1891)*

2. "I've never travelled," Dona Consolation blandly confessed, "but I dare say, dear, you can't judge Egypt by *Aida*."
—*Ronald Firbank, The Eccentricities of Cardinal Pirelli (1926)*

3. People are wrong when they say that the opera isn't what it used to be. It is what it used to be—that's what's wrong with it.
—*Noël Coward, Design for Living (1933)*

4. I wish I could write librettos for the rest of my life. It is the purest of human pleasures, a heavenly hermaphroditism of being both writer and musician. No wonder that selfish beast Wagner kept it all to himself.
—*Sylvia Townsend Warner, letter, 7 April 1949*

5. No opera plot can be sensible, for in sensible situations people do not sing. An opera plot must be, in both senses of the word, a melodrama.
—*W. H. Auden, Times Literary Supplement, 2 November 1967*

6. Sweet monster opera, I am in your whirlpool kiss. You have sucked me deep into your contralto throat, drawn me down into identifications with your characters by your sheer liquid expressiveness of their emotions.
—*Brigid Brophy, In Transit (1969)*

7. If music in general is an imitation of history, opera in particular is an imitation of human willfulness; it is rooted in the fact that we not only have feelings but insist upon having them at whatever cost to ourselves.
—*W. H. Auden, A Certain World (1970)*

8. Stephen: The moment I saw him, even before he'd seen me, before we were introduced, I knew he was going to be the one. He was my destiny and I was his. I saw my future flash before me and it was all him. It was like the first act of *Carmen*. Don José sees her, she throws him the acacia flower, and his fate is sealed.

MENDY: Carmen isn't gay.

STEPHEN: She is when a certain mezzo's singing her.

—*TERRENCE MCNALLY, The Lisbon Traviata (1985)*

9. We "Octavians" get some very peculiar fan mail.

—*BRIGITTE FASSBAENDER, in Helena Matheopoulos, Diva (1991)*

10. I find myself becoming more and more acutely aware of, and aroused by, her femininity. The very butchness with which she tackles, say, a role like Octavian—the sheer, absolutist bravado of the impersonation—infuses it with a dizzying homosexual charge. The more dashingly Fassbaender pretends, the more completely she fails—with the result that a new stage illusion takes shape: that of a woman robustly in love with another woman.

—*TERRY CASTLE, on Brigitte Fassbaender in the trouser role of Octavian in Richard Strauss's*

Der Rosenkavalier; The Apparitional Lesbian: Female Homosexuality and Modern Culture (1993)

11. I devoted my twenty-first winter to Mozart's *Don Giovanni* . . . and to the search for a boyfriend. In my dorm room, I listened to Donna Elvira's "Ah! chi mi dice mai" again and again; I wanted the boy next door to hear it, through the thin wall separating our bedrooms, while he slept and studied. . . . I feared my love affair with the boy next door would end any moment and that I would become Donna Elvira, crying on the streets. . . . In order to speak to myself about boy meets boy, I entered the vocal consciousness of a woman who can sing boldly about her erotic life only because she's been deserted.

—*WAYNE KOESTENBAUM, The Queen's Throat: Opera, Homosexuality, and the Mystery of Desire (1993)*

Opinions

1. A plague of opinion! A man may wear it on both sides, like a leather jerkin.
   —*WILLIAM SHAKESPEARE, Troilus and Cressida (1602)*

2. There are as many points of view in the world as there are people of sense to take them.
   —*HENRY JAMES, Portrait of a Lady (1881)*

3. It is only about things that do not interest one, that one can give a really unbiased opinion; and this is no doubt why an unbiased opinion is always valueless.
   —*OSCAR WILDE, in Speaker, 22 March 1890*

4. A fashionable milieu is one in which everybody's opinion is made up of the opinion of all the others. Has everybody a different opinion? Then it is a literary milieu.
   —*MARCEL PROUST, Pleasures and Regrets (1896)*

5. No man's opinions can be worth holding unless he knows how to deny them easily and gracefully upon occasion in the cause of charity.
   —*SAMUEL BUTLER (d. 1902), The Way of All Flesh (1903)*

6. A woman whose dresses are made in Paris and whose marriage has been made in heaven might be equally biased for and against free imports.
   —*SAKI [H. H. Munro], The Unbearable Bassington (1912)*

7. The opinions which we hold of one another, our relations with friends and kinsfolk are in no sense permanent, save in appearance, but are as eternally fluid as the sea itself.
   —*MARCEL PROUST, Remembrance of Things Past: The Guermantes Way (1921)*

8. Literature is strewn with the wreckage of men who have minded beyond reason the opinions of others.
   —*VIRGINIA WOOLF, A Room of One's Own (1929)*

9. It rarely adds anything to say, "In my opinion"—not even modesty. Naturally a sentence is only your opinion; and you are not the Pope.
   —*PAUL GOODMAN, Five Years (1959)*

10. I've never had a humble opinion. If you've got an opinion, why be humble about it.
    —*JOAN BAEZ, in Scotland on Sunday, 1992*

Oppression and Repression

1. To pardon the oppressor is to deal harshly with the oppressed.
—SA'DI, *Gulistan (1258)*

2. Man lording it over man, man kneeling to man, is a spectacle that Gabriel might well travel hitherward to behold; for never did he behold it in heaven.
—HERMAN MELVILLE, *Mardi (1849)*

3. Society knows very well how to go about suppressing a man and has methods more subtle than death.
—ANDRÉ GIDE, "In Memoriam Oscar Wilde" (1901)

4. One cannot serve this Eros without becoming a stranger in society as it is today; one cannot commit oneself to this form of love without incurring a mortal wound.
—KLAUS MANN (d. 1949), in Marcel Reich-Ranicki, *Thomas Mann and His Family (1989)*

5. Obviously the most oppressed of any oppressed group will be its women.
—LORRAINE HANSBERRY (1959), in Adrienne Rich, *Bread, Blood, and Poetry (1986)*

6. It is precisely because certain groups have no representation in a number of recognized political structures that their position tends to be so stable, their oppression so continuous.
—KATE MILLETT, *Sexual Politics (1969)*

7. You know, it's not the world that was my oppressor, because what the world does to you, if the world does it to you long enough and effectively enough, you begin to do to yourself.
—JAMES BALDWIN, *A Dialogue, with Nikki Giovanni (1973)*

8. Feminists who still sleep with men are delivering their most vital energies to the oppressor.
—JILL JOHNSTON, *Lesbian Nation: The Feminist Solution (1973)*

9. If repression has indeed been the fundamental link between power, knowledge, and sexuality since the classical age, it stands to reason that we will not be able to free ourselves from it except at considerable cost.
—MICHEL FOUCAULT, *The History of Sexuality, Vol. 1 (1976)*

10. Tell a man what he may not sing and he is still half free; even all free, if he never wanted to sing it. But tell him what he must sing, take up his

time with it so that his true voice cannot sound even in secret—there, I have seen slavery.
> —*MARY RENAULT, The Praise Singer (1978)*

11. In order to perpetuate itself, every oppression must corrupt or distort those various sources of power within the culture of the oppressed that can provide energy for change.
> —*AUDRE LORDE, Uses of the Erotic (1978)*

12. The possibility of a woman who does not exist sexually for men— the lesbian possibility—is buried, erased, occluded, distorted, misnamed, and driven underground.
> —*ADRIENNE RICH, "Compulsory Heterosexuality and Lesbian Existence" (1980)*

13. It is the responsibility of the oppressed to teach the oppressors their mistakes.
> —*AUDRE LORDE, Sister Outsider (1984)*

14. I've spent fifteen years of my life fighting for our right to be free and make love whenever, wherever. . . . And you're telling me that all those years of what being gay stood for is wrong . . . and I'm a murderer. We have been so oppressed! Don't you remember how it was? Can't you see how important it is for us to love openly, without hiding and without guilt?
> —*LARRY KRAMER, The Normal Heart (1986)*

15. Tyranny sets up its own echochamber.
> —*BRUCE CHATWIN, Utz (1988)*

16. You may be repressed / but you're remarkably dressed.
> —*MORRISSEY, "Hairdresser on Fire" (1988)*

17. What you try to bury just ends up burying you.
> —*JANE WAGNER, My Life, So Far (1994)*

Optimism and Pessimism

1. It is wisdom in prosperity, when all is as thou wouldst have it, to fear and suspect the worst.
> —DESIDERIUS ERASMUS (d. 1536), Proverbs or Adages of Erasmus (1545)

2. The basis of optimism is sheer terror.
> —OSCAR WILDE, The Picture of Dorian Gray (1891)

3. People who "view with alarm" never build anything.
> —ELEANOR ROOSEVELT (d. 1962), Tomorrow Is Now (1963)

4. Pessimists are people who have no hope for themselves or for others. Pessimists are also people who think the human race is beneath their notice, that they're better than other human beings.
> —JAMES BALDWIN, A Dialogue, with Nikki Giovanni (1973)

5. What goes up must come down. But don't expect it to come down where you can find it.
> —JANE WAGNER [words spoken by Lily Tomlin], The Search for Signs of Intelligent Life in the Universe (1985)

6. The taste for worst-case scenarios reflects the need to master fear of what is felt to be uncontrollable. It also expresses an imaginative complicity with disaster.
> —SUSAN SONTAG, AIDS and Its Metaphors (1989)

Out

1. Nowadays to be intelligible is to be found out.
> —OSCAR WILDE, Lady Windermere's Fan (1892)

2. No one is more trustworthy than the repentant sinner who has been found out.
> —ETHEL SMYTH, What Happened Next (1940)

3. We must declare ourselves, become known; allow the world to discover this subterranean life of ours which connects kings and farm boys, artists and clerks. Let them see that the important thing is *not* the object of love but the emotion itself.

> —GORE VIDAL, *The City and the Pillar (1948)*

4. If all Lesbians suddenly turned purple today, society would be surprised at the number of purple people in high places.

> —SYDNEY ABBOTT AND BARBARA LOVE, *Sappho Was a Right-on Woman (1972)*

5. I never said I was a dyke even to a dyke because there wasn't a dyke in the land who thought she should be a dyke or even that she was a dyke so how could we talk about it.

> —JILL JOHNSTON, *Lesbian Nation (1973)*

6. Being queer is like being on lifetime assignment as a secret agent in some foreign country. No matter how careful you are, no matter how practiced you are at emulating the natives, you know that at any minute you may be uncovered.

> —NORETTA KOERTGE, *Who Was That Masked Woman? (1981)*

7. I am absolutely convinced that if everyone would come out at once and stay out we could put an end to most of our problems.

> —BARBARA GRIER, in Margaret Cruikshank, ed., *The Lesbian Path (1985)*

8. I have decided to give up heterosexuality. I have decided that, while the project of altering the balance of power within heterosexual relationships is still a valid one, it is no longer one I can espouse—so to speak. There is no revolutionary hope for the heterosexual, and I have therefore decided to love myself and become a lesbian.

> —MICHELENE WANDOR, "Meet My Mother" (1987)

9. I regard the greatest villains today to be those famous closet cases who are not being open about their lives. These people could make an enormous difference in enlightening the general public about the nature of homosexuality. And I'm tired of hearing their feeble excuses for why this isn't possible. It almost always boils down to money in the long run.

> —ARMISTEAD MAUPIN, in *Outlines,* August 1990

Outsiders

1. The stranger has no friend, unless it be a stranger.
   —SA'DI, *Gulistan* (1258)

2. When in disgrace with Fortune and men's eyes / I all alone beweep my outcast state, / And trouble deaf heaven with my bootless cries, / And look upon myself and curse my fate.
   —WILLIAM SHAKESPEARE, *Sonnet 29* (1609)

3. And this the burthen of his song, / For ever us'd to be, / I care for nobody, not I, / If no one cares for me.
   —ISAAC BICKERSTAFFE, *Love in a Village* (1762)

4. I have not loved the world, nor the world me.
   —GEORGE GORDON, LORD BYRON, *Childe Harold's Pilgrimage* (1812–18)

5. What a life! True life is elsewhere. We are not in the world.
   —ARTHUR RIMBAUD, "*Délires I*," *Une Saison en Enfer* (1874)

6. Shot? so quick, so clean an ending? / Oh that was right, lad, that was brave: / Yours was not an ill for mending, / 'Twas best to take it to the grave.
   —A. E. HOUSMAN, poem 44, *A Shropshire Lad* (1896)

7. And alien tears will fill for him / Pity's long-broken urn, / For his mourners will be outcast men, / And outcasts always mourn.
   —OSCAR WILDE, *The Ballad of Reading Gaol* (1898) *[These lines are the epitaph on Wilde's grave.]*

8. And now what shall become of us without any barbarians? Those people were a kind of solution.
   —CONSTANTINE P. CAVAFY, "*Expecting the Barbarians*" (1898)

9. I'm an unspeakable of the Oscar Wilde sort.
   —E. M. FORSTER, *Maurice* (1914; published 1971)

10. I am one of those whom God marked on the forehead. Like Cain, I am marked and blemished.
    —RADCLYFFE HALL, *The Well of Loneliness* (1928)

11. The world would condemn but they would rejoice; glorious outcasts, unashamed, triumphant!
    —RADCLYFFE HALL, *The Well of Loneliness* (1928)

12. I'm fundamentally, I think, an outsider. I do my best work and feel most braced with my back to the wall. It's an odd feeling though, writing against the current: difficult entirely to disregard the current. Yet of course I shall.
—*VIRGINIA WOOLF (1938); in Leonard Woolf, ed., A Writer's Diary (1953)*

13. To be an outsider is the one unbearable humiliation.
—*KLAUS MANN, The Turning Point (1942)*

14. This was the summer when for a long time she had not been a member. She belonged to no club and was a member of nothing in the world. Frankie had become an unjoined person who hung around in the doorways, and she was afraid.
—*CARSON MCCULLERS, The Member of the Wedding (1946)*

15. Excluded by my birth and tastes from the social order, I was not aware of its diversity. I wondered at its perfect coherence, which rejected me.
—*JEAN GENET, The Thief's Journal (1948)*

16. All of life is a foreign country.
—*JACK KEROUAC, letter, 24 June 1949*

17. I was much too far out all my life / And not waving but drowning.
—*STEVIE SMITH, "Not Waving but Drowning" (1957)*

18. I was like a cat always climbing the wrong tree.
—*CARSON MCCULLERS, Clock Without Hands (1961)*

19. I am not an eccentric. It's just that I am more alive than most people. I am an unpopular electric eel in a pool of catfish.
—*EDITH SITWELL, in Life (1963)*

20. In an expanding universe, time is on the side of the outcast.
—*QUENTIN CRISP, The Naked Civil Servant (1968)*

21. Be nobody's darling; / Be an outcast.
—*ALICE WALKER, "Be Nobody's Darling" (1971)*

22. I am in exile in my own land.
—*MARILYN HACKER, "Exiles" (1974)*

23. Strangers are an endangered species.
—*ADRIENNE RICH, "The Spirit of the Place" (1981)*

24. When you are a member of an out-group, and you challenge others with whom you share this outsider position to examine some aspect of their lives that distorts differences between you, then there can be a great deal of pain.
—*AUDRE LORDE, in Claudia Tate, Black Women Writers at Work (1983)*

25. A black woman singing aloud about unhappiness in love with the consciousness that she was outcast because of her race was sure to attract the attention and empathy of gay men.
> —MICHAEL BRONSKI, *Culture Clash: The Making of Gay Sensibility (1984)*

26. She always knew she was an outlaw, but she could never figure out which one.
> —SARAH SCHULMAN, *Girls, Visions and Everything (1986)*

27. Displaced, I am. And not like a girl who didn't quite make it but like someone they missed out on, someone they missed their shot on when they once had her in their sights for the bead of a rifle will never have at its disposal the powers of a mirror.
> —NICOLE BROSSARD, *The Aerial Letter (1988)*

28. [A pariah is] something like a martyr with more suffering and less class.
> —RITA MAE BROWN, *Bingo (1988)*

29. Living on borders and in margins, keeping intact one's shifting and multiple identity and integrity, is like trying to swim in a new element, an "alien" element. . . . And yes, the "alien" element has become familiar—never comfortable, not with society's clamor to uphold the old, to rejoin the flock, to go with the herd. No, not comfortable but home.
> —GLORIA ANZALDÚA, *Borderlands/La Frontera (1989)*

Pain

1. If you wish me to shed tears / You must first feel pain yourself.
> —HORACE, *Ars Poetica (c. 19 BCE)*

2. Give us back our suffering, we cry to Heaven in our hearts—suffering rather than indifferentism, for out of nothing comes nothing. Better have pain than paralysis!
> —FLORENCE NIGHTINGALE, *"Cassandra" (1852)*

3. After great pain, a formal feeling comes— / The Nerves sit ceremonious, like Tombs—

—EMILY DICKINSON, no. 341
(c. 1862), Complete Poems (1955)

4. I know that pain is the one nobil-
ity / upon which Hell itself cannot
encroach.
—CHARLES BAUDELAIRE,
"Bénédiction," Les Fleurs du Mal
(1857)

5. Even pain / Pricks to livelier
living.
—AMY LOWELL, "Happiness" (1914)

6. My soul is a broken field /
Ploughed by pain.
—SARA TEASDALE, "The Broken
Field" (1920)

7. There is no limit to human suffering. When one thinks "Now I have
touched the bottom of the sea—now
I can go no deeper," one goes deeper.
—KATHERINE MANSFIELD (1920),
Journal of Katherine Mansfield
(1927)

8. On the outskirts of every agony sits
some observant fellow who points.
—VIRGINIA WOOLF, The Waves
(1931)

9. My pain was the horse that I must
learn to ride. I flicked my cigarette
out of the window and watched it
drop and die. I thought of throwing

myself after it. I was no rider and
pain was no horse.
—JAMES BALDWIN, Tell Me How
Long the Train's Been Gone
(1968)

10. They can rule the world while
they can persuade us / our pain
belongs in some order.
—ADRIENNE RICH, "Power Hunger,"
The Dream of a Common
Language (1978)

11. In the country of pain we are
each alone.
—MAY SARTON, "The Country of
Pain" (1980)

12. If I cannot air this pain and alter
it, I will surely die of it.
—AUDRE LORDE, quoted in Claudia
Tate, Black Women Writers at
Work (1983)

13. I believe that we often disguise
pain through ritual and it may be the
only solace we have.
—RITA MAE BROWN, Starting from
Scratch (1988)

14. I have secret scars in places
you'll never see.
—WAYNE KOESTENBAUM, "Haunting
Tune That Ends Too Soon,"
Rhapsodies of a Repeat Offender
(1994)

Parents

1. I am the slave of my baptism. Parents, you have caused my misfortune, and you have caused your own.
    —*Arthur Rimbaud, "Nuit de l'Enfer," Une Saison en Enfer (1874)*

2. Through the survival of their children, happy parents are able to think calmly, and with a very practical affection, of a world in which they are to have no direct share.
    —*Walter Pater, Marius the Epicurean (1885)*

3. To lose one parent, Mr Worthing, may be regarded as a misfortune; to lose both looks like carelessness.
    —*Oscar Wilde, The Importance of Being Earnest (1895)*

4. How often do we not see children ruined through the virtues, real or supposed, of their parents?
    —*Samuel Butler (d. 1902), Note Books (1912)*

5. It is not a bad thing that children should occasionally, and politely, put parents in their place.
    —*Colette, My Mother's House (1922)*

6. Parents have too little respect for their children, just as the children have too much for the parents.
    —*Ivy Compton-Burnett, Two Worlds and Their Ways (1949)*

7. Parents—especially step-parents—are sometimes a bit of a disappointment to their children. They don't fulfill the promise of their early years.
    —*Anthony Powell, A Buyer's Market (1952)*

8. Compassion for our parents is the true sign of maturity.
    —*Anaïs Nin (1954), The Diary of Anaïs Nin, Vol. 5 (1974)*

9. I was born in 1896 and my parents were married in 1919.
    —*J. R. Ackerley (d. 1967), My Father and Myself (1968)*

10. Oh, I'm glad my parents are dead. This would've killed them.
    —*Joe Orton (d. 1967), What the Butler Saw (1969)*

11. If one is not going to take the necessary precautions to avoid having parents, one must undertake to bring them up.

—QUENTIN CRISP, *The Naked Civil Servant (1968)*

12. We are never done with thinking about our parents, I suppose, and come to know them better long after they are dead than we ever did when they were alive.

—MAY SARTON, *At Seventy (1982)*

13. Your father don't approve of the way you live, but that don't mean he don't love you. Lord . . . parents love their children. They can't help it. That's what the Lord put us here for—to love our children and make them miserable. . . . That was a joke.

—LARRY DUPLECHAN, *Captain Swing (1993)*

Parties

1. Whether a party can have much success without a woman present I must ask others to decide, but one thing is certain, no party is any fun unless seasoned with folly.

—DESIDERIUS ERASMUS, *Praise of Folly (1509)*

2. Come, / Let's have one other gaudy night. Call to me / All my sad captains. Fill our bowls once more, / Let's mock the midnight bell.

—WILLIAM SHAKESPEARE, *Antony and Cleopatra (1606)*

3. On with the dance! let joy be unconfined; / No sleep till morn, when Youth and Pleasure meet / To chase the glowing hours with flying feet.

—GEORGE GORDON, LORD BYRON, *Childe Harold's Pilgrimage (1812–18)*

4. I am for those who believe in loose delight, I / share the midnight orgies of young men, / I dance with the dancers and drink with the / drinkers.

—WALT WHITMAN, *"Native Moments" (1860)*

5. I adore political parties. They are the only place left to us where people don't talk politics.

—OSCAR WILDE, *An Ideal Husband (1895)*

6. We give lovely parties that last through the night, / I dress as a woman and scream with delight.

—NOËL COWARD, *"Bright Young People" (1931)*

7. At a dinner party one should eat wisely but not too well, and talk well but not too wisely.

—W. SOMERSET MAUGHAM, *A Writer's Notebook (1949)*

Passion

▼

1. Love/(the fall of wind on a mountain,/of a storm on a steep wooded
slope,/of a hurricane force, of rustling
oak/of deep-rooted trees uptorn) /
took me by the heart and shook hard.
  —SAPPHO (7th century BCE),
    Fragment 47; trans. Anita
    George

2. In the fevered course of my pursuit / You faltered, turned, and ten-
derly / Shaded my burning heart with
your breast.
  —SAPPHO (7th century BCE),
    Fragment 48; trans. Anita
    George

3. I felt my soul on my lips as I was
kissing Agathon. / The poor thing
came there in the hope of crossing
over.
  —PLATO (4th century BCE),
    Epigraph 6, "To Agathon"; trans.
    Dennis Kratz

4. Jupiter, not wanting man's life to
be wholly gloomy and grim, has
bestowed far more passion than reason—you could reckon the ration as
twenty-four to one. Moreover, he con-
fined reason to a cramped corner of
the head and left all the rest of the
body to the passions.

  —DESIDERIUS ERASMUS, Praise of
    Folly (1509)

5. But I can love, and love at such a
pitch, / As I dare boast it will ev'n you
enrich.
  —KATHERINE PHILIPS, "To my Lady
    M. Cavendish, chusing the Name
    of Polycrite" (1664)

6. That sweet fury, that rage of active
delight which crowns the enjoyments
of a mutual love-passion.
  —JOHN CLELAND, Memoirs of a
    Woman of Pleasure (1749)

7. How little do they know human
nature who think they can say to passion, so far shalt thou go, and no further!
  —SARAH SCOTT, The History of
    Cornelia (1750)

8. They declaim against the passions
without bothering to think that it is
from their flame philosophy lights its
torch.
  —MARQUIS DE SADE, L'Histoire de
    Juliette, ou les Prospérités du
    Vice (1797)

9. For each ecstatic instant / We must
an anguish pay / In keen and quivering ratio / To the ecstasy . . .

—EMILY DICKINSON, no. 125
(c. 1859), Complete Poems
(1955)

10. Not to discriminate every moment some passionate attitude in those about us, and in the brilliance of their gifts some tragic dividing of forces on their ways is, on this short day of frost and sun, to sleep before evening.
—WALTER PATER, Studies in the
History of the Renaissance
(1873)

11. Passion, that thing of beauty, that flowering without roots, has to be born, live and die without reason.
—GEORGETTE LEBLANC (1898), in
Souvenirs (1932);
trans. Janet Flanner

12. Well, the whole summer she was mine—a mad and irresponsible summer of moonlight nights, and infinite escapades, and passionate letters, and music, and poetry. Things were not tragic for us then, because although we cared passionately we didn't care deeply—not like now, though it was deepening all the time.
—VITA SACKVILLE-WEST (on her
affair with Violet Trefusis), diary
entry, 29 September 1920; quoted
in Nigel Nicholson, Portrait of a
Marriage (1973)

13. Like a barrier of fire her passion for the woman flared up to forbid her the love of the man; for as great as the mystery of virginity itself, is sometimes the power of the one who has destroyed it.
—RADCLYFFE HALL, The Well of
Loneliness (1928)

14. Night and day, you are the one / Only you beneath the moon and under the sun.
—COLE PORTER, "Night and Day"
(1932 song)

15. Mad About the Boy
—NOËL COWARD, song title (1932)

16. Nothing is real but those ten days in Paris when I held you in my arms and taught you to love, when your heart beat close against my heart, and your mouth was on mine, and our arms were round each other straining our bodies closer & more close, until there was agony in our loving.
—RADCLYFFE HALL, letter to
Evguenia Souline,
3 October 1934

17. I've Got You Under My Skin
—COLE PORTER, song title (1936)

18. At the climax, you were lit up with a quiet ecstasy, which enveloped your blessed body in a supernatural nimbus, like a cloak that you pierced with your head and feet.

—JEAN GENET, *Our Lady of the Flowers (1949)*

19. Love was a burning fence / about my house.
—AUDRE LORDE, *"Gemini" (1956)*

20. Passion is more important than justice.
—CARSON MCCULLERS, *Clock Without Hands (1961)*

21. To give oneself, one must annihilate oneself.
—VIOLETTE LEDUC, *Therese and Isabelle (1968)*

22. To hide a passion totally (or even to hide, more simply, its excess) is inconceivable: not because the human subject is too weak, but because passion is in essence made to be seen: the hiding must be seen: *I want you to know that I am hiding something from you,* that is the active paradox I must resolve: *at one and the same time* it must be known and not known: I want you to know that I don't want to show my feelings: that is the message I address to the other.
—ROLAND BARTHES, *A Lover's Discourse (1977)*

23. With each touch of you / I am fresh bread / warm and rising.
—PAT PARKER, *"I Have" (1978)*

24. Somewhere between the swamp and the mountains. Somewhere between fear and sex. Somewhere between God and the Devil passion is and the way there is sudden and the way back is worse.
—JEANETTE WINTERSON, *The Passion (1987)*

Past, Present, Future

1. I did love you once, Atthis, / But that was long ago. / I thought you were a little thing: / A girl without grace.
—SAPPHO *(7th century BCE), Fragment 49; trans. Anita George*

2. Past and to come, seems best; things present, worst.
—WILLIAM SHAKESPEARE, *2 Henry IV (1597–98)*

3. The Past—the dark unfathom'd retrospect! / The teeming gulf—the

sleepers and the shadows! / The past! the infinite greatness of the past! / For what is the present after all but a growth out of the past?
    —WALT WHITMAN, *"Passage to India" (1871)*

4. The past is of no importance. The present is of no importance. It is with the future that we have to deal. For the past is what man should not have been. The present is what man ought not to be. The future is what artists are.
    —OSCAR WILDE, *"The Soul of Man Under Socialism" (1895)*

5. Those who do not remember the past are condemned to repeat it.
    —GEORGE SANTAYANA, *The Life of Reason (1906)*

6. Our faith in the present dies out long before our faith in the future.
    —RUTH BENEDICT (1913), in *Margaret Mead, An Anthropologist at Work (1959)*

7. The past not merely is not fugitive, it remains present.
    —MARCEL PROUST, *Remembrance of Things Past: The Guermantes Way (1921)*

8. Each had his past shut in him like the leaves of a book known to him by heart; and his friends could only read the title.
    —VIRGINIA WOOLF, *Jacob's Room (1922)*

9. The past is immortalized; that is to say, it is dead; and death is the root of all godliness and all abiding significance.
    —THOMAS MANN, *"Disorder and Early Sorrow" (1925)*

10. There is something about the present which we would not exchange, though we were offered a choice of all past ages to live in.
    —VIRGINIA WOOLF, *"How It Strikes a Contemporary," The Common Reader (1925)*

11. I love my past, I love my present. I'm not ashamed of what I've had, and I'm not sad because I have it no longer.
    —COLETTE, *The Last of Cheri (1926)*

12. In me past, present, future meet.
    —SIEGFRIED SASSOON, *The Heart's Journey (1928)*

13. We can never go back again, that much is certain. The past is still too close to us.
    —DAPHNE DU MAURIER, *Rebecca (1938)*

14. The future will one day be the present and will seem as unimportant as the present does.
    —W. SOMERSET MAUGHAM, *The Summing Up (1938)*

15. We will let the dead past bury its dead, and go back to the old days and the old ways and the old happiness.
—*IVY COMPTON-BURNETT, Two Worlds and Their Ways (1949)*

16. The past is a foreign country: they do things differently there.
—*L. P. HARTLEY, The Go-Between (1953)*

17. Like camels, we lived on our past.
—*ALICE B. TOKLAS, The Alice B. Toklas Cookbook (1954)*

18. The future is the most expensive luxury in the world.
—*THORNTON WILDER, The Matchmaker (1954)*

19. Love only what you do, / And not what you have done.
—*ADRIENNE RICH, "The Diamond Cutters" (1955)*

20. The future is like heaven— everyone exalts it but no one wants to go there now.
—*JAMES BALDWIN, Nobody Knows My Name (1961)*

21. Every journey into the past is complicated by delusions, false memories, false namings of real events.
—*ADRIENNE RICH, Of Woman Born (1976)*

22. We cannot live in the past, nor can we re-create it. Yet as we unravel the past, the future also unfolds before us, as though they are mirrors without which neither can be seen or happen.
—*JUDY GRAHN, Another Mother Tongue (1984)*

23. Yes, I have inherited the past because I have acknowledged it at last. And, now that I have come to understand it, I no longer need to look back.
—*PETER ACKROYD, English Music (1992)*

24. It is the great past, and not the dizzy present, that is the best door to the future.
—*CAMILLE PAGLIA, Sex, Art, and American Culture (1992)*

Perfection

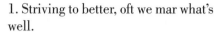

1. Striving to better, oft we mar what's well.
   —*WILLIAM SHAKESPEARE, King Lear (1605–6)*

2. The condition of perfection is idleness: the aim of perfection is youth.
   —*OSCAR WILDE, "Phrases and Philosophies for the Use of the Young" (1894)*

3. He whose preoccupation is with excellence longs fervently to find rest in perfection; and is not nothingness a form of perfection?
   —*THOMAS MANN, Death in Venice (1911)*

4. Perfection is a trifle dull.
   —*W. SOMERSET MAUGHAM, The Summing Up (1938)*

5. In the matter of love, too, I hold for perfection unadorned.
   —*MARGUERITE YOURCENAR, Coup de Grâce (1939)*

6. Perfection is no more a requisite to art than to heroes. Frigidaires are perfect. Beauty limps. My frigidaire has had to be replaced.
   —*NED ROREM, Music from Inside Out (1967)*

Personality

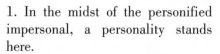

1. In the midst of the personified impersonal, a personality stands here.
   —*HERMAN MELVILLE, Moby-Dick (1851)*

2. What's the matter with this country is the matter with the lot of us individually—our sense of personality is a sense of outrage.
   —*ELIZABETH BOWEN, The Last September (1929)*

3. She had to confess inexperience; her personality was still too much for her, like a punt-pole.

—*ELIZABETH BOWEN, Friends and Relations (1931)*

4. We do not accept ourselves for what we are, we retreat from our real selves, and then we erect a personality to bridge the gap.
  —*SUSAN SONTAG, The Benefactor (1963)*

5. Humility is no substitute for a good personality.
  —*FRAN LEBOWITZ, Metropolitan Life (1978)*

6. I had to leave home so I could find myself, find my own intrinsic nature buried under the personality that had been imposed on me.
  —*GLORIA ANZALDÚA, Borderlands/La Frontera (1987)*

Perspective

▼

1. Nothing is perfect from every point of view.
  —*HORACE (1st century BCE), Odes II, 16*

2. I / Keep both my eyes in my two hands, / And see no more than I can touch.
  —*SOR JUANA INÉS DE LA CRUZ, "Hope" (c. 1680); trans. Kate Flores*

3. A bystander often sees more of the game than those who play.
  —*HORACE WALPOLE, The Castle of Otranto (1764)*

4. Man may be said to look out on the world from a sentry-box with two joined sashes for his window.
  —*HERMAN MELVILLE, Moby-Dick (1851)*

5. What one reads, or rather all that comes to us, is surely only of interest and value in proportion as we find ourselves therein,—form given to what was vague, what slumbered stirred to life.
  —*ALICE JAMES (1889), in Anna Robeson Burr, Alice James (1934)*

6. Certain people and certain things need to be approached on an angle.
  —*ANDRÉ GIDE, Journals, 26 October 1924*

7. This life's idiotic: we're seeing far too much of each other and yet we never see each other properly.
  —*COLETTE, The Cat (1933)*

8. No man ever looks at the world with pristine eyes. He sees it edited

by a definite set of customs and institutions and ways of thinking.
> —*RUTH BENEDICT, Patterns of Culture (1934)*

9. No object is mysterious. The mystery is your eye.
> —*ELIZABETH BOWEN, The House in Paris (1935)*

10. If you look at life one way, there is always cause for alarm.
> —*ELIZABETH BOWEN, The Death of the Heart (1938)*

11. I am a camera with its shutter open, quite passive, recording, not thinking.
> —*CHRISTOPHER ISHERWOOD, Goodbye to Berlin (1939)*

Perversion and Perversity

1. I am not so nice / To change true rules for odd inventions.
> —*WILLIAM SHAKESPEARE, The Taming of the Shrew (1593)*

2. No man can tickle himself.
> —*FRANCIS BACON (d. 1626), Sylva Sylvarum (1627)*

3. I can scarcely be accused of shirking reality, but I do not wish to spend the rest of my life with my nose nailed to other people's lavatories.
> —*EDITH SITWELL (d. 1964), on William S. Burroughs's The Naked Lunch, quoted in The Independent (1994)*

4. Perversity is the muse of modern literature.
> —*SUSAN SONTAG, Against Interpretation (1966)*

5. How would you describe a man who mauls young boys, importunes policemen and lives on terms of intimacy with a woman who shaves twice a day?
> —*JOE ORTON (d. 1967), What the Butler Saw (1969)*

6. I insist upon my sickness, even arguing its value, turning it into a perversity, something clung to. Because it is mine, because it is my whole life now, my obsession.
> —*KATE MILLETT, Sita (1976)*

7. If that's perverse, / there are, you'll guess, perversions I'd prefer.

—MARILYN HACKER, *Love, Death,
and the Changing of the Seasons
(1986)*

8. Profanation and violation are part of the perversity of sex, which never will conform to liberal theories of benevolence. Every model of morally or politically correct sexual behavior *will be subverted,* by nature's daemonic law.
　　—CAMILLE PAGLIA, *Sexual Personae
　　(1990)*

9. Sick and perverted always appeals to me.
　　—MADONNA, *in Paul Zollo,
　　Songwriters on Songwriting
　　(1991)*

10. Only people with a profound aversion to bodily fluids could have invented the bidet.
　　—LISA ALTHER, *Five Minutes in
　　Heaven (1995)*

Pleasure

▼

1. May you drowse on the breast of a tender girlfriend.
　　—SAPPHO *(7th century* BCE*),
　　Fragment 126; trans. Anita
　　George (1995)*

2. Is there any greater or keener pleasure than that of sexual love?
　　—SOCRATES *(5th century* BCE*), in
　　Plato (4th century* BCE*), The
　　Republic*

3. Everyone is dragged on by their favourite pleasure.
　　—VIRGIL, *Eclogues (43–37* BCE*)*

4. Variety is the soul of pleasure.
　　—APHRA BEHN, *The Rover (1681)*

5. Novelty ever makes the strongest impressions, and in pleasures, especially.
　　—JOHN CLELAND, *Memoirs of a
　　Woman of Pleasure (1749)*

6. Pleasure's a sin, and sometimes / Sin's a pleasure.
　　—GEORGE GORDON, LORD BYRON,
　　Don Juan (1819–24)

7. I don't care for the great questions. I care for pleasure—for amusement.
　　—HENRY JAMES, *The Europeans
　　(1878)*

8. Pleasure is the only thing worth having a theory about.

—OSCAR WILDE, *The Picture of Dorian Gray (1891)*

9. Pleasure after all is a safer guide than either right or duty.
—SAMUEL BUTLER *(d. 1902), The Way of All Flesh (1903)*

10. All this fuss about sleeping together. For physical pleasure I'd sooner go to my dentist any day.
—EVELYN WAUGH, *Vile Bodies (1930)*

11. The essential delight of blood drawn from ageless springs . . . / Never to deny its pleasure in the morning single light.
—STEPHEN SPENDER, *"I Think Continually of Those Who Were Truly Great" (1933)*

12. The spirit is often most free when the body is satiated with pleasure; indeed, sometimes the stars shine more brightly seen from the gutter than from the hilltop.
—W. SOMERSET MAUGHAM, *The Summing Up (1938)*

13. Anticipation of pleasure is a pleasure in itself.
—SYLVIA TOWNSEND WARNER, *letter, 1960*

14. Pleasure is by no means an infallible critical guide, but it is the least fallible.

—W. H. AUDEN, *The Dyer's Hand (1962)*

15. Marred pleasure's best, shadow makes the sun strong.
—STEVIE SMITH, *"The Queen and the Young Princess" (1964)*

16. Pleasure is continually disappointed, reduced, deflated, in favor of strong, noble virtues: Truth, Death, Progress, Struggle, Joy, etc. Its victorious rival is Desire: we are always being told about Desire, never about Pleasure.
—ROLAND BARTHES, *The Pleasure of the Text (1966)*

17. There are some elements in life—above all, sexual pleasure—about which it isn't necessary to have a position.
—SUSAN SONTAG, *in Village Voice, 22 March 1976*

18. As to sex, the original pleasure, I cannot recommend too highly the advantages of androgyny.
—JAN MORRIS, *Pleasures of a Tangled Life (1989)*

19. I've seen Puritans going past a theatre where all was merriment and pleasure and holding their starched linen to their noses for fear they might smell pleasure and be infected by it.
—JEANETTE WINTERSON, *Sexing the Cherry (1989)*

Police

1. You are thought here to be the most senseless and fit man for the constable of the watch, therefore bear you the lantern.
> —*WILLIAM SHAKESPEARE, Much Ado About Nothing (1598)*

2. With their souls of patent leather, / they come down the road.
> —*FEDERICO GARCÍA LORCA, "Romance de la Guardia Civil Española" (1935–36)*

3. [The police] learned something from them Harlem riots. They used to beat your head right in public, but now they only beat it after they get you down to the station house.
> —*LANGSTON HUGHES, Simple Speaks His Mind (1950)*

4. You won't find a policeman around here; they're all over on the west side of the park chasing fairies down from trees or out of the bushes. That's all they do. That's their function.

> —*EDWARD ALBEE, The Zoo Story (1958)*

5. A *functioning* police state needs no police.
> —*WILLIAM S. BURROUGHS, The Naked Lunch (1959)*

6. Reading isn't an occupation we encourage among police officers. We try to keep the paperwork down to a minimum.
> —*JOE ORTON, Loot (1966)*

7. However low a man sinks he never reaches the level of the police.
> —*QUENTIN CRISP, The Naked Civil Servant (1968)*

8. He may be a very nice man. But I haven't got the time to figure that out. All I know is, he's got a uniform and a gun and I have to relate to him that way. That's the only way to relate to him because one of us may have to die.
> —*JAMES BALDWIN, A Dialogue, with Nikki Giovanni (1973)*

Politics and Politicians

1. There are some whom the applause of the multitudes has deluded into the belief that they are really statesmen.
> —*PLATO (4th century BCE), The Republic*

2. Nothing is so foolish, they say, as for a man to stand for office and woo the crowd to win its vote, buy its support with presents, court the applause of all those fools and feel self-satisfied when they cry their approval, and then in his hour of triumph to be carried round like an effigy for the public to stare at, and end up cast in bronze to stand in the market place.
> —*DESIDERIUS ERASMUS, Praise of Folly (1509)*

3. There have been many great men that have flattered the people who ne'er loved them.
> —*WILLIAM SHAKESPEARE, Coriolanus (1608)*

4. It will be impossible to establish a higher political life than the people themselves crave.
> —*JANE ADDAMS, Twenty Years at Hull House (1910)*

5. The friend of humanity cannot recognize a distinction between what is political and what is not. There is nothing that is not political.
> —*THOMAS MANN, The Magic Mountain (1924)*

6. Would the world ever be run by anything better than personal passion, and the scoring off each other of amoral schoolboys?
> —*KATE O'BRIEN, That Lady (1946)*

7. In a society like ours, politics is improvisation. To the artful dodger rather than the true believer goes the prize.
> —*GORE VIDAL, Rocking the Boat (1962)*

8. We cannot cure the evils of politics with politics. . . . Fifty years ago if we had gone the way of Freud (to study and tackle hostility within ourselves) instead of Marx, we might be closer to peace than we are.
> —*ANAÏS NIN, The Diary of Anaïs Nin, Vol. 5 (1974)*

9. Lesbians have historically been deprived of a political existence through "inclusion" as female versions of male homosexuality. To equate lesbian existence with male

homosexuality because each is stigmatized is to erase female reality once again.

> —ADRIENNE RICH, "Compulsory
> Heterosexuality and Lesbian
> Existence" (1980)

10. I think a lot of gay people who are not dealing with their homosexuality get into right-wing politics.

> —ARMISTEAD MAUPIN, quoted in
> the Guardian (London),
> 22 April 1988

11. My anti-liberal position should not be mistaken for conservatism.

> —CAMILLE PAGLIA, Sex, Art, and
> American Culture (1992)

Pornography   and   Erotica

1. Who knows what a degrading, vulgar life you lead; / how horrible the surroundings must have been / when you posed to have this picture taken; / what a cheap soul you must have.

> —CONSTANTINE P. CAVAFY, "The
> Photograph" (1913)

2. There's only one good test of pornography. Get twelve normal men to read the book, and then ask them, "Did you get an erection?" If the answer is "Yes" from a majority of the twelve, then the book is pornographic.

> —W. H. AUDEN, "March 17, 1947,"
> The Table Talk of W. H. Auden,
> ed. Alan Ansen and Nicholas
> Jenkins (1990)

3. What I wanted to get at is the value difference between pornographic playing-cards when you're a kid and pornographic playing-cards when you're older. It's that when you're a kid you use the cards as a substitute for a real experience, and when you're older you use real experience as a substitute for fantasy.

> —EDWARD ALBEE, The Zoo Story
> (1958)

4. What pornographic literature does is precisely to drive a wedge between one's existence as a full human being and one's existence as a sexual being—while in ordinary life a healthy person is one who prevents such a gap from opening up.

—SUSAN SONTAG, "The
Pornographic Imagination,"
Styles of Radical Will (1966)

5. Straightforward commercial pornography: and what's wrong with that?
—BRIGID BROPHY, In Transit
(1969)

6. I see the function of true Erotica (writing which is pro-, not antisexual) as one not only permissible but worthy of encouragement and social approval, as its laudable and legitimate function is to increase sexual appetite just as culinary prose encourages other appetites.
—KATE MILLETT, Sexual Politics
(1969)

7. Pornography is a direct denial of the power of the erotic, for it represents the suppression of true feeling. Pornography emphasizes sensation without feeling.
—AUDRE LORDE, Uses of the Erotic
(1978)

8. This negative morality which pervades our society is the root not only of homophobia but of the punishing violence of much pornography. We won't move freely in the world until all people are required to confront their sexual natures in order to understand, take responsibility for and celebrate them, as we have had to.
—JANE RULE, A Hot-Eyed Moderate
(1985)

9. Pornography is the first place a lot of gay men are exposed to gay sex. It functions as a kind of cookbook for sexual technique and allows us to build a catalog of images of how it can be when males touch each other.
—FRANK BROWNING, The Culture of
Desire: Paradox and Perversity
in Gay Lives Today (1993)

10. Pornography exists for the lonesome, the ugly, the fearful. . . . It's made for the losers.
—RITA MAE BROWN, in Ms., 1994

Poverty

1. Wealth and poverty: the one is the parent of luxury and indolence, and the other of meanness and viciousness, and both of discontent.
—*PLATO (4th century BCE), The Republic*

2. O world, how apt the poor are to be proud!
—*WILLIAM SHAKESPEARE, Twelfth Night (1601)*

3. Come away! Poverty's catching.
—*APHRA BEHN, The Rover (1677)*

4. Too poor for a bribe, and too proud to importune, / He had not the method of making a fortune.
—*THOMAS GRAY, "Sketch of His Own Character" (1761)*

5. As for the virtuous poor, one can pity them, of course, but one cannot possibly admire them.
—*OSCAR WILDE, "The Soul of Man Under Socialism" (1895)*

6. I have no money at all: I live, or am supposed to live, on a few francs a day. . . . Like dear St. Francis of Assisi I am wedded to Poverty: but in my case the marriage is not a success.
—*OSCAR WILDE, letter, June 1899*

7. 'Tis the superfluity of one man which makes the poverty of the other.
—*VERNON LEE, Limbo (1908)*

8. We are not concerned with the very poor. They are unthinkable, and only to be approached by the statistician or the poet.
—*E. M. FORSTER, Howards End (1910)*

9. Poverty keeps together more homes than it breaks up.
—*SAKI [H. H. MUNRO], "Esmé," The Chronicles of Clovis (1911)*

10. Privation prevents all thought, substitutes of any other mental image than of a hot, sweet-smelling dish, and reduces hope to the shape of a rounded loaf set in rays of glory.
—*COLETTE, Music Hall Sidelights (1913)*

11. He knew now, more than ever, that money was everything, the wall that stood between all he loathed and all he wanted.
—*WILLA CATHER, "Paul's Case" (1920)*

12. People don't resent having nothing nearly as much as too little.
—*IVY COMPTON-BURNETT, A Family and a Fortune (1939)*

13. Hunger allows no choice / To the citizen or the police.
   —W. H. AUDEN,
      "September 1, 1939" (1940)

14. I have two enemies in all the world . . . / The hunger of the hungry and the fullness of the full.
   —MARINA TSVETAEVA (d. 1941), "If the Soul Was Born with Pinions," Swans' Encampment (1957)

15. You can be young without money but you can't be old without it.
   —TENNESSEE WILLIAMS, Cat on a Hot Tin Roof (1955)

16. We're really all of us bottomly broke. I haven't had time to work in weeks.
   —JACK KEROUAC, On the Road (1957)

17. Anyone who has ever struggled with poverty knows how extremely expensive it is to be poor.
   —JAMES BALDWIN, Nobody Knows My Name (1961)

18. Poverty is an expensive luxury. We cannot afford it.
   —ELEANOR ROOSEVELT (d. 1962), Tomorrow Is Now (1963)

19. The heartless stupidity of those who have never known a great and terrifying poverty.
   —EDITH SITWELL (d. 1964), Taken Care Of (1965)

20. Once poor, always wantin'. Rich is just a way of wantin' bigger.
   —LILY TOMLIN, as her character "Wanda V.," in Rolling Stone, 24 October 1974

21. When we are not physically starving, we have the luxury to realize psychic and emotional starvation.
   —CHERRÍE MORAGA, "La Güera" (1983)

22. We are all more blind to what we have than to what we have not.
   —AUDRE LORDE, "Trip to Russia," Sister Outsider (1984)

Power

1. They that have power to hurt and will do none, / That do not do the thing they most do show, / Who moving others are themselves as stone, / Unmovèd, cold, and to temptation slow— / They rightly do inherit heaven's graces, / And husband nature's riches from expense; / They

are the lords and owners of their faces.

—WILLIAM SHAKESPEARE, *Sonnet 94 (1609)*

2. It is a strange desire to seek power and to lose liberty.

—FRANCIS BACON, *"Of Great Place," Essays (1625)*

3. Power, when invested in the hands of knaves or fools, generally is the source of tyranny.

—CHARLOTTE CHARKE, *A Narrative of the Life of Mrs Charlotte Charke (1755)*

4. It is natural for men to want power. But to seek power actively takes a temperament baffling to both the simple and the wise. The simple cannot fathom how any man would dare presume to prevail, while the wise are amazed that any reasonable man would want the world, assuming he could get it.

—GORE VIDAL, *Rocking the Boat (1962)*

5. When the world changes and one day women are capable of seizing power and devoting themselves to the exercise of arms and letters in which they will doubtless soon excel, woe betide us.

—MONIQUE WITTIG, *Les Guérillères (1969)*

6. Power is not an institution, and not a structure; neither is it a certain strength we are endowed with; it is the name that one attributes to a complex strategical situation in a particular society.

—MICHEL FOUCAULT, *The History of Sexuality, Vol. 1 (1976)*

7. I call the discourse of power a discourse that engenders blame, hence guilt, in its recipient.

—ROLAND BARTHES, *lecture, Collège de France, 7 January 1977*

8. Power is the test. Some, once they have it, are content to buy the show of liking, and punish those who withhold it; then you have a despot. But some keep a true eye for how they seem to others, and care about it, which holds them back from much mischief.

—MARY RENAULT, *The Praise Singer (1978)*

9. Bodies in power tend to stay in power, unless external forces disturb them.

—CATHARINE R. STIMPSON, *"The Power to Name" (1979)*

10. Nobody is as powerful as we make them out to be.

—ALICE WALKER, *In Search of Our Mothers' Gardens (1983)*

11. "Power may be at the end of a gun," but sometimes it's also at the end of the shadow or the image of a gun.

—JEAN GENET, *Prisoner of Love (1986)*

12. Power is far more exciting than sex.
>—*GORE VIDAL, in Chicago Tribune, 22 June 1987*

13. Three hundred homosexuals rule the world and I know every one of them.
>—*DAVID HOCKNEY, in Manchester Guardian Weekly, 21 May 1989*

P r e j u d i c e

1. Prejudice is the sole author of infamies: how many acts are so qualified by an opinion forged out of nought but prejudice!
>—*MARQUIS DE SADE, L'Histoire de Juliette, ou les Prospérités du Vice (1797)*

2. Whenever we discover a dislike in us toward anyone, we should ever be a little suspicious of ourselves.
>—*HERMAN MELVILLE, Redburn (1849)*

3. The paradoxes of today are the prejudices of tomorrow, since the most benighted and most deplorable prejudices have had their moment of novelty when fashion lent them its fragile grace.
>—*MARCEL PROUST, Pleasures and Regrets (1896)*

4. The paradox is here: when cultivated people do stay away from a certain portion of the population, when all social advantages are persistently withheld, it may be for years, the result itself is pointed to as a reason and is used as an argument for continued withholding.
>—*JANE ADDAMS, Twenty Years at Hull House (1910)*

5. They're despised and rejected of their fellow-men today. What they suffer in a world not yet ready to admit their right to existence, their right to love, no normal person can realize; but I believe that the time is not so far distant when we shall recognize in the best of our intermediate types the leaders and masters of the race.
>—*A. T. FITZROY, Despised and Rejected (1918)*

6. We must exclude someone from our gathering, or we shall be left with nothing.
>—*E. M. FORSTER, A Passage to India (1924)*

7. A very great many have very many prejudices concerning loving. . . . This is very common. Not very many are very well pleased with other people's ways of having loving in them. Some are very much pleased with some ways of having loving and not with other ways of having loving. Some are wanting people to be very nice in having loving being in them. Some are pretty well ready to let most people do the kind of loving they have naturally in them but are not ready to let all people do the loving the way loving naturally comes to be in them.

> —GERTRUDE STEIN, *The Making of Americans (1925)*

8. And wherefore is he wearing such a conscience-stricken air? / Oh they're taking him to prison for the colour of his hair.

> —A. E. HOUSMAN *(d. 1936), no. 18, Additional Poems, Collected Poems (1939)*

9. If we—and now I mean the relatively conscious whites and the relatively conscious blacks, who must, like lovers, insist on, or create the consciousness of others—do not falter in our duty now, we may be able, handful that we are, to end the racial nightmare, and achieve our country, and change the history of the world.

> —JAMES BALDWIN, *The Fire Next Time (1963)*

10. There will still be a stigma attached to "the love that dare not speak its name" in the minds of millions of people for generations to come.

> —NOËL COWARD, *Song at Twilight (1966)*

11. Instead of being presented with stereotypes by age, sex, color, class, or religion, children must have the opportunity to learn that within each range, some people are loathsome and some are delightful.

> —MARGARET MEAD, *Twentieth Century Faith (1972)*

12. Well, if I were a dyke and a pair of Podhoretzes came waddling toward me on the beach, copies of Leviticus and Freud in hand, I'd get in touch with the nearest Alsatian dealer pronto.

> —GORE VIDAL, *on Norman Podhoretz's invective against lesbians at the Island of Pines, Pink Triangle and Yellow Star (1982)*

13. Of course it is extremely difficult to like oneself in a culture which thinks you are a disease.

> —CHRYSTOS, *"I Don't Understand Those Who Have Turned Away from Me" (1983)*

Press and the Media

1. To a philosopher all news, as it is called, is gossip, and they who edit it and read it are old women over their tea.

—HENRY DAVID THOREAU, "Where I Lived, and What I Lived For," Walden (1854)

2. I cannot imagine how a pure hand can touch a newspaper without disgust.

—CHARLES BAUDELAIRE (d. 1867), Mon Coeur Mis à Nu (1887)

3. Newspapers, even, have degenerated. They may now be absolutely relied upon.

—OSCAR WILDE, "The Decay of Lying" (1891)

4. Journalism is unreadable, and literature is not read.

—OSCAR WILDE, "The Critic as Artist" (1891)

5. To read a newspaper is to refrain from reading something worth while. The first discipline of education must therefore be to refuse resolutely to feed the mind with canned chatter.

—ALEISTER CROWLEY, The Confessions of Aleister Crowley (1929)

6. News is what a chap who doesn't care much about anything wants to read. And it's only news until he has read it. After that it's dead.

—EVELYN WAUGH, Scoop (1938)

7. If newspapers were written by people whose sole object in writing was to tell the truth about politics and the truth about art we should not believe in war, and we should believe in art.

—VIRGINIA WOOLF, Three Guineas (1938)

8. You must always start by refusing to give an interview to anybody. Then later you can fill the front page.

—COLETTE, Gigi (1944)

9. The next day's headlines were the talk of Troy:/BIG BIRD SENSATION, MISSING LOCAL BOY.

—WILLIAM PLOMER, "Ganymede" (1945)

10. It is very difficult to have a free, fair and honest press anywhere in the world. In the first place, as a rule, papers are largely supported by advertising, and that immediately gives the advertisers a certain hold over the medium which they use.

—*ELEANOR ROOSEVELT,*
If You Ask Me (1946)

11. Never lose your temper with the Press or the public.
   —*CHRISTABEL PANKHURST (d. 1958),*
   Unshackled (1959)

12. Say what you like, there's lots to be learned from television. I know it's for profits, but in its way it's a big universal education.
   —*COLIN MacINNES, Absolute*
   Beginners (1959)

13. We are given in our newspapers and on TV and radio exactly what we, the public, insist on having, and this very frequently is mediocre information and mediocre entertainment.
   —*ELEANOR ROOSEVELT (1959), My*
   Day, Vol. 3 (1991)

14. What the mass media offer is not popular art, but entertainment which is intended to be consumed like food, forgotten, and replaced by a new dish.
   —*W. H. AUDEN, The Dyer's Hand*
   (1962)

15. The aim of so much journalism is to exploit the moral prejudices of the reader, to say nothing of those of the proprietor.
   —*GORE VIDAL, in Nova (1969)*

16. Television is for appearing on, not for watching.
   —*NOËL COWARD (d. 1973),*
   quoted in the Guardian,
   28 November 1988

17. Radio news is bearable. This is due to the fact that while the news is being broadcast the disc jockey is not allowed to talk.
   —*FRAN LEBOWITZ, Metropolitan*
   Life (1978)

18. The press is too often a distorting mirror, which deforms the people and events it represents, making them seem bigger or smaller than they really are.
   —*MARGUERITE YOURCENAR, With*
   Open Eyes (1980)

19. In Czechoslovakia there is no such thing as freedom of the press. In the United States there is no such thing as freedom from the press.
   —*MARTINA NAVRATILOVA, in Lee*
   Green, Sportswit (1984)

Privacy and Secrecy

1. Nakedness is uncomely, as well in mind as body, and it addeth no small reverence to men's manners and actions if they be not altogether open. Therefore, set it down: *That a habit of secrecy is both politic and moral.*

> —FRANCIS BACON, "Of Simulation and Dissimulation," Essays (1625)

2. Love ceases to be a pleasure, / When it ceases to be a secret.

> —APHRA BEHN, "Four O'Clock," The Lover's Watch (1696)

3. So long as the laws remain such as they are today, employ some discretion: loud opinion forces us to do so; but in privacy and silence let us compensate ourselves for that cruel chastity we are obliged to display in public.

> —MARQUIS DE SADE, Philosophy in the Bedroom (1795)

4. I have grown to love secrecy. It seems to be the one thing that can make modern life mysterious or marvellous to us. The commonest thing is delightful if only one hides it.

> —OSCAR WILDE, The Picture of Dorian Gray (1891)

5. I might have been a gold-fish in a glass bowl for all the privacy I got.

> —SAKI [H. H. Munro], "The Innocence of Reginald," Reginald (1904)

6. Secrecy has this disadvantage: we lose the sense of proportion; we cannot tell whether our secret is important or not.

> —E. M. FORSTER, A Room with a View (1908)

7. A room with a view—and you / And no one to worry us.

> —NOËL COWARD, "A Room with a View" (1929)

8. I have always had something to live besides a private life.

> —MARGARET ANDERSON, My Thirty Years' War (1930)

9. The best letters of our time are precisely those that can never be published.

> —VIRGINIA WOOLF, "Modern Letters" (1930)

10. I am ill at ease with people whose lives are an open book.

—*IVY COMPTON-BURNETT, More Women than Men (1933)*

11. There is nothing that gives more assurance than a mask.

—*COLETTE, My Apprenticeships (1936)*

12. The inside room was a very private place. She could be in the middle of a house full of people and still feel like she was locked up by herself.

—*CARSON MCCULLERS, The Heart Is a Lonely Hunter (1940)*

13. May we agree that private life is irrelevant? Multiple, mixed, ambiguous at best—out of it we try to fashion the crystal clear, the singular, the absolute, and that is what is relevant; that is what matters.

—*MAY SARTON, Mrs. Stevens Hears the Mermaids Singing (1965)*

14. In large Victorian houses with many rooms and heavy doors, the occupants could be mysterious and exciting to one another in a way that those who live in rackety developments can never hope to be. Not even the lust of a Lord Byron could survive the fact of Levittown.

—*GORE VIDAL, New York Review of Books, 31 March 1966*

15. Isn't privacy about keeping taboos in their place?

—*KATE MILLETT, speech, Women Writers' Conference, Los Angeles, 22 March 1975*

Procreation

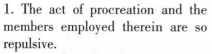

1. The act of procreation and the members employed therein are so repulsive.

—*LEONARDO DA VINCI, Dell'Anatomia Fogli (c. 1500)*

2. This type of man who is devoted to the study of wisdom is always most unlucky in everything, and particularly when it comes to procreating children; I imagine this is because Nature wants to ensure that the evils of wisdom shall not spread further throughout mankind.

—*DESIDERIUS ERASMUS, Praise of Folly (1509)*

3. Get thee to a nunnery. Why wouldst thou be a breeder of sinners?

—*WILLIAM SHAKESPEARE, Hamlet
(1600–1601)*

4. Do not breed. Nothing gives less pleasure than childbearing.
　—*MARQUIS DE SADE, L'Histoire de
　　Juliette, ou les Prospérités du
　　Vice (1797)*

5. A hen is only an egg's way of making another egg.
　—*SAMUEL BUTLER, Life and Habit
　　(1877)*

6. If people waited to know one another before they married, the world wouldn't be so grossly over-populated as it is now.
　—*W. SOMERSET MAUGHAM, Mrs. Dot
　　(1912)*

7. The night my father got me / His mind was not on me.
　—*A. E. HOUSMAN, no. 14 ["The
　　Culprit"], Last Poems (1922)*

8. It will all go on as long as women are stupid enough to go on bringing men into the world.
　—*DOROTHY RICHARDSON,
　　Pilgrimage: The Tunnel (1919)*

9. I'm one of the blind alleys off the main road of procreation.

—*EVELYN WAUGH, Decline and Fall
(1928)*

10. One wonders how they ever brought themselves to commit the grotesque act necessary to beget children.
　—*VITA SACKVILLE-WEST, Grand
　　Canyon (1942)*

11. Let us therefore respect these variants of the species who offer us their gifts: those singular beings who created works of genius instead of more dubious offspring, for it is known that the genius excels in production rather than reproduction. May those "blossoming peaks" of our race, whose only fruit are their works of art, console us for the multiplying mediocrity of humanity.
　—*NATALIE CLIFFORD BARNEY, Traits
　　et Portraits (1963)*

12. Breeding and bohemianism do not mix. For breeding you need a steady job, you need a mortgage, you need credit, you need insurance. And don't you dare die, either, until the family's future is provided for.
　—*CHRISTOPHER ISHERWOOD, A
　　Single Man (1964)*

13. To bring into the world an unwanted human being is as antisocial an act as murder.
　—*GORE VIDAL, in Esquire,
　　October 1968*

14. Posterity trembles like a leaf / and we go on making heirs and heirlooms.
> —ADRIENNE RICH, "The Demon Lover" (1969)

15. Your parents should have thought of the overpopulation problem.

16. Disgust is reason's proper response to the grossness of procreative nature.
> —CAMILLE PAGLIA, Sexual Personae (1990)

> —CHARLES LUDLAM, Hot Ice (1974)

Progress

1. Only mediocrities progress.
> —OSCAR WILDE, in Pall Mall Gazette, 25 September 1894

2. All progress is based upon a universal innate desire on the part of every organism to live beyond its income.
> —SAMUEL BUTLER (d. 1902), Note Books (1912)

3. There is an unlucky tendency to allow every new invention to add to life's complications, and every new power to increase life's hustling; so that, unless we can dominate the mischief, we are really the worse off instead of the better.
> —VERNON LEE, Hortus Vitae (1904)

4. Progress, far from consisting in change, depends on retentiveness. When change is absolute there remains no being to improve and no direction is set for possible improvement.
> —GEORGE SANTAYANA, The Life of Reason (1906)

5. No progress of humanity is possible unless it shakes off the yoke of authority and tradition.
> —ANDRÉ GIDE, Journals, 17 March 1931

6. Progress—progress is the dirtiest word in the language.
> —EDNA ST. VINCENT MILLAY, "We Have Gone Too Far," Collected Poems (1949)

7. Don't you see there isn't any real progress, there is only one large circle that we march in, around and around, each of us with our own little picture—in front of us—our own little mirage that we think is the future.

—LORRAINE HANSBERRY, *A Raisin in*
the Sun (1958)

—ALICE WALKER, in Claudia Tate,
ed., *Black Women Writers at*
Work (1983)

8. People tend to think that life really does progress for everyone eventually, the people progress, but actually only some people progress. The rest of the people don't.

9. Whoever said progress was a positive thing has never been to Florida or California.
—RITA MAE BROWN, *Bingo (1988)*

Prostitution and Hustling

1. I made a vice of necessity, from the constant fears I had of being turned out to starve.
   —JOHN CLELAND, *Memoirs of a*
   Woman of Pleasure (1749)

2. Be composed—be at ease with me—I am Walt / Whitman, liberal and lusty / as Nature, / Not till the sun excludes you do I exclude you, / Not till the waters refuse to glisten for you and the leaves to rustle for you, / do my words refuse to glisten and rustle for you.
   —WALT WHITMAN, *"To a Common*
   Prostitute" (1860)

3. And this is of a poor lad born in the slums, who with achingly lonely heart once walked the streets of London. / Many spoke to him because he was fair—asked him to come and have a drink, and so forth; but still it

was no satisfaction to him; for they did not give him that which he needed.
   —EDWARD CARPENTER, *"A Mightier*
   than Mammon," Towards
   Democracy (1883)

4. The commercial prostitution of love is the last outcome of our whole social system, and its most clear condemnation. It flaunts in our streets, it hides in the garment of respectability under the name of matrimony.
   —EDWARD CARPENTER, *Love's*
   Coming of Age (1911)

5. If you want to buy my wares, / Follow me and climb the stairs.
   —COLE PORTER, *"Love for Sale,"*
   The New Yorkers (1930)

6. The world is full of whores. What it really needs is a good bookkeeper.
   —JEAN GENET, *The Balcony (1956)*

7. So long as we were in a room in a brothel, we belonged to our fantasies, but once having exposed them, we're now tied up with human beings, tied to you and forced to go on with this adventure according to the laws of visibility.
> —*JEAN GENET, The Balcony (1956)*

8. A country without bordels is like a house without bathrooms.
> —*MARLENE DIETRICH, Marlene Dietrich's ABC (1962)*

9. Will you sell your sex for the sake of your pen? . . . I would sell everything for greater exactness.
> —*VIOLETTE LEDUC, Mad in Pursuit (1971)*

10. All women have to sell their bodies. They have to do it on one level or another. . . . We can't make a decent living in this society.
> —*KATE MILLETT, in Claudia Dreifus, Radical Lifestyles (1971)*

11. Hustling is linked to narcissism and being paid is proof that one is very strongly desired and desirable.
> —*JOHN RECHY, in Gay News, December 1975*

12. I was kind of a Hershey Bar whore—there wasn't much I wouldn't do for a nickel's worth of chocolate.
> —*TRUMAN CAPOTE (d. 1984), Answered Prayers (1986)*

13. "Easy meat" / but a reasonably good buy
> —*MORRISSEY, "Piccadilly Parlare" (1990)*

14. Prostitution testifies to the amoral power struggle of sex, which religion has never been able to stop. Prostitutes, pornographers, and their patrons are marauders in the forest of archaic night.
> —*CAMILLE PAGLIA, Sexual Personae (1990)*

15. Pocket full of green / bottom full of cum
> —*JONATHAN WILLIAMS, Quantulumcumque (1991)*

Psychology and Psychiatry

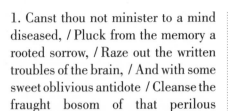

1. Canst thou not minister to a mind diseased, / Pluck from the memory a rooted sorrow, / Raze out the written troubles of the brain, / And with some sweet oblivious antidote / Cleanse the fraught bosom of that perilous stuff / Which weighs upon the heart?
    —WILLIAM SHAKESPEARE, Macbeth (1606)

2. The more one analyses people, the more all reasons for analysis disappear. Sooner or later one comes to that dreadful universal thing called human nature.
    —OSCAR WILDE, "The Decay of Lying" (1891)

3. Here was a big constructive imagination; here was a mere doctor laying bare the origins of Greek drama as no classical scholar had ever done, teaching the anthropologist what was really meant by his totem and taboo, probing the mysteries of sin, of sanctity, of sacrament—a man who, because he understood, purged the human spirit from fear. I have no confidence in psycho-analysis as a method of therapeutics but I am equally sure that for generations almost every branch of human knowledge will be enriched and illumined by the imagination of Freud.
    —JANE HARRISON, Reminiscences of a Student's Life (1925)

4. What doctor can know the entire truth? Many times they meet only the neurasthenics, those of us for whom life has proved too bitter. They are good, these doctors—some of them very good; they work hard trying to solve our problem, but half the time they must work in the dark—the whole truth is known only to the normal invert. The doctors cannot make the ignorant think, cannot hope to bring home the sufferings of millions; only one of ourselves can do that.
    —RADCLYFFE HALL, The Well of Loneliness (1928)

5. All the art of analysis consists in saying a truth only when the other person is ready for it, has been prepared for it by an organic process of gradation and evolution.
    —ANAÏS NIN (1932), Diary of Anaïs Nin, Vol. 1 (1966)

6. The Freudian theory is one of the most important foundation stones for an edifice to be built by future gen-

erations, the dwelling of a freer and wiser humanity.
> —THOMAS MANN, in New York
> Times, 21 June 1939

7. To us he is no more a person / Now but a whole climate of opinion.
> —W. H. AUDEN, "In Memory of
> Sigmund Freud" (1940)

8. It is almost impossible to be a doctor and an honest man, but it is obscenely impossible to be a psychiatrist without at the same time bearing the stamp of the most incontestable madness: that of being unable to resist that old atavistic reflex of the mass of humanity, which makes any man of science who is absorbed by this mass a kind of natural and inborn enemy of all genius.
> —ANTONIN ARTAUD, "Van Gogh, the
> Man Suicided by Society" (1947)

9. Psychoanalysis can unravel some of the forms of madness; it remains a stranger to the sovereign enterprise of unreason. It can neither limit nor transcribe, nor most certainly explain, what is essential in this enterprise.
> —MICHEL FOUCAULT, Madness and
> Civilization (1961)

10. Mrs. Strunk . . . is trained in the new tolerance, the technique of annihilation by blandness. Out comes her psychology book—bell and candle are no longer necessary. Reading from it in sweet singsong she proceeds to exorcise the unspeakable out of George. No reason for disgust, she intones, no cause for condemnation. Nothing here that is wilfully vicious. All is due to heredity, early environment (shame on those possessive mothers, those sex-segregated British schools!), arrested development at puberty, and / or glands. Here we have a misfit, debarred forever from the best things of life, to be pitied, not blamed.
> —CHRISTOPHER ISHERWOOD, A
> Single Man (1964)

11. I suspect that our own faith in psychiatry will seem as touchingly quaint to the future as our grandparents' belief in phrenology seems now to us.
> —GORE VIDAL, Reflections upon a
> Sinking Ship (1969)

12. Thanks to medical technology, major breakthroughs in psychiatric care, I'm no longer a woman obsessed with an unnatural craving. Just another normal very socially acceptable alcoholic.
> —LILY TOMLIN, as her character
> "The Rubber Freak," in Rolling
> Stone, 24 October 1974

13. A large part of the popularity and persuasiveness of psychology comes from its being a sublimated spiritualism: a secular, ostensibly scientific way of affirming the primacy of "spirit" over matter.
> —SUSAN SONTAG, Illness as
> Metaphor (1978)

Public Opinion

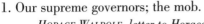

1. Our supreme governors; the mob.
   —HORACE WALPOLE, *letter to Horace Mann, 7 September 1743*

2. Uncertain is the air of popular applause, and a moment suffices to make him today the detestation of the world who yesterday was its idol.
   —MATTHEW G. LEWIS, *The Monk (1795)*

3. Public Opinion . . . an attempt to organise the ignorance of the community, and to elevate it to the dignity of physical force.
   —OSCAR WILDE, *"The Critic as Artist" (1891)*

4. It is because the public are a mass—inert, obtuse, and passive— that they need to be shaken up from time to time so that we can tell from their bear-like grunts where they are—and also where they stand. They are pretty harmless, in spite of their numbers, because they are fighting against intelligence.
   —ALFRED JARRY, *in La Revue Blanc, January 1897*

5. If forty million people say a foolish thing it does not become a wise one, but the wise man is foolish to give them the lie.
   —W. SOMERSET MAUGHAM (1901), *A Writer's Notebook (1949)*

6. An opinion, though it is original, does not necessarily differ from the accepted opinion; the important thing is that it does not try to conform to it.
   —ANDRÉ GIDE, *Journals, 6 February 1929*

7. Great bodies of people are never responsible for what they do.
   —VIRGINIA WOOLF, *A Room of One's Own (1929)*

8. It is all the question of identity. . . . As long as the outside does not put a value on you it remains outside but when it does put a value on you then it gets inside or rather if the outside puts a value on you then all your inside gets to be outside.
   —GERTRUDE STEIN, *Everybody's Autobiography (1937)*

9. What the public wants is the image of passion, not passion itself.
   —ROLAND BARTHES, *in Esprit (1952)*

10. To see yourself as the world sees you may be very brave, but it can be very foolish. Why should you accept the world's view of you as a weak-willed neurotic—better dead than alive?
> —TERENCE RATTIGAN, *The Deep Blue Sea* (1952)

11. What the public really loathes in homosexuality is not the thing itself but having to think about it.
> —E. M. FORSTER, *"Terminal Note" (1960) to Maurice (1914; published 1971)*

12. The public will believe any-thing—so long as it is not founded on the truth.
> —EDITH SITWELL (d. 1964), *Taken Care Of* (1965)

13. I was and I always shall be ham-pered by what I think other people will say.

> —VIOLETTE LEDUC, *La Bâtard* (1965)

14. When the reviews are bad I tell my staff that they can join me as I cry all the way to the bank.
> —LIBERACE, *Autobiography* (1973)

15. I have come to represent a sad person's view of a gay person.
> —QUENTIN CRISP, *An Evening with Quentin Crisp* (1978)

16. We reserve our most fervent admiration for famous people who destroy their lives as well as their tal-ent. The fatal flaws of Elvis, Judy, and Marilyn register much higher on our national applause meter than their living achievements.
> —FLORENCE KING, *Lump It or Leave It* (1990)

Punishment

1. The reward of sin is death: that's hard.
> —CHRISTOPHER MARLOWE, *The Tragical History of Dr. Faustus* (c. 1592)

2. Why, what a ruthless thing is this in him, for the rebellion of a codpiece to take away the life of a man!
> —WILLIAM SHAKESPEARE, *Measure for Measure* (1603)

3. What would have become of
Aristides, Solon, Themistocles,
Harmodius and Aristogiton, Xeno-
phon, Cato, Socrates, Titus—the
delights of Mankind, Cicero, Pliny,
Trajan, Hadrian &c., &c.—these
idols of their Country and ornaments
of human Nature? They would have
perished on your Gibbets.
    —JEREMY BENTHAM,
      "Nonconformity" (c. 1774)

4. Any punishment that does not correct, that can merely rouse rebellion
in whoever has to endure it, is a
piece of gratuitous infamy which
makes those who impose it more
guilty in the eyes of humanity, good
sense and reason, nay a hundred
times more guilty than the victim on
whom the punishment is inflicted.
    —MARQUIS DE SADE, letter from
      prison, 21 May 1781

5. All punishment is mischief: all
punishment in itself is evil.
    —JEREMY BENTHAM, Principles of
      Morals and Legislation (1789)

6. One is absolutely sickened, not by
the crimes that the wicked have committed, but by the punishments that
the good have inflicted; and a community is infinitely more brutalised
by the habitual employment of punishment than it is by the occasional
occurrence of crime.
    —OSCAR WILDE, "The Soul of Man
      Under Socialism" (1895)

7. Many men would take the death-
sentence without a whimper to escape the life-sentence which fate
carries in her other hand.
    —T. E. LAWRENCE (d. 1935), The
      Mint (1955)

8. We're all of us sentenced to solitary confinement inside our own
skins, for life!
    —TENNESSEE WILLIAMS, Orpheus
      Descending (1958)

9. People who cannot feel punish
those who do.
    —MAY SARTON, Mrs. Stevens Hears
      the Mermaids Singing (1965)

10. Swine! How dare you enter my
room without knocking? *[Lashes
whip.]* Have you forgotten the House
of Pain?
    —CHARLES LUDLAM, Bluebeard
      (1970)

11. I'm all for bringing back the
birch, but only between consenting
adults.
    —GORE VIDAL, quoted in the
      Sunday Times Magazine,
      16 September 1973

12. In its function, the power to punish is not essentially different from
that of curing or educating.
    —MICHEL FOUCAULT, Discipline and
      Punish: The Birth of the Prison
      (1975)

13. He said "Next time can I bring my friend?" And I thought "Does he mean friend?" And I thought "Yes he *does* mean friend." Which was quite bold in those days. It was the Dark Ages. Men and men. And they could still put you in prison for it. And did, dear.

  —ALAN BENNETT, *Prick Up Your*
   Ears: The Screenplay (1987)

14. Historically, societies that have condemned the woman who is lesbian have dealt with her in several ways. At times they have tried to destroy her: by burning her at the stake, by hanging her, by guillotining her. At times they have tried to "cure" her: by asking her to remove from her life any type of eroticism, or by asking her to change her erotic orientation.

  —DOLORES KLAICH, *Woman Plus*
   Woman (1989)

Queens

▼

1. I would not be a queen / For all the world.

  —WILLIAM SHAKESPEARE, *Henry VIII*
   (1613)

2. In truth, a mature man who uses hair-oil, unless medicinally, that man has probably got a quoggy spot in him somewhere.

  —HERMAN MELVILLE, *Moby-Dick*
   (1851)

3. One has a right to be frivolous, if it's one's nature.

  —HENRY JAMES, *The Europeans*
   (1878)

4. Let us follow these bright ornaments.

  —RONALD FIRBANK, *Vainglory*
   (1916)

5. His Weariness the Prince entered the room in all his tinted orders.

  —RONALD FIRBANK, *The Flower*
   Beneath the Foot (1923)

6. And of lavender, my nature's got just a dash in it.

  —COLE PORTER, "I'm a Gigolo"
   (1929)

7. PANSY. *Pheonix pheonixissima formosissima arabiana.* This rare and

fabulous bird is UNIQUE. The World's Oldest Bachelor. Has no mate and doesn't want one. When old, sets fire to itself and emerges miraculously reborn. Specially imported from the East.

> —SYLVIA TOWNSEND WARNER, "The Phoenix" (1940)

8. I raised my right hand and waved the palm-open, finger-wiggling backward wave I'd used from time to time since first seeing Liza Minnelli do it near the end of *Cabaret*. I think it's a smart little gesture.

> —LARRY DUPLECHAN, Captain Swing (1993)

Q u e e r

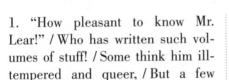

1. "How pleasant to know Mr. Lear!" / Who has written such volumes of stuff! / Some think him ill-tempered and queer, / But a few think him pleasant enough.

> —EDWARD LEAR, preface, Nonsense Songs (1871)

2. The world is damned queer—it really is. But people won't recognize the immensity of its queerness.

> —LYTTON STRACHEY, letter to Duncan Grant, June 1908

3. We're queer because we're queer because we're queer.

> —CHRISTOPHER ISHERWOOD, The World in the Evening (1954)

4. America, I'm putting my queer shoulder to the wheel.

> —ALLEN GINSBERG, "America," Howl (1956)

5. His wife, a former beauty queer, regarded him with a strange but burly look.

> —JOHN LENNON, In His Own Write (1964)

6. There are dozens of ways of being queer and you have to find what your kind is and then make something of it.

> —MAUREEN DUFFY, The Microcosm (1965)

7. If homosexuality is a disease, let's all call in queer to work. "Hello, can't work today, still queer."

> —ROBIN TYLER, speech, March on Washington for Lesbian, Gay, and Bi Rights, 25 April 1993

Reality

1. If one doesn't talk about a thing, it has never happened. It is simply expression that gives reality to things.
—*OSCAR WILDE, The Picture of Dorian Gray (1891)*

2. Ugliness was the one reality.
—*OSCAR WILDE, The Picture of Dorian Gray (1891)*

3. The longer you wear pearls, the realer they become.
—*COLETTE, Cheri (1920)*

4. What is meant by "reality"? It would seem to be something very erratic, very undependable.
—*VIRGINIA WOOLF, A Room of One's Own (1929)*

5. My greatest enemy is reality. I have fought it successfully for thirty years.
—*MARGARET ANDERSON, My Thirty Years' War (1930)*

6. My unreality is chiefly this: I have never felt much like a human being. It's a splendid feeling.
—*MARGARET ANDERSON, My Thirty Years' War (1930)*

7. The unreal is natural, so natural that it makes of unreality the most natural of anything natural.
—*GERTRUDE STEIN, "I Came and Here I Am" (1936)*

8. A naked lunch is natural to us, / we eat reality sandwiches.
—*ALLEN GINSBERG, "On Burroughs' Work" (1954)*

9. There's nothing like eavesdropping to show you that the world outside your head is different from the world inside your head.
—*THORNTON WILDER, The Matchmaker (1954)*

10. We take our shape, it is true, within and against that cage of reality bequeathed to us at our birth.
—*JAMES BALDWIN, Notes of a Native Son (1955)*

11. They say that there is not reality before it has been given shape by words rules regulations.
—*MONIQUE WITTIG, Les Guérillères (1969)*

12. Before I was shot, I always thought that I was more half-there

than all-there—I always suspected that I was watching TV instead of living life. Right when I was being shot and ever since, I knew that I was watching television.

> —ANDY WARHOL, *The Philosophy of Andy Warhol: From A to B and Back Again (1975)*

13. I made some studies, and reality is the leading cause of stress amongst those in touch with it. I can take it in small doses, but as a lifestyle I found it too confining.

> —JANE WAGNER *[words spoken by Lily Tomlin], The Search for Signs of Intelligent Life in the Universe (1985)*

14. The lesbian is a threatening *reality* for reality.

> —NICOLE BROSSARD, *The Aerial Letter (1988);* trans. Marlene Wildeman

15. Reality is something the human race doesn't handle very well.

> —GORE VIDAL, in *Radio Times,* 3 January 1990

Reason

▼

1. Strong reasons make strange actions.

> —WILLIAM SHAKESPEARE, *King John (1596)*

2. Reason, an *ignus fatus* in the mind, / Which leaving light of nature, sense behind, / Pathless and dangerous wandering ways it takes, / Through error's fenny bogs and brakes.

> —JOHN WILMOT, EARL OF ROCHESTER, *"A Satire Against Reason and Mankind" (1679)*

3. Sense makes few martyrs.

> —HORACE WALPOLE, *letter to Horace Mann, 7 February 1772*

4. Mankind are not reasoning beings, if reason won't do with them.

> —HERMAN MELVILLE, *The Confidence-Man (1857)*

5. I don't care anything about reasons, but I know what I like.

> —HENRY JAMES, *Portrait of a Lady (1881)*

6. I can stand brute force, but brute reason is quite unbearable. There is something unfair about its use. It is hitting below the intellect.

—OSCAR WILDE, *The Picture of Dorian Gray (1891)*

7. Logic is like the sword—those who appeal to it shall perish by it.
—SAMUEL BUTLER (d. 1902), *Note Books (1912)*

8. Reason and happiness are like other flowers—they wither when plucked.
—GEORGE SANTAYANA, *The Life of Reason (1906)*

9. Logic must look after itself.
—LUDWIG WITTGENSTEIN, *Tractatus Logico-Philosophicus (1922)*

10. The want of logic annoys. Too much logic bores.
—ANDRÉ GIDE, *Journals, 12 May 1927*

11. A little simplification would be the first step toward rational living, I think.
—ELEANOR ROOSEVELT, *My Days (1938)*

12. You can't be a rationalist in an irrational world. It isn't rational.
—JOE ORTON (d. 1967), *What the Butler Saw (1969)*

13. If the world were a logical place, men would ride side-saddle.
—RITA MAE BROWN, *Sudden Death (1983)*

14. Logic is the key to an all-inclusive spiritual well-being.
—MARLENE DIETRICH, *Marlene (1989)*

Regret

1. If one good deed in all my life I did / I do repent it from my very soul.
—WILLIAM SHAKESPEARE, *Titus Andronicus (1592)*

2. Things without all remedy / Should be without regard. What's done is done.
—WILLIAM SHAKESPEARE, *Macbeth (1606)*

3. Make the most of your regrets; never smother your sorrow, but tend and cherish it till it come to have a separate and integral interest. To regret deeply is to live afresh.
—HENRY DAVID THOREAU, *Journal, 13 November 1839*

4. Remorse—is Memory—awake— / Her Parties all astir— / A Presence

of Departed Acts— / At window— and at Door—

—*EMILY DICKINSON, no. 744 (c. 1863), Complete Poems (1955)*

5. It's no use crying over spilt milk, because all the forces of the universe were bent on spilling it.

—*W. SOMERSET MAUGHAM, Of Human Bondage (1915)*

6. There is no man, however wise, who has not at some period of his youth said things, or lived in a way the consciousness of which is so unpleasant to him in later life that he would gladly, if he could, expunge it from his memory.

—*MARCEL PROUST, Remembrance of Things Past: Within a Budding Grove (1918)*

7. I have made it a rule of my life never to regret and never to look back. Regret is an appalling waste of energy.

—*KATHERINE MANSFIELD, "Je Ne Parle Pas Français" (1920)*

8. It's the things I might have said that fester.

—*CLEMENCE DANE, A Bill of Divorcement (1921)*

R e l a t i o n s h i p s

1. "My father is deceased. Come, Gaveston, / And share the kingdom with thy dearest friend." / Ah, words that make me surfeit with delight! / What greater bliss can hap to Gaveston / Than live and be the favourite of a king? / Sweet prince, I come; these, these thy amorous lines / Might have enforced me to have swum from France, / And, like Leander, gasped upon the sand, / So thou woulds't smile, and take me in thy arms.

—*CHRISTOPHER MARLOWE, Edward II (c. 1591)*

2. I cannot content myself without sending you this present, praying God that I may have a joyful and comfortable meeting with you and that we may make at this Christmas a new marriage ever to be kept hereafter; for, God so love me, as I desire only to live in this world for your sake, and that I had rather live banished in any part of the earth with you than I live a sorrowful widow's life without you. And so God bless you, my sweet child and wife, and grant that ye may ever be a comfort to your dear dad and husband.

—KING JAMES I OF ENGLAND AND VI
OF SCOTLAND, *letter to George
Villiers, Duke of Buckingham,
December 1623*

3. Our changed and mingled souls are grown / To such acquaintance now, / That if each would resume their own, / Alas! we know not how. / We have each other so engrost / That each is in the union lost.
—KATHERINE PHILIPS,
"To Mrs. M. A. at Parting" (1664)

4. Two old Bachelors were living in one house; / One caught a Muffin, the other caught a Mouse.
—EDWARD LEAR, "Two Old
Bachelors," Nonsense Songs
(1871)

5. There is too little courtship in the world. . . . For courtship means a wish to stand well in the other person's eyes, and, what is more, a readiness to be pleased with the other's ways; a sense on each side of having had the better of the bargain; an undercurrent of surprise and thankfulness at one's good luck.
—VERNON LEE, Hortus Vitae (1904)

6. Personal relations are the important thing for ever and ever, and not this outer life of telegrams and anger.
—E. M. FORSTER, Howards End
(1910)

7. When married people don't get on they can separate, but if they're not married it's impossible. It's a tie that only death can sever.
—W. SOMERSET MAUGHAM,
The Circle (1921)

8. To be fierce and tender to be warm and established, to have celebrations and to lean closely all these establish a past a present and a future. The history of establishment is a history of bliss.
—GERTRUDE STEIN, "Didn't Nelly
and Lilly Love You" (1922)

9. Unconsecrated unions produce relationships that are just as numerous and complicated as those created by marriage, but more solid.
—MARCEL PROUST (d. 1922),
Remembrance of Things Past:
The Captive (1923)

10. The bonds that unite another person to ourselves exist only in our mind.
—MARCEL PROUST (d. 1922),
Remembrance of Things Past:
The Sweet Cheat Gone (1925)

11. The heart of another is a dark forest, always, no matter how close it has been to one's own.
—WILLA CATHER, The Professor's
House (1925)

12. All things they would be the one to the other, should they stand in that limitless relationship; father, mother, friend, and lover; all things—the amazing completeness of it; and

Mary, the child, the friend, the belovèd. With the terrible bonds of her dual nature, she could bind Mary fast, and the pain would be sweetness, so that the girl would cry out for that sweetness, hugging her chains always closer to her.
> —RADCLYFFE HALL, *The Well of Loneliness (1928)*

13. Intimacy is a difficult art.
> —VIRGINIA WOOLF, *"Geraldine and Jane," The Second Common Reader (1932)*

14. No one worth possessing / Can be quite possessed.
> —SARA TEASDALE, *"Advice to a Girl," Strange Victory (1933)*

15. Sexual fidelity is more important in a homosexual relationship than in any other. In other relationships there are a variety of ties. But here, fidelity is the only bond.
> —W. H. AUDEN *(1947), quoted in Alan Ansen and Nicholas Jenkins, The Table Talk of W. H. Auden (1990)*

16. The relationship is only a shadow, but a shadow is not always easy to elude.
> —IVY COMPTON-BURNETT, *Two Worlds and Their Ways (1949)*

17. There is probably nothing like living together for blinding people to each other.
> —IVY COMPTON-BURNETT, *Mother and Son (1955)*

18. What kind of life can two men have together, anyway?
> —JAMES BALDWIN, *Giovanni's Room (1956)*

19. Almost all of our relationships begin and most of them continue as forms of mutual exploitation, a mental or physical barter, to be terminated when one or both parties run out of goods.
> —W. H. AUDEN, *The Dyer's Hand (1962)*

20. Two's company—three's a ménage.
> —MART CROWLEY, *The Boys in the Band (1968)*

21. No partner in a love relationship (whether homosexual or heterosexual) should feel that he has to give up an essential part of himself to make it viable.
> —MAY SARTON, *Journal of a Solitude (1973)*

22. Cleaving is an activity which should be left to snails for cleaning ponds and aquariums.
> —JANE RULE, *Lesbian Images (1975)*

23. Human relations just are not fixed in their orbits like the planets—they're more like galaxies, changing all the time, exploding into light for years, then dying away.
> —MAY SARTON, *Crucial Conversations (1975)*

24. It is explained that all relationships require a little of give and take. This is untrue. Any particular partnership demands that we give and give and give and at the last, as we flop into our graves exhausted, we are told that we didn't give enough.
— *Quentin Crisp, How to Become a Virgin (1981)*

25. Do you know the difference between involvement and commitment? Think of ham and eggs. The chicken is involved. The pig is committed.
— *Martina Navratilova, in Observer, 1982*

26. Breath is life, and the intermingling of breaths is the purpose of good living. This is in essence the great principle on which all productive living must rest, for relationships among all the beings of the universe must be fulfilled; in this way each individual life may also be fulfilled.
— *Paula Gunn Allen, The Sacred Hoop (1986)*

27. I'd like to throw my laundry in with yours. / I'd like to put my face between your legs.
— *Marilyn Hacker, Love, Death, and the Changing of the Seasons (1986)*

28. Darling, love is more than just sex. I mean, even trolls can have sex. What you need is a boyfriend. Someone to nest with, wake up with, just lie around the beach house with.
— *Paul Rudnick, Jeffrey (1994)*

Religion

1. From foolish devotions may God deliver us!
— *Teresa of Avila, Life (1565)*

2. I count religion but a childish toy, / And hold there is no sin but ignorance.
— *Christopher Marlowe, The Jew of Malta (c. 1589)*

3. Convents seem calculated to make numbers really miserable, and only to hide from the world that they are so.
— *Sarah Scott, The History of Cornelia (1750)*

4. Jesus has on the whole field of sexual irregularity preserved an uninterrupted silence.

—JEREMY BENTHAM,
"Nonconformity" (c. 1774)

5. Christians have burned each other quite persuaded / That all the Apostles would have done as they did.
—GEORGE GORDON, LORD BYRON,
Don Juan (1819–24)

6. But in truth, in no instance has a system in regard to religion been ever established, but for the purpose, as well as with the effect of its being made an instrument of intimidation, corruption, and delusion, for the support of depredation and oppression in the hands of government.
—JEREMY BENTHAM, Constitutional
Code (1827)

7. The duty of sitting in a whitewashed meeting-house and listening to a nasal Puritan! That's difficult. But it's not sublime.
—HENRY JAMES, Roderick Hudson
(1876)

8. Religion is the fashionable substitute for belief.
—OSCAR WILDE, The Picture of
Dorian Gray (1891)

9. Christianity, above all, consoles; but there are naturally happy souls who do not need consolation. Consequently Christianity begins by making such souls unhappy, for otherwise it would have no power over them.

—ANDRÉ GIDE, Journals,
10 October 1893

10. I endeavoured to drown the yearnings of my heart with the ordinary pleasures and vices that usually attract the young. I had to choose a profession. I became a priest.
—JOHN FRANCIS BLOXHAM, "The
Priest and the Acolyte" (1894)

11. The fashion just now is a Roman Catholic frame of mind with an Agnostic conscience; you get the mediaeval picturesqueness of the one with the modern convenience of the other.
—SAKI [H. H. Munro], "Reginald at
the Theatre," Reginald (1904)

12. "There is no Holiness here," George interrupted, in that cold, white, candent voice which was more caustic than silver nitrate and more thrilling than a scream.
—FREDERICK WILLIAM ROLFE
["Baron Corvo"], Hadrian VII
(1904)

13. Claude's such an extremist, you know. They say that when he kissed the Pope's slipper he went on to do considerably *more.* . . .
—RONALD FIRBANK, The Princess
Zoubaroff (1920)

14. I remember the average curate at home was something between a eunuch and a snigger.
—RONALD FIRBANK, The Flower
Beneath the Foot (1923)

15. I know that a creed is the shell of a lie.

> —AMY LOWELL, "Evelyn Ray,"
> What's O'Clock (1925)

16. Religion is different from everything else; *because in religion seeking is finding.*

> —WILLA CATHER, My Mortal Enemy
> (1926)

17. Religion is like music, one must have an ear for it. Some people have none at all.

> —CHARLOTTE MEW (d. 1928), in
> Penelope Fitzgerald, Charlotte
> Mew and Her Friends (1984)

18. While analyzing so many people I realized the constant need of a mother, or a god (the same thing) is really immaturity. It is a childish need, a human need, but so universal that I can see how it gave birth to all religions.

> —ANAÏS NIN (1935), The Diary of
> Anaïs Nin, Vol. 2 (1967)

19. I am not sure that Christ would have been very satisfied to foresee that He would be looked upon principally as a *redeemer* and nailed forever upon the cross by human ignorance. It seems to me that He above all desired to bring men a message of truth, that He wanted to heal them of their faults by making an appeal to all their energy; He shook them up as much as He could, He did not seek to spare them the trouble.

> —ADRIENNE MONNIER (1938), in
> The Very Rich Hours of Adrienne
> Monnier (1976); trans. Richard
> McDougall

20. To this day I do not know whether the power which has inspired my works is something related to religion, or is indeed religion itself.

> —KÄTHE KOLLWITZ (d. 1945), in
> Hans Kollwitz, ed., The Diaries
> and Letters of Käthe Kollwitz
> (1955)

21. It was the East that should have sent us missionaries.

> —JEAN COCTEAU, Diary of an
> Unknown (1952)

22. I was raised on the good book Jesus / till I read between the lines.

> —LAURA NYRO, "Stoney End"
> (1966)

23. It's Life that defeats the Christian Church. She's always been well-equipped to deal with Death.

> —JOE ORTON, The Erpingham
> Camp (1966)

24. Religion is probably, after sex, the second oldest resource which

human beings have available to them for blowing their minds.
—SUSAN SONTAG, "The Pornographic Imagination," Styles of Radical Will (1966)

25. How shocking! His abnormal condition has driven him to seek refuge in religion. Always the last ditch stand of a man on the brink of disaster.
—JOE ORTON (d. 1967), What the Butler Saw (1969)

26. Vicar, you are supposed to be preparing me for Confirmation. When I have received the gift of the Holy Spirit, if I'm in the mood, I'll telephone you.
—NOËL COWARD, in response to the clergyman who fondled him during Confirmation class; interview with David Frost (1969)

27. [Catholicism] is so wrapped up in symbolism, and indeed drag, the priests in their robes, the colorful saints, the beautiful cathedrals. I think stylistically it made my writing very elaborate, filled it with metaphors and symbolism. Beyond that my books are formed around the idea of confession.
—JOHN RECHY, in Gay News, December 1974

28. Religions are manipulated by those who govern society and not the

other way around. This is a brand-new thought to Americans, whether once or twice or never bathed in the Blood of the Lamb.
—GORE VIDAL, Pink Triangle and Yellow Star (1982)

29. Just because I don't harass it like some peoples us know don't mean I ain't got religion.
—ALICE WALKER, The Color Purple (1982)

30. That country's been sodomized by religion.
—HANIF KUREISHI, filmscript, My Beautiful Laundrette (1985)

31. Religion has sadly become irrelevant, something of a joke, in the lives of many people who reacted against its frequent double-standard moral taboos and insufferably bad theology.
—MALCOLM BOYD, Gay Priest: An Inner Journey (1986)

32. For a while I went into our churches because they were built from the heart. . . . I'm never tempted by God but I like his trappings. Not tempted but I begin to understand why others are. With this feeling inside, with this wild love that threatens, what safe places might there be? Where do you store gunpowder? How do you sleep at night again? If I were

a little different I might turn passion into something holy and then I would sleep again.
—JEANETTE WINTERSON, *The Passion (1987)*

33. Piety is like garlic: a little goes a long way.
—RITA MAE BROWN, *Bingo (1988)*

34. Catholicism is not a soothing religion. It's a painful religion. We're all gluttons for punishment.
—MADONNA, *in Rolling Stone, 23 March 1989*

35. The locations, rituals, and myths of Catholicism are fertile ground for the homoerotic imagination: candlelit cloisters, dark wood booths in which secrets are confessed, stories of self-flagellation and of the "passion" of men tortured on crosses. And like the armed services, college fraternities, and other sex-segregated institutions, the Catholic priesthood has always been ripe for sexual innuendo. What do all those men *do* together?
—JOHN PRESTON (d. 1993), *Flesh and the Word 3 (1995)*

Reputation

1. Reputation is an idle and most false imposition; oft got without merit and lost without deserving.
—WILLIAM SHAKESPEARE, *Othello (1603–4)*

2. One can survive everything nowadays, except death, and live down anything except a good reputation.
—OSCAR WILDE, *A Woman of No Importance (1893)*

3. You and I must keep from shame / In London streets the Shropshire name; / On banks of Thames they must not say / Severn breeds worse men than they.

—A. E. HOUSMAN, *poem 37, A Shropshire Lad (1896)*

4. I don't give a hoot about posterity. Why should I worry about what people think of me when I'm dead as a doornail anyway?
—NOËL COWARD, *Present Laughter (1943)*

5. It's harder to maintain a reputation for being pretty than for being a great artist.
—NED ROREM, *The Paris Diary of Ned Rorem (1966)*

Resistance

1. Nothing so aggravates an earnest person as a passive resistance.
   —*HERMAN MELVILLE*, "Bartleby the
   Scrivener" (1853)

2. Not, I'll not, carrion comfort, Despair, not feast on thee; / Not untwist—slack they may be—these last strands of man / In me or, most weary, cry I can no more. I can; / Can something, hope, wish day come, not choose not to be.
   —*GERARD MANLEY HOPKINS*,
   "Carrion Comfort" (1885)

3. Agitators are a set of interfering, meddling people, who come down to some perfectly contented class of the community and sow the seeds of discontent amongst them. That is the reason why agitators are so absolutely necessary. Without them, in our incomplete state, there would be no advance towards civilisation.
   —*OSCAR WILDE*, "The Soul of Man
   Under Socialism" (1895)

4. If we must die, let it not be like hogs / Hunted and penned in an inglorious spot / While round us bark the mad and hungry dogs, / Making their mock at our accursed lot.
   —*CLAUDE MCKAY*, "If We Must
   Die," Harlem Shadows (1922)

5. There are two kinds of men and women, those who have in them resisting as their way of winning and those who have in them attacking as their way of winning.
   —*GERTRUDE STEIN*, The Making of
   Americans (1925)

6. We are adhering to life now with our last muscle—the heart.
   —*DJUNA BARNES*, Nightwood
   (1936)

7. "I will not cease from mental fight," Blake wrote. Mental fight means thinking against the current, not with it.
   —*VIRGINIA WOOLF*, in New
   Republic, 21 October 1940

8. When you get to the end of your rope—tie a knot in it and hang on.
   —*ELEANOR ROOSEVELT*, You Learn
   by Living (1960)

9. Despite all the evils they wished to crush me with / I remain as steady as the three-legged cauldron.
   —*MONIQUE WITTIG*, Les Guérillères
   (1969)

10. For a woman to be a lesbian in a male-supremacist, capitalist, misogynist, racist, homophobic, imperialistic culture, such as that of North America, is an act of resistance.
> —CHERYL CLARKE, in Cherríe Moraga and Gloria Anzaldúa, *This Bridge Called My Back* (1981)

11. Agoraphobia was my quirky armor against a gregarious America.
> —FLORENCE KING, *When Sisterhood Was in Flower* (1982)

12. This struggle of people against their conditions, this is where you find the meaning in life.
> —KIM CHERNIN, *In My Mother's House* (1983)

13. What we resist persists.
> —SONIA JOHNSON, *Going out of Our Minds* (1987)

14. If patriarchy can take what exists and make it not, surely we can take what exists and make it be.
> —NICOLE BROSSARD, *The Aerial Letter* (1988); trans. Marlene Wildeman

15. I believe in a lively disrespect for most forms of authority.
> —RITA MAE BROWN, *Starting from Scratch* (1988)

16. *Resistance* is the secret of joy!
> —ALICE WALKER, *Possessing the Secret of Joy* (1992)

17. Did I survive? I guess I did. But only because I knew I might get home to you.
> —LESLIE FEINBERG, *Stone Butch Blues* (1993)

Revenge

1. O God, that I were a man! I would eat his heart in the market-place.
> —WILLIAM SHAKESPEARE, *Much Ado About Nothing* (1598)

2. A man that studieth revenge keeps his own wounds green.
> —FRANCIS BACON, "Of Revenge," *Essays* (1625)

3. I would pay him in his own coin.
> —APHRA BEHN, *The Lucky Chance* (1686)

4. You made love to pieces of white bread, you stupid man, and not only that, but I made your toast out of it in the morning. HAH! I trust you'll be more careful next time I say something is just marmalade.
> —CHRISTOPHER DURANG, *Titanic* (1974)

5. Once the tables are turned, only a humiliator can appreciate humiliation's sweeter edges.

—TRUMAN CAPOTE (d. 1984), *Answered Prayers* (1986)

6. And she asked me to remember that a woman, if cheated, will never forget and will someday pay you back, even if it takes years.
> —JEANETTE WINTERSON, *Sexing the Cherry* (1989)

Revolution

1. If there be fuel prepared, it is hard to tell whence the spark shall come that shall set it on fire.
> —FRANCIS BACON, *"Of Seditions and Troubles"* (1625)

2. A successful revolution establishes a new community. A missed revolution makes irrelevant the community that persists. And a compromised revolution tends to shatter the community that was without an adequate substitute.
> —PAUL GOODMAN, *Growing Up Absurd* (1960)

3. The two things we are trying to do—set up a counterculture and

make a revolution—it's hard to do both things at the same time.
> —JUNE ARNOLD, *The Cook and the Carpenter* (1973)

4. In America the word revolutionary is used to sell pantyhose.
> —RITA MAE BROWN, *In Her Day* (1976)

5. "Progress" affects few. Only revolution can affect many.
> —ALICE WALKER (1978), in *Gloria T. Hull, Patricia Bell Scott, and Barbara Smith, eds., All the Women Are White, All the Blacks Are Men, but Some of Us Are Brave* (1982)

6. The revolution begins at home.
   —*CHERRÍE MORAGA AND GLORIA
   ANZALDÚA, This Bridge Called
   My Back (1983)*

7. Revolution is not a one-time event.
   —*AUDRE LORDE, "Learning from
   the '60s," Sister Outsider (1984)*

R i g h t s

1. An absolute and unlimited right over any object of property would be the right to commit nearly every crime. If I had such a right over the stick I am about to cut, I might employ it as a mace to knock down the passengers, or I might convert it into a sceptre as an emblem of royalty, or into an idol to offend the national religion.
   —*JEREMY BENTHAM (d. 1832),
   Principles of the Civil Code, in
   Works (1838–43)*

2. Natural rights is simple nonsense: natural and imprescriptable rights, rhetorical nonsense—nonsense upon stilts.
   —*JEREMY BENTHAM (d. 1832),
   Anarchical Fallacies, in Works
   (1838–43)*

3. There will never be a free and enlightened State until the State comes to recognize the individual as a higher and independent power, from which all its own power and authority are derived, and treats him accordingly.
   —*HENRY DAVID THOREAU, Civil
   Disobedience (1849)*

4. How long you women have been trying for the vote. For my part, I mean to get it.
   —*CHRISTABEL PANKHURST (c. 1890),
   childhood remark to her mother,
   in Emmeline Pankhurst, My Own
   Story (1914)*

5. Where, after all, do human rights begin? They begin in small places, close to home—so close and so small that they cannot be seen on any map of the world.
   —*ELEANOR ROOSEVELT (d. 1962),
   in New York Times,
   26 December 1965*

6. I may have to go on calling myself a lesbian into great old age, not

because it is any longer true but because it takes such a long time to make the simple point that I have the right to be.

> —*JANE RULE, A Hot-Eyed Moderate (1985)*

7. It must become a right of every person to die of old age. And if we secure this right for ourselves, we can, coincidentally, assure it for the planet.

> —*ALICE WALKER, Living by the Word (1988)*

8. Understand that sexuality is as wide as the sea. Understand that your morality is not law. Understand that we are you. Understand that to have sex whether safe, safer, or unsafe, it is our decision and you have no rights in our lovemaking.

> —*DEREK JARMAN, At Your Own Risk: A Saint's Testament (1992)*

Romance

1. The worst of having a romance is that it leaves one so unromantic.

> —*OSCAR WILDE, The Picture of Dorian Gray (1891)*

2. Twenty years of romance make a woman look like a ruin; but twenty years of marriage make her something like a public building.

> —*OSCAR WILDE, A Woman of No Importance (1893)*

3. Romance only dies with life. No pair of pincers will ever pull it out of us.

> —*E. M. FORSTER, Where Angels Fear to Tread (1902)*

4. Romance is having what is where it is which is not where you are stay where it is.

> —*GERTRUDE STEIN, What Are Masterpieces (1940)*

5. Romantic love has always seemed to me unaccountable, unassailable, unforgettable, and nearly always unattainable.

> —*MARGARET ANDERSON, The Fiery Fountains (1953)*

6. I used to think romantic love was a neurosis shared by two, a supreme

foolishness. I no longer thought that. There's nothing foolish in loving anyone. Thinking you'll be loved in return is what's foolish.

    —RITA MAE BROWN, *Bingo (1988)*

7. I felt the unordinary romance of / women who love women for the first time.

    —DIONNE BRAND, *"Hard Against the Soul" (1990)*

R o u g h   T r a d e

1. I am rough, and woo not like a babe.

    —WILLIAM SHAKESPEARE, *The Taming of the Shrew (1593)*

2. I was walking along, fists in my torn pockets; / my overcoat also was entering the realm of the ideal.

    —ARTHUR RIMBAUD, *"Ma Bohème" (1870)*

3. After I left you I went to the Tube and saw there a very nice red-cheeked black-haired youth of the lower classes—nothing remarkable in that—*but* he was wearing a heavenly shirt, which transported me. . . . I thought it so exactly your goût that I longed to get one for you. At last on the platform I made it an épreuve to go up to him and ask him where he got it. Pretty courageous, wasn't it? You see he was not alone, but accompanied by two rather higher-class youths in billycock hats, who I had to

brush aside in order to reach him. I adopted the well-known John style—with great success. It turned out . . . that it was simply a football jersey—he belonged to the Express Dairy team.

    —LYTTON STRACHEY, *letter to Henry Lamb, 20 February 1914*

4. I did not want them to start getting rough, so I said, pacifically, "Dear sweet clodhoppers, if you knew anything of sexual psychology you would know that nothing could give me keener pleasure than to be manhandled by you meaty boys. It would be an ecstasy of the very naughtiest kind. So if any of you wishes to be my partner in joy come and seize me. If, on the other hand, you simply wish to satisfy some obscure and less easily classified libido and see me bathe, come with me quietly, dear louts, to the fountain."

—*EVELYN WAUGH, Brideshead Revisited (1945)*

5. It's not that I'm inimical to sleaze. / I most fondly remember getting it on / with her, crammed standing in an airplane john, / airsprayed, spotlit, jeans bunched around our knees.

—*MARILYN HACKER, Love, Death, and the Changing of the Seasons (1986)*

6. They were a challenge, skinheads, and made me feel shifty as they stood about the streets and shopping precincts, magnetising the attention they aimed to repel. Cretinously simplified to booted feet, bum and bullet head, they had some, if not all, of the things one was looking for.

—*ALAN HOLLINGHURST, The Swimming-Pool Library (1988)*

S a i n t s

1. I shall never be virtuous enough to be a saint, nor infamous enough to pretend to be one.

—*CHRISTINA, QUEEN OF SWEDEN, letter to Cardinal Azzolino (c. 1667)*

2. There is no sinner like a young saint.

—*APHRA BEHN, The Rover (1681)*

3. A saint's bastard may be no saint himself.

—*HORACE WALPOLE, The Castle of Otranto (1764)*

4. Our manners have been corrupted by communication with the saints.

—*HENRY DAVID THOREAU, "Economy," Walden (1854)*

5. She is a saint, and a persecution is all that she needs to bring out her saintliness and make her perfect.

—*HENRY JAMES, The American (1877)*

6. The only difference between the saint and the sinner is that every saint has a past, and every sinner has a future.

—*OSCAR WILDE, A Woman of No Importance (1893)*

7. The medieval saints would scarcely have been pleased if they could have foreseen that their names would be associated nowadays chiefly with racehorses and the cheaper clarets.

—SAKI [H. H. MUNRO], "Reginald
at the Carlton," Reginald (1904)

8. It is easier to make a saint out of a libertine than out of a prig.
—GEORGE SANTAYANA, The Life of
Reason (1906)

9. Humility has its origin in an awareness of unworthiness, and sometimes too in a dazzled awareness of saintliness.
—COLETTE (d. 1954), Belles
Saisons (1955)

10. People who are born even-tempered, placid and untroubled—secure from violent passions or

temptations to evil—those who have never needed to struggle all night with the Angel to emerge lame but victorious at dawn, never become great saints.
—EVA LE GALLIENNE, The Mystic in
the Theatre: Eleanora Duse
(1965)

11. I'm an alcoholic. I'm a drug addict. I'm homosexual. I'm a genius. Of course, I could be all four of these dubious things and still be a saint. But I shonuf ain't no saint yet, naw-suh.
—TRUMAN CAPOTE, Music for
Chameleons (1980)

Sanity and Insanity

▼

1. I doubt if a single individual could be found from the whole of mankind free from some form of insanity. The only difference is one of degree. A man who sees a gourd and takes it for his wife is called insane because this happens to very few people.
—DESIDERIUS ERASMUS, Praise of
Folly (1509)

2. Much Madness is divinest Sense— / To a discerning Eye— / Much Sense—the starkest Madness—

—EMILY DICKINSON, no. 435
(c. 1862), Complete Poems (1955)

3. Sanity is madness put to good uses; waking life is a dream controlled.
—GEORGE SANTAYANA,
Interpretations of Poetry and
Religion (1900)

4. Everything great in the world comes from neurotics. They alone have founded our religions and com-

posed our masterpieces. Never will the world know all it owes to them nor all that they have suffered to enrich us.
> —MARCEL PROUST, *Remembrance of Things Past: The Guermantes Way (1921)*

5. Those comfortably padded lunatic asylums which are known, euphemistically, as the stately homes of England.
> —VIRGINIA WOOLF, *"Lady Dorothy Nevill," The Common Reader (1925)*

6. I have a horror, I think, of not being, and of my friends not being, quite perfectly balanced.
> —ELIZABETH BOWEN, *The Hotel (1928)*

7. But mad dogs and Englishmen / Go out in the midday sun.
> —NOËL COWARD, *"Mad Dogs and Englishmen" (1938)*

8. There is in every madman a misunderstood genius whose idea, shining in his head, frightened people, and for whom delirium was the only solution to the strangulation that life had prepared for him.
> —ANTONIN ARTAUD, *"Van Gogh, the Man Suicided by Society" (1947)*

9. I saw the best minds of my generation destroyed by madness, starving hysterical naked.
> —ALLEN GINSBERG, *"Howl" (1956)*

10. Sanity is a cozy lie.
> —SUSAN SONTAG, *"Against Interpretation" (1961)*

11. A touch of madness is, I think, almost always necessary for constructing a destiny.
> —MARGUERITE YOURCENAR, *With Open Eyes (1980)*

12. Insanity is doing the same thing over and over again, but expecting different results.
> —RITA MAE BROWN, *Sudden Death (1983)*

13. Frankly, goin' crazy was the *best* thing that ever happened to me. I don't say it's for everybody; some people couldn't cope.
> —JANE WAGNER *[words spoken by Lily Tomlin], The Search for Signs of Intelligent Life in the Universe (1985)*

14. The more I fear my own insanity the more I must punish yours.
> —KATE MILLETT, *The Loony-Bin Trip (1990)*

15. I envy paranoids; they actually feel people are paying attention to them.
> —SUSAN SONTAG, *in Time Out, 19 August 1992*

Scandal

1. Expose not the secret failings of mankind, otherwise you must verily bring scandal upon them and distrust upon yourself.
  —SA'DI, *Gulistan (1258)*

2. Verily the sin lieth in the scandal.
  —APHRA BEHN, *Roundheads (1682)*

3. The basis of every scandal is an immoral certainty.
  —OSCAR WILDE, *The Picture of Dorian Gray (1891)*

4. One should never make one's début with a scandal. One should reserve that to give an interest to one's old age.
  —OSCAR WILDE, *The Picture of Dorian Gray (1891)*

5. Scandal is merely the compassionate allowance which the gay make to the humdrum. Think how many blameless lives are brightened by the blazing indiscretions of other people.
  —SAKI [H. H. MUNRO], *"Reginald at the Carlton," Reginald (1904)*

6. Any truth creates a scandal.
  —MARGUERITE YOURCENAR, *Memoirs of Hadrian (1951)*

7. If one is not scandalous it is difficult to write at all.
  —J. R. ACKERLEY, *in Neville Braybrooke, ed., The Ackerley Letters (1975)*

8. I don't want to be involved in some sort of scandal, but I've covered the waterfront.
  —TENNESSEE WILLIAMS, *when asked if he was a homosexual, television interview with David Frost, 1970*

Seduction

1. Come, woo me, woo me, for now I am in a holiday humour, and like enough to consent.
    —*WILLIAM SHAKESPEARE, As You Like It (1599–1600)*

2. When she raises her eyelids it's as if she were taking off all her clothes.
    —*COLETTE, Claudine et Annie (1903)*

3. A woman: take her or leave her, but do not take her and leave her.
    —*NATALIE CLIFFORD BARNEY, Éparpillements (1910)*

4. I am being led I am being led I am being gently led to bed.
    —*GERTRUDE STEIN, "Didn't Nelly and Lilly Love You" (1922)*

5. The seduction emanating from a person of uncertain or dissimulated sex is powerful.
    —*COLETTE, The Pure and the Impure (1932)*

6. "L for Love," Beebo said, looking in space. "L for Laura." She turned and smiled at her. "L for Lust and L for the L of it. L for Lesbian, L for Let's—let's," she said.
    —*ANN BANNON, I Am a Woman (1959)*

7. Most virtue is a demand for greater seduction.
    —*NATALIE CLIFFORD BARNEY, "My Country 'tis of Thee" (1962)*

8. When he turned his face my way it was dark, indistinguishable; his back and shoulders were carving up strips of light, carving them this way and that as he twisted and bobbed. The water was dark, opaque, but it caught the sun's gold light, the wavy dragon scales writhing under a sainted knight's halo. At last Kevin swam up beside me; his submerged body looked small, boneless. He said we should go down to the store and buy some Vaseline.
    —*EDMUND WHITE, A Boy's Own Story (1982)*

9. Fifteen minutes with you / well, I wouldn't say no.
    —*MORRISSEY, "Reel Around the Fountain" (1984)*

10. "I'm a woman," I said, lifting up my shirt and risking the catarrh.
    She smiled. "I know."
    I didn't go home. I stayed.
    —*JEANETTE WINTERSON, The Passion (1987)*

11. She put on rhumba records and we danced around laughing and drinking from the bottle in between sloppy, drunken kisses. Then Elvis sang, "Wise men say, even fools fall in love." That's when I murmured "Don't be cruel," and fell on my knees at Priscilla's feet, burying my face in her polyester.

—SARAH SCHULMAN, *After Delores
(1988)*

12. Pursuit and seduction are the essence of sexuality. It's part of the sizzle.

—CAMILLE PAGLIA, *Sex, Art, and the
American Culture (1992)*

Self-Denial and Self-Sacrifice

1. How seek the way which leadeth to our wishes? By renouncing our wishes. The crown of excellence is renunciation.

—HAFIZ (14th century),
Ghazal 15, Divan

2. The principle of asceticism never was, nor ever can be, consistently pursued by any living creature. Let but one tenth part of the inhabitants of the earth pursue it consistently, and in a day's time they will have turned it into a Hell.

—JEREMY BENTHAM, *The Principles
of Morals and Legislation (1789)*

3. Asceticism is the trifling of an enthusiast with his power, a puerile coquetting with his selfishness or his vanity, in the absence of any sufficiently great object to employ the first or overcome the last.

—FLORENCE NIGHTINGALE, *letter to
Dr. Sutherland, 1858*

4. Renunciation—is a piercing Virtue— / The letting go / A Presence—for an Expectation.

—EMILY DICKINSON, *no. 745
(c. 1863), Complete Poems (1955)*

5. Self-denial is simply a method by which man arrests his progress, and self-sacrifice a survival of the mutilation of the savage.

—OSCAR WILDE, *"The Critic as
Artist" (1891)*

6. If a hermit lives in a state of ecstasy, his lack of comfort becomes the height of comfort. He must relinquish it.

—JEAN COCTEAU, *Opium (1929)*

7. The very act of sacrifice magnifies the one who sacrifices himself to the point where his sacrifice is much more costly to humanity than would have been the loss of those for whom he is sacrificing himself. But in his abnegation lies the secret of his grandeur.
> —ANDRÉ GIDE, *Journals,*
> *23 June 1931*

8. I never know why self-sacrifice is noble. Why is it better to sacrifice oneself than someone else?
> —IVY COMPTON-BURNETT, *Mother*
> *and Son (1955)*

9. Renouncement: the heroism of mediocrity.

—NATALIE CLIFFORD BARNEY, "Gods," in Adam International Review, 1962

10. He who despises himself esteems himself as a self-despiser.
> —SUSAN SONTAG, *Death Kit (1967)*

11. Those who believe they are ugly / objectify the rest of us.
> —JUDY GRAHN, *The Queen of*
> *Swords (1967)*

12. To give oneself, one must annihilate oneself.
> —VIOLETTE LEDUC, *Therese and*
> *Isabelle (1968)*

Self-Determination

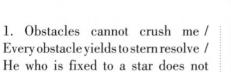

1. Obstacles cannot crush me / Every obstacle yields to stern resolve / He who is fixed to a star does not change his mind.
> —LEONARDO DA VINCI, *Notebooks*
> *(c. 1500)*

2. I celebrate myself, and sing myself.
> —WALT WHITMAN, "Song of
> Myself," Leaves of Grass (1855)

3. Happiest of all, surely, are those Uranians, ever numerous, who have no wish nor need to fly society—or themselves. Knowing what they are, understanding the natural, moral strength of their position as homosexuals; sure of right on their side, even if it be never accord to them in the lands where they must live; fortunate in either due self-control or private freedom—day by day, they go

through their lives, self-respecting and respected, in relative peace.

—EDWARD IRENAEUS PRIME-
STEVENSON [Xavier Mayne], The
Intersexes (1908)

4. I'm gonna do just as I want to anyway / I don't care if they all despise me.

—BESSIE SMITH, "T'ain't Nobody's
Biz-Ness If I Do" (1922)

5. No one can make you feel inferior without your own consent.

—ELEANOR ROOSEVELT, This Is My
Story (1937)

6. To be one's own master is to be the slave of self.

—NATALIE CLIFFORD BARNEY,
"Samples from Almost Illegible
Notebooks" (1962)

7. I am sure that the impulse of desire towards someone of the same sex is not in itself wrong: it is not an offence in any degree—neither against God nor Man. And although for a short time I took pleasure in thinking I was flouting Society, it was exactly the same degree of pleasure that I felt when I wore a daringly low-cut dress, or first wore trousers and walked in Mecklenburgh Square (in 1926 this was a startling thing to do).

—VALENTINE ACKLAND (d. 1969),
For Sylvia: An Honest Account
(1985)

8. When did we begin to dress ourselves?

—ADRIENNE RICH, "Blood-Sister,"
Diving into the Wreck (1973)

9. The nature of gay life is that it is philosophical. Like Nietzsche, though in a different sense, we could speak of "gay science," that obligatory existentialism forced on people who must invent themselves. . . . Once one discovers one is gay one must choose everything, from how to walk, dress and talk to where to live, with whom and on what terms.

—EDMUND WHITE, States of Desire:
Travels in Gay America (1980)

10. Walls protect and walls limit. It is in the nature of walls that they should fall. That walls should fall is the consequence of blowing your own trumpet.

—JEANETTE WINTERSON, Oranges
Are Not the Only Fruit (1985)

11. I want the freedom to carve and chisel my own face, to staunch the bleeding with ashes, to fashion my own gods out of my entrails.

—GLORIA ANZALDÚA,
Borderlands / La Frontera
(1987)

12. Self-determination has to mean that the leader is your individual gut, and heart, and mind or we're talking about power, again, and its rather well-known impurities. Who is really

going to care whether you live or die and who is going to know the most intimate motivation for your laughter and your tears is the only person to be trusted to speak for you and to decide what you will or will not do.

—*JUNE JORDAN, Moving Towards Home (1989)*

Self-Knowledge

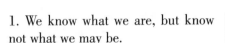

1. We know what we are, but know not what we may be.

—*WILLIAM SHAKESPEARE, Hamlet (1600–1601)*

2. Be so true to thyself as thou be not false to others.

—*FRANCIS BACON, "Of Wisdom for a Man's Self," Essays (1625)*

3. I believed, when I entered this convent, I was escaping from myself, but alas, poor me, I brought myself with me!

—*SOR JUANA INÉS DE LA CRUZ (c. 1680), in Violeta Miqueli, Women in Myth and History (1962)*

4. I have said that the soul is not more than the body, / And I have said that the body is not more than the soul, / And nothing, not God, is greater to one than one's self is.

—*WALT WHITMAN, "Song of Myself," Leaves of Grass (1855)*

5. If a man really knew himself he would utterly despise the ignorant notions others might form on a subject in which he had such matchless opportunities for observation.

—*GEORGE SANTAYANA, The Life of Reason (1906)*

6. He would not—and this was the test—pretend to care about women when the only sex that attracted him was his own. He loved men and always had loved them. He longed to embrace them and mingle his being with theirs. Now that the man who returned his love had been lost, he admitted this.

—*E. M. FORSTER, Maurice (1914; published 1971)*

7. Know thyself! A maxim as pernicious as it is ugly. Whoever observes himself arrests his own development. A caterpillar who wanted to know itself well would never become a butterfly.

—*ANDRÉ GIDE, Les Nouvelles Nourritures (1935)*

8. "Know thyself" is a most superfluous direction. We can't avoid it. We can only hope that no one else knows.

> —IVY COMPTON-BURNETT, *A Family and a Fortune (1939)*

9. Nobody knows what I am trying to do but I do and I know when I succeed.

> —GERTRUDE STEIN (d. 1946), in John Malcolm Brinnin, *The Third Rose (1959)*

10. Between the ages of twenty and forty we are engaged in the process of discovering who we are, which involves learning the difference between accidental limitations which it is our duty to outgrow and the necessary limitations of our nature beyond which we cannot trespass with impunity.

> —W. H. AUDEN, *The Dyer's Hand (1962)*

11. Every man, deep down, knows he's a worthless piece of shit.

> —VALERIE SOLANAS, *SCUM Manifesto (1968)*

12. It is my theory that if you have authority, know your business and know you have authority, you have the authority.

> —DOROTHY ARZNER, in *New York Times, 15 June 1972*

13. I have searched for myself across time and have not found myself anywhere.

> —HÉLÈNE CIXOUS, *Prénoms du Soleil (1974)*

14. Until we can understand the assumptions in which we are drenched we cannot know ourselves.

> —ADRIENNE RICH, "When We Dead Awaken: Writing as Re-Vision," *On Lies, Secrets, and Silences (1979)*

15. Every woman I have ever loved has left her print upon me, where I loved some invaluable piece of myself apart from me—so different that I had to stretch and grow in order to recognize her. And in that growing, we came to separation, that place where work begins.

> —AUDRE LORDE, *Zami: A New Spelling of My Name (1982)*

16. The next time you feel you have to say "I love you" to someone, say it to yourself—and see if you believe it.

> —HARVEY FIERSTEIN, *Torch Song Trilogy (1982)*

17. Was I searching for a dancer whose name I did not know or was I searching for the dancing part of myself?

> —JEANETTE WINTERSON, *Sexing the Cherry (1989)*

18. I'm the kind of woman that likes to enjoy herselves in peace.

> —ALICE WALKER, *The Temple of My Familiar (1989)*

Self-Pity

1. I am stale, a garment out of fashion.

—*WILLIAM SHAKESPEARE, Cymbeline (1610)*

2. There is nothing so slipperily alluring as sadness; we become sad in the first place by having nothing stirring to do; we continue in it, because we have found a snug sofa at last.

—*HERMAN MELVILLE, Pierre, or the Ambiguities (1852)*

3. Shall a man go and hang himself because he belongs to the race of pygmies, and not be the biggest pygmy that he can?

—*HENRY DAVID THOREAU, "Conclusion," Walden (1854)*

4. The world is quickly bored by the recital of misfortune, and willingly avoids the sight of distress.

—*W. SOMERSET MAUGHAM, The Moon and Sixpence (1919)*

5. I'm a fart in a gale of wind, a humble violet under a cow pat.

—*DJUNA BARNES, Nightwood (1936)*

6. Please get over the notion that your particular "thing" is something that only the deepest, saddest, the most nobly tortured can know. It ain't. It's just one kind of sex—that's all. And, in my opinion, the universe turns regardless.

—*LORRAINE HANSBERRY, The Sign in Sidney Brustein's Window (1964)*

7. I'm just a poor soul looking for friendship on this bitch of an earth out in the middle of this bitch of a sea.

—*CHRISTOPHER DURANG, Titanic (1974)*

8. You're a selfish, inconsiderate, self-centered stereotypical, aging, immature queen. No wonder you don't have any friends. Yes, all that because you won't bring a goddamn record album over here or let me come over there and get it! Besides, the Maria Callas Lisbon *Traviata* is not just another goddamn record album. Right now, at this particular moment in my not so terrific life, it's probably the most goddam important thing in the world to me, but I wouldn't expect an insensitive faggot whose idea of a good time is sitting around listening to Angela Lansbury shrieking on about "The Worst Pies in London" like yourself to understand what I'm talking about.

—*Terrence McNally, The Lisbon Traviata (1985)*

9. Oh Mother, I can feel the soil falling over my head / as I climb into an empty bed.

—*Morrissey, "I Know It's Over" (1985)*

10. Self-pity is the simplest luxury.
—*Rita Mae Brown, Bingo (1988)*

Sensuality and the Senses

1. I was afraid that by observing objects with my eyes and trying to comprehend them with each of my other senses I might blind my soul altogether.
—*Socrates (5th century BCE), in Plato (4th century BCE), Phaedo*

2. All sensuality is one, though it takes many forms; all purity is one. It is the same whether a man eat, or drink, or cohabit, or sleep sensually. They are but one appetite.
—*Henry David Thoreau, "Higher Laws," Walden (1854)*

3. Seeing, hearing, feeling, are miracles, and each part and tag of me is a miracle.
—*Walt Whitman, "Song of Myself," Leaves of Grass (1855)*

4. Scents, colors, and sounds echo one another.

—*Charles Baudelaire, "Correspondances," Les Fleurs du Mal (1857)*

5. Nothing can cure the soul but the senses, just as nothing can cure the senses but the soul.
—*Oscar Wilde, The Picture of Dorian Gray (1891)*

6. How much more sensuality invites to art than does sentimentality.
—*André Gide, Journals, 1912*

7. We are what we are, the spirit afterwards, but first the touch.
—*Charlotte Mew (d. 1928), in Penelope Fitzgerald, Charlotte Mew and Her Friends (1984)*

8. All the world of feminine voluptuousness seemed to be gathered up and released in that one divine curving of the loosened lips. There was no humour in it, but there was an indescribable caress.

—VITA SACKVILLE-WEST, *The Edwardians (1930)*

9. Touch is the most demystifying of all senses, different from sight which is the most magical.
> —ROLAND BARTHES, *Mythologies (1957)*

10. Sensuality, wanting a religion, invented Love.
> —NATALIE CLIFFORD BARNEY, *"Gods" (1962)*

11. Devils can be driven out of the heart by the touch of a hand on a hand, or a mouth on a mouth.

—TENNESSEE WILLIAMS, *The Milk Train Doesn't Stop Here Anymore (1963)*

12. One wakes only to the touch of love. Before then, we are only gardens without sorrows, spaces swarming with erotic bodies, landscapes of seas full of fish, flesh without cares.
> —HÉLÈNE CIXOUS, *La (1976)*

13. Smell remembers and tells the future. Smell is home or loneliness. Confidence or betrayal.
> —CHERRÍE MORAGA, *"La Orenda" (1993)*

Separation and Absence

1. Dapple-throned Aphrodite, / eternal daughter of God, / snare-knitter! Don't, I beg you, / cow my heart with grief! Come
> —SAPPHO *(7th century BCE), Fragment 38; trans. Mary Barnard (1958)*

2. The moon has gone down / And the Dovestars. / It is mid night. / Time passes. / And I, / I sleep alone.
> —SAPPHO *(7th century BCE), Fragment 168(b); trans. Anita George*

3. Oh ship, you who owe us Virgil, entrusted to you, bring him back safely to Attic shores, I pray, and preserve the half of my own life.
> —HORACE *(1st century BCE), Odes 1, 3*

4. Farewell—thou art too dear for my possessing, / And like enough thou know'st thy estimate. / The charter of thy worth gives thee releasing; / My bonds in thee are all determinate.
> —WILLIAM SHAKESPEARE, *Sonnet 87 (1609)*

5. How like a winter hath my absence been / From thee, the pleasure of the fleeting year! / What freezings I have felt, what dark days seen.
> —WILLIAM SHAKESPEARE,
> Sonnet 97 (1609)

6. O never say that I was false of heart, / Though absence seemed my flame to qualify.
> —WILLIAM SHAKESPEARE,
> Sonnet 109 (1609)

7. I cannot live with You— / It would be Life— / And Life is over there— / Behind the Shelf.
> —EMILY DICKINSON, no. 640
> (c. 1862), Complete Poems (1955)

8. I remember the way we parted, / The day and the way we met; / You hoped we were both brokenhearted, / And knew we should both forget.
> —ALGERNON CHARLES SWINBURNE,
> "An Interlude" (1866)

9. Parting is all we know of heaven, / And all we need of hell.
> —EMILY DICKINSON (d. 1886), no.
> 1732 (undated), Complete Poems
> (1955)

10. The cost runs into millions, but a woman must have something to console herself for a broken heart.
> —AMY LOWELL, "Malmaison"
> (1916)

11. My hands have not touched water since your hands— / No;—nor my lips freed laughter since "farewell."
> —HART CRANE, "Carrier Letter"
> (1918)

12. After all, my erstwhile dear, / My no longer cherished, / Need we say it was not love, / Just because it perished?
> —EDNA ST. VINCENT MILLAY,
> "Passer Mortuus Est" (1921)

13. It is seldom indeed that one parts on good terms, because if one were on good terms one would not part.
> —MARCEL PROUST (d. 1922),
> Remembrance of Things Past:
> The Sweet Cheat Gone (1925)

14. The heart may think it knows better: the senses know that absence blots people out.
> —ELIZABETH BOWEN, The Death of
> the Heart (1938)

15. Absence becomes the greatest Presence.
> —MAY SARTON, "Difficult Scene"
> (1948)

16. Once you have lived with another it is a great torture to have to live alone.
> —CARSON MCCULLERS, The Ballad
> of the Sad Café (1953)

S e x

▼

1. There is no greater nor keener pleasure than that of bodily love—and none which is more irrational.
>   —PLATO (4th century BCE), The
>   Republic

2. I break wild roses, scatter them over her. / The thorns between us sting like love's pain. / Her flesh, bitter and salt to my tongue, / I taste with endless kisses and taste again.
>   —ELSA GIDLOW, "For the Goddess
>   Too Well Known" (1919)

3. But beyond the bounds of this turbulent river would lie gentle and most placid harbours of refuge; harbours in which the body could repose with contentment, while the lips spoke low, indolent words, and the eyes beheld a dim, golden haze that blinded the while it revealed all beauty. Then Stephen would stretch out her hand and touch Mary where she lay, happy only to feel her nearness.
>   —RADCLYFFE HALL, The Well of
>   Loneliness (1928)

4. If sex isn't a joke, what is it?
>   —NELLA LARSEN, Passing (1929)

5. Surely the sex business isn't worth all this damned fuss? I've met only a handful of people who cared a biscuit for it.
>   —T. E. LAWRENCE (d. 1935), on
>   Lady Chatterley's Lover; in
>   Christopher Hassall, Edward
>   Marsh (1959)

6. I'm always amazed at the American practice of allowing one party to a homosexual act to remain passive—it's so undemocratic. Sex must be mutual.
>   —W. H. AUDEN (1947), quoted in
>   Alan Ansen and Nicholas
>   Jenkins, The Table Talk of W. H.
>   Auden (1990)

7. That pathetic short-cut suggested by Nature the supreme joker as a remedy for our loneliness, that ephemeral communion which we persuade ourselves to be of the spirit when it is in fact only of the body—durable not even in memory!
>   —VITA SACKVILLE-WEST, No
>   Signposts in the Sea (1961)

8. Sex: In America an obsession. In other parts of the world a fact.
>   —MARLENE DIETRICH, Marlene
>   Dietrich's ABC (1962)

9. Sex was delightful and of prime importance, the distance between

the mouth and the crotch must be bridged at once, clothes must come off as soon as possible, no courtship, no nonsense, no beating, so to speak, about the bush.

> —*J. R. ACKERLEY, My Father and Myself (1968)*

10. Sex is the last refuge of the miserable.

> —*QUENTIN CRISP, The Naked Civil Servant (1968)*

11. Well, one thing you can say for masturbation . . . you certainly don't have to look your best.

> —*MART CROWLEY, The Boys in the Band (1968)*

12. In the release of the bed there lies an ecstasy so strong and a satisfaction so profound that it seems that it is everything that life can offer a man, the very purpose of his existence on earth.

> —*TERENCE RATTIGAN, A Bequest to the Nation (1970)*

13. *"Post coitum homo tristis"* / What nonsense!

> —*W. H. AUDEN, "City Without Walls" (1970)*

14. There is nothing mysterious or magic about Lesbian lovemaking. . . . The mystery and the magic come from the person with whom you are making love.

> —*DEL MARTIN AND PHYLLIS LYON, Lesbian / Woman (1972)*

15. What's it like for two women to make love? Pretty much as you would expect.

> —*ELANA NACHMAN [Elana Dykewomon], Riverfinger Women (1974)*

16. When people used to learn about sex at fifteen and die at thirty-five, they obviously were going to have fewer problems than people today who learn about sex at eight or so, I guess, and live to be eighty. That's a long time to play around with the same concept. The same boring concept.

> —*ANDY WARHOL, The Philosophy of Andy Warhol: From A to B and Back Again (1975)*

17. How did people ever think of doing this?

> —*ANDY WARHOL, on sex, The Philosophy of Andy Warhol: From A to B and Back Again (1975)*

18. His imagery for a big orgasm was winning the sailboat race, the Renaissance, high mountains.

> —*JOHN CHEEVER, Falconer (1977)*

19. In homosexual sex you know exactly what the other person is feeling, so you are identifying with the other person completely. In heterosexual sex you have no idea what the other person is feeling.

—WILLIAM S. BURROUGHS, *in Victor*
 Bockris, ed., With William
 Burroughs: A Report from the
 Bunker (1981)

20. Sex? I'd rather have a cup of tea—any day!
 —BOY GEORGE *(attributed, 1983)*

21. For flavor, Instant Sex will never supercede the stuff you had to peel and cook.

—QUENTIN CRISP, *in Cosmopolitan,*
 October 1984

22. In the South, Sunday morning sex is accompanied by church bells.
 —FLORENCE KING, *Confessions of a*
 Failed Southern Lady (1985)

23. Clea was a woman who adored love. Hormones had always been her recreational drug of choice.
 —LISA ALTHER, *Bedrock (1990)*

Sexuality

1. Man was not created for celibacy: were love a crime, God never would have made it so sweet, so irresistible.
 —MATTHEW G. LEWIS, *The Monk*
 (1795)

2. I love man with the same distinction that I love woman—as if my friend were of some third sex—some other or some stranger and still my friend.
 —HENRY DAVID THOREAU, *Journal,*
 5 May 1846

3. Sexuality is the lyricism of the masses.
 —CHARLES BAUDELAIRE *(d. 1867),*
 Intimate Journals (1930); trans.
 Christopher Isherwood

4. WHAT am I suffering from? Sexuality. . . . Will it destroy me? . . . How can I rid myself of Sexuality?
 —THOMAS MANN *(1896), quoted in*
 Marcel Reich-Ranicki, Thomas
 Mann and His Family (1989)

5. Between exclusive homosexuality and exclusive heterosexuality, there is every intermediate shading.
 —ANDRÉ GIDE, *Corydon (1924)*

6. My own view, for what it's worth, is that sexuality is lovely, there cannot be too much of it, it is self-limiting if it is satisfactory, and satisfaction diminishes tension and clears the mind for attention and learning.
 —PAUL GOODMAN, *Compulsory*
 Miseducation (1964)

7. One could plausibly argue that it is for quite sound reasons that the whole capacity for sexual ecstasy is inaccessible to most people—given that sexuality is something, like nuclear energy, which may prove amenable to domestication through scruple, but then again may not.
—SUSAN SONTAG, "The Pornographic Imagination," Styles of Radical Will (1966)

8. For our highly repressive and Puritan tradition has almost hopelessly confused sexuality with sadism, cruelty, and that which is in general inhumane and antisocial. This is a deplorable state of affairs.
—KATE MILLETT, Sexual Politics (1969)

9. Admittedly, a homosexual can be conditioned to react sexually to a woman, or to an old boot, for that matter. In fact, both homo- and heterosexual experimental subjects *have* been conditioned to react sexually to an old boot, and you can save a lot of money that way.
—WILLIAM S. BURROUGHS, The Adding Machine (1985)

10. Sexuality, whether hetero or homo, does not arrive only once, in that moment of revelation and proclamation that we call "coming out." Every time is the first time. Every performance is a debut.
—WAYNE KOESTENBAUM, The Queen's Throat (1993)

Silence

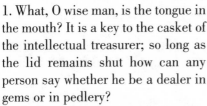

1. What, O wise man, is the tongue in the mouth? It is a key to the casket of the intellectual treasurer; so long as the lid remains shut how can any person say whether he be a dealer in gems or in pedlery?
—SA'DI, Gulistan (1258)

2. I do know of these / That therefore only are reputed wise / For saying nothing.

—WILLIAM SHAKESPEARE, The Winter's Tale (1609)

3. Silence is the virtue of fools.
—FRANCIS BACON, De Dignitae et Augmentis Scientiarum (1623)

4. I have been breaking silence these twenty-three years and have hardly made a rent in it.

—HENRY DAVID THOREAU, *Journal,*
9 February 1841

5. In brighter days to come / Such
men as I would not lie dumb.
—WILLIAM CORY, "A Separation,"
Ionica (1858)

6. For words divide and rend; / But
silence is most noble till the end.
—ALGERNON CHARLES SWINBURNE,
Atalanta in Corydon (1865)

7. Silence is all we dread. / There's
Ransom in a Voice— / But Silence is
Infinity.
—EMILY DICKINSON, poem *(1873)*

8. What can be said at all can be said
clearly; and whereof one cannot
speak, thereon one must remain
silent.
—LUDWIG WITTGENSTEIN, *Tractatus
Logico-Philosophicus (1922)*

9. There are some kinds of people in
whose presence you should shut up
like an oyster: people with strong
moral views, members of Watch-
Committees or Purity Leagues, natural policemen, schoolmasters.
—W. H. AUDEN, in *Listener,*
22 December 1937

10. Silences can be as different as
sounds.
—ELIZABETH BOWEN, *Collected
Impressions (1950)*

11. An audience of twenty thousand,
sitting on its hands, could not have
produced such an echoing silence.
—MARY RENAULT, *The Mask of
Apollo (1966)*

12. But this same silence is become
speech / With the speed of darkness.
—MURIEL RUKEYSER, "The Speed of
Darkness" *(1968)*

13. If we don't sit down and shut up
once in a while we'll lose our minds
even earlier than we had expected.
Noise is an imposition on sanity, and
we live in very noisy times.
—JOAN BAEZ, *Daybreak (1968)*

14. "Lesbianism" would appear to be
so little a threat at the moment that it
is hardly ever mentioned. Whatever
its potentiality in sexual politics,
female homosexuality is currently so
dead an issue that while male homosexuality gains a grudging tolerance,
in women the event is observed in
scorn or in silence.
—KATE MILLETT, *Sexual Politics
(1969)*

15. The shadows cannot speak.
—PAULA GUNN ALLEN, "Shadows"
(1974)

16. While we wait in silence for that
final luxury of fearlessness, the
weight of that silence will choke us.
—AUDRE LORDE, in *Sinister Wisdom
(1978)*

17. Silence and invisibility go hand in hand with powerlessness.
> —*AUDRE LORDE, The Cancer Journals (1980)*

18. We must be the last generation to live in silence.
> —*PAUL MONETTE, The Politics of Silence (1993)*

S i n

1. If it be sin to love a lovely lad / Oh there sin I.
> —*RICHARD BARNFIELD, The Affectionate Shepherd (1594)*

2. We cannot do well without our sins; they are the highway of our virtue.
> —*HENRY DAVID THOREAU, Journal, 22 March 1842*

3. In some sort, Sin hath its sacredness, not less than holiness. And great Sin calls forth more magnanimity than small Virtue.
> —*HERMAN MELVILLE, Pierre (1852)*

4. O seasons, O castles! / What soul is without faults?
> —*ARTHUR RIMBAUD, "O Saisons, O Châteaux" (1872)*

5. They do not sin at all / Who sin for love.
> —*OSCAR WILDE, The Duchess of Padua (1883)*

6. Nothing makes one so vain as being told that one is a sinner.
> —*OSCAR WILDE, The Picture of Dorian Gray (1891)*

7. *Sins* cut up boldly through every class in society, but mere misdemeanors show a certain level in life.
> —*ELIZABETH BOWEN, The Death of the Heart (1938)*

8. On a sofa upholstered in panther skin / Mona did researches in original sin.
> —*WILLIAM PLOMER, "Mews Flat Mona" (1960)*

9. So much attention is paid to the aggressive sins, such as violence and cruelty and greed with all their tragic effects, that too little attention is paid to the passive sins, such as apathy and laziness, which in the long run can have a more devastating and destructive effect upon society than the others.
> —*ELEANOR ROOSEVELT, You Learn by Living (1960)*

10. There are different kinds of wrong. The people sinned against are not always the best.
> —*IVY COMPTON-BURNETT, The Mighty and Their Fall (1961)*

11. Sin recognized—but that—may keep us humble, / But oh, it keeps us nasty.

> —*STEVIE SMITH, "Recognition Not Enough" (1962)*

12. There was nothing to confess.
> —*UNA TROUBRIDGE (d. 1963), on how she and Radclyffe Hall reconciled their relationship with their Catholicism, in Michael Baker, Our Three Selves: A Life of Radclyffe Hall (1985)*

S o c i e t y

1. Man seeketh in society comfort, use, and protection.
> —*FRANCIS BACON, The Advancement of Learning (1605)*

2. Society is no comfort / To one not sociable.
> —*WILLIAM SHAKESPEARE, Cymbeline (1610)*

3. No two things are more opposite than a crowd and society.
> —*SARAH SCOTT, A Description of Millenium Hall (1762)*

4. What men call social virtues, good fellowship, is commonly but the virtue of pigs in a litter, which lie close together to keep each other warm.

> —*HENRY DAVID THOREAU, Journal, 23 October 1851*

5. To be in it is merely a bore. But to be out of it simply a tragedy.
> —*OSCAR WILDE, A Woman of No Importance (1893)*

6. At the heart of our friendly or purely social relations, there lurks a hostility cured but recurring by fits and starts.
> —*MARCEL PROUST, Remembrance of Things Past: Cities of the Plain (1922)*

7. Society itself is an accident to the spirit, and if society in any of its forms is to be justified morally it must be justified at the bar of the individual conscience.

—GEORGE SANTAYANA, *Dialogues in Limbo (1925)*

8. If this is Society, thought Anguetil, God help us, for surely no fraud has ever equalled it.
—VITA SACKVILLE-WEST, *The Edwardians (1930)*

9. Society in its full sense is never an entity separate from the individuals who compose it. No individual can arrive even at the threshold of his potentialities without a culture in which he participates.
—RUTH BENEDICT, *Patterns of Culture (1934)*

10. You shall love your crooked neighbour / With your crooked heart.
—W. H. AUDEN, *"As I Walked Out One Evening" (1940)*

11. The whole trouble with Western society today is the lack of anything worth concealing.
—JOE ORTON (d. 1967), in John Lahr, *Prick Up Your Ears: The Biography of Joe Orton (1978)*

12. Within any society men and women develop differently and have, each, a subculture of their own that is overbalanced in the importance it places on particular jobs, attitudes, amounts of aggressiveness, roles it plays, amounts of expressed physicality and tenderness. . . . One of the major homosexual / shamanic functions in any society is to *cross over* between these two essentially different worlds and reveal them to each other.
—JUDY GRAHN, *Another Mother Tongue (1984)*

Sodomy

▼

1. Then give me health, wealth, mirth, and wine, / And, if busy love entrenches, / There's a sweet, soft page of mine / Does the trick worth forty wenches.
—JOHN WILMOT, EARL OF ROCHESTER, *"Song: Love a woman? You're an ass!" (1680)*

2. Here it is quite accepted. One admits one's sodomy, and it is spoken of at table in the hotel. Sometimes you do a bit of denying, and then everybody teases you and you end up confessing. Travelling as we are for educational purposes, and charged with a mission by the government, we

have considered it our duty to indulge in this form of ejaculation.
—*GUSTAVE FLAUBERT, on his travels in Egypt, letter to Louis Bouilhet, 15 January 1850*

3. I have no doubt myself the absorption of semen implies a real modification of the person who absorbs it, and that, in these homosexual relations, this constitutes an important basis for subsequent conditions—both spiritual and corporeal.
—*JOHN ADDINGTON SYMONDS, letter to Edward Carpenter, 29 December 1892*

4. All roads lead to Sodom.
—*EVELYN WAUGH, letter to Dudley Carew, 1924*

5. Impotence and sodomy are socially O.K. but birth control is flagrantly middle-class.
—*EVELYN WAUGH, in Nancy Mitford, Noblesse Oblige (1956)*

6. Should you find yourself in a compromising situation largely of your own making, you should stop defending your virtue and start worrying about your maturity. It will give you something to think about while the savage pumper bangs away.
—*QUENTIN CRISP, Manners from Heaven (1984)*

Soldiers and Sailors

1. If a city or an army could be made up only of lovers and their beloved, it would excel all others. For they would refrain from everything shameful, rivalling one another in honor; and men like these, fighting at each other's side, might well conquer the world. For the lover would rather be seen by anyone than by his beloved, flying or throwing away his arms; rather he would be ready a thousand times to die.
—*PLATO (4th century BCE), The Symposium*

2. Of arms and the man I sing.
—*VIRGIL, Aeneid (19 BCE)*

3. Great armies are nothing but a collection of weakness.
—*CHRISTINA, QUEEN OF SWEDEN, Maxims (1660–80), in Pensées de Christine, Reine de Suède (1825)*

4. What too many seamen are when ashore is very well known: but what some them become when completely cut off from shore indulgences can hardly be imagined by landsmen. The sin for which the cities of the plain were overthrown still lingers in some of these wooden-walled Gomorrahs of the deep.
　—HERMAN MELVILLE, *White Jacket* (1850)

5. I made an acquaintance last autumn in Venice with a Corporal of the 2nd Life Guard who was travelling with a man I knew. . . . [He] said that some men "listed on purpose to indulge their propensities." An Italian Colonel told me the same thing—i.e. that young men of the best families, after serving as volunteers, or in the natural course of conscription, would sometimes remain on in the ranks with a view to the opportunities afforded by barracks.
　—JOHN ADDINGTON SYMONDS, letter to Edward Carpenter, 5 February 1893

6. Soldiers are citizens of death's gray land, / Drawing no dividend from time's tomorrows.
　—SIEGFRIED SASSOON, "Dreamers" (1917)

7. I 'listed at home for a lancer, / *Oh who would not sleep with the brave?*
　—A. E. HOUSMAN, no. 1 ["Lancer"], *Last Poems* (1922)

8. Has anybody seen our ship? The H.M.S. Peculiar.
　—NOËL COWARD, "Has Anybody Seen Our Ship" (1935 song)

9. His preoccupation with the soldier grew in him like a disease. As in cancer, when the cells unaccountably rebel and begin the insidious self-multiplication that will ultimately destroy the body, so in his mind did the thought of the soldier grow out of all proportion to their normal sphere.
　—CARSON MCCULLERS, *Reflections in a Golden Eye* (1941)

10. I felt, in fact, about the Army, much as I had felt, in early adolescence, about sex: it was something difficult, rather disgusting and ultimately inevitable, which I dreaded yet longed to experience.
　—JOCELYN BROOKE, *A Mine of Serpents* (1949)

11. What they're claiming is that us queers are unfit for their beautiful pure Army and Navy—when they ought to be glad to have us.
　—CHRISTOPHER ISHERWOOD, *The World in the Evening* (1954)

12. Are you joining the Army? Good, it'll make a woman of you.
　—JOE ORTON, *Up Against It* (1966)

13. The Army with its male relationships was simply an extension of my public school.

—*J. R. ACKERLEY (d. 1967), My Father and Myself (1968)*

14. Even in childhood I was mad about men in uniform.
   —*QUENTIN CRISP, in Guy Kettelhack, ed., The Wit and Wisdom of Quentin Crisp (1984)*

15. We know that priorities are amiss in the world when a man gets a military medal of honor for killing another man and a dishonorable discharge for loving one.
   —*CHARLOTTE BUNCH, Passionate Politics (1987)*

Solidarity

1. There is a star above us which unites souls of the first order, though worlds and ages separate them.
   —*CHRISTINA, QUEEN OF SWEDEN, Maxims (1660–80)*

2. Come; let us squeeze hands all around; nay, let us all squeeze ourselves into each other; let us squeeze ourselves universally into the very milk and sperm of kindness.
   —*HERMAN MELVILLE, Moby-Dick (1851)*

3. I dream'd in a dream I saw a city invincible to the attacks of the whole of the rest of the earth, / I dream'd that was the new city of Friends.
   —*WALT WHITMAN, "I Dream'd in a Dream" (1860)*

4. Whoever degrades another degrades me.
   —*WALT WHITMAN, preface, Leaves of Grass (1872 ed.)*

5. Only connect! . . . Only connect the prose and the passion, and both will be exalted, and human love will be seen at its height. Only connect, and the beast and the monk, robbed of the isolation that is life to either, will die.
   —*E. M. FORSTER, Howards End (1910)*

6. The most dangerous word in any human tongue is the word for brother. It's inflammatory.
   —*TENNESSEE WILLIAMS, Camino Real (1953)*

7. If they take you in the morning, they will be coming for us that night.
   —*JAMES BALDWIN, "Open Letter to My Sister, Angela Davis" (1971)*

8. They had won, she and the other woman; the victory was orange and the afterworld green. . . . Her old battered mind had stood up and now she and . . . all women swam in a field of brilliant green, buoyed up by unbelievable green—gathered in a giant sweep all yellow and blue and scooped it into one untouchable safe sea of women.

—*JUNE ARNOLD, Sister Gin (1972)*

9. They were history, this moving blanket of women. The March showed strength and unity. Sisterhood in more than words, a political statement of determination in planting the seeds for a new southern woman. No doubt, there was a silent legion of lesbians striding along with her, dreaming of a different southern march someday for another purpose.

—*ANN ALLEN SHOCKLEY, Say Jesus and Come to Me (1982)*

10. The only way we'll have real pride is when we demand recognition of a culture that isn't just sexual. It's all there—all through history we've been there; but we have to claim it, and identify who was in it, and articulate what's in our minds and hearts and all our creative contributions to

this earth. And until we do that, and until we organize ourselves block by neighborhood by city by state into a united visible community that fights back, we're doomed.

—*LARRY KRAMER, The Normal Heart (1986)*

11. Snowflakes, leaves, humans, plants, raindrops, stars, molecules, microscopic entities all come in communities. The singular cannot in reality exist.

—*PAULA GUNN ALLEN, Grandmothers of the Light (1991)*

12. When the bigots came it was time to fight, and fight we did. Fought hard—femme and butch, women and men together.

—*LESLIE FEINBERG, Stone Butch Blues (1993)*

13. The more people come out, the less it will be an issue. If we are ashamed of ourselves, how the hell can we expect the rest of the world not to be ashamed of us?

—*MARTINA NAVRATILOVA, in New York, 10 May 1993*

Solitude

1. While you are alone you are entirely your own master and if you have one companion you are but half your own, and the less so in proportion to the indiscretion of his behavior.
　　—LEONARDO DA VINCI, *Notebooks (c. 1500)*

2. Whosoever is delighted in solitude is either a wild beast or a god.
　　—FRANCIS BACON, *"Of Friendship," Essays (1625)*

3. If from society we learn to live, / 'Tis Solitude should teach us how to die; / It hath no flatterers.
　　—GEORGE GORDON, LORD BYRON, *Childe Harold's Pilgrimage (1812–18)*

4. If any individual live too much in relations, so that he becomes a stranger to the resources of his own nature, he falls, after a while, into a distraction, or imbecility, from which he can only be cured by a time of isolation, which gives the renovating fountains time to rise up.
　　—MARGARET FULLER, *Woman in the Nineteenth Century (1845)*

5. I would rather sit on a pumpkin and have it all to myself than be crowded on a velvet cushion.
　　—HENRY DAVID THOREAU, *"Economy," Walden (1854)*

6. There are days when solitude is a heady wine that intoxicates you with freedom, others when it is a bitter tonic, and still others when it is a poison that makes you beat your head against the wall.
　　—COLETTE, *Les Vrilles de la Vigne (1908)*

7. A solitary, unused to speaking of what he sees and feels, has mental experiences which are at once more intense and less articulate than those of a gregarious man.
　　—THOMAS MANN, *Death in Venice (1911)*

8. Perhaps it would be better to go the whole hog and cut oneself off entirely from the outside world. A merely negative form of protest, I fear, against conditions one does not like; for resentment is vain unless one has an alternative to offer. Flight is no alternative; it is only a personal

solution. But as a personal experiment it certainly offers material for reflection to the curious.

— *VITA SACKVILLE-WEST, Twelve Days (1928)*

9. I want to be alone.

— *GRETA GARBO, in Grand Hotel (1932); script by William A. Drake*

10. Greatness and loneliness. "Puissant et solitaire." To live above the crowd in loneliness. To be condemned to loneliness by the greatness of one's qualities. To be condemned to live apart, however much one wanted the contact of warm human companionship. . . . Strange and dreadful fate!

— *OLIVIA [Dorothy Strachey Bussy], Olivia (1949)*

11. I have never, in all my life, been so odious as to regard myself as "superior" to any living being, human or animal. I just walked alone—as I have always walked alone.

— *EDITH SITWELL (d. 1964), Taken Care Of (1965)*

12. I don't see anything wrong with being alone. . . . The biggest price you pay for love is that you have somebody around, you can't be on your own, which is always so much better.

— *ANDY WARHOL, The Philosophy of Andy Warhol: From A to B and Back Again (1975)*

13. He travels fastest who travels alone, and that goes double for she.

— *FLORENCE KING, With Charity Toward None (1992)*

14. What others regard as retreat from them or rejection of them is not those things at all but instead a breeding ground for greater friendship, a culture for deeper involvement, eventually, with them.

— *DORIS GRUMBACH, Fifty Days of Solitude (1994)*

Sorrow

1. That sorrow which is the harbinger of joy is preferable to the joy which is followed by sorrow.
— SA'DI, *Gulistan (1258)*

2. Give sorrow words. The grief that does not speak / Whispers the o'er-fraught heart and bids it break.
— WILLIAM SHAKESPEARE, *Macbeth (1606)*

3. I'm so entangl'd and so lost a thing / By all the shocks my daily sorrow bring.
— KATHERINE PHILIPS, "Orinda to Lucasia parting October, 1661, at London" *(1664)*

4. Sorrows are only for a time.
— JOHN CLELAND, *Memoirs of a Woman of Pleasure (1749)*

5. Grief should be the instructor of the wise; / Sorrow is knowledge: they who know the most / Must mourn the deepest o'er the fatal truth, / The tree of knowledge is not that of Life.
— GEORGE GORDON, LORD BYRON, *Manfred (1817)*

6. I measure every Grief I meet / With narrow, probing Eyes— / I wonder if it weighs like Mine— / Or has an Easier size.
— EMILY DICKINSON, no. 561 *(c. 1862), Complete Poems (1955)*

7. But, truly, I have wept too much! The Dawns are heartbreaking. Every moon is atrocious and every sun bitter.
— ARTHUR RIMBAUD, "Le Bateau Ivre" *(1871)*

8. A lean sorrow is hardest to bear.
— SARAH ORNE JEWETT, "All My Sad Captains" *(1895)*

9. Where there is sorrow there is holy ground.
— OSCAR WILDE, *De Profundis (1897)*

10. Rapture's self is three parts sorrow.
— AMY LOWELL, "Happiness," *Sword Blades and Poppy Seeds (1914)*

11. There is in this world in which everything wears out, everything perishes, one thing that crumbles into dust, that destroys itself still more completely, leaving behind still fewer traces of itself than Beauty: namely Grief.
— MARCEL PROUST (d. 1922), *Remembrance of Things Past: The Sweet Cheat Gone (1925)*

12. A man's sorrow runs uphill; true it is difficult for him to bear, but it is also difficult for him to keep.
> —*DJUNA BARNES, Nightwood (1936)*

13. There is no doubt that sorrow brings one down in the world. The aristocratic privilege of silence belongs, you soon find out, to only the happy state—or, at least, to the state when pain keeps within bounds.
> —*ELIZABETH BOWEN, The Death of the Heart (1938)*

14. Many people misjudge the permanent effect of sorrow, and their capacity to live in the past.
> —*IVY COMPTON-BURNETT, Mother and Son (1955)*

Speech

1. Talk to me god-like lyre / Find your voice in mine.
> —*SAPPHO (7th century BCE), Fragment 118; trans. Anita George*

2. In the faculty of speech man excels the brute; but if thou utterest what is improper, the brute is thy superior.
> —*SA'DI, Gulistan (1258)*

3. Talkers are no good doers.
> —*WILLIAM SHAKESPEARE, Richard III (1592–93)*

4. The speaking in a perpetual hyperbole is comely in nothing but love.
> —*FRANCIS BACON, "Of Love," Essays (1625)*

5. Their tongues quivered like aspen leaves.
> —*WILLIAM BECKFORD, Vathek (1786)*

6. How fond you are of saying dangerous things!
> —*OSCAR WILDE, The Picture of Dorian Gray (1891)*

7. On an occasion of this kind it becomes more than a moral duty to speak one's mind. It becomes a pleasure.
> —*OSCAR WILDE, The Importance of Being Earnest (1895)*

8. All those beautiful sentiments that I've uttered have made me feel genuinely upset.
> —*COLETTE, "The Journey" (1905)*

9. Love? I make it constantly but I never talk about it.
>—*MARCEL PROUST, Remembrance of Things Past: The Guermantes Way (1921)*

10. Speech is civilization itself. The word, even the most contradictious word, preserves contact—it is silence which isolates.
>—*THOMAS MANN, The Magic Mountain (1924)*

11. Sappho would speak, I think, quite openly. . . .
>—*AMY LOWELL, "The Sisters" (1925)*

12. Her sarcasm was so quick, so fine at the point—it was like being touched by a metal so cold that one doesn't know whether one is burned or chilled.
>—*WILLA CATHER, My Mortal Enemy (1926)*

13. Our tongues recant like beaten weather vanes.
>—*HART CRANE, "The Tunnel," The Bridge (1930)*

14. She had the fluency of tongue and action meted out by divine providence to those who cannot think for themselves.
>—*DJUNA BARNES, Nightwood (1936)*

15. But no one would possibly listen to her. No one ever listened to one unless one said the wrong thing.
>—*SYLVIA TOWNSEND WARNER, "Fenella" (1966)*

16. Great people talk about ideas, average people talk about things, and small people talk about wine.
>—*FRAN LEBOWITZ, Social Studies (1981)*

Sports

1. The mere athlete becomes too much of a savage.
>—*PLATO (4th century BCE), The Republic*

2. Forasmuch as there is great noise in the city caused by hustling over large balls, from which many evils may arise, which God forbid, we

command and forbid on behalf of the King, on pain of imprisonment, such game to be used in the city in the future.

—*EDWARD II, KING OF ENGLAND, royal proclamation banning football (1314)*

3. You base football player.

—*WILLIAM SHAKESPEARE, King Lear (1605–6)*

4. Tennis is a game of no use in itself.

—*FRANCIS BACON, The Advancement of Learning (1605)*

5. O the joy of the strong-brawn'd fighter, towering / in the arena in perfect condition, conscious of / power, thirsting to meet his opponent.

—*WALT WHITMAN, "A Song of Joys," Leaves of Grass (1855)*

6. The English country gentleman galloping after a fox—the unspeakable in full pursuit of the uneatable.

—*OSCAR WILDE, A Woman of No Importance (1893)*

7. Night after night I went to sleep murmuring, "Tomorrow I will be easy, strong, quick, supple, accurate, dashing and self-controlled all at once!" for not less than this is necessary in the Game of Life called Golf.

—*ETHEL SMYTH, What Happened Next (1940)*

8. There are people who think that wrestling is an ignoble sport.

Wrestling is not sport, it is a spectacle, and it is no more ignoble to attend a wrestled performance of suffering than a performance of the sorrows of Arnolphe or Andromaque.

—*ROLAND BARTHES, Mythologies (1957)*

9. The great difference between sport and art is that sport, like a sonnet, forces beauty within its own system. Art, on the other hand, cyclically destroys boundaries and breaks free.

—*RITA MAE BROWN, Sudden Death (1983)*

10. People in the States used to think that if girls were good at sports their sexuality would be affected. Being feminine meant being a cheerleader, not being an athlete.

—*MARTINA NAVRATILOVA, Martina Navratilova—Being Myself (1985)*

11. Anyone who says that softball is a boring game to watch isn't looking at the right things.

—*YVONNE ZIPTER, Diamonds Are a Dyke's Best Friend (1988)*

12. When I was fifteen I believed that sex was nearly the same thing as softball.

—*LUCY JANE BLEDSOE, "State of Grace" (1992)*

Stage and Screen

1. O, it offends me to the soul to hear a robustious periwig-pated fellow tear a passion to tatters, to very rags, to split the ears of the groundlings.
   —WILLIAM SHAKESPEARE, *Hamlet (1600–1601)*

2. It is not good for one's morals to see bad acting.
   —OSCAR WILDE, *The Picture of Dorian Gray (1891)*

3. It's extraordinary how they keep so young. Actresses I mean. I think it's because they are always playing different parts.
   —W. SOMERSET MAUGHAM, *The Circle (1921)*

4. When I asked her where she had learnt to read so quickly she replied, "On the screens at cinemas."
   —RONALD FIRBANK, *The Flower Beneath the Foot (1923)*

5. We'll trot down to the movies and see how girls with wax faces live.
   —THORNTON WILDER, *The Skin of Our Teeth (1942)*

6. If his new film *Jailhouse Rock* reaches Cambridge I think you would not find the evening entirely wasted if you got one of your young friends to take you. [Elvis] is a handsome boy and dances and sings most provocatively. A surprisingly good actor too. And the moral of the story good: love and honour win the day over ambition and the golden calf.
   —J. R. ACKERLEY, *letter to E. M. Forster, 1958*

7. A film is a petrified fountain of thought.
   —JEAN COCTEAU, *in Esquire, February 1961*

8. [Peter O'Toole in *Lawrence of Arabia* is] far more attractive than Lawrence could ever hope to be. I said to him afterwards that if Lawrence had looked like him there would have been many more than twelve Turks queueing up for the buggering scene.
   —NOËL COWARD, *diary, 4 December 1962*

9. I have yet to see one completely unspoiled star, except for the animals—like Lassie.
   —EDITH HEAD, *in Saturday Evening Post, 1963*

10. Thanks to the silver screen your neurosis has style.
    —MART CROWLEY, *The Boys in the Band (1968)*

11. There is a point in portraying surface vulgarity where tragedy and comedy are very close.
> —*BARBARA STANWYCK, in Ella Smith, Starring Miss Barbara Stanwyck (1974)*

12. Lesbians are sharks, vampires, creatures from the deep lagoon, godzillas, hydrogen bombs, inventions of the laboratory, werewolves—all of whom stalk Beverly Hills by night. Christopher Lee in drag, in the Hammar [*sic*] Films middle-period, is my ideal lesbian.
> —*BERTHA HARRIS, in Sinister Wisdom, spring 1977*

13. All Americans born between 1890 and 1945 wanted to be movie stars.
> —*GORE VIDAL, The Second American Revolution and Other Essays (1982)*

14. [Kenneth] Tynan said I had only two gestures, the left hand up, the right hand up—what did he want me to do, bring out my prick?
> —*JOHN GIELGUD, in John Mortimer, In Character (1983)*

15. I can't be absolutely certain, thirty years ago . . . I made the decision to become an actor, but certainly one of the reasons was it was the way to meet other queer men.
> —*IAN MCKELLEN, in San Francisco Chronicle, 16 August 1992*

16. When we were doing it, [my character] was supposed to be very, very drunk. I said, "Why does she have to be very, very drunk?" I mean, if you're going to bed with a woman . . . and she looks like Catherine Deneuve, and she's as charming as Catherine Deneuve, why make [my character] drunk?
> —*SUSAN SARANDON, on the lesbian sex scene in The Hunger (1983); in The Advocate, 6 October 1992*

Stories

1. An honest tale speeds best being plainly told.
> —*WILLIAM SHAKESPEARE, Richard III (1592–93)*

2. She was telling some one, who was loving every story that was charming.

Some one who was living was almost always listening. Some one who was loving was almost always listening. That one who was loving was almost always listening. That one who was loving was telling about being one then listening. That one being lov-

ing was then telling stories having a beginning and a middle and an ending.
　　—GERTRUDE STEIN, *Ada (1908)*

3. Isn't it queer: there are only two or three human stories, and they go on repeating themselves as fiercely as if they had never happened before.
　　—WILLA CATHER, *O Pioneers!*
　　(1913)

4. Neanderthal man listened to stories, if one may judge by the shape of his skull.
　　—E. M. FORSTER, *Aspects of the*
　　Novel (1927)

5. A person can be fully involved in a story without understanding it.
　　—THOMAS MANN, *Joseph and His*
　　Brothers (1933)

6. Oh, it's a grand bad story, and who says I'm a betrayer? I say, tell the story of the world to the world!
　　—DJUNA BARNES, *Nightwood*
　　(1936)

7. The universe is made of stories, / not of atoms.
　　—MURIEL RUKEYSER, *"The Speed of*
　　Darkness" (1968)

8. The bearers of fables are always welcome.
　　—MONIQUE WITTIG, *Les Guérillères*
　　(1969)

9. All classes, all human groups, have their narratives, enjoyment of which is very often shared by men with different, even opposing, cultural backgrounds.
　　—ROLAND BARTHES, *Music, Image,*
　　Text (1977)

Straight

▼

1. Leave the pretty women for men without imagination.
　　—MARCEL PROUST *(d. 1922),*
　　Remembrance of Things Past:
　　The Sweet Cheat Gone (1925)

2. You will never succumb to the charms of any of your sex—What an arid garden the world must be for you!

　　—VIRGINIA WOOLF, *letter to her*
　　sister Vanessa Bell, 22 May 1927

3. What is straight? A line can be straight, or a street, but the human heart, oh, no. It's curved like a road through the mountains.
　　—TENNESSEE WILLIAMS, *A Streetcar*
　　Named Desire (1947)

4. Nearly all my loves are married, and parents of children I have no desire to meet. Why distress the tranquil vegetation of middle-aged Darbies and Joans? No home-breaker I, no cuckoo in other nests. I culled the *prémices,* and it is a subtle satisfaction, even in retrospect, to have kindled flames in Elgin marble breasts.

—HAROLD ACTON, *Memoirs of an Aesthete (1948)*

5. There is probably no sensitive heterosexual alive who is not preoccupied with his latent homosexuality.

—NORMAN MAILER, *Advertisements for Myself (1959)*

6. [The] problem that confronts homosexuals is that they set out to win the love of a "real" man. If they succeed, they fail. A man who "goes with" other men is not what they would call a real man.

—QUENTIN CRISP, *The Naked Civil Servant (1968)*

7. Straight! He's about as straight as the Yellow Brick Road.

—MART CROWLEY, *The Boys in the Band (1968)*

8. RANCE: Ruin follows the accusation not the vice. Had you committed the act you wouldn't now be facing the charge.

PRENTICE: I couldn't commit the act. I'm a heterosexual.

RANCE: I wish you wouldn't use these Chaucerian words. It's most confusing.

—JOE ORTON (d. 1967), *What the Butler Saw (1969)*

9. If you're straight then I'm crooked, but if I'm gay then you're morose.

—ROBIN TYLER, *recording Always a Bridesmaid Never a Groom (1979)*

10. Bob and I were talking about how hard it was to find Ten Straight Men, and somebody said that should be my next portfolio—ten men who've never had a homosexual experience.

—ANDY WARHOL, *diary, 27 October 1980*

11. Straight ladies can be very dangerous. They tend to toy with our affections.

—JANE CHAMBERS, *Last Summer at Blue Fish Cove (1981)*

12. Such figures as Boy George do not disturb me nearly so much as do those relentlessly hetero (sexual?) keepers of the keys and seals, those who know what the world needs in the way or order and who are ready and willing to supply that order.

—JAMES BALDWIN, *The Price of the Ticket (1985)*

13. I think it's very much harder to be heterosexual, from the inward point of view. It's easier from the social, outer point of view. Of course,

I am a lesbian. But if you are a heterosexual woman, you are taking the stranger in; you are taking into you, even physically, somebody very different from you.

> —MAY SARTON, interview in
> Margaret Cruikshank, The
> Lesbian Path (1985)

14. It's funny how heterosexuals have lives and the rest of us have "lifestyles."

> —SONIA JOHNSON, Going Out of
> Our Minds (1987)

15. All men are homosexual, some turn straight. It must be very odd to be a straight man because your sexuality is hopelessly defensive. It's like an ideal of racial purity.

> —DEREK JARMAN, At Your Own
> Risk: A Saint's Testament (1992)

16. I became a lesbian out of devout Christian charity. All those women out there are praying for a man and I gave them my share.

> —RITA MAE BROWN, Venus Envy
> (1993)

Success and Failure

1. It is charming to totter into vogue.
> —HORACE WALPOLE, letter to George
> Selwyn, 2 December 1765

2. I also say it is good to fall, battles are lost in the same spirit in which they are won.
> —WALT WHITMAN, "Song of Myself"
> Leaves of Grass (1855)

3. Success is counted sweetest / By those who ne'er succeed.
> —EMILY DICKINSON, no. 67
> (c. 1859), Complete Poems (1955)

4. To burn always with the hard, gemlike flame, to maintain this ecstasy, is success in life.

> —WALTER PATER, Studies in the
> History of the Renaissance
> (1873)

5. The success or failure of a life, as far as posterity goes, seems to lie in the more or less luck of seizing the right moment of escape.
> —ALICE JAMES (1891), in Anna
> Robeson Burr, Alice James
> (1934)

6. When we can begin to take our failures nonseriously, it means we are ceasing to be afraid of them. It is of immense importance to learn to laugh at ourselves.

—KATHERINE MANSFIELD (1922),
Journal of Katherine Mansfield
(1927)

7. I find it's as hard to live down an early triumph as an early indiscretion.

—EDNA ST. VINCENT MILLAY (1922),
in Allan Ross Macdougall, ed.,
Letters of Edna St. Vincent
Millay (1952)

8. Worldly wisdom teaches that it is better for the reputation to fail conventionally than to succeed unconventionally.

—JOHN MAYNARD KEYNES, *The*
General Theory of Employment,
Interest and Money (1936)

9. The common idea that success spoils people by making them vain, egotistic and self-complacent is erroneous; on the contrary it makes them, for the most part, humble, tolerant and kind. Failure makes people bitter and cruel.

—W. SOMERSET MAUGHAM,
Summing Up (1938)

10. More people are ruined by victory, I imagine, than by defeat.

—ELEANOR ROOSEVELT, *My Days*
(1938)

11. There are so many ways of earning a living and most of them are failures.

—GERTRUDE STEIN, *Ida (1941)*

12. The face of victory often resembles the face of defeat.

—JANE BOWLES, *Two Serious Ladies*
(1943)

13. To think of losing is to lose already.

—SYLVIA TOWNSEND WARNER
(1951), in William Maxwell, ed.,
Letters: Sylvia Townsend Warner
(1982)

14. What frightened him, and kept him more than ever on his knees, was the knowledge that, once having fallen, nothing would be easier than to fall again.

—JAMES BALDWIN, *Go Tell It on the*
Mountain (1953)

15. The mystery of life is not solved by success, which is an end in itself, but in failure, in perpetual struggle, in becoming.

—PATRICK WHITE, *Voss (1957)*

16. In a total work, the failures have their not unimportant place.

—MAY SARTON, *Mrs. Stevens Hears*
the Mermaids Singing (1965)

17. Whenever a friend succeeds, a little something in me dies.

—GORE VIDAL, *in Sunday Times*
Magazine, 16 September 1973

18. It is not enough to succeed. Others must fail.

—GORE VIDAL, *quoted in G. Irvine,*
Antipanegyric for Tom Driberg
(1976)

19. Why is it we are always hearing about the tragic cases of too much, too soon? What about the rest of us? Too little, too late.
> —*LILY TOMLIN, in Time,*
> *28 March 1977*

20. Nothing succeeds like address.
> —*FRAN LEBOWITZ, Metropolitan*
> *Life (1978)*

21. Sometimes I worry about being a success in a mediocre world.
> —*LILY TOMLIN, in New Times,*
> *9 January 1978*

22. No honest work of man or woman "fails"; / It feeds the sum of all human action.

> —*MICHELENE WANDOR, Aurora*
> *Leigh (1979)*

23. For you to be successful, sacrifices must be made. It's better that they are made by others but failing that, you'll have to make them yourself.
> —*RITA MAE BROWN, Starting from*
> *Scratch (1988)*

24. What does so-called success or failure matter if only you have succeeded in doing the thing you set out to do. The DOING is all that really counts.
> —*EVA LE GALLIENNE (d. 1991), in*
> *Robert A. Schanke, Shattered*
> *Applause (1991)*

Taste

1. There are as many preferences as there are men.
> —*HORACE (1st century BCE),*
> *Satires II, 1*

2. Taste and distinction, if they do not justify, they at least ennoble weakness.
> —*JOHN CLELAND, Memoirs of a*
> *Coxcomb (1751)*

3. One of the greatest geniuses that ever existed, Shakespeare, undoubtedly wanted taste.
> —*HORACE WALPOLE, letter to*
> *Christopher Wren, 1764*

4. What is exhilarating in bad taste is the aristocratic pleasure of giving offense.

—CHARLES BAUDELAIRE (d. 1867),
*Intimate Journals (1930); trans.
Christopher Isherwood*

5. Absolute catholicity of taste is not without its dangers. It is only an auctioneer who should admire all schools of art.
—OSCAR WILDE, *in Pall Mall
Gazette, 8 February 1886*

6. Beautiful things, when taste is formed, are obviously and unaccountably beautiful.
—GEORGE SANTAYANA, *The Life of
Reason (1906)*

7. Between friends differences in taste or opinion are irritating in direct proportion to their triviality.
—W. H. AUDEN, *The Dyer's Hand
(1962)*

8. Taste tends to develop very unevenly. It's rare that the same person has good visual taste *and* good taste in people *and* taste in ideas.
—SUSAN SONTAG, *"Notes on 'Camp,'"
Against Interpretation (1964)*

9. Good taste is the worst vice ever invented.
—EDITH SITWELL (d. 1964), *in
Elizabeth Salter, The Last Years
of a Rebel (1967)*

Temptation

1. O cunning enemy, that, to catch a saint, / With saints dost bait thy hook! Most dangerous / Is that temptation that doth goad us on / To sin in loving virtue.
—WILLIAM SHAKESPEARE, *Measure
for Measure (1603)*

2. Not all that tempts your wand'ring eyes / And heedless hearts, is lawful prize.
—THOMAS GRAY, *"Ode on the Death
of a Favourite Cat" (1747)*

3. I beg you let me be quiet, for I am not over-fond of resisting temptation.
—WILLIAM BECKFORD, *Vathek
(1786)*

4. I can resist everything except temptation.

—OSCAR WILDE, *Lady Windermere's Fan (1891)*

5. The only way of getting rid of temptation is to yield to it.
    —OSCAR WILDE, *The Picture of Dorian Gray (1891)*

6. Temptations came to him, in middle age, tentatively and without insistence, like a neglected butcher-

boy who asks for a Christmas box in February for no more hopeful reason than he didn't get one in December.
    —SAKI [H. H. Munro], *"The Reticence of Lady Anne," The Chronicles of Clovis (1911)*

7. No temptation can ever be measured by the value of its object.
    —COLETTE (d. 1954), *The Earthly Paradise (1966)*

Thought

1. Toward you comely girls / My thoughts are ever constant.
    —SAPPHO *(7th century BCE), Fragment 41; trans. Anita George*

2. There is nothing either good or bad, but thinking makes it so.
    —WILLIAM SHAKESPEARE, *Hamlet (1600–1601)*

3. All thought is immoral. Its very essence is destruction.
    —OSCAR WILDE, *A Woman of No Importance (1893)*

4. I send you my thoughts—the air between us is laden, / My thoughts

fly in at your window, a flock of wild birds.
    —SARA TEASDALE, *"At Night" (1915)*

5. We have too much sex on the brain and too little of it elsewhere.
    —NORMAN DOUGLAS, *An Almanac (1942)*

6. A thinking woman sleeps with monsters.
    —ADRIENNE RICH, *"Snapshots of a Daughter-in-Law" (1963)*

7. Thought is never free. It is bought in pain, / loneliness.

—MAUREEN DUFFY, *"For The Freethinker Centenary" (1980)*

8. Original thought is like original sin: both happened before you were born to people you could not possibly have met.
—FRAN LEBOWITZ, *Social Studies (1981)*

T i m e

1. Time bears away all things, even the mind.
—VIRGIL *(1st century BCE), Eclogues*

2. I wasted time, and now doth time waste me.
—WILLIAM SHAKESPEARE, *Richard II (1595)*

3. One hour of right-down love / Is worth an hour of dully living on.
—APHRA BEHN, *The Rover (1677)*

4. As if you could kill time without injuring eternity.
—HENRY DAVID THOREAU, *"Economy," Walden (1854)*

5. Remember! Time, that tireless gambler, wins / on every turn of the wheel: that is the law.
—CHARLES BAUDELAIRE, *"L'Horloge," Les Fleurs du Mal (1857)*

6. Time is a Test of Trouble— / But not a Remedy— / If such it prove, it prove too / There was no Malady—.
—EMILY DICKINSON, *no. 683 (c. 1863), Complete Poems (1955)*

7. What has the actual lapse of time got to do with the past?
—OSCAR WILDE, *The Picture of Dorian Gray (1891)*

8. Time is the only true purgatory.
—SAMUEL BUTLER *(d. 1902), Note Books (1912)*

9. If we take eternity to mean not infinite temporal duration but time-lessness, then eternal life belongs to those who live in the present.
—LUDWIG WITTGENSTEIN, *Tractatus Logico-Philosophicus (1922)*

10. Although time changes people, it cannot change the image we have already made of them.

—MARCEL PROUST (d. 1922),
Remembrance of Things Past:
Time Regained (1926)

11. Time has no divisions to mark its passage, there is never a thunderstorm or blare of trumpets to announce the beginning of a new month or year. Even when a new century begins it is only we mortals who ring bells and fire off pistols.
—THOMAS MANN, The Magic
Mountain (1924)

12. And what is time but shadows that were cast / By these storm-sculptured stones while centuries fled?
—SIEGFRIED SASSOON, The Heart's
Journey (1928)

13. Time was our banker once, and on our credit / Like an indulgent father let us draw.
—VITA SACKVILLE-WEST, King's
Daughter (1929)

14. To be quite oneself one must first waste a little time.
—ELIZABETH BOWEN, The House in
Paris (1935)

15. A distraction is to avoid the consciousness of the passage of time.
—GERTRUDE STEIN, Everybody's
Autobiography (1937)

16. You must live through the time when everything hurts.
—STEPHEN SPENDER, "The Double
Shame" (1939)

17. Time is the reef upon which all of our frail mystic ships are wrecked.
—NOËL COWARD, Blithe Spirit
(1941)

18. I didn't go to the moon, I went much further—for time is the longest distance between two places.
—TENNESSEE WILLIAMS, The Glass
Menagerie (1945)

19. Time has too much credit. It is not a great healer. It is an indifferent and perfunctory one. Sometimes it does not heal at all. And sometimes when it seems to, no healing has been necessary.
—IVY COMPTON-BURNETT, Darkness
and Day (1951)

20. What is this thing about time? Why is it better to be late than early? People are always saying, we must wait, we must wait. What are they waiting for?
—JAMES BALDWIN, Giovanni's Room
(1956)

21. In reality, *killing time* / Is only the name for another of the multifarious ways / By which Time kills us.
—OSBERT SITWELL, "Milordo
Inglese" (1958)

22. Since we're not young, weeks have to do time for years of missing each other. Yet only this odd warp in time tells me we're not young.
—ADRIENNE RICH, "Twenty-One
Love Poems," The Dream of a
Common Language (1978)

23. Time moves slowly, but passes quickly.
>—ALICE WALKER, *The Color Purple (1982)*

24. It may be true that the preoccupation with time has been the downfall of Western man, but it can also be argued that conjecture about eternity is a waste of time.

>—QUENTIN CRISP, *in Guy Kettelhack, ed., The Wit and Wisdom of Quentin Crisp (1984)*

25. Time has passed through me and become a song.
>—HOLLY NEAR, *Fire in the Rain . . . Singer in the Storm (1990)*

Tolerance and Intolerance

1. Tolerance is the virtue of the weak.
>—MARQUIS DE SADE, *La Nouvelle Justine (1797)*

2. I cherish the greatest respect towards everybody's religious obligations, never mind how comical.
>—HERMAN MELVILLE, *Moby-Dick (1851)*

3. The public is wonderfully tolerant. They forgive everything except genius.
>—OSCAR WILDE, *Intentions (1891)*

4. Tolerance is only another name for indifference.

>—W. SOMERSET MAUGHAM (1896), *A Writer's Notebook (1949)*

5. Intolerance itself is a form of egoism, and to condemn egoism intolerantly is to share it.
>—GEORGE SANTAYANA, *Winds of Doctrine (1913)*

6. Traditional Anglo-Saxon intolerance is a local and temporal culture-trait like any other. We have failed to understand the relativity of cultural habits, and we remain debarred from much profit and enjoyment in our human relations with people of different standards, and untrustworthy in our dealings with them.

—RUTH BENEDICT, *Patterns of Culture (1934)*

7. Tolerance is a very dull virtue. It is boring. Unlike love it has a bad press. It is negative. It merely means putting up with people, being able to stand things.
  —E. M. FORSTER, *Two Cheers for Democracy (1951)*

T r a g e d y

1. All tragedies are finished by a death, / All comedies are ended by a marriage.
  —GEORGE GORDON, LORD BYRON, *Don Juan (1819–24)*

2. It often happens that the real tragedies of life occur in such an inartistic manner that they hurt us by their crude violence, their absolute incoherence, their absurd want of meaning, their entire lack of style. They affect us just as vulgarity affects us. They give us an impression of sheer brute force, and we revolt against that. Sometimes, however, a tragedy that possesses artistic elements of beauty crosses our lives. If these elements of beauty are real, the whole thing simply appeals to our sense of dramatic effect. Suddenly we find that we are no longer the actors, but the spectators of the play. Or rather we are both.
  —OSCAR WILDE, *The Picture of Dorian Gray (1891)*

3. In this world there are only two tragedies. One is not getting what one wants and the other is getting it. The last is much the worst, the last is the real tragedy.
  —OSCAR WILDE (d. 1900), in *Hesketh Pearson, Oscar Wilde (1946)*

4. The actual tragedies of life bear no relation to one's preconceived ideas. In the event, one is always bewildered by their simplicity, their grandeur of design, and by that element of the bizarre which seems inherent in them.
  —JEAN COCTEAU, *Les Enfants Terribles (1929); trans. Rosamond Lehmann*

5. The great tragedy of life is not that men perish, but that they cease to love.
  —W. SOMERSET MAUGHAM, *The Summing Up (1938)*

6. Like all very handsome men who die tragically, he left not so much a character behind him as a legend. Youth and death shed a halo through which it is difficult to see a real face.
　　—VIRGINIA WOOLF, "A Sketch of the Past" (1940)

7. All tragedies deal with fated meetings; how else could there be a play? Fate deals its stroke; sorrow is purged, or turned to rejoicing; there is death, or triumph; there has been a meeting, and a change. No one will

ever make a tragedy—and that is as well, for one could not bear it— whose grief is that the principals never meet.
　　—MARY RENAULT, The Mask of Apollo (1966)

8. Tragedy is a vision of nihilism, a heroic or ennobling vision of nihilism.
　　—SUSAN SONTAG, "The Death of Tragedy," Against Interpretation (1966)

Transsexuality

▼

1. What a pity one can't now and then change sexes! I should love to be a dowager Countess.
　　—LYTTON STRACHEY, letter to Clive Bell, 21 October 1909

2. Some ninety hours afterwards the said young novice brought into the world the Blessed St Elizabeth Bathilde, who, by dint of skipping, changed her sex at the age of forty and became a man.
　　—RONALD FIRBANK, Valmouth (1919)

3. The sound of trumpets died away and Orlando stood stark naked. No human being since the world began,

has ever looked more ravishing. His form combined in one the strength of a man and a woman's grace. . . . Orlando had become a woman— there is no denying it. But in every other respect, Orlando remained precisely as he had been.
　　—VIRGINIA WOOLF, Orlando (1928)

4. If Myra Myron is dead as a doornail why when I lost those ugly things it was like a ship losing its anchor and I've been sailing ever since.
　　—GORE VIDAL, Myra Breckinridge (1968)

5. So help me god she stands up and hikes up her dress and pulls down

her goddam panties and shows me this scar where cock and balls should be and says quote Uncle Buck I am Myron Breckinridge unquote period paragraph I like to have fainted at the sight.
> —*GORE VIDAL, Myra Breckinridge (1968)*

6. I believe the transsexual urge, at least as I have experienced it, to be far more than a social compulsion, but biological, imaginative, and essentially spiritual, too.
> —*JAN MORRIS, Conundrum (1974)*

7. If you have a psychotic fixation and you go to the doctor and you want these two fingers amputated, he will not cut them off. But he *will* remove your genitals. I have more trouble getting a prescription for Valium than I do having my uterus lowered and made into a penis.
> —*LILY TOMLIN, in Rolling Stone, 24 October 1974*

8. How many modern transsexuals are unacknowledged shamans? Perhaps it is to poets they should go for counsel, rather than surgeons.
> —*CAMILLE PAGLIA, Sexual Personae (1990)*

9. I know I'm not a man—about that I'm very clear, and I've come to the conclusion that I'm probably not a woman either, at least not according to a lot of people's rules on this sort of thing. The trouble is, we're living in a world that insists that we be one or the other—a world that doesn't bother to tell us exactly what one or the other is.
> —*KATE BORNSTEIN, Gender Outlaw (1994)*

10. *Man Enough to Be a Woman*
> —*JAYNE [WAYNE] COUNTY, book title (1995)*

Trust

1. Love all, trust a few.
> —*WILLIAM SHAKESPEARE, All's Well That Ends Well (1604–5)*

2. I wonder men trust themselves with men.

—*WILLIAM SHAKESPEARE, Timon of Athens (1605)*

3. He's mad that trusts in the tameness of a wolf, a horse's health, a boy's love, or a whore's oath.

—WILLIAM SHAKESPEARE, *King Lear*
(1605–6)

4. We have to distrust each other. It's
our only defense against betrayal.
—TENNESSEE WILLIAMS, *Camino
Real (1953)*

5. How can the people trust the har-
vest, unless they see it sown?
—MARY RENAULT, *The King Must
Die (1958)*

6. How desperately we wish to maintain our trust in those we love! In the
face of everything, we try to find reasons to trust. Because losing faith is
worse than falling out of love.
—SONIA JOHNSON, *From Housewife
to Heretic (1981)*

7. I'm telling you stories. Trust me.
—JEANETTE WINTERSON, *The
Passion (1987)*

Truth

1. They deem him their worst enemy
who tells them the truth.
—PLATO *(4th century BCE), The
Republic*

2. A Hair perhaps divides the False
and True.
—OMAR KHAYYÁM, *Rubáiyát
(11th–12th century); trans.
Edward FitzGerald*

3. Truth is powerful, and it is not
always that we do not believe what
we eagerly wish.
—JOHN CLELAND, *Memoirs of a
Woman of Pleasure (1749)*

4. Truth is irresistible. The vivacity
of its coloring has quite a different
effect from the daub of falsity or
invention.
—JOHN CLELAND, *Memoirs of a
Coxcomb (1751)*

5. 'Tis strange but true; for truth is
always stranger; / Stranger than fiction.
—GEORGE GORDON, LORD BYRON,
Don Juan (1819–24)

6. Between whom there is hearty
truth there is love.
—HENRY DAVID THOREAU, *"The
Atlantides," A Week on the
Concord and Merrimack Rivers
(1849)*

7. It is not for man to follow the trail
of truth too far, since by so doing he

entirely loses the directing compass of his mind.
> —HERMAN MELVILLE, *Pierre* (1852)

8. Whatever satisfies the soul is truth.
> —WALT WHITMAN, preface, *Leaves of Grass* (1855 ed.)

9. Tell the Truth but tell it slant— / Success in Circuit lies / Too bright for our infirm Delight / the Truth's superb surprise.
> —EMILY DICKINSON, no. 1129 (c. 1868), *Complete Poems* (1955)

10. The truth is rarely pure, and never simple.
> —OSCAR WILDE, *The Importance of Being Earnest* (1895)

11. A thing is not necessarily true because a man dies for it.
> —OSCAR WILDE (d. 1900), *Sebastian Melmoth* (1904)

12. There is no permanent absolute unchangeable truth; what we should pursue is the most convenient arrangement of our ideas.
> —SAMUEL BUTLER (d. 1902), *Note Books* (1912)

13. We can't be content with telling the truth—we must tell the whole truth.
> —LYTTON STRACHEY, letter to John Maynard Keynes, 8 April 1906

14. The stupid believe that to be truthful is easy; only the artist, the great artist, knows how difficult it is.
> —WILLA CATHER, *The Song of the Lark* (1915)

15. The truth is cruel, but it can be loved, and it makes free those who have loved it.
> —GEORGE SANTAYANA, "Ideal Immortality" (1920)

16. It is in our idleness, in our dreams, that the submerged truth sometimes comes to the top.
> —VIRGINIA WOOLF, *A Room of One's Own* (1929)

17. Anything difficult to say must be shouted from the rooftops.
> —NATALIE CLIFFORD BARNEY, *Adventures of the Mind* (1929)

18. Nobody speaks the truth when there's something they must have.
> —ELIZABETH BOWEN, *The House in Paris* (1935)

19. Truth is a flower in whose neighbourhood others must wither.
> —E. M. FORSTER, *Abinger Harvest* (1936)

20. If truth is a value it is because it is true and not because it is brave to speak it.
> —W. SOMERSET MAUGHAM, *The Summing Up* (1938)

21. To love the truth is to refuse to let oneself be saddened by it.

—ANDRÉ GIDE, *Journals,*
    14 October 1940

22. Truth is so impossible. Something has to be done for it.
    —IVY COMPTON-BURNETT, *Darkness*
        and Day (1951)

23. The truth is balance, but the opposite of truth, which is unbalance, may not be a lie.
    —SUSAN SONTAG, *Against*
        Interpretation (1966)

24. The truths of the past are the clichés of the present.
    —NED ROREM, *Music from Inside*
        Out (1967)

25. What would happen if one woman told the truth about her life? / The world would split open.
    —MURIEL RUKEYSER, *"Käthe*
        Kollwitz" (1968)

26. There are two sexes. The unpalatable truth must be faced.
    —JOE ORTON (d. 1967), *What the*
        Butler Saw (1969)

27. At some point I believe one has to stop holding back for fear of alienating some imaginary reader or real relative or friend, and come out with personal truth.
    —MAY SARTON, *Journal of a*
        Solitude (1973)

28. There is at least one thing more brutal than the truth, and that is the consequence of saying less than the truth.
    —TI-GRACE ATKINSON, *Amazon*
        Odyssey (1974)

29. Lady . . . Lady, I do not make up things. That is lies. Lies is not true. But the truth could be made up if you know how. And that's the truth.
    —LILY TOMLIN, *as her character*
        "Edith Ann," in Rolling Stone,
        24 October 1974

30. There are certain truths so true that they are practically unbelievable.
    —GORE VIDAL, *The Second*
        American Revolution and Other
        Essays (1982)

31. So often the truth is told with hate, and lies are told with love.
    —RITA MAE BROWN, *Bingo (1988)*

32. Gay truths are different from straight truths. And most of the straight world does not wish to hear gay truths. Because, as all truth should, it often contains enough hurt for everyone.
    —LARRY KRAMER, *Just Say No*
        (1989)

33. But the truth is other as truth always is.
    —JEANETTE WINTERSON, *"The*
        Poetics of Sex" (1993)

Understanding

▼

1. Happy the man who could understand the causes of things.
> —*VIRGIL (1st century BCE),*
> *Georgics II*

2. Nothing can be loved or hated unless it is first known.
> —*LEONARDO DA VINCI, Notebooks*
> *(c. 1500)*

3. Who understandeth thee not, loves thee not.
> —*WILLIAM SHAKESPEARE, Love's*
> *Labour's Lost (1594–95)*

4. In human intercourse the tragedy begins, not when there is misunderstanding about words, but when silence is not understood.
> —*HENRY DAVID THOREAU, "The*
> *Atlantides," A Week on the*
> *Concord and Merrimack Rivers*
> *(1849)*

5. The world only goes round by misunderstanding.
> —*CHARLES BAUDELAIRE (d. 1867),*
> *Intimate Journals (1930); trans.*
> *Christopher Isherwood*

6. I like people who understand what one says to them, and also what one doesn't say.
> —*HENRY JAMES, Princess*
> *Casamassima (1886)*

7. Where there is no exaggeration there is no love, and where there is no love there is no understanding.
> —*OSCAR WILDE, in Speaker,*
> *22 March 1890*

8. Understanding is the beginning of approving.
> —*ANDRÉ GIDE, Journals (1902)*

9. The worst tragedy for a poet is to be admired through being misunderstood.
> —*JEAN COCTEAU, Le Rappel à*
> *l'Ordre (1926)*

10. In daily life we never understand each other, neither complete clairvoyance nor complete confessional exists.
> —*E. M. FORSTER, Aspects of the*
> *Novel (1927)*

11. The light of understanding / has made me discreet.
> —*FEDERICO GARCÍA LORCA, "The*
> *Faithless Wife" (1928)*

12. Perfect understanding will sometimes almost extinguish pleasure.
> —*A. E. HOUSMAN, The Name and*
> *Nature of Poetry (1933)*

13. One never discusses anything with anybody who can understand

one discusses things with people who cannot understand.
> —GERTRUDE STEIN, *Everybody's Autobiography (1937)*

14. Insight—the titillating knack for hurting!
> —COLETTE (d. 1954), *The Earthly Paradise (1966)*

15. You always admire what you don't really understand.

> —ELEANOR ROOSEVELT, *television interview, Meet the Press, 16 September 1956*

16. At the moment you are most in awe of all there is about life that you don't understand, you are closer to understanding it all than at any other time.
> —JANE WAGNER [words spoken by Lily Tomlin], *The Search for Signs of Intelligent Life in the Universe (1985)*

Vice   and   Virtue

1. Even virtue followed beyond reason's rule / May stamp the just man knave, the sage a fool.
> —HORACE (1st century BCE), *Epistles I, 6*

2. To the eye of enmity virtue appears the ugliest blemish.
> —SA'DI, *Gulistan (1258)*

3. I am not a slut, though I thank the gods I am foul.
> —WILLIAM SHAKESPEARE, *As You Like It (1599–1600)*

4. Virtue? A fig! 'Tis in ourselves that we are thus or thus. Our bodies are our gardens to which our wills are gardeners.

> —WILLIAM SHAKESPEARE, *Othello (1603–4)*

5. Virtue is like precious odours—most fragrant when they are incensed or crushed.
> —FRANCIS BACON, *"Of Adversity," Essays (1625)*

6. Vices are the harpies that infect and foul the feast.
> —JOHN CLELAND, *Memoirs of a Woman of Pleasure (1749)*

7. Your two friends, Prudence and Reflection, I am informed, have lately ventured to pay you a visit; for which I heartily congratulate you, as

nothing can possibly be more joyous to the heart than the return of absent friends, after a long and painful peregrination.
> —CHARLOTTE CHARKE, *A Narrative of the Life of Mrs. Charlotte Charke (1755)*

8. His virtues were always ready to operate when his passions did not obscure his reason.
> —HORACE WALPOLE, *The Castle of Otranto (1764)*

9. You were virtuous from vanity, not principle.
> —MATTHEW G. LEWIS, *The Monk (1795)*

10. Virtue knows to a farthing what it has lost by not having been vice.
> —HORACE WALPOLE (d. 1797), in L. Kronenberger, *The Extraordinary Mr Wilkes (1974)*

11. Be warm, but pure; be amorous, but chaste.
> —GEORGE GORDON, LORD BYRON, *English Bards and Scotch Reviewers (1809)*

12. I never was so rapid in my virtue but my vice kept up with me.
> —HENRY DAVID THOREAU, *Journal, 8 February 1841*

13. Look at the poor lives we lead. It is a wonder that we are so good as we are, not that we are so bad.
> —FLORENCE NIGHTINGALE, *"Cassandra" (1852)*

14. Come down and redeem us from virtue, / Our Lady of Pain.
> —ALGERNON CHARLES SWINBURNE, *"Dolores" (1866)*

15. I find that forgiving one's enemies is a most curious morbid pleasure; perhaps I should check it.
> —OSCAR WILDE, *letter, 20 April 1894*

16. My virtue's still far too small, I don't trot it out and about yet.
> —COLETTE, *Claudine at School (1900)*

17. I would sooner have fifty unnatural vices, than one unnatural virtue. It is unnatural virtue that makes the world, for those who suffer, such a premature Hell.
> —OSCAR WILDE (d. 1900), in Hesketh Pearson, *Oscar Wilde (1946)*

18. Half the vices which the world condemns most loudly have seeds of good in them and require moderate use rather than total abstinence.
> —SAMUEL BUTLER (d. 1902), *The Way of All Flesh (1903)*

19. Honesty is a selfish virtue. Yes, I am honest enough.
> —GERTRUDE STEIN, *Q.E.D. (1903)*

20. Life as a child and then as a girl had taught her patience, hope, silence; and given her a prisoner's proficiency in handling these virtues as weapons.
—COLETTE, *Cheri (1920)*

21. Those who practice the same profession recognize each other instinctively; likewise those who practice the same vice.
—MARCEL PROUST, *Remembrance of Things Past: Cities of the Plain (1922)*

22. Some out of their own virtue make a god who sometimes later is a terror to them.
—GERTRUDE STEIN, *The Making of Americans (1925)*

23. How pure are those who have never forced anything open!
—COLETTE, *La Naissance du Jour (1928)*

24. Chastity has, even now, a relative importance in a woman's life, and has so wrapped itself round with nerves and instincts that to cut it free and bring it to the light of day demands courage of the rarest.
—VIRGINIA WOOLF, *A Room of One's Own (1929)*

25. The distortions of ingrown virginity.
—W. H. AUDEN, *"Sir, No Man's Enemy" (1930)*

26. Chastity more rarely follows fear, or a resolution, or a vow, than it is the mere effect of lack of appetite and, sometimes even, of distaste.
—ANDRÉ GIDE, *Journals, 12 March 1938*

27. A person who can really be called an unselfish person has no place in life.
—IVY COMPTON-BURNETT, *Elders and Betters (1944)*

28. I'm as pure as the driven slush.
—TALLULAH BANKHEAD, *in Saturday Evening Post, 1 April 1947*

29. Here's a rule I recommend. Never practice two vices at once.
—TALLULAH BANKHEAD, *Tallulah (1952)*

30. Never support two weaknesses at the same time. It's your combination sinners—your lecherous liars and your miserly drunks—who dishonor the vices and bring them into bad repute.
—THORNTON WILDER, *The Matchmaker (1954)*

31. Vice is its own reward.
—QUENTIN CRISP, *The Naked Civil Servant (1968)*

32. The American vice is explanation.
—GORE VIDAL, *"Rich Kids," The Second American Revolution and Other Essays (1982)*

Victims

1. Alas, regardless of their doom, / The little victims play! / No sense have they of ills to come, / Nor care beyond to-day.
> —THOMAS GRAY, Ode on a Distant
> Prospect of Eton College (1742)

2. What is the offense of a lamb that we should rear it, and tend it, and lull it into security, for the express purpose of killing it? Its offense is the misfortune of being something which society wants to eat, and which cannot defend itself.
> —SAMUEL BUTLER, Erewhon (1872)

3. It is well for his peace that the saint goes to his martyrdom. He is spared the sight of his harvest.
> —OSCAR WILDE, Intentions (1891)

4. Why should he have been murdered? He was not clever enough to have enemies.
> —OSCAR WILDE, The Picture of
> Dorian Gray (1891)

5. Every reformation must have its victims. You can't expect the fatted calf to share the enthusiasm of the angels over the prodigal's return.
> —SAKI [H. H. Munro], "Reginald
> on the Academy," Reginald
> (1904)

6. If the crowd has to choose someone to crucify, it will always save Barabbas.
> —JEAN COCTEAU, Le Coq et
> l'Arlequin (1918)

7. One likes people much better when they're battered down by a prodigious siege of misfortune than when they triumph.
> —VIRGINIA WOOLF, A Writer's Diary,
> 13 August 1921

8. A man must be sacrificed now and again / To provide for the next generation of men.
> —AMY LOWELL, A Critical Fable
> (1922)

9. Wandering people the world over found her profitable in that she could be sold for a price forever, for she carried her betrayal money in her own pocket.
> —DJUNA BARNES, Nightwood
> (1936)

10. It pains me physically to see a woman victimized, rendered pathetic, by fashion.
> —YVES SAINT LAURENT, in Ritz
> (1984)

Violence

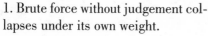

1. Brute force without judgement collapses under its own weight.
> —HORACE (1st century BCE), Odes III, 4

2. These violent delights have violent ends.
> —WILLIAM SHAKESPEARE, Romeo and Juliet (1595)

3. Violence is a symptom of impotence.
> —ANAÏS NIN (1960), The Diary of Anaïs Nin, Vol. 6 (1976)

4. The only thing that's been a worse flop than the organization of nonviolence has been the organization of violence.
> —JOAN BAEZ, Daybreak (1968)

5. The people in power will not disappear voluntarily, giving flowers to the cops just isn't going to work. This thinking is fostered by the establishment; they like nothing better than love and nonviolence. The only way I like to see cops given flowers is in a flower pot from a high window.
> —WILLIAM S. BURROUGHS, in The Job: Interviews with Daniel Odier (1969)

6. Today, together, let us repeat as our slogan that all trace of violence must disappear from this earth, then the sun will be honey-colored and music good to hear.
> —MONIQUE WITTIG, Les Guérillères (1969)

7. It is possible, I suppose, that we are returning to a Dark Age. What is frightening is that violence is not only represented by nations, but everywhere walks among us freely.
> —MAY SARTON, The House by the Sea: A Journal (1977)

8. Want of passion is, I think, a very striking characteristic of Americans, not unrelated to their predilection for violence. For very few people truly have a passionate desire to achieve, and violence serves as a kind of substitute.
> —MARGUERITE YOURCENAR, With Open Eyes (1980)

Vulgarity

1. Give thy thoughts no tongue, / Nor any unproportioned thought his act. / Be thou familiar but by no means vulgar.
> —*William Shakespeare, Hamlet (1600–1601)*

2. Don't joke about your poverty. That is quite as vulgar as to boast of it.
> —*Henry James, The Europeans (1878)*

3. Vulgarity is simply the conduct of other people.
> —*Oscar Wilde, An Ideal Husband (1895)*

4. Very notable was his distinction between coarseness and vulgarity (coarseness, revealing something; vulgarity, concealing something).
> —*E. M. Forster, The Longest Journey (1907)*

5. Explain yourself without gestures. The moment you gesticulate you look common.
> —*Colette, Gigi (1944)*

6. I can't stand a naked light bulb, any more than I can a rude remark or a vulgar action.
> —*Tennessee Williams, A Streetcar Named Desire (1947)*

7. You can be in the Horseguards and still be common, dear.
> —*Terence Rattigan, Separate Tables (1954)*

8. Vulgarity is, in reality, nothing but a modern, chic, pert descendent of the goddess Dullness.
> —*Edith Sitwell (d. 1964), Taken Care Of (1965)*

9. I have no concern for the common man except that he should not be so common.
> —*Angus Wilson, No Laughing Matter (1967)*

War

1. The most disadvantageous peace is better than the most just war.
> —DESIDERIUS ERASMUS, *Adagia (1500)*

2. Blood is the god of war's rich livery.
> —CHRISTOPHER MARLOWE, *Tamburlaine the Great (1587)*

3. That bloody spendthrift, War.
> —HERMAN MELVILLE, *The Confidence-Man (1857)*

4. As long as war is regarded as wicked, it will always have its fascination. When it is looked upon as vulgar, it will cease to be popular.
> —OSCAR WILDE, *"The Critic as Artist" (1891)*

5. To delight in war is a merit in the soldier, a dangerous quality in the captain, and a positive crime in the statesman.
> —GEORGE SANTAYANA, *The Life of Reason (1906)*

6. If you could hear, at every jolt, the blood / Come gargling from the froth-corrupted lungs, / Bitter as the cud / Of vile, incurable sores on innocent tongues,— / My friend, you would not tell with such high zest / To children ardent for some desperate glory / The old Lie: *Dulce et decorum est/Pro patria mori.*
> —WILFRED OWEN, *"Dulce et Decorum Est" (1918)*

7. Who live under the shadow of a war, / What can I do that matters?
> —STEPHEN SPENDER, *"Who live under the shadow of a war" (1933)*

8. If we justify war, it is because all peoples always justify the traits of which they find themselves possessed, not because war will bear an objective examination of its merits.
> —RUTH BENEDICT, *Patterns of Culture (1934)*

9. Every war already carries within it the war which will answer it. Every war is answered by a new war, until everything, everything is smashed.
> —KÄTHE KOLLWITZ (1944), in Hans Kollwitz, ed., *The Diaries and Letters of Käthe Kollwitz (1955)*

10. War is never fatal but always lost.
> —GERTRUDE STEIN, *Wars I Have Seen (1945)*

11. I cannot believe that war is the best solution. No one won the last war, and no one will win the next war.

—ELEANOR ROOSEVELT, *letter to Harry S. Truman, 1948*

12. When money rolled in / and blood rolled out.
—LANGSTON HUGHES, *"Green Memory" (1951)*

13. Out of that bungled, unwise war / An alp of unforgiveness grew.
—WILLIAM PLOMER, *"The Boer War" (1960)*

14. There's a consensus out that it's OK to kill when your government decides who to kill. If you kill inside the country you get in trouble. If you kill outside the country, right time, right season, latest enemy, you get a medal.
—JOAN BAEZ, *Daybreak (1968)*

15. All wars are useless to the dead.
—ADRIENNE RICH, *"Implosions," Leaflets (1969)*

16. What if someone gave a war & Nobody came? / Life would ring the bells of Ecstasy and Forever be Itself again.

—ALLEN GINSBERG, *"Graffiti 12th Cubicle Men's Room Syracuse Airport," The Fall of America (1973)*

17. War is, undoubtedly, hell, but there is no earthly reason why it has to start so early in the morning.
—FRAN LEBOWITZ, *Social Studies (1981)*

18. How many are dying / from the taxes I've paid?
—CHRYSTOS, *"Down," Dream On (1991)*

19. War is bestowed like electroshock on the depressive nation: thousands of volts jolting the system, an artificial galvanizing, one effect of which is loss of memory. War comes at the end of the twentieth century as absolute failure of imagination, scientific and political. That a war can be represented as helping a people to "feel good" about themselves, their country, is a measure of that failure.
—ADRIENNE RICH, *What is Found There (1993)*

W i t

1. Brevity is the soul of wit.
   —*William Shakespeare, Hamlet*
   (1600–1601)

2. He's winding up the watch of his wit. / By and by it will strike.
   —*William Shakespeare, The*
   Tempest (1611)

3. Yet if thou didst but know how little wit governs this mighty universe.
   —*Aphra Behn, Roundheads (1682)*

4. Shrink not from blasphemy—it will pass for wit.
   —*George Gordon, Lord Byron,*
   English Bards and Scotch
   Reviewers (1806)

5. That is not wit which needs explaining.
   —*Herman Melville, Redburn*
   (1849)

6. The quality of wit inspires more admiration than confidence.
   —*George Santayana, The Sense of*
   Beauty (1896)

7. Impropriety is the soul of wit.
   —*W. Somerset Maugham, The*
   Moon and Sixpence (1919)

8. To be wildly enthusiastic, or deadly serious—both are wrong.
Both pass. One must keep ever present a sense of humour.
   —*Katherine Mansfield (1922),*
   Journal of Katherine Mansfield
   (1927)

9. When a creature is witty enough, he will occasionally say something that smacks of the profound.
   —*Rose O'Neill, Garda (1929)*

10. A laugh is a terrible weapon.
   —*Kate O'Brien, The Last of*
   Summer (1943)

11. If evolution was worth its salt, by now it should've evolved something better than the survival of the fittest. Yeah, I told 'em I think a better idea would be survival of the wittiest. At least, that way, the creatures that didn't survive could've died *laughing*.
   —*Jane Wagner [words spoken by*
   Lily Tomlin], The Search for
   Signs of Intelligent Life in the
   Universe (1985)

12. Humor comes from self-confidence. There's an aggressive element to wit.

—*RITA MAE BROWN, Starting from Scratch (1988)*

13. Wit destroys eroticism and eroticism destroys wit, so women must choose between taking lovers and taking no prisoners.

—*FLORENCE KING, Reflections in a Jaundiced Eye (1989)*

W o m e n

1. Two women placed together makes cold weather.

—*WILLIAM SHAKESPEARE, Henry VIII (1613)*

2. Nuns and married women are equally unhappy, if in different ways.

—*CHRISTINA, QUEEN OF SWEDEN, Maxims (1660–80)*

3. We are always ready to esteem a woman who will give us leave to do so.

—*SARAH SCOTT, A Description of Millenium Hall (1762)*

4. Why have women Passion, intellect, moral activity—these three—and a place in society where no one of the three can be exercised?

—*FLORENCE NIGHTINGALE, "Cassandra" (1852)*

5. Women have no sympathy . . . and my experience of women is almost as large as Europe.

—*FLORENCE NIGHTINGALE, letter, 13 December 1861*

6. Went out last night with a crowd of my friends, / They must've been women, 'cause I don't like no men.

—*MA RAINEY, "Prove It on Me Blues" (1928)*

7. Why are women . . . so much more interesting to men than men are to women?

—*VIRGINIA WOOLF, A Room of One's Own (1929)*

8. It is true that I only want to show off to women. Women alone stir my imagination.

—*VIRGINIA WOOLF, letter to Ethel Smyth, 19 August 1930, The Letters of Virginia Woolf, Vol. 4, Ed. Nigel Nicolson and Joanne Trautmann (1980)*

9. Intimacies between women often go backwards, beginning in revelations and ending up in small talk without loss of esteem.

> —ELIZABETH BOWEN, *The Death of the Heart (1938)*

10. One is not born a woman: one becomes a woman. No biological, psychological or economic destiny can determine how the human female will appear in society.

> —SIMONE DE BEAUVOIR, *The Second Sex (1949)*

11. "I don't see what women see in other women," I'd told Doctor Nolan in my interview the noon. "What does a woman see in a woman that she doesn't see in a man?"

Doctor Nolan paused. Then she said, "Tenderness."

> —SYLVIA PLATH (d. 1963), *The Bell Jar (1966)*

12. Consider the "new" woman. She's trying to be Pollyanna Borgia, clearly a conflict of interest. She's supposed to be a ruthless winner at work and a bundle of nurturing sweetness at home.

> —RITA MAE BROWN, *In Her Day (1976)*

13. Through centuries of suckling men emotionally at our breasts we have also been told that we were polluted, devouring, domineering, masochistic, harpies, butches, dykes, and whores.

> —ADRIENNE RICH, *Of Woman Born (1976)*

14. Some of the finest women I know, I have kissed. Women who were lonely, women I didn't know and didn't want to, but kissed because that was a way to say yes we are still alive and lovable, though separate.

> —JUDY GRAHN, *"A Woman Is Talking to Death" (1978)*

15. Being a woman is of special interest only to aspiring male transsexuals. To actual women, it is merely a good excuse not to play football.

> —FRAN LEBOWITZ, *Metropolitan Life (1978)*

16. One feature of lesbian oppression consists precisely of making women out of reach for us, since women belong to men. Thus a lesbian *has* to be something else, a not-woman, a not-man, a product of society, not a product of nature, for there is no nature in society.

> —MONIQUE WITTIG, *"One Is Not Born a Woman" (1981)*

17. I would like so much to be a woman without thinking about it.

> —HÉLÈNE CIXOUS, *Le Livre de Promethea (1983)*

18. Women are in league with each other, a secret conspiracy of hearts and pheromones.

> —CAMILLE PAGLIA, *Sex, Art, and American Culture (1992)*

Words and Names

1. What's in a name? That which we call a rose / By any other name would smell as sweet.
    —WILLIAM SHAKESPEARE, *Romeo and Juliet (1595)*

2. Here are a few of the unpleasant'st words / That ever blotted paper.
    —WILLIAM SHAKESPEARE, *The Merchant of Venice (1596–97)*

3. Thy words are too precious to be cast away upon curs. Throw some of them at me.
    —WILLIAM SHAKESPEARE, *As You Like It (1599–1600)*

4. The accomplished languages of Europe in the nineteenth century supply no terms for this persistent feature of human psychology, without imparting some implications of disgust, disgrace, vituperation.
    —JOHN ADDINGTON SYMONDS, on homosexuality, *A Problem in Modern Ethics (1891)*

5. My words are little jars / For you to take and put upon a shelf.
    —AMY LOWELL, *"Gift" (1914)*

6. Both legally and familiarly, as well as in my books, I now have only one name, which is my own.
    —COLETTE, *"La Naissance du Jour" (1928)*

7. Words are weapons, and it is dangerous in speculation, as in politics, to borrow them from our enemies.
    —GEORGE SANTAYANA, *Obiter Scripta (1936)*

8. And the words which carry most knives are the blind / Phrases searching to be kind.
    —STEPHEN SPENDER, *"The Double Shame" (1939)*

9. It's when the thing itself is missing that you have to supply the word.
    —HENRY DE MONTHERLANT, *Queen After Death (1942)*

10. A word is the carving and colouring of a thought, and gives it permanence.
    —OSBERT SITWELL, *Laughter in the Next Room (1949)*

11. Words should be an intense pleasure just as leather should be to a shoemaker.
    —EVELYN WAUGH, *in The New York Times, 19 November 1950*

12. You don't know what love means. To you it's just another four-letter word.

—TENNESSEE WILLIAMS, *Cat on a
Hot Tin Roof (1955)*

13. We must use words as they are
used, or stand aside from life.
   —IVY COMPTON-BURNETT, *Mother
   and Son (1955)*

14. If dirty words frighten you, I
really don't know how you have managed to live so long. People are full of
dirty words. The only time they do
not use them, most people, I mean, is
when they are describing something
dirty.
   —JAMES BALDWIN, *Giovanni's Room
   (1956)*

15. To be destructive, words must be
irrefutable. Print was less effective
than the spoken word because the
blast was greater; eyes could ignore,
slide past, dangerous verbs and
nouns. But if you could lock the
enemy into a room somewhere, and
fire the sentence at them you could
get a sort of seismic disturbance.
   —JOE ORTON, *The Vision of
   Gombold Proval (1961)*

16. Some words / bedevil me.
   —AUDRE LORDE, *"Coal" (1962)*

17. MIKE: There's no word in the Irish
language for what you were doing.
   WILSON: In Lapland they have no
word for snow.
   —JOE ORTON, *The Ruffian on the
   Stair (rev. ed. 1967)*

18. They say that in the first place
the vocabulary of every language is
to be examined, modified, turned
upside down, that every word must
be screened.
   —MONIQUE WITTIG, *Les Guérillères
   (1969)*

19. I wanted to choose words that even
you / would have to be changed by.
   —ADRIENNE RICH, *"Implosions,"
   Leaflets (1969)*

20. People are able to live with only
half a heart, to live without real compassion, because they are able to use
words that are only forms.
   —ANGUS WILSON, *in Iowa Review,
   February 1972*

21. *Lifestyle.* Not a word at all,
really—rather a wordette. A genuine
case of more is less. The word *life*
and the word *style* are, except in rare
cases (and chances are that *you're*
not one of them), mutually exclusive.
   —FRAN LEBOWITZ, *in Interview
   magazine (1975)*

22. Adjectives are the curse of
America.
   —RITA MAE BROWN, *In Her Day
   (1976)*

23. The word *lesbian* must be af-
firmed because to discard it is to col-
laborate with silence and lying about
our very existence; with the closet-
game, the creation of the *unspeakable.*

—ADRIENNE RICH, "It Is the Lesbian in Us . . ." (1976)

24. The dictionary is only a rough draft.
—MONIQUE WITTIG and SANDE ZEIG, *Lesbian Peoples* (1976)

25. How can we describe the most exalted experience of our physical lives, as if—jack, wrench, hubcap, and nuts—we were describing the changing of a flat tire?
—JOHN CHEEVER, "A Miscellany of Characters That Will Not Appear" (1978)

26. Homosexual desire is specific; there are homosexual utterances. But homosexuality is nothing; it's only a word. So let's take the word seriously, let's go with it and make it yield all the possibilities it contains.
—GILLES DELEUZE, in George Stambolian and Elaine Marks, *Homosexualities and French Literature* (1979)

27. Euphemisms are not, as many young people think, useless verbiage for that which can and should be said bluntly; they are like secret agents on a delicate mission, they must airily pass by a stinking mess with barely so much as a nod of the head, make their point of constructive criticism and continue on in calm forbearance. Euphemisms are unpleasant truths wearing diplomatic cologne.
—QUENTIN CRISP, *Manners from Heaven* (1984)

28. Few words are as guaranteed to set off an explosion of fear in her belly as the word *bulldike* when it is used on a woman like a whip.
—JUDY GRAHN, *Another Mother Tongue* (1984)

29. The condition that is now called gay was then called queer. The operative word was *faggot* and, later, pussy, but those epithets really had nothing to do with the question of sexual preference: You were being told simply that you had no balls.
—JAMES BALDWIN, *The Price of the Ticket* (1985)

30. Naming is a difficult and time-consuming process; it concerns essences, and it means power. But on the wild nights who can call you home? Only the one who knows your name.
—JEANETTE WINTERSON, *Oranges Are Not the Only Fruit* (1985)

31. Lesbian . . . No word more terrifying, in my mother's mouth it is a snake hissing, Lesbian, intake of breath the unspeakable word.
—KATE MILLETT, *Flying* (1990)

32. These names: gay, queer, homosexual are limiting. I would love to finish with them. We're going to have to decide which terms to use and where we use them. . . . For me to use

the word "queer" is a liberation; it was a word that frightened me, but no longer.

—DEREK JARMAN, *At Your Own Risk: A Saint's Testament (1992)*

33. *Lesbian* and *homosexual* may indeed be neologisms, but there have always been *other* words—a whole slangy mob of them—for pointing to (or taking aim at) the lover of women: *tribade, fricatrice, sapphist, roaring girl, amazon, freak, romp, dyke, bull dagger, tommy.* Even the seemingly innocent *odd woman* or *odd girl* occur with such enticing regularity in early lesbian-themed writing as to suggest the possibility of a host of lost or suppressed code terms.

—TERRY CASTLE, *The Apparitional Lesbian: Female Homosexuality and Modern Culture (1993)*

34. Next to "I win," "I told you so," are the sweetest words.

—GORE VIDAL, "United States," *Essays 1952–1992 (1993)*

Work

1. Hard work conquered everything, / And need pressing in straightened circumstances.

—VIRGIL *(1st century BCE)*, *Georgics I*

2. Thou, O God, dost sell us good things at the price of labor.

—LEONARDO DA VINCI, *Notebooks (c. 1500)*

3. 'Tis a sure sign that work goes on merrily, when folks sing at it.

—ISAAC BICKERSTAFFE, *The Maid of the Mill (1765)*

4. The really efficient laborer will be found not to crowd his day with work, but will saunter to his task surrounded by a wide halo of ease and leisure.

—HENRY DAVID THOREAU, *Journal, 31 March 1842*

5. Toil is man's allotment; toil of brain, or toil of hands, or a grief that's more than either, the grief and sin of idleness.

—HERMAN MELVILLE, *Mardi (1849)*

6. It is necessary to work, if not from inclination, at least from despair. Everything considered, work is less boring than amusing oneself.

—CHARLES BAUDELAIRE *(d. 1867)*, *Mon Coeur Mis à Nu (1887)*

7. Work is the curse of the drinking classes.
>—OSCAR WILDE (d. 1900), in Hesketh Pearson, The Life of Oscar Wilde (1946)

8. No longer diverted by other emotions, I work the way a cow grazes.
>—KÄTHE KOLLWITZ (1910), Diaries and Letters (1955)

9. To work—to work! It is such infinite delight to know that we still have the best things to do.
>—KATHERINE MANSFIELD, letter to Bertrand Russell, 7 December 1917

10. I made up my mind long ago that life was too short to do anything for myself that I could pay others to do.
>—W. SOMERSET MAUGHAM, A Writer's Notebook (1949)

11. Work is much more fun than fun.
>—NOËL COWARD, in Observer, 1963

12. In order that people may be happy in their work, these three things are needed: They must be fit for it: they must not do too much of it: and they must have a sense of success in it—not a doubtful sense, such as needs some testimony of others for its confirmation, but a sure sense, or rather knowledge, that so much work has been done well, and fruitfully done, whatever the world may say or think about it.
>—W. H. AUDEN, A Certain World (1970)

13. I suppose I have a really loose interpretation of "work," because I think that just being alive is so much work at something you don't always want to do. The machinery is always going. Even when you sleep.
>—ANDY WARHOL, The Philosophy of Andy Warhol: From A to B and Back Again (1975)

Writing

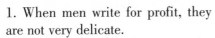

1. When men write for profit, they are not very delicate.
>—HORACE WALPOLE, letter, 1 September 1778

2. Authorship is a mania, to conquer which no reasons are sufficiently strong. As easily persuade not to love as not to write.
>—MATTHEW G. LEWIS, The Monk (1795)

3. Camerado, this is no book, / Who touches this touches a man, / (Is it

night? Are we here together alone?) / It is I you hold and who holds you.
  —WALT WHITMAN, "So Long!" (1860)

4. You must find your own quiet center of life, and write from that to the world.
  —SARAH ORNE JEWETT, letter to Willa Cather, 1908

5. Whatever is felt upon the page without being specifically named there—that, one might say, is created. It is the inexplicable presence of the thing not named, of the overtone divined by the ear but not heard by it, the verbal mood, the emotional aura of the fact or the thing or the deed, that gives high quality to the novel or drama, as well as to poetry itself.
  —WILLA CATHER, "The Novel Démeublé" (1922)

6. I write for myself and strangers.
  —GERTRUDE STEIN, The Making of Americans (1925)

7. I adore italics, don't you?
  —RONALD FIRBANK (d. 1926), in Siegfried Sassoon, Siegfried's Journey (1945)

8. The child is never far to seek in the author.
  —RADCLYFFE HALL, The Well of Loneliness (1928)

9. Every secret of a writer's soul, every experience of his life, every

quality of his mind is written large in his works, yet we require critics to explain the one and biographers to expound the other. That time hangs heavy on people's hands is the only explanation of the monstrous growth.
  —VIRGINIA WOOLF, Orlando (1928)

10. How rare, how precious is frivolity! How few writers can prostitute all their powers! They are always implying "I am capable of higher things."
  —E. M. FORSTER, "Ronald Firbank," Abinger Harvest (1936)

11. When I am happy I live and despise writing / For my Muse this cannot be but dispiriting.
  —STEVIE SMITH, "My Muse," Selected Poems (1962)

12. The role of the writer is not to say what we can all say, but what we are unable to say.
  —ANAÏS NIN (1954), The Diaries of Anaïs Nin, Vol. 5 (1974)

13. In my writing I am acting as a map maker, an explorer of psychic areas . . . a cosmonaut of inner space, and I see no point in exploring areas that have already been thoroughly surveyed.
  —WILLIAM S. BURROUGHS (1964), in Eric Mottram, William Burroughs, the Algebra of Need (1977)

14. To write is to inform against others.

—VIOLETTE LEDUC, *Mad in Pursuit*
(1971)

15. I wrote at a steady pace three hours a day, with Isabelle's river tresses in my mouth, in my throat. . . . There was more to be said, and I was unable to say it. I failed; there is no doubt in my mind about that. I don't regret my labors. It was an attempt. Other women will go on from there, others will succeed where I failed.
   —VIOLETTE LEDUC, on her novel
      Thérèse et Isabelle; Mad in
      Pursuit (1971)

16. Writers are usually in the unfortunate predicament of having to speak the truth without the authority to speak it.
   —W. H. AUDEN (d. 1973), in
      Charles Osborne, W. H. Auden:
      The Life of a Poet (1979)

17. Contrary to what many of you might imagine, a career in letters is not without its drawbacks—chief among them the unpleasant fact that one is frequently called upon to actually sit down and write.
   —FRAN LEBOWITZ, *Metropolitan*
      Life (1978)

18. We have let rhetoric do the job of poetry.
   —CHERRÍE MORAGA, *"La Guëra"*
      (1983)

19. Writing is the passageway, the entrance, the exit, the dwelling place of the other in me.

—HÉLÈNE CIXOUS, *The Newly Born*
   Woman (1986)

20. The writer is either a practicing recluse or a delinquent, guilt-ridden one; or both. Usually both.
   —SUSAN SONTAG, in *The New York*
      Times Book Review, 1986

21. Writing is one-tenth perspiration and nine-tenths masturbation.
   —ALAN BENNETT, *film script, Prick*
      Up Your Ears (1987); words
      spoken by Gary Oldman as
      Joe Orton

22. Show me a writer, any writer, who hasn't suffered and I'll show you someone who writes in pastels as opposed to primary colors.
   —RITA MAE BROWN, *Starting from*
      Scratch (1988)

23. How do I write? With a woman's gaze resting on me. Or with the body inclined towards her.
   —NICOLE BROSSARD, *The Aerial*
      Letter (1988)

24. Poetry is not an expression of the party line. It's that time of night, lying in bed, thinking what you really think, making the private world public, that's what the poet does.
   —ALLEN GINSBERG, in *Barry Miles,*
      Ginsberg (1989)

25. Prose is the respectable, grown-up form of written communication. Poetry is reserved for children and

others brave or foolish enough to refuse the mainstream's ability to stipulate what color cows must be, which notes girls may sing, who can make love with whom.
> —*TONI MCNARON, I Dwell in Possibility (1992)*

26. Even when I cannot write, I know I am still a writer, just the way I know I am still sexual even if I have not had a lover for many months.
> —*OLGA BROUMAS, in Bonnie Friedman, Writing Past Dark (1993)*

Youth

1. Boy who casts a girlish glance, / I am pursuing you.
> —*ANACREON (5th century BCE), Fragment PMG 360; trans. Dennis Kratz*

2. The right way to begin is to pay attention to the young, and make them just as good as possible.
> —*SOCRATES (5th century BCE), in Plato (4th century BCE), Euthyphro*

3. The democratic youth lives along day by day, gratifying the desire that occurs to him, at one time drinking and listening to the flute, at another downing water and reducing, now practicing gymnastics, and again idling and neglecting everything; and sometimes spending his time as though he were occupied in philosophy.
> —*PLATO (4th century BCE), The Republic*

4. Alas, that Spring should vanish with the Rose! / That Youth's sweet-scented Manuscript should close!
> —*OMAR KHAYYÁM, Rubáiyát (11th–12th century); trans. Edward FitzGerald*

5. A man loves the meat in his youth that he cannot endure in his age.
> —*WILLIAM SHAKESPEARE, Much Ado About Nothing (1598)*

6. Young men are fitter to invent than to judge, fitter for execution than for counsel, fitter for new projects than for settled business.
> —*FRANCIS BACON, "Of Youth and Age," Essays (1625)*

7. I avoid talking before the youth of the age as I would dancing before them: for if one's tongue don't move in the steps of the day, and thinks to please by its old graces, it is only an object of ridicule.

—HORACE WALPOLE, letter,
15 April 1768

8. The youth gets together his materials to build a bridge to the moon, or, perchance, a palace or temple on the earth, and, at length, the middle-aged man concludes to build a woodshed with them.
—HENRY DAVID THOREAU, Journal,
14 July 1852

9. Idle youth, enslaved to everything; by being too sensitive I have wasted my life.
—ARTHUR RIMBAUD, "The Song of the Highest Tower" (1872)

10. It's our peculiar good luck that we don't see the limits of our minds. We're young, compared with what we may one day be. That belongs to youth; it's perhaps the best part of it.
—HENRY JAMES, Roderick Hudson (1876)

11. In America, . . . lads of twenty-five and thirty have old heads and young hearts, or at least young morals; here [in Europe] they have young heads and very aged hearts, morals the most grizzled and wrinkled.
—HENRY JAMES, The American (1877)

12. Contentment who had known youth as a child and never seen him since.
—RUPERT BROOKE, "The Funeral of Youth" (1914)

13. If youth did not matter so much to itself, it would never have the heart to go on.
—WILLA CATHER, The Song of the Lark (1915)

14. It is an illusion that youth is happy, an illusion of those who have lost it.
—W. SOMERSET MAUGHAM, Of Human Bondage (1915)

15. Youth condemns; maturity condones.
—AMY LOWELL, Tendencies in Modern American Poetry (1917)

16. The old Happiness is unreturning. / Boys' griefs are not so grievous as youth's yearning. / Boys have no sadness sadder than our hope.
—WILFRED OWEN (d. 1918), "Happiness," Collected Poems (1920)

17. If one could recover the uncompromising spirit of one's youth, one's greatest indignation would be for what one has become.
—ANDRÉ GIDE, The Counterfeiters (1925); trans. Dorothy Bussy

18. This is not so strange when you reflect that from the earliest times the old have rubbed it into the young that they are wiser than they, and before the young had discovered what nonsense this was they were old too, and it profited them to carry on the imposture.

—W. SOMERSET MAUGHAM, *Cakes
and Ale (1930)*

19. My youth is escaping me without giving me anything it owes me.
—IVY COMPTON-BURNETT, *A
Heritage and Its History (1959)*

20. The situation of our youth is not mysterious. Children have never been very good at listening to their elders, but they have never failed to imitate them. They must, they have no other models.
—JAMES BALDWIN, *Nobody Knows
My Name (1961)*

21. Youth is not a question of years: one is young or old from birth.
—NATALIE CLIFFORD BARNEY, *in
Adam International Review,
1962*

22. You are only young once. At the time it seems endless, and is gone in a flash; and then for a very long time you are old.
—SYLVIA TOWNSEND WARNER,
*"Swans on an Autumn River"
(1966)*

23. No position is impossible when you're young and healthy.
—JOE ORTON (d. 1967), *What the
Butler Saw (1969)*

24. The young always have the same problem—how to rebel and conform at the same time. They have now solved this by defying their parents and copying one another.
—QUENTIN CRISP, *The Naked Civil
Servant (1968)*

25. I worry about kids today. Because of the sexual revolution they're going to grow up and never know what dirty means.
—LILY TOMLIN, *in Time,
28 March 1977*

I n d e x

About the Editor

Patricia Juliana Smith is a visiting assistant professor of English at the University of California, Los Angeles, where she teaches twentieth-century British literature and gay and lesbian studies.

She is a graduate of California State University, Dominguez Hills, and received her M.A. and Ph.D. from UCLA. Her other books include *Lesbian Panic: Homoeroticism in Modern British Women's Fiction; The Queer Sixties;* and *En Travesti: Women, Gender Subversion, and Opera.* Dr. Smith has also published numerous articles and given public lectures on a variety of literary topics, on opera, and on popular culture. She is currently working on a study of the effects of the end of empire and the "permissive society" of the 1960s on British literature and culture, and also on a filmscript based on her experiences as a used-car dealer.